*Eroding
the Commons*

EASTERN AFRICAN STUDIES

Eroding the Commons

The Politics of Ecology in Baringo, Kenya 1890s–1963

DAVID M. ANDERSON

Senior Lecturer in History
School of Oriental & African Studies (SOAS)
University of London

James Currey
OXFORD

E.A.E.P.
NAIROBI

Ohio University Press
ATHENS

PUBLISHED IN COLLABORATION WITH
THE OHIO UNIVERSITY PRESS ECOLOGY AND HISTORY SERIES

James Currey Ltd	EAEP	Ohio University Press
73 Botley Road	Kijabe Street	Scott Quadrangle
Oxford	PO Box 45314	Athens,
OX2 0BS	Nairobi	Ohio 45701

Published in collaboration with
the Ohio University Press
Ecology and History Series

© David M. Anderson 2002
First published 2002

1 2 3 4 5 06 05 04 03 02

British Library Cataloguing in Publication Data
Anderson, David, 1957-
  Eroding the commons : the politics of ecology in Baringo,
  Kenya, 1890s-1963. - (East African studies)
  1.Range ecology - Political aspects - Kenya - Baringo,
  Lake, Region 2.Rangelands - Kenya - Baringo, Lake, Region
  3.Baringo, Lake, Region (Kenya) - Social conditions 4.Kenya
  - Politics and government 5.Kenya - History - 1895-1963
  I.Title
  333.7'4'0967627

        ISBN 0-85255-469-9 (James Currey cloth)
        ISBN 0-85255-468-0 (James Currey paper)

**Library of Congress Cataloging-in-Publication Data is available
from the Library of Congress**
Anderson, David, 1957-
  Eroding the commons : the politics of ecology in Baringo, Kenya, 1890s-1963 /David
M. Anderson.
  p. cm. -- (Eastern African studies) (Ohio University Press series in ecology and history)
Includes bibliographical references and index.
  ISBN 0-8214-1479-8 (alk. paper) -- ISBN 0-8214-1480-1 (pbk.: alk. paper)
    1. Environmental policy--Kenya--Baringo District--History--20th century. 2. Baringo
District (Kenya)--Environmental conditions--History--20th century. 3. Baringo District
(Kenya)--politics and government--20th century. I. Title. II. Series. III. Eastern African
studies (London, England)

GE190.K4 A53 2002
307.1'412'0967627--dc21   2002075504

        ISBN 0-8214-1479-8 (Ohio University Press cloth)
        ISBN 0-8214-1480-1 (Ohio University Press paper)

Typeset in 10/11pt Baskerville
by Long House Publishing Services, Cumbria, UK
Printed and bound in Britain
by Woolnough, Irthlingborough

Dedicated
to the memory
of my daughter
Moya
born and died
21 October 1990

Contents

Contents

Nine
Watering the Shamba
The Perkerra Irrigation Scheme, 1952–63

Conclusion
Colonial Development in Lowland Baringo
Misreading History

Appendix
The Baringo Historical Texts

Maps, Tables & Figures

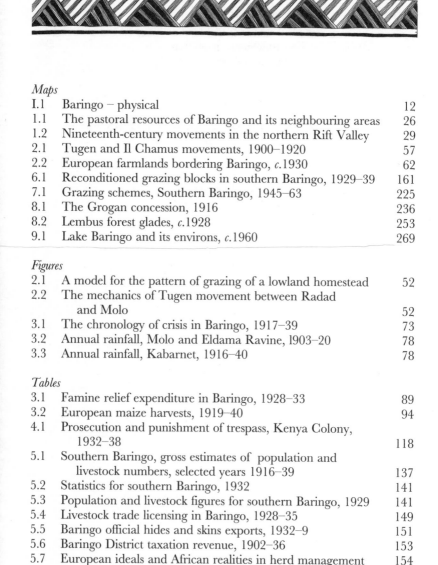

Maps, Tables & Figures

Abbreviations

ADC	African District Council	AG	Attorney General
AI	Agricultural Inspector	BAR	Baringo District
AgPC	Acting Provincial Commissioner	CNC	Chief Native Commissioner
ALDEV	African Land Development and Settlement Board	CS	Chief Secretary
		CVO	Chief Veterinary Officer
ALMO	African Livestock Marketing Organisation	DC	District Commissioner
		DO	District Officer
BDAR	Baringo District Annual Report	ER	Eldama Ravine
BHT	Baringo Historical Texts	ERD	Eldama Ravine District
CH	Chamus	Laik.	Laikipia District
ES	European Settler	LO	Land Office
NB	Nubian	NKU	Nakuru District
SW	Swahili	PC	Provincial Commissioner
TG	Tugen	PRB	Political Record Book
DARA	Development and Reconstruction Authority	PWD	Public Works Department
		RVP	Rift Valley Province
ESA	Entebbe Secretariat Archives	LC	Livestock Control
ESM	Equator Sawmills Ltd	LegCo	Legislative Council
FA	Farmers' Association	LNC	Local Native Council
KLC	Kenya Land Commission	MMB	Meat Marketing Board
KLC:EM	Kenya Land Commission: Evidence and Memoranda	PAO	Provincial Agricultural Officer
		PIS	Perkerra Irrigation Scheme
KMC	Kenya Meat Commission	PRO	Public Records Office
KNA	Kenya National Archives	PVO	Provincial Veterinary Officer
ADC	Assistant District Commissioner	CO	Colonial Office
		FO	Foreign Office
AR	Annual Report	RH	Rhodes House, Oxford
ARC	(FOR) Forest Department	RO	Reconditioning Officer
ARC	(MAWR) Ministry of Agriculture and Water Resources	RSD	Ravine Station Diary
		SCS	Soil Conservation Service
		VO	Veterinary Officer

Preface & Acknowledgements

Writing is a lonely business, but research is a collective activity. The collaboration, cooperation and support of other people are what make the journey of discovery so enjoyable, and I cannot be alone in needing the warm memories of the friendships and adventures of research to nurture me through the long hours with only my notecards and computer for company. Over the years I have studied Kenya's and Baringo's histories, I have come to owe considerable debts of gratitude to many people. Their contribution to this book can be sincerely acknowledged here, but I will do my best to repay it in other ways.

My interest in Baringo first began as a project of doctoral research, and from 1980 to 1981 I completed nine months of fieldwork in Kenya's northern Rift Valley and seven months of archival research in Nairobi. The doctorate was completed in 1982, but the available archives were then only open up to 1950 and I had only examined them up to 1940. Trinity College, Cambridge, where I had spent three years as a graduate student, then generously provided for a year of post-doctoral research, which included support for another stint at the Kenya National Archives. This gave me the opportunity to explore more widely, and it was at this time that I realized that Baringo's story needed to be taken up to the ending of colonialism in 1963 if its full significance was to be appreciated. The archive sources would not be fully open on this period until 1990, so over the next few years I returned to Kenya several times, on each occasion working my way through the latest batch of archives to be opened – often alarmed by their mounting quantity as we moved through the 1950s – and returning to Baringo to visits old friends and familiar haunts.

Whilst gathering these materials from 1983, I was first supported as a Research Fellow at New Hall, Cambridge. After a very happy year there, during which Cambridge University's Smuts Memorial Fund awarded me a further travel grant, I left in 1984 to take up a teaching post at Birkbeck College, London. Thanks to the support of Birkbeck, the Central Research Fund of the University of London and the British Academy, I was able to make further research visits to Kenya in 1986 and 1988. During the academic year 1990–91 I held a Leverhulme Trust Research Fellowship, and was able to collect what turned out to be the final batch of primary data for this study during a visit to Kenya in the summer of 1990. In 1991,

I took up my present post at the School of Oriental and African Studies, London, and since then have made annual visits to Kenya, but not for research directly connected with this project.

During my many visits to Nairobi the staff of the Kenya National Archive have been unfailingly helpful and supportive. I am very grateful to the archivist, Mr Musembi, and all the staff in the reading-room, most especially Richard Ambani, for their professionalism, courtesy and friendship. In 1980–81, I was attached to the History Department of the University of Nairobi as a Research Associate, and since then members of the department have continued to take an interest in my work. Professor Godfrey Muriuki was especially supportive in the early stages of the project, when I had little idea what I was doing or how to do it. Karim Janmohammed and Atieno Odhiambo, both of whom have since moved on to other places, were then stern critics and have remained respected friends. More recently, Henry Mutoro and David Sperling found time to be welcoming and helpful, even when burdened by the almost intolerably heavy teaching loads that now afflict all staff at Nairobi University. Beyond the university, I have been fortunate in being able to use the British Institute in Eastern Africa (BIEA) as my base in Nairobi for many years now. The late Neville Chittick, then director of the BIEA, first introduced me to the excellent library and comfortable facilities of the Institute's Chiromo building – once the home of Ewart Grogan. Subsequently the Institute has moved out a little way from the university campus, to equally pleasant surroundings in Kileleshwa, where John Sutton, Director from 1984 to 1998, has been a generous host on more occasions than any visitor should reasonably expect. I am grateful to John for tolerating my post-archival rantings each evening with such grace, and for sharing liberal quantities of his fine home-brewed beer. During earlier periods in Kenya, Dave Salter's flat was a lively base from which to escape the heat and dust of Baringo, and Ed Steinhart and Suzie Duffy were always quick to offer a meal and their very good company.

While working in Baringo, life was made easier by a number of friends. My research assistants Kipronoh Toroitich and Samuel ole Sekue did a marvellous job. The results of the fieldwork are due to their efforts in locating our informants. They tolerated my slow-wittedness with language over the many hours spent transcribing tapes, and their good humour did much to sustain my sometimes flagging spirits as yet another interview drifted away from its intended subject. In Marigat, Father Joseph of the Catholic Mission was kind enough to let me pitch my tent within his compound, where I was based for four months. In Mogotio, Peter Kibiego helped me in a number of ways, with transport, with sound advice and with the companionship of his blossoming family. There, living in a one-room block on the edge of the Somali compound and adjacent to a butchery, I learned more about livestock trading than I really needed to know. When I needed rest and relaxation, Jeff and Jay Lewis and Will and Sue Critchley

provided a haven by the shores of the lake at Kampi-ya-Samaki. The advice and guidance they offered was invaluable, and without their patient assistance I doubt if the project could have been successfully completed. During the early part of my fieldwork in Baringo, I shared my tent with another researcher, Peter Little, then of the University of Indiana. I was grateful for Peter's companionship, and for many stimulating discussions about our research topics. His subsequent string of publications on Il Chamus have served both as an inspiration and an admonishment. Most importantly of all, I must offer a very great debt of gratitude to all those in Baringo who gave up their time to be interviewed by a persistently curious, determinedly stubborn and sometimes downright stupid researcher. Without their tolerance and indulgence, I would never have made sense of anything.

At an early stage in my research, the late A.T. Matson offered me great encouragement and made available many of his personal papers and notes for my use. Mat then read early drafts of chapters and exchanged ideas in letters and conversations, saving me from many careless errors of chronology and detail. Mat epitomized all that is best in the tradition of the amateur historian, and his enthusiasm is much missed. Many others also helped shape my thoughts on Baringo, and there are some who must be mentioned here: Philip Amis, Narendhra Morar and John Overton helped with the collection of archival data in Nairobi, and John also drew the original set of maps and worked with me on the Survey Department records; Bill Adams helped me to understand the importance of the relationship between ecological ideas and rural development; David Throup has sharpened my awareness of Kenya's many political struggles, past and present; and Richard Waller has, more than anyone else, shared my thoughts and ideas on this project and many, many others besides. His influence has been so deep over such a long time that it is now difficult to fathom; no one could wish for a more stimulating critic or a more amiable friend. But the thanks I owe to John Lonsdale transcend all of the above. In an academic world that is too often riven by pettiness and backbiting, John's generosity of spirit shines like a beacon. There is no better teacher in the field of African history, and no finer example of imaginative and dedicated scholarship. It was he who first pointed me towards the northern Rift Valley, though I first thought that sending a pale, freckle-faced, red-headed Scot to fry on the Rift Valley floor in temperatures above 30°C might have been an act of malicious cruelty! He has had a hand in guiding everything I have done since, and his wisdom has saved me from myself on more occasions than I care to admit. I still struggle to match the insights of his writings in my own work, but have grown to accept that I never shall. I can only hope that this book will show at least some sign of his influence.

Having families and writing books are not easily compatible activities. The preciousness of authorship can be difficult to live with; and obsession grows as the word count mounts. My family has handled this in the best

possible way: by completely ignoring it. I am fortunate to have in Angela a partner who always keeps such things in perspective. And Callum, Megan, Fraser and Rhona have at times driven me mad, but in the end it is they who keep me sane. I am grateful to them all for their love and tolerance.

This book has taken me far too long to write. Virtually all the data were collected by 1990, and it was then my intention to complete the project during a period of sabbatical leave from September 1990 to August 1991. That did not prove possible. Now, several years on, I have finally drawn a line under what is, I now realize, a very different book from the one I first sat down to write. It is dedicated to the memory of Moya, whose shade has been with me on every page.

St Albans

Introduction

Development, Environment & Colonial History

This book is about the history of rural development in the lowlands of Kenya's Baringo District during the years of colonial rule. In many respects colonial Baringo was an unexceptional place. Lying in the semi-arid Rift Valley, between the more prosperous highlands of west and central Kenya, Baringo appeared to be a colonial backwater, distant from larger markets and lacking the intensive cultivation of cash crops that brought comparative wealth to other regions. On these dry, rocky lowlands African herders made only a frugal living while doing their best to avoid the exactions of the state. But in the middle years of colonial rule Baringo's anonymity gave way to notoriety. Prolonged drought and localized famine in the district, from the mid-1920s to mid-1930s, led to claims that the lowlands were rapidly eroding. Baringo was becoming a desert, it was alleged, as a result of over-crowding and mismanagement. The degradation of the lowlands was contrasted with a past image of Baringo as a land of tall grasses, abundant wildlife and rural productivity. In short, Baringo was portrayed as a land in dramatic decay.

In response to the alarm over erosion, the state embarked upon a programme for the 'reconditioning' of pastures in lowland Baringo. Beginning in the late 1920s, these were among the earliest schemes of their kind anywhere under British rule in Africa. Following these first experiments in rural rehabilitation, a succession of development initiatives aimed at improving land husbandry and carrying capacity were mounted in Baringo over the next thirty years. As one of the first districts in which rehabilitation, conservation and development programmes were implemented, Baringo became both a symbol of the essential need for colonial intervention in African land husbandry and a testing ground for colonial

1

ideas on how reform should be implemented. Already by the end of the 1930s, the supposed successes of rehabilitation in Baringo were being modelled for application elsewhere in Kenya Colony. In the years after the Second World War, as the colonial state carried forward a dramatically enlarged programme of rural development, Baringo's experience became an important point of reference for others.

Because of the longevity of colonial interventions in Baringo, the district provides an excellent focus for the study of the broader evolution of colonial ideologies and practices of development. These ideologies and practices are fundamental to an understanding of the history of development in all parts of Africa. In the latter phase of colonial rule, after 1945, the ethos of 'development' was placed at the very heart of government, with the colonial state adopting far-reaching policies of reform in almost every area of African life. During the 1950s, more than in any other decade of the twentieth century, the state in Africa was concerned with the 'management' of the rural environment – with the rehabilitation of ecologies, with conservation, with controlled improvements in agricultural production – and took a direct role in enforcing policies that would both protect the productive capacity of the land and bring about the social and economic reforms that were then considered desirable. This was 'the new colonialism',[1] designed by a state that was ready to jettison the comfortable passivity of indirect rule for an ambitious and interventionist reforming programme.

The implications of this were very far-reaching. It is evident that the purpose of rural development in the period after 1945 was not just to foster economic growth but also to bring about an accelerated transformation of African society, with new patterns of land tenure, new ideas of property, of labour and of social organization. These policies were the product of nearly 50 years of colonial rule, the application of the accumulated wisdom of the colonial mind to tackling the ills of rural Africa. Increasingly convinced of its own authority and of the urgent need for reform after 1945, the colonial state in East Africa advocated 'scientific agriculture' in tandem with an ambitious programme for 'social engineering'. Land-tenure reform was the central element of this push for modernization – the ending of communal tenure in rangelands, such as lowland Baringo, and the consolidation of plots and introduction of individual title in agricultural areas such as Kenya's Central Highlands.[2] As we shall see, some of the policies brought in after 1945 were rooted in the earlier experience of rural rehabilitation in Baringo. The wider application of 'the new colonialism' brought a common process of social, economic and political change throughout East Africa.[3]

---

[1] John Iliffe, *A Modern History of Tanganyika* (Cambridge, 1979), 436.

[2] African Land Development and Settlement Board [ALDEV], *African Land Development in Kenya 1946–62* (Nairobi, 1962); R.J.M. Swynnerton, *A Plan to Intensify the Development of African Agriculture in Kenya [Swynnerton Plan]* (Nairobi, 1954).

[3] Good introductory outlines of these processes within East Africa are to be found in Michael McWilliam, 'The managed economy: agricultural change, development and finance in

This transformation has been fittingly characterized by John Lonsdale in the phrase 'the second colonial occupation'.[4] The phrase is appropriate in more than one sense, for not only did the 1940s see the emergence of a new kind of colonial rule, the state reinforced by an army of officials and technicians keen to impose a new order, but it also saw new forms of African resistance to this invasion. The actions of the colonial state after 1945 were not always popular with Africans and, in many places, including Baringo, the emergence of the politics of African nationalism was fuelled in the rural areas by opposition to colonial development and conservation policies.[5] In Baringo the politics of the nationalist era was essentially the politics of ecology, revolving around conflicts over access to and control of environmental resources, most especially rights in land.

From the grandly overambitious goals of the early schemes of the 1920s, to the compromises that would be forced upon frustrated colonial staff by the politics of decolonization in the late 1950s, Baringo's experience therefore offers a study in the history of colonial rural development that is exceptional in its duration but typical in its form. Over time, Baringo's problems came to be seen to epitomize those of degrading semi-arid lands elsewhere in Africa. The district became a frequently cited example of the need for state intervention in environmental management, its development programmes offered as models for others to follow. In this way, Baringo formed an important and surprisingly enduring element in the shaping of the colonial 'blueprint' for the rehabilitation and development of eroded pasturelands.[6] The process by which wider 'colonial knowledge' of the

---

3 (cont.) Kenya', and Margaret Bates, 'Social engineering, multi-racialism, and the rise of TANU', both in D.A. Low & Alison Smith (eds), *Oxford History of East Africa* (Oxford, 1976), iii, 251–89 and 157–95. For southern African comparisons, see William Beinart, 'Soil erosion,conservationism and ideas about development: a southern African exploration 1900–60', *Journal of Southern African Studies*, 11 (1984), 52–83, and the response from Ian Phimister, 'Discourse and the disciplines of historical context: conservation and ideas about development in Southern Rhodesia, 1930–1950', *Journal of Southern African Studies*, 12 (1986), 263–75. The work of William Allan was influential in shaping colonial understandings throughout eastern and central Africa of what might be achieved through 'scientific agriculture'. See his *Studies in Africa Land Usage in Northern Rhodesia* (Lusaka, 1949), but also *The African Husbandman* (Edinburgh, 1965) for an important retrospective summary.

4 D.A. Low & John M. Lonsdale, 'Introduction: towards the new order 1945–63', in Low & Smith (eds), *Oxford History of East Africa*, iii, 1–64.

5 For examples of African reactions, see David W. Throup, *The Economic and Social Origins of Mau Mau* (London, Nairobi and Athens, OH. 1987), esp. ch.6; Steven Feierman, *Peasant Intellectuals: Anthropology and History in Tanzania* (Madison, 1990); Isaria N. Kimambo, *Penetration and Protest in Tanzania: The Impact of the World Economy on the Pare, 1860–1960* (London, Nairobi, Dar es Salaam and Athens, OH., 1991); Fiona Mackenzie, *Land, Ecology and Resistance in Kenya, 1880–1952* (Portsmouth, 1998). All owe a debt to the pioneering study by Lionel Cliffe, 'Nationalism and the reaction to enforced agricultural change in Tanganyika during the colonial period', in Lionel Cliffe & John Saul (eds), *Socialism in Tanzania: An Interdisciplinary Reader* (Dar es Salaam, 1972), 17–24.

6 The work of Emery Roe has been central to my understanding of this issue: '"Development

---

processes of degradation in semi-arid lands was defined, assembled and then applied to the specific problems of Baringo is therefore a central concern of this book.

Agency, knowledge & politics

Interest in the history of ecological change and rural development, and the links between them, has been galvanized by a concern to understand what are very real and dramatic problems of environmental degradation, drought and famine in contemporary Africa. In the words of Michael Mortimore, 'The problem is not whether there is a crisis in rural Africa, but what its nature really is.'[7] History can help us address this fundamental question, and historians, along with others in the humanities and social sciences who have adopted a historical perspective, have begun to offer descriptions of *and* explanations for the processes of environmental change.[8] Some have gone further, consciously seeking to contribute to the process of development planning and policy-making by suggesting prescriptions for the solution to Africa's environmental and developmental problems that are based upon historical evidence. Among those working in applied development, the historical dimension has even come to be accepted as a legitimate (and increasingly essential) component in research and planning.[9] An

[6 (cont.)] narratives" or making the best of blueprint development', *World Development*, 19 (1991), 287–300. Melissa Leach & Robin Mearns (eds), *The Lie of the Land: Challenging Received Wisdom on the African Environment* (Oxford & Portsmouth NH, 1996), elaborate the significance of 'blueprint' development.

[7] Michael Mortimore, *Adapting to Drought: Farmers, Famines and Desertification in West Africa* (Cambridge, 1989), 1.

[8] For the most important recent literature on eastern Africa, see Helge Kjekshus, *Ecology Control and Economic Development in East African History: The Case of Tanganyika 1850–1950* (London, 1977: 2nd edn, with a new introduction, Oxford, 1997); Juhani Koponen, *People and Production in Late Precolonial Tanzania: History and Structures* (Helsinki, 1988). James Giblin, *The Politics of Environmental Control in Northeastern Tanzania 1840–1940* (Philadelphia, 1993); Gregory Maddox, James Giblin & Isaria N. Kimambo (eds), *Custodians of the Land: Ecology and Culture in the History of Tanzania* (London, Dar Es Salaam & Athens OH., 1996); MacKenzie, *Land, Ecology and Resistance*; Douglas H. Johnson & David M. Anderson (eds), *The Ecology of Survival: Case Studies from Northeast African History* (London and Boulder, 1988); James C. McCann, *People of the Plow: An Agricultural History of Ethiopia, 1800–1990* (Madison, 1995). A comparable literature on the environmental history of Uganda and the lakes region is only now emerging. See David L. Schoenbrun, *A Green Place, a Good Place: Agrarian Change and Social Identity in the Great Lakes Region to the 15th Century* (Portsmouth, NH, Oxford & Nairobi, 1999). And for an excellent study that explores a variety of African cases, James C McCann, *Green Land, Brown Land, Black Land: An Environmental History of Africa, 1800–1990* (Oxford & Portsmouth, NH, 1999).

[9] An excellent East African example is Mary Tiffen, Michael Mortimore & Frances Gichuki, *More People, Less Erosion: Environmental Recovery in Kenya* (Chichester & Nairobi, 1994). See also Grace Carswell, 'Farmers, agricultural change and sustainability in colonial Kigezi,

understanding of ecological change is now firmly on the historian's agenda in eastern Africa, and history is increasingly seen as relevant by those involved in the implementation of development.

Ideas emanating from the various critiques of development, clustering around the issues of participation, indigenous knowledge and sustainability, have had a profound impact upon historical writing in eastern Africa. The work of writers such as Chambers, Hyden, Richards and others posed the challenge to contemporary development in deliberately polemical and populist tones, advocating a voice for Africans in determining development priorities and practices and insisting upon greater awareness of African contexts.[10] This body of critical writing first stimulated historical enquiry into the problems of rural development in the early 1980s, just at a time when a general broadening of the scope of history as a discipline was rapidly opening up new sub-fields of investigation into areas such as environmental history and gender history.[11]

Two issues emerged from this conjuncture that have particular importance for defining the parameters of this study: the first concerns African agency. The previous tendency in eastern African historical writing to portray the African purely as a 'victim' of colonialism was then giving way to an approach that emphasized African agency, demonstrating the multiple means by which rural Africans had delayed, deflected and avoided the intentions of the colonial state: in Kjekshus's words, 'people living close to their environments, but as masters and shapers of them, not as their prisoners.'[12] Reflecting this now well-established historiographical shift, a principal impulse behind this study has therefore been to determine the role that the people of Baringo played in shaping their own history.

In a context where so much of what had previously been written about Baringo denied the indigenous dynamic of that historical experience, no

---

9 (cont.) south-western Uganda' (PhD thesis, University of London, 1997). Of wider comparative relevance are Paul Richards, *Indigenous Agricultural Revolution: Ecology and Food Production in West Africa* (London, 1985), esp. ch 1; Michael Watts, *Silent Violence: Food, Famine and Peasantry in Northern Nigeria* (Berkeley, 1983); Piers Blaikie, *The Political Economy of Soil Erosion in Developing Countries* (London, 1985); 'The politics of conservation in Southern Africa', *Journal of Southern African Studies* (Special issue, ed. William Beinart), xv (1989); David M. Anderson & Richard Grove (eds), *Conservation in Africa: People, Policies and Practice* (Cambridge, 1987); James Fairhead & Melissa Leach, *Misreading the African Landscape: Society and Ecology in a Forest–Savanna Mosaic* (Cambridge, 1996).

10 Robert Chambers, *Rural Development: Putting the Last First* (London, 1983); Goran Hyden, *No Shortcuts to Progress: African Development Management in Perspective* (London, 1983); Richards, *Indigenous Agricultural Revolution*. William M. Adams, *Green Development: Environment and Sustainability in the Third World* (London & New York, 1990), provides an excellent overview of this wider 'intellectual history'.

11 Penelope Hetherington, 'Explaining the crisis of capitalism in Kenya', *African Affairs*, 92 (1993), 89–105, but also David M. Anderson, 'The "crisis of capitalism" and Kenya's social history: a comment', *African Affairs*, 92 (1993), 285–90.

12 Kjekshus, *Ecology Control*, xxx.

apology will be offered for a tendency to adopt the tones of advocacy in this task.[13] The taking of sides this implies – 'taking the part of the peasant', in Gavin Williams' now famous phrase[14] – serves a constructive purpose where an orthodox or received view of historical change and causation is being substantially challenged. There are, however, dangers of populism to be avoided. An emphasis upon African agency should not obscure the fact that the disempowerment of African communities in the face of colonial policy-making was real enough. Nowhere in colonial Africa were Africans participants in the colonial decision-making processes that defined development goals.[15] If it is in some ways misleading to represent Africans as the 'victims' of colonial rural development, then they were certainly marginalized by its processes.[16]

This leads to the second issue that defines this study: indigenous knowledge. Under colonialism, the marginalizing of African interests was evident in terms of both power and knowledge. The solution to rural problems – the 'gift' of development – was defined solely in terms of western (colonial) science, with little or no sensitivity to indigenous African husbandry practices or prevailing systems of social organization. Indigenous knowledge systems were not recognized as having any validity or any relevance in relation to progress and modernization under colonialism.[17] Colonial development programmes therefore too often proved to be experiments – conducted Heath Robinson-style in the under-resourced laboratory that was rural Africa – that were doomed to failure because of errors, ignorance, misjudgements and simple misunderstandings on the part of developers.[18]

---

[13] For example, David M. Anderson, 'Rehabilitation, resettlement and restocking: ideology and practice in pastoral development', in David M. Anderson & Vigdis Broch-Due (eds), *The Poor Are Not Us: Poverty and Pastoralism in Eastern Africa* (Oxford, Kampala, Nairobi, Dar es Salaam & Athens, OH, 1999), 240–56. For two other recent works that have displayed this tendency to admirable effect, see McCann, *Green Land*, and Dorothy L. Hodgson, 'Taking stock: state control, ethnic identity and pastoralist development in Tanganyika, 1948–58', *Journal of African History*, 41 (2000), 35–54.

[14] Gavin Williams, 'Taking the part of the peasants: rural development in Nigeria and Tanzania', in P. Gutkind & I. Wallerstein (eds), *The Political Economy of Contemporary Africa* (Beverley Hills, 1976), 131–54.

[15] The excellent collection of essays to be found in Samuel N. Chipungu (ed.), *Guardians in Their Time: Experiences of Zambians under Colonial Rule, 1890–1964* (London & Basingstoke, 1992) has no East African parallel, but the points raised are entirely applicable to Kenya.

[16] For striking examples, see John McCracken, 'Experts and expertise in colonial Malawi', *African Affairs*, 81 (1982), 101–16, on cotton planting; and James L. Giblin, 'Trypanosomiasis control in African history: an evaded issue?', *Journal of African History*, 31 (1990), 59–80, and Richard D. Waller, 'Tsetse fly in Western Narok', *Journal of African History*, 31 (1990), 81–102, on colonial efforts to deal with the tsetse problem.

[17] For an excellent discussion of the wider implications of this, Frederick Cooper & Randall Packard (eds), *International Development and the Social Sciences – Essays on the History and Politics of Knowledge* (Berkeley, 1997). And for an example of the construction of colonial knowledge, see MacKenzie, *Land, Ecology and Resistance*, 98–124.

[18] The most infamous example of failure of this kind is surely the East African Groundnut

This should not lead us to dismiss colonial science, or to replace it with a romanticized presentation of an invariably superior indigenous knowledge system. For this historical reconstruction it will be important to understand the interaction between these two sets of views, colonial and indigenous, and to see how the differences were made manifest in terms both of policy implementation and the reaction to policy.[19]

There were dissenting voices within the colonial project. Most notable among them were William Allen and John Ford, who argued for the appropriateness of indigenous solutions in the management of agricultural and ecological systems, but it is ironic that the value of their insightful work did not begin to be appreciated until more than a decade after the ending of colonialism in eastern Africa.[20] Allen and Ford have each hugely influenced academic scholarship on rural Africa. Paul Richards was most prominent among the group of scholars whose critique of agrarian development sought to popularize the value of indigenous knowledge systems, not by presenting them as an alternative to western science, but by showing, as Allen and Ford had done before, that past practice was an important basis for future development.[21] For historians, the significance of this has been manifest in the recovery of indigenous histories of ecological management, resource conservation and decision-making. These ideas have been most usefully deployed in historical research when harnessed with an approach that gives emphasis to what Richards has termed 'ecological particularism'. The value of this approach has most recently been demonstrated in exemplary fashion in the work of writers such as Giblin, Fairhead and Leach and Feierman.[22] An appreciation of local context is the common and crucial element in each of these studies, and it is a factor that will be emphasized in our examination of Baringo.

Helge Kjekshus's presentation of East Africa's 'traditional indigenous

---

18 (cont.) Scheme. For a firsthand account of 'the groundnutters', see Alan Wood, *The Groundnut Affair* (London, 1950). For a balanced but highly critical assessment, see Jan S. Hogendorn & K.M. Scott, 'Very large-scale agricultural projects: the lessons of the East African Groundnut Scheme', in Robert I. Rotberg (ed.), *Imperialism, Colonialism and Hunger: East and Central Africa* (Lexington, MA & Toronto, 1983), 167–98.

19 For an example of the dangers, see Leach & Mearns (eds), *Lie of the Land*, esp. 1–33, and many of the subsequent chapters.

20 John Ford, *The Role of Trypanosomiasis in African Ecology* (Oxford, 1971); Allan, *African Husbandman*.

21 Richards, *Indigenous Agricultural Revolution*; Paul Richards, 'Ecological change and the politics of African land use', *African Studies Review*, 26, ii (1983), 1–72. An earlier statement of the position had a strong East African element: David W. Brokensha, D.M. Warren and O. Werner (eds), *Indigenous Knowledge Systems and Development* (Washington, 1980); and, for an example directly relevant to Baringo, Peter D. Little & David W. Brokensha, 'Local institutions, tenure and resource management in East Africa', in Anderson & Grove (eds), *Conservation in Africa*, 193–210.

22 Fairhead & Leach, *Misreading the African Landscape*; Giblin, *Politics of Environmental Control*; and Feierman, *Peasant Intellectuals*.

systems' in his groundbreaking study of *Ecology Control and Economic Development in East African History*, first published in 1977, did not deploy the idea of indigenous knowledge in the same manner as Richards would popularize, being less centred in 'ecological particularism'; but Kjekshus' emphasis upon African agency in managing the environment – 'ecology control' as he termed it – raised a similar set of questions in a specifically historical context.[23] While this book perhaps overstressed the destructive impact of colonialism upon African production systems and ecology at the turn of the nineteenth century, its great achievement was to provide a framework for the analysis of the short- and medium-term impact of colonial interventions. The burgeoning field of environmental history in eastern Africa since the early 1980s has continued to productively address the agenda set down by Kjekshus,[24] although fewer scholars have followed Kjekshus in directly linking the causes of ecological change and the trajectory of rural development within a single analysis. Our study of Baringo will endeavour to do this.

But giving prominence to African *agency*, and appreciating the value of indigenous knowledge are not enough if all that is achieved is the presentation of an alternative history that denies the significance of colonial ideas and actions: it is the interaction between African agency and colonial ideas that matters. The structures of colonial rule – ideologies, systems and practices – cannot be ignored in a reconstruction of the history of colonial development. The difficulties in marrying agency and indigenous knowledge with the motivation and operationalization of development practice have been neatly encapsulated by William Adams, who characterizes the relationship between the developers and the developed as being that of 'the blind and the dumb': the developers unwilling or unable to see beyond the end of their own ideologies and preconceptions (their 'learned' practices), the developed unable or denied the right to voice an opinion or have a role in the development process.[25] If this remains true for modern Africa in Adams' representation, and much in the writing of Ferguson, Havnevik and others surely underlines the point, then it was certainly more strongly the case in colonial Africa.[26] Expressing the importance of agency in reconstructing the history of Baringo begins by emphasizing the need to examine the experience of the developed, but it must also engage with the perceptions and intentions of the developers. Such an approach will allow us to evaluate the extent of the 'blindness' of colonial developers, whilst also giving voice to the 'dumb': or, to put it another way, to understand what

[23] Kjekshus, *Ecology Control*, xvii–xxi.

[24] For a wide variety of examples, see the contributions to Johnson & Anderson, *Ecology of Survival*, and Maddox, Giblin & Kimambo, *Custodians of the Land*.

[25] Adams, *Green Development*, ch. 8.

[26] James Ferguson, *The Anti-Politics Machine: 'Development', Depoliticization and Bureaucratic State Power in Lesotho* (Cambridge, 1990); Kjell J. Havnevik, *Tanzania: The Limits to Development from Above* (Uppsala, 1993).

constrained colonial policy and what motivated African response.

This takes us to the question of politics. Relations between developers and the developed in Baringo were mediated by an evolving *politics of ecology*.[27] This politics of ecology is dealt with on two levels in this study: the first imperial, the second local. On the level of imperial policy, there is now a large literature on the history of development planning relating to British experience, which draws upon metropolitan archives to trace the wider international influences of environmental and natural science in the colonial context.[28] In the areas of forestry policy, soil conservation and rangeland management, this wider discourse of development had a direct bearing upon development practice in colonial Baringo.[29]

This body of material therefore also informs questions of policy-making within Kenya colonial administration at the local level. How did the colonizer perceive the rural landscape? What problems were identified and how were these defined? What did government intend to achieve through rural development and by what mechanisms were programmes to be implemented? How did the ideologies behind development translate into the politics of local action? To appreciate the politics of ecology at this local level, a quite different set of sources must be examined. Local colonial archives map out the daily actions of the state in implementing development and record the reactions of Africans as these were perceived by European officers and their informants. From these sources we shall see the way in which the ideological intentions of wider imperial policies were often distorted by the practicalities of the local politics of implementation. These colonial archives often reveal African voices and visions almost despite

---

[27] I have avoided the term 'political ecology', as it implies a more holistic view that sees all ecological issues as political. In Baringo, ecological issues were increasingly politicized as a more strident and pervasive anticolonial politics emerged. See Chapters Seven and Eight below.

[28] Michael Havinden & David Meredith, *Colonial Development: Britain and its Tropical Colonies, 1850–1960* (London & New York, 1993), offer the best overview. D.J. Morgan, *The Official History of Colonial Development*, 5 vols (London, 1980) is an indispensable work of reference. Stephen Constantine, *The Making of British Colonial Development Policy, 1914–1940* (London, 1984), provides a good and detailed account of policies in the 1930s, while J.M. Lee & Martin Petter, *The Colonial Office, War and Development Policy: Organisation and the Planning of a Metropolitan Initiative* (London, 1982), and J.M. Lee, *Colonial Development and Good Government: A Study of the Ideas Expressed by the British Official Classes in Planning Decolonization 1939–64* (Oxford, 1967), take the story forward into the 1940s and 1950s. Robert D. Pearce, *The Turning Point in Africa: British Colonial Policy 1938–1948* (London, 1982), examines the background to the emergence of new development policies at the end of the Second World War with an African focus. David Fieldhouse, *Black Africa 1945–1980: Economic Decolonization and Arrested Development* (London, 1986), wrestles with the economics of development, but Ralph Austen, *African Economic History* (London & Portsmouth, NH, 1987), 197–271, offers a more balanced and insightful analysis.

[29] David M. Anderson, 'Depression, dust bowl, demography and drought: the colonial state and soil conservation in East Africa during the 1930s', *African Affairs*, 83 (1984), 321–43.

themselves, portraying those dissenting from the colonial model of progress and modernity as conservative, reactionary traditionalists. But the local politics of ecology also has a distinctly African aspect, reflected in the oral histories of the implementation of development – the individual and public memories of the interaction between the developers and the developed. In these histories we find rejections of colonial imposition, compulsion, coercion and constraint; but we also find a lively discourse about the divergent meanings of modernity, some keen to accelerate colonial programmes for land reform and social change, others determined to thwart such policies. These memories reveal subtle and nuanced African voices of dissent and African visions of alternative futures.[30]

The local politics of ecology therefore reveal conflicts between and within the African communities of Baringo, and between those Africans and their European settler neighbours. Much of this conflict revolves around the perceived 'rewards' and 'losses' of development – the reallocation of resources.[31] Issues of land use, of resource allocation and of the control of access to land remain as critical to the politics of Baringo today as they were 60 and more years ago.[32] The history of ecological change has been and still is inseparable from the politics of African life: access to and control of land and its basic resources are, of essence, political issues in all societies, but are especially important where the bulk of the population continues to gain its direct subsistence from agricultural production. In the colonial history of Baringo, disputes over access to land were the dominant political issue of the lives of the African communities inhabiting the lowlands, sharpened as some Africans came to actively support and campaign for the

---

[30] For examples of recent work that has developed these same points: MacKenzie, *Land, Ecology and Resistance, passim*; Giblin, *Politics of Environmental Control*, 136–52; Kimambo, *Penetration and Protest*, 96–116, 141–53; Feierman, *Peasant Intellectuals*, 181–99; Pamela Maack, '"We don't want terraces!" Protest and identity under the Uluguru Land Usage Scheme', in Maddox, Giblin & Kimambo, *Custodians of the Land*, 152–68.

[31] A large body of literature now addresses this question for the late colonial and early independence periods in East Africa. The best examples are Tiffen, Mortimore & Gichuki, *More People, Less Erosion*; Havnevik, *Limits to Development*; Thomas Spear, *Mountain Farmers: Moral Economies of Land and Agricultural Development in Arusha and Meru* (Oxford, Berkeley, Los Angeles & Dar es Salaam, 1997); Dorothy Hodgson, 'Images and interventions: the "problem" of pastoralist "development"', in Anderson & Broch-Due (eds), *The Poor Are Not Us*, 221–39; Christopher Conte, 'Nature reorganised: ecological history in the plateau forests of the West Usambara Mountains, 1850–1935', in Maddox, Giblin & Kimambo (eds), *Custodians of the Land*, 96–122. The centrality of these questions to current research in African history has been emphasized in a recent issue of the *Journal of African History*, 41, i (2000), which carried five articles under the collective heading 'Development experiences in the late colonial period'.

[32] Richards, 'Ecological change', offers an excellent discussion of the key points, even though the examples used are now rather dated. For more recent examples, of direct relevance to Baringo, see Charles R. Lane (ed.), *Custodians of the Commons: Pastoral Land Tenure in East and West Africa* (London, 1998).

changes in land tenure and property rights advocated by the colonial state. The history of rural development in Baringo between the 1920s and 1963 charts the intensification of disputes within African communities.

The politics of ecology in Baringo (or anywhere else in colonial Africa) were not, therefore, simply a product of colonial imposition: the colonial state in Kenya was never as powerful as it wished to be or (in the final analysis) needed to be. Of course, the new forces of colonialism brought about significant changes in the ways in which most African communities mediated disputes over land and land-related questions, but it is too easy to portray these disputes as being a conflict between colonizer and colonized – 'an interaction between two major sets of initiatives, European and African'[33] – in which the ideas of an oppressive and overbearing colonial government were imposed upon a reluctant and sometimes recalcitrant African people. Nationalist historians have liked to present things in this simple formulation,[34] but it has long been widely recognized that the reality was a good deal more complex, as the case of Baringo illustrates. European colonialists and the African communities over which they established hegemony 'each comprised several groups of actors with different conventions, institutions, and goals, all of which were subject to change over time'.[35] Like all politics, the politics of ecology in Africa was mutable, divisible and biddable. Colonial development policies were, accordingly, sometimes opposed, sometimes not; but most commonly they worked their way insidiously into the fabric of social reality through the active support and participation of Africans whom the colonial state liked to term 'progressive' or 'modernizing'.[36] To present African communities as the hapless victims of colonialism would be to deny the complexity of the social relations upon which the policies of development impinged and to deny the power of *agency*, *knowledge* and *politics*.

With these wider issues firmly in mind, let us turn to the specifics of Baringo's story.

> *'Upesi, upesi,*
> *Hata Baringo'*
> (19th century Swahili marching song)[37]

---

[33] J. Forbes Munro, *Colonial Rule and the Kamba: Social Change in the Kenya Highlands, 1889–1939* (Oxford, 1975), 1.

[34] A tendency evident in Isaria Kimambo, *Mbiru: Popular Protest in Colonial Tanzania* (Nairobi, 1971); Benaventure Swai, 'Colonial development policy and agrarian protest in Tanganyika territory: the Usambara case, 1920–1960', *Transafrican Journal of History*, 12 (1983), 153–74; and Cliffe, 'Nationalism and the reaction'.

[35] Munro, *Colonial Rule and the Kamba*, 1.

[36] Terence Ranger, *Voices from the Rocks: Nature, Culture and History in the Matopos Hills of Zimbabwe* (Harare, Oxford, Bloomington & Indianapolis, 1999), 162–226, and Iliffe, *Modern History of Tanganyika*, 436–520, each offer masterful elaborations of this point. See also G. Andrew Maguire, *Toward Uhuru in Tanzania: The Politics of Participation* (Cambridge, 1969).

[37] Mrs R.T. Lambert, 'A political history of Baringo and Eldama Ravine' (typescript, 1947), 1, Rhodes House Library Oxford [RH], Lambert Papers, MSS.Afr.s.1388.

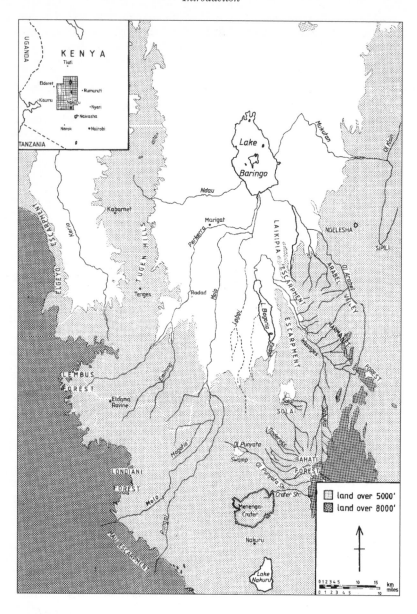

Map I.1 Baringo – physical

Baringo: a land in decay?

Among the most influential critiques of contemporary development to emerge in recent years has been the notion of the 'development narrative'. This has been characterized in the writings of Emery Roe and others as a 'story' that describes the causes of a development problem, its consequences and the likely outcome if the problem is not effectively dealt with. The 'story' may have its origins in a specific, historical example, but its power lies in its generalization to all other cases where the basic ingredients of the problem appear broadly similar. The problem, not the place, becomes the defining factor in determining an appropriate response, and so long as the problem can be categorized the response is predetermined.[38] The narrative thus provides a justification for intervention along lines that move away from the specifics of Richards' environmental particularism and instead foster generalizations based upon 'learned' experience of other cases. So it is that developers carry broad assumptions from one place to another, standardizing the solutions they offer as they go and adopting 'blueprint' programmes to deal with identifiable problems. This phenomenon has its roots deep in the colonial experience of rural development.[39]

Baringo's 'story' is entwined with a development narrative *par excellence*, the narrative of overstocking, which told the tale of a precolonial Eldorado of environmental stability ruined by the excesses of herders who exploited the common pasture beyond its capacity to endure and whose actions therefore needed to be controlled to prevent a once rich land turning into a desert. The power of such a narrative derives from its apparent simplicity, its 'known' logic.[40] The Baringo narrative presents an apparent paradigmal case of a 'tragedy of the commons' which thereby justified a particular set of development interventions and which remained unquestioned until the 1980s.[41] But was the narrative correct? The argument of this book sets out to demonstrate the inaccuracy of this narrative, but also to explain how the story first emerged and why it has endured for so long.

---

[38] Emery Roe, 'Development narratives'.

[39] Leach & Mearns, *Lie of the Land*, 1–33.

[40] On this point, see Alan Hoben, 'The cultural construction of environmental policy: paradigms and politics in Ethiopia', in Leach & Mearns, *Lie of the Land*, 186–208; and McCann, *Green Land*, 79–84.

[41] G. Hardin, 'The tragedy of the commons', *Science*, 162 (1968), 1243–8. For critiques: B. McKay & J. Acheson (eds), *The Question of the Commons: The Culture and Ecology of Communal Resources* (Tucson, 1987), esp ch. by Pauline Peters, 'Embedded systems and rooted models', 171–94; J.T. McCabe, 'Turkana pastoralism: a case against the tragedy of the commons', *Human Ecology*, 18 (1990), 81–103. For the application of the 'new ecology' to the Baringo case, see Katherine Homewood & W.A. Rodgers, 'Pastoralism, conservation and the over-grazing controversy', in Anderson & Grove (eds), *Conservation in Africa*, 111–26; and Katherine Homewood & A. Hurst, 'Comparative ecology of pastoralist livestock in Baringo, Kenya', *Pastoral Development Network Paper*, 21b (Overseas Development Institute, London, 1986).

Lying immediately north of the equator in the northern portion of Kenya's vast Rift Valley Province, Baringo District sprawls over more than 10,000 sq. km of beautifully rugged country.[42] Distant from Kenya's railway and not connected by a decent trunk road to the major highways until the early 1980s, it long seemed isolated and not a little remote from broader currents of political and economic change. But a good road from Nakuru, the nearest town of any importance, now brings steadily growing numbers of tourists speedily through the southern lowlands to view the spectacular bird life of lakes Bogoria and Baringo, before passing on to the game parks of Samburu District or to Lake Turkana in the north. Some take the excellent, winding new road up the escarpment of the Tugen Hills to Kabarnet, admiring the magnificent views of the Rift Valley and its lakes far below. Despite the scenic attractions, few Kenyans yet find reason to visit Baringo, although the district is well known to all: Central Baringo is the parliamentary constituency and birthplace of Kenya's President since 1978, Daniel Toroitich arap Moi.[43] The district's spanking new roads have all been constructed since President Moi came to office, and over this time Baringo has enjoyed something of an upturn in its economic fortunes, the formerly small trading centres of Kabarnet, Marigat and Mogotio now thriving small towns, boasting business communities, hotels and busy petrol stations where before there had been only the humble, ubiquitous rural *duka*.

But the surprising ostentation of Kabarnet cannot disguise the rural poverty that pervades much of the district. There are three zones within the district, each characterized by a different ecology and with a distinct

---

[42] Several changes occurred in the administrative arrangements of the district during the first half of the twentieth century. Baringo was transferred to the East Africa Protectorate from Uganda as part of Naivasha Province in 1902. In 1921, it was removed from Naivasha with the creation of the Kerio Province, incorporating all the African lands in the northern Rift Valley and administered from Eldama Ravine. Between 1921 and 1923 the name 'Suk-Kamasia Reserve' was more generally used, but after 1923, Kerio Province was adopted as the official title. Finally, in 1929, Baringo was included as part of the newly created Rift Valley Province, with its administrative headquarters at Nakuru. Up until 1933, the internal administration of the district was divided between two subunits: North Baringo, centred at Kabarnet from 1914, government headquarters having previously been situated at Loiminagi, Arabel, and then Mukutan (all in the vicinity of Lake Baringo); and South Baringo, headquartered at Eldama Ravine. After 1933, the Eldama Ravine station was closed and Kabarnet became the sole government station responsible for all of Baringo District's administration. After 1948, a district officer was again based at Eldama Ravine. These details are summarized from: Lambert, 'Political History', RH Lambert Papers, MSS.Afr.s.1388; A.R. Champion, 'Boundaries of Baringo Reserve', Jan. 1929, Kenya National Archives [KNA], Political Record Book [PRB] BAR/1/3; Kenneth Ingham, 'Uganda's old Eastern Province: the transfer to the East Africa Protectorate in 1902', *Uganda Journal*, 21 (1957), 41–7; A.T. Matson, 'The eastern boundary of Uganda in 1902', *Uganda Journal*, 24 (1960), 128–9; Robert G. Gregory, Robert M. Maxon & Leon P. Spencer, *A Guide to the Kenya National Archives* (Syracuse, 1969), 9–19.

[43] Andrew Morton's *Moi: the Making of an African Statesman* (London, 1998) is the only biography, but it lacks insight and critical edge.

production system.[44] To the west lies the Kerio Valley, the river running along the valley floor marking the boundary of Baringo and Elgeyo-Marakwet Districts. Moving east, the land rises sharply from 3,500 ft on the Kerio valley floor to peaks of over 8,000 ft in the Tugen Hills, these forming the second zone. The hills run north to south through Baringo, and form a secondary fault escarpment lying within the Rift Valley. At the southern extreme of the Tugen Hills, surrounding Eldama Ravine, lies the Lembus Forest, a portion of the larger Londiani Forest Reserve. In this southern area land was excised for a large European timber concession in 1905 (the consequences of which we shall return to in some detail in Chapter Eight).[45] The Lembus area is the most developed in the district in terms of commercial agriculture. Moving further north, along the spine of the Tugen Hills, altitude ranges from 6,000 ft to more than 8,000 ft. The hills enjoy a moderate and cool climate, and with rainfall of over 40 inches per annum the agricultural potential appears good.[46] However, the steep-sloped hills are extremely rugged. Farmers cultivate wherever they can, and much of the best land has been terraced since the 1950s to minimize the effects of soil erosion (which has been severe in some unprotected areas). Until the 1950s the crop regime in the hills was limited to sorghums, millets and varieties of vegetables, but pyrethrum and coffee are now successfully grown. The hilltops are generally reserved as grazing for livestock. This hill region is known by the name *Masop* to the Tugen who live there.[47]

To the east, the hills drop very rapidly to the broad expanse of the dry, bush-infested, rocky Rift Valley floor – the Baringo lowlands. It is with this third zone, known as *Soi*, that the present study is primarily concerned. The land here has a bare, inhospitable, parched appearance, and since the colonial period has come to be characterized as 'goat country' – although whether it is a country made by the goat or a country made for the goat is a question to which we shall return in Chapter Five. But when the rains come to the lowlands the appearance of the landscape can be remarkably transformed, with a rapidly grown and verdant flush of grazing. Two rainfall seasons are expected in this region – the long rains from April to July and the short rains from October to November – although the limited rainfall records we have indicate this to be a very unreliable regime. Rainfall on the lowlands is notoriously variable between points only a short distance apart, and an average of less than 30 inches is all that can be expected to fall in a year. The soils of the plains are not especially fertile, the vegetational

---

[44] J.C. de Wilde et al. *Experiences with Agricultural Development in Tropical Africa, Vol. II, The Case Studies* (Baltimore, 1967).

[45] David M. Anderson, 'Managing the forest: the conservation history of Lembus, Kenya, 1904–63', in Anderson & Grove, *Conservation in Africa*, 249–68.

[46] De Wilde et al., *Experiences with Agricultural Development*.

[47] Colin Maher, *Soil Erosion and Land Utilisation in the Kamasia, Njemps, and East Suk Reserves* (Nairobi, 1937), 14–28.

cover being dominated by *Acacia* species.[48] Alongside the numerous flocks of sheep and goats, cattle are herded on the lowlands. Since the late 1950s, land consolidation has been expanding through the lowlands (see Chapter Seven), and cultivation of cereals (now almost exclusively maize) has increased significantly, although the unreliability of rainfall makes this a hazardous business.[49]

Two major rivers flow across the rugged plains of the Rift Valley floor from south to north: the Perkerra and the Molo. The former rises in the Lembus Forest, west of Eldama Ravine, and the latter descends on to the Baringo lowlands from the Mau Escarpment to the south. Many smaller rivers also water the plains, but the majority of these are seasonal, and even the more reliable among them in the south, the Emining, Mogotio and Esageri Rivers, are prone to run dry if the rains are too long delayed. The Molo and Perkerra both feed Lake Baringo, the two rivers merging in the fertile swamplands on the Njemps Flats along the southern margins of lake. This swamp provides an important reserve grazing area for cattle in the dry season.[50] Beyond the lake, which marks the northern limit of our study, the plains descend gradually towards Lake Turkana, with aridity increasing as altitude falls.

Although Baringo has never been densely settled, population has concentrated in the more fertile parts of the hills and on the lowlands in the south. According to the 1969 government population census, the inhabitants of Baringo District then numbered approximately 162,000, predominantly comprised of three main ethnic groups, the Kalenjin-speaking Tugen and Pokot and the Maa-speaking Chamus.[51] The main focus of the study rests upon those Tugen living on the southern Baringo lowlands within the area bounded to the north by Lake Baringo, to the south by Menengai Crater and the upland areas of Rongai, by the Lembus Forest and the Tugen Hills to the west, and by the Rift Valley escarpments of Laikipia and Solai to the east. By the later colonial period approximately 30 per cent of Baringo's population lived within this zone, numbering more than 40,000 people. Also included within this region are Il Chamus Maasai, who inhabit the alluvial flats between Lakes Baringo and Bogoria, their settlements extending towards the Laikipia Escarpment by way of Mukutan, Arabel and

---

[48] Peter D. Little, *The Elusive Granary: Herder, Farmer and State in Northern Kenya* (Cambridge, 1992), 18–24. For a detailed survey of local ecology, Republic of Kenya, *Baringo Semi-Arid Area Pilot Project*, Parts 1 and 2 (Ministry of Agriculture, Marigat 1984). For rainfall data, see J.C. Bille & A.H. Heemstra, 'An Illustrated Introduction to the Rainfall Patterns of Kenya' (ILCA Kenya, Working Document No. 12, Nairobi, 1979); and H.E. Carrick & A.E. Tetley, 'Report on the Perkerra River Irrigation Project', 25 June 1936, KNA PC/RVP.6A/ll/26.

[49] De Wilde et al., *Experiences with Agricultural Development*, ii, 172.

[50] Little, *Elusive Granary*, 22–4; Homewood & Hurst, 'Comparative ecology'; Katherine Homewood and J.G. Lewis, 'Impact of drought on pastoral livestock in Baringo, 1983–85', *Journal of Applied Ecology*, 24 (1987), 615-31.

[51] Republic of Kenya, *Kenya Population Census, 1969. Vol. IV – Analytical Report* (Central Bureau of Statistics, Nairobi, 1970).

Ngelesha. Recent population counts reckon the Chamus to number some 9,000, but during the colonial period their population was probably never greater than 4,500. Renowned in the nineteenth century as productive and skilled agriculturalists who irrigated their lands, the colonial experience of Il Chamus will be examined in greatest detail in Chapter Nine.[52] A smaller community of Uasin Gishu Maasai also occupied lands to the west of Eldama Ravine on the southern lowlands from the 1890s, but all bar a handful of this population had been moved to the Trans-Mara region under colonial directive by the 1950s.[53] The Maa dialect spoken by the Chamus is close to that of Samburu, a fact evident in the close historical relationship between these two groups. But clan histories of Il Chamus also reveal close connections with other Maa-speakers and with the neighbouring Tugen.[54] The Kalenjin dialect of Tugen varies markedly from north to south through the district, reflecting a wider pattern of dialect variability evident among all six of the major clusters of Kalenjin-speakers in Kenya – Tugen, Nandi, Kipsigis, Keyo, Marakwet and Pokot.[55]

Kalenjin history has to date received only slight scholarly attention, and what research has been conducted has focused in the main upon Nandi and

---

[52] Two recent books have focused upon the Chamus: Paul Spencer, *The Pastoral Continuum: The Marginalization of Tradition in East Africa* (Oxford, 1998), 129–204, with a discussion of demographics at 140–41, n13; and Little, *Elusive Granary*.

[53] Richard D. Waller, 'Interaction and identity on the periphery: the Trans-Mara Maasai', *International Journal of African Historical Studies*, 17 (1984), 243–84; A.T. Matson, 'The early history of the Uasin Gishu', *Kenya Weekly News*, 23 Feb. 1963.

[54] Rainer Vossen, 'Linguistic evidence regarding the territorial history of the Maa-speaking peoples: some preliminary remarks', *Kenya Historical Review*, 6 (1978), 34–52, notes the Samburu connection. See also Gabriele Sommer & Rainer Vossen, 'Dialects, sectiolects, or simply lects? the Maa language in time perspective', in Thomas Spear & Richard D. Waller (eds), *Being Maasai: Ethnicity and Identity in East Africa* (London, Nairobi, Dar es Salaam, & Athens, OH, 1993), 25–36. For further ethnographic details, see Spencer, *Pastoral Continuum*, esp. 134–48.

[55] R.O. Moore, 'Unraveling the Kalenjin Riddle' (University of Nairobi, History Department Staff Seminar No. 6, 1977), discusses some of the problems presented by the regional differences in Kalenjin dialects. There is no good ethnographic survey of the Kalenjin peoples, but see G.W.B. Huntingford, *The Southern Nilo-Hamites* (London, 1953), and Benjamin Kipkorir, *People of the Rift Valley – Kalenjin* (Nairobi, 1978), a short text written for use in schools. Ethnographies containing useful historical material include: C.W. Hobley, *Eastern Uganda: An Ethnological Survey* (London, 1902); A.C. Hollis, *The Nandi: Their Language and Folklore* (Oxford, 1909); Mervyn W.H. Beech, *The Suk: Their Language and Folklore* (Oxford, 1911); J.A. Massam, *The Cliff Dwellers of Kenya* [Keyo] (London, 1927); J.G. Peristiany, *The Social Institutions of the Kipsigis* (London, 1939); G.W.B. Huntingford, *Nandi Work and Culture* (London, 1950); G.W.B. Huntingford, *The Nandi of Kenya: Tribal Control in a Pastoral Society* (London, 1953); I.Q. Orchardson, *The Kipsigis* (Nairobi, 1961); W. Goldschmidt, *The Culture and Behaviour of the Sebei* (Berkeley, 1976); Benjamin E. Kipkorir & F.B. Welbourn, *The Marakwet of Kenya: a Preliminary Survey* (Nairobi, 1973); M. Langley, *The Nandi of Kenya* (London, 1979); Henrietta L. Moore, *Space, Text and Gender: An Anthropological Study of the Marakwet of Kenya* (Cambridge, 1986).

Kipsigis, with a concentration upon precolonial history[56] and the impact of colonial conquest.[57] The experience of the Tugen in the twentieth century has been almost wholly neglected.[58] The early colonial literature refers to the Tugen of the southern locations of Baringo by the derogatory Maasai name 'Kamasia', although it is evident that several names relating to the smaller political units of Tugen society, the *pororosiek*, were in general use up until the early 1900s. These names, such as Lembus, Kakamor and Ewalel, were known to early colonial administrators at Eldama Ravine, and appear regularly in their diaries and correspondences.[59] Such names were

---

[56] For examples: William R. Ochieng, *An Outline History of the Rift Valley of Kenya up to AD 1900* (Nairobi, 1975); Henry A. Mwanzi, *A History of the Kipsigis* (Nairobi, 1977); Taaitta Toweett, *Oral Traditional History of the Kipsigis* (Nairobi, 1979); S.C. Lang'at, 'Some aspects of Kipsigis history before 1914', in B.G. McIntosh (ed.), *Ngano: Studies in Traditional and Modern East African History* (Nairobi, 1969), 73–94; Benjamin E. Kipkorir, 'The Kalenjin phenomenon and the Misri legends' (University of Nairobi, History Dept. Staff Seminar Paper, 1971); Kipketer Chirchir-Chuma, 'Aspects of Nandi society and culture in the 19th century', *Kenya Historical Review*, 3 (1975), 23–38; B.K. Kipkulei, 'The origin, migration, and settlement of the Tugen people, with special reference to the Aror, from the earliest times to the turn of the twentieth century' (BA dissertation, University of Nairobi, 1972); Isaac Tarus, 'An outline history of the Keiyo people from 1700 to 1919' (BA dissertation, University of Nairobi, 1988); J.A. Distefano, 'Lagokap Miot (The Children of Miot): An Enquiry into Kalenjin Pre-Colonial History' (University of Nairobi, History Dept. Staff Seminar No.7, 1976); J.E.G. Sutton, *The Archaeology of the Western Highlands of Kenya* (Nairobi, 1973).

[57] For example, Henry Mwanzi, 'Koitalel arap Samoie and Kipchomber arap Koilege: southern Kalenjin rulers and their encounters with British imperialism', in Benjamin E. Kipkorir (ed.), *Imperialism and Collaboration in Colonial Kenya* (Nairobi, 1980), 15–36; P.K. arap Magut, 'The rise and fall of the Nandi orkoiyot 1850–1957', in McIntosh (ed.), *Ngano*, 95–110; Samuel arap Ng'eny, 'Nandi resistance to the establishment of British administration, 1893–1906', in B.A. Ogot (ed.), *Hadith 2* (Nairobi, 1970), 104–26; Alice Gold, 'The Nandi in transition: background to the Nandi resistance to the British, 1895–1906', *Kenya Historical Review*, 6 (1978), 84–104; A.T. Matson, *Nandi Resistance to the British*, Vol. 1 (Nairobi, 1972); A.T. Matson, *The Nandi Campaign Against the British, 1895–1906* (Nairobi, 1974); A.T. Matson, *Nandi Resistance to British Rule: Vol. 2 The Volcano Erupts* (Cambridge, 1993); David M. Anderson, 'Visions of the vanquished: prophets and colonialism in Kenya's western highlands', in David M. Anderson & Douglas H. Johnson (eds), *Revealing Prophets: Prophecy in East African History* (London, Kampala, Nairobi, and Athens, OH, 1995), 164–95.

[58] I am not aware of any explicitly historical work on Baringo in the twentieth century. R.O. Hennings, *African Morning* (London, 1951) is the memoirs of a colonial officer who served in Baringo, and went on to be secretary to ALDEV in the 1950s; Elspeth Huxley, *The New Earth: An Experiment in Colonialism* (London, 1960), has a chapter on 1950s development in Baringo. De Wilde et al., *Experiences with Agricultural Development* takes Baringo as one of its case-studies, with material mostly relating to the 1960s. And two unpublished doctoral theses each contain some useful historical background material: R. Ott, 'Decisions and development: the lowland Tugen of Baringo district, Kenya' (PhD thesis, State University of New York at Stoney Brook, 1979); Bonnie Kettel, 'Time is money: the social consequences of economic change in Seretunin, Kenya' (PhD thesis, University of Illinois, 1980).

[59] See Matson, *Nandi Resistance*, I, 224–34, for several examples, mostly cited from the Austen diaries and the Ravine Station Diaries, copies of which are located in RH, Matson Papers MSS.Afr.s.1272/4/45.

subsequently adopted as locational divisions under colonial administration.[60] The means by which colonial administration ascribed names to African peoples, labelling and lumping groups to create spatially discrete political entities, has become a familiar theme in recent historical writing on the colonial period. The ethnic markers ascribed to Baringo's peoples bore some indigenous socio-economic and cultural meaning, although the agents of colonialism would put these labels of identity to entirely novel purposes. The ethnic taxonomy of colonial rule in Baringo therefore was not 'invented' by European officials, but was constructed out of the interactions with the Africans whom they encountered.[61]

While the definition of ethnic identity within Baringo was negotiated, it must be acknowledged that the category of 'Kalenjin' was the creation of a more self-conscious and overtly political process. Until the 1940s, those now called Kalenjin had been referred to collectively as 'the Nandi-speaking peoples'. In wartime they formed a large element of the African recruits to military service, and when the Office of Information decided to initiate radio broadcasts in vernacular languages they targeted each of the central areas of recruitment. According to the account given by Kipkorir, the term 'Kalenjin' emerged from these broadcasts, being a bowdlerization of a frequently used phrase, *kalenjok* ('I tell you'). The term was quickly taken up at the Alliance High School in Nairobi, where 'the newly emerging Kalenjin educated elite' formed a Kalenjin Club in 1944. Four years later, John arap Chemallan, who had been the Nandi voice in the wartime broadcasts, joined others, many of them ex-servicemen, to form a political organization based in Eldoret, which they called the Kalenjin Union. This, argues Kipkorir, marked the beginning of the emergence of a political identity, which was consolidated during the Mau Mau emergency of the 1950s and thereafter in the tense politics of Kenya's final years under colonial rule, when the Kalenjin Union became part of the Kenya African Democratic Union (KADU).[62] Kalenjin identity was born out of linguistic similarity and cultural affinity, nurtured by geographical proximity in the

---

[60] Baringo Political Record Book, vol. 1, ch. 2, KNA PRB/1 BAR/13.

[61] Iliffe, *Modern History of Tanganyika*, 318–41, remains the best discussion, although T.O. Ranger, 'The invention of tradition in colonial Africa', in Eric Hobsbawm & T.O. Ranger (eds), *The Invention of Tradition* (Cambridge, 1983) is more often credited as the principal source of the idea. See also Leroy Vail, 'Ethnicity in Southern African history', in Leroy Vail (ed.) *The Creation of Tribalism in Southern Africa* (London, Berkeley & Los Angeles, 1989), 1–18. For East African examples: Bill Bravman, *Making Ethnic Ways: Communities and Their Transformations in Taita, Kenya, 1800–1950* (Portsmouth NH, Oxford & Nairobi, 1998); Justin Willis, *Mombasa, the Swahili and the Making of the Mijikenda* (Oxford, 1993); and T.O. Ranger's, 'European attitudes and African realities: the rise and fall of the Matola chiefs of southeast Tanganyika', *Journal of African History*, 20 (1979), 63–82. Kipkorir & Welbourn, *Marakwet of Kenya*, 1–5, provide a Kalenjin example.

[62] Kipkorir & Welbourn, *Marakwet of Kenya*, 70–76. For additional information: Benjamin E. Kipkorir, 'The Alliance High School and the making of an African elite, 1926–62' (PhD thesis, University of Cambridge, 1969).

Rift Valley Province, but brought to maturity by political intent.

When asked in the 1980s to categorize their own communities and to place these in relation to their neighbours, lowland Tugen interviewed for this study did not then emphasize any sense of being Kalenjin.[63] They commonly identified the Tugen people as comprising three broad sections; the *Aror*, of the poor and barren lands to the north; and the *Samorr*, of the richer southern locations, this group being further subdivided into groups of herders who reside on *Soi* (the lowlands), and agriculturalists, who inhabit *Masop* (the hills). The differentiation between people from *Aror* and those from *Samorr* was believed to be long-standing, while the *Soi* Tugen were said only to have emerged as a recognizable group since the early part of the century.[64] These internal distinctions were acknowledged to be social constructions, a perception of group identities working as a continuously changing process, mobilized by shifting ecological and economic conditions as well as by cultural and political factors. But by the mid-1990s many in Baringo had developed a much sharper sense of themselves as a bounded group, more conscious of the threat from outsiders than of internal fissures. All were still *Aror*, *Masop* or *Soi*, and all were Tugen, but more importantly all were by then unquestionably Kalenjin, and this had become the ethnic label people preferred to attach to themselves, especially when talking with strangers. There are, of course, many elements involved in so rapid a transformation of self-projection and perception, but this was most overtly a product of Kenya's changing political kaleidoscope. For the people of Baringo, politics had been given a dramatic immediacy through the person of the President, and reinforced after 1990 as Kenya stumbled towards multi-partyism through a thickening fog of ethnic particularism.[65] Whether ethnic markers were ascribed through the negotiations with colonialism or are taken up more directly by communities to describe themselves, they have considerable importance for the politics of the day.

In colonial Baringo the politics of the day was inevitably linked to the question of access to land. As elsewhere in Kenya, this was primarily determined by race and secondarily by ethnicity. In contrast to the harsh environment of the Baringo lowlands, the neighbouring areas to the east and south comprise good arable farming lands, containing a number of well-watered pastures. In these areas the land rises to over 5,000 ft, and with this the rainfall regime becomes both more plentiful and more reliable.[66] The areas of Solai and Subukia, bounding Baringo to the east, and Ol Pun-

[63] Details of the collection of these oral histories can be found in the Appendix to this volume.
[64] The same distinctions are described in Kipkulei, 'Origin, migration, and settlement'; D.W.W. Kettel, 'Passing like flowers: the marriage regulations of the Tugen of Kenya and their implications for a theory of Crow Omaha' (PhD thesis, University of Illinois, 1975); and Ott, 'Decisions and development'.
[65] David Throup & Charles Hornsby, *Multi-Party Politics in Kenya* (Oxford, Nairobi and Athens, OH, 1998).
[66] For rainfall figures from a number of farms in these areas, see the Meteorological Department Annual Reports, 1902–1929 (Ministry of Agriculture Library, Nairobi).

yata, Lomolo, Rongai, Esageri and Eldama Ravine, lying along the south-ern marches, were all alienated as areas of European settlement prior to 1920. These farmlands came to mark the administrative limits of Baringo District, but more importantly they marked the limit of lands that could be freely used by the African herder. In taking possession of these lands the European settler community had seized seasonal grazing areas and watering points that were crucial to the survival of the African herders on the lowlands of southern Baringo. Their property in this land was reinforced by the might of the state, and they sought to keep it to themselves. The alienation of these uplands from African control marked the beginnings of Baringo's 'decay'.

To understand why this should have been so, it is neccessary to contrast the land-use patterns of the nineteenth century in this part of the northern Rift Valley with those brought about under colonialism. The opening two chapters of this book describe and analyse the dramatic changes in the settlement of the Baringo lowlands that occurred as a consequence of colonialism. Chapter One reconstructs pastoral land-use patterns of the nineteenth century to illustrate that the Baringo lowlands formed part of a wider ecological system, seasonally exploited by transhumant herders. After 1900, the waning of Maasai power in the Rift Valley created opportunities for the expansion of Tugen herders, eastwards and southwards from the Tugen Hills. For African herders making this move the exploitation of a wider pattern of seasonal grazing was the critical dynamic in the economic management of their livestock. The story of their experience in the twentieth century has largely centred on their struggles to cope with the denial of access to those upland areas. The Baringo lowlands were part of a wider production system, one which colonial incursion permanently fractured. From the viewpoint of the African in Baringo, their troubles after 1900 were without doubt the consequence of colonialism. But this was not how the colonial administration saw things: from a colonial perspective, the apparent decay of the Baringo lowlands, mapped out in the discussion of the impact of drought and the practice of trespass (Chapters Three and Four) and culminating in the desiccation of the lowlands described in evidence before the Kenya Land Commission in 1932 (Chapter Five), was an inevitable product of the mismanagement of the African herder.

In the second half of the book, the focus shifts to the development programmes mounted in the lowlands by the colonial state between 1929 and the 1950s to solve what was by then widely accepted as Baringo's environmental decay. From 1929, a scheme for reconditioning pasture was introduced and, by the end of the 1930s, covered very extensive areas of the southern lowlands. As the earliest example of development initiatives in pastoral lands in East Africa, and as the basis for larger projects applied to many other districts after 1940, these reconditioning schemes will be closely examined in Chapter Six. In 1940, a more ambitious scheme for the reha-bilitation of the rangelands was devised and was implemented after the end of the war. Chapter Seven examines the various grazing and rehabilitation

schemes implemented in this postwar phase, the successors to the reconditioning project of the 1930s. The two principal schemes were located on the Solai border and at Esageri, near Eldama Ravine. Administration and regulation on these schemes were much tighter than had been the case before 1940, as the state struggled to impose limits on livestock numbers by enforced culling. African herders resisted these initiatives in several ways, and by the late 1950s opposition to the grazing control schemes had become deeply politicized. At the same time, many prominent individuals had taken advantage of colonial encouragement to fence lands from the common pasturage and carve out what were, in effect, smallholdings. These actions bred new, internal conflicts and added further to the politics of land in this period. Chapter Eight focuses upon similar issues with regard to the Lembus Forest Resettlement Scheme, a project that became the focus of much African political activity in the years immediately before independence. The third element of postwar development to be considered is the Perkerra Irrigation Scheme. Quite different in character from the various reconditioning and resettlement schemes elsewhere in the district, this project was, however, directly linked to the same set of concerns. Originally mooted in the 1920s, the scheme was only begun in the 1950s when the labour of Mau Mau detainees was used to construct the main dam works on the Perkerra River near Marigat, to the immediate south of Lake Baringo. While administrators saw the potential for using the scheme as a model for smallholder agriculture and as encouragement of individual tenure, they ignored the long historical tradition of indigenous irrigation among Il Chamus and brought in others to farm the irrigated lands. Chapter Nine will examine the deeper history of this scheme in the context of later colonial attitudes toward rural development, bringing us full circle, back to the irrigated agriculture by Lake Baringo that first drew traders to the area in the mid-nineteenth century.

In telling this story we shall challenge the deeply embedded orthodox 'narrative' of Baringo's environmental and development history. It is still widely believed today that the area around Lake Baringo was a rich and fertile agricultural zone in the nineteenth century and that the lowland pastures were of a quality to sustain large herds. Neither was in fact the case: agriculture at Lake Baringo, even with irrigation, was a fragile system, prone to failure and periodic famine; and the lowland pastures had rainfall only adequate to support seasonal use. Under colonial rule it came to be believed that Baringo's environment had been degraded by the actions of the cattle and goat herds kept by irresponsible African herders, whose overstocking promoted rapid desiccation. The struggle for existence on the lowlands of Baringo was real enough by the mid-colonial years, but the apocalyptic scenarios of European commentators vastly exaggerate the extent and nature of the environmental changes they supposed had taken place. The development 'narrative' of Baringo was shaped by these European perceptions of a dramatically decaying landscape, and it was this vision that provided the impetus and justification for colonial interventions.

One

Baringo
in the Nineteenth Century
c. 1840s–1900

The patterns of settlement and land use in lowland Baringo during the colonial period represented a radical transformation from the circumstances of the nineteenth century. Conflicts between African and European under colonial rule would revolve around African attempts to re-create a nineteenth-century model of land use and European determination to prevent them from doing so. This chapter opens with an account of the movements of Maa-speaking groups through Baringo in the second half of the nineteenth century, illustrating the position of the Baringo lowlands in a wider seasonal system of pastoralist land use. From the 1840s onwards the pastoralist communities of the Rift Valley were disrupted by demographic changes, which led to an escalation in raiding and ultimately to warfare. Drought and outbreaks of serious cattle disease heightened their difficulties in the wake of internecine warfare, left the pastoral Maa sections vulnerable to their agricultural neighbours and paved the way for colonial incursions. The second part of the chapter will sketch out the circumstances of the colonial conquest of the region in the 1890s and early 1900s. By the turn of the century the territorial map of Baringo had been radically redrawn, setting the scene for the protracted conflict that was to follow between African herders and European settlers.

The Baringo lowlands before 1900

Our reconstruction of the history of Baringo in the nineteenth century relies upon the oral histories of the several Maa-speaking and Kalenjin-speaking peoples, who lived in and around the central and northern Rift Valley at

that time. From the 1870s, these sources can sometimes be augmented by the written accounts of European travellers and by information on historical events collected by colonial officials in the early years of the twentieth century, and they can be cross-referenced to provide a surprisingly detailed catalogue of events for the period before the intrusion of European influences.

At the centre of all these accounts stand the struggles among Maa-speakers and between them and their neighbours, which ebbed and flowed through the lowlands from the 1840s to the 1880s. This protracted series of conflicts have come to be collectively known as the 'Iloikop Wars'. This term encapsulates a very diverse and complex sequence of events, in which several different sections of Maa-speakers were drawn into conflict over control of seasonal pastures and access to watering points. We know more about their consequences than about their causes, but it is likely that the conflicts were initially prompted by the very success of Maasai pastoralism in the early part of the nineteenth century. After a period of successful territorial expansion at the expense of their non-Maa neighbours, by mid-century Maasai sections turned upon one another in an effort to secure key resources. What began as sporadic and opportunistic raids of the strong upon the weak escalated, as counter-raids were mounted and those harried by stronger neighbours looked elsewhere to make good their losses.[1]

Before we examine the chain of events that made up the Iloikop Wars, something must be said about ethnicity, community and the nature of warfare in the nineteenth century. Our earliest information on the Iloikop Wars derives from the writings of European missionaries on the East African coast, such as Krapf, Wakefield and Farler, who received their news of events in the interior at second or third hand. These writers, along with others, tended to characterize the conflicts of the Iloikop Wars as being fought out between feuding sections (*il-oshon*) of Maasai, one side comprising pastoralists, the other agriculturalists. The agricultural Maasai sections were described by the term *Kwavi*, and hence the Iloikop Wars are sometimes also written about as the Kwavi wars.[2] More recently, historians using Maasai oral histories have recognized that the supposed division between agricultural and pastoral sections, if it was ever meaningful in these broad terms, was the product of struggle, not its delimiting factor. The Iloikop Wars were fought to secure cattle and access to pasture and water for cattle. It seems most likely that conflict was generated by the overcrowding of key grazing areas – by too great a competition for limited pastoral resources.

---

[1] The essential starting point remains Richard D. Waller, 'The Lords of East Africa: the Maasai in the mid-nineteenth century, *c.*1840–1885' (PhD thesis, University of Cambridge, 1978).

[2] J. Ludwig Krapf, *Travels, Researches and Missionary Labours during Eighteen Years Residence in Eastern Africa* (London & Boston, 1860); T. Wakefield, 'Routes of native caravans from the coast to the interior of East Africa', *Journal of the Royal Geographical Society*, 40 (1870), 303–38; J.P. Farler, 'Native routes in East Africa from Pangani to the Masai country and the Victoria Nyanza', *Proceedings of the Royal Geographical Society*, 4 (1882), 730–42.

Those defeated in the Iloikop Wars were made destitute in cattle and were, inevitably, absorbed by the victors or forced to flee to neighbouring communities as refugees. Either way, without cattle the defeated were likely to find themselves dependent upon agriculture for as long as it might take them to acquire new livestock and build up their herds.[3]

The Iloikop Wars were not, then, struggles in which the principal aim was to inflict large numbers of casualties upon your enemies. Rather, the struggles were territorial and strategic. Those who lost cattle could not sustain themselves through pastoralism and were accordingly compelled to take up agriculture or seek refuge with other communities. This has great significance for our wider understanding of East African history in two respects. First, and in marked contrast to assumptions made in much of the earlier work on the history of pastoralist peoples in East Africa, ethnic identity was not defined solely in terms of production. Maa-speakers were principally cattle-keepers, yes, but many were also agriculturalists. Movement between herding and cultivating was essential in ensuring the long-term security of pastoralism. All herding communities in the Rift Valley maintained close relationships with neighbouring cultivators, some of whom were Maa-speakers, others of whom were not. Ethnic identity in the Rift Valley was seldom a barrier to peaceful contacts and interpenetration, and can best be understood, in the words of Berntsen, 'if likened to an osmotic membrane through which people passed according to their needs and according to the pressures placed upon them or the opportunities opened to them at a given time'.[4] Thus, identity was not fixed, but mutable. The ability of a society to assimilate and incorporate incoming individuals and families acted as an important social dynamic. This allowed Tugen and Il Chamus to accommodate numbers of Maasai refugees during the second half of the nineteenth century, peoples who had been displaced by the Maasai wars in the Rift Valley around Nakuru and Menengai and, later in the century, by the social dislocations of drought and disease, as we shall

---

[3] For various oral histories: Waller, 'Lords of East Africa'; Richard D. Waller, 'The Maasai and the British 1895–1905: the origins of an alliance', *Journal of African History*, 17 (1976), 529–53; Richard D. Waller, 'Economic and social relations in the Central Rift Valley: the Maa-speakers and their neighbours in the nineteenth century', in B.A. Ogot (ed.), *Kenya in the Nineteenth Century* (Nairobi, 1985), 83–151; John L. Berntsen, 'Pastoralism, raiding and Prophets: Maasailand in the nineteenth century' (PhD thesis,University of Wisconsin, 1979); Neal P. Sobania, 'The historical traditions of the peoples of the Eastern Lake Turkana Basin, *c*.1840–1925' (PhD thesis, University of London, 1980); Paul Spencer, *Nomads in Alliance: Symbiosis and Growth among the Rendille and Samburu of Kenya* (London 1973); K.R. Dundas, 'Notes on the Tribes inhabiting the Baringo District, East African Protectorate', *Journal of the Royal Anthropological Institute*, 40 (1910), 49–72, is based upon oral histories collected before 1910. For linguistic evidence: Vossen, 'Linguistic evidence', 34–52; and Sommer & Vossen, 'Dialects, sectiolects, or simply lects?', 25–37.

[4] John L. Berntsen, 'The Maasai and their neighbours: variables of interaction', *African Economic History*, 2 (1976), 8. In many senses, the entire project of Spear & Waller's *Being Maasai* is an elaboration of this point.

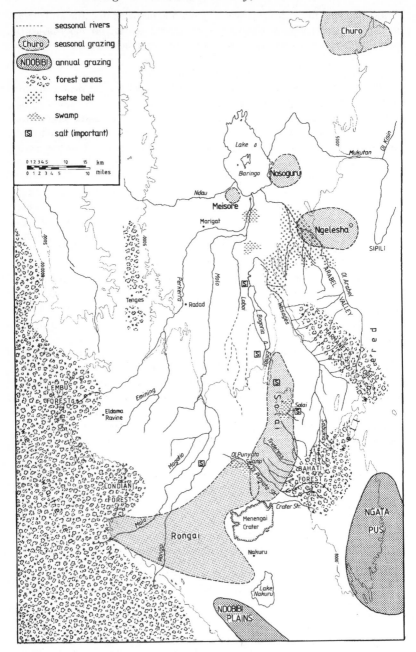

Map 1.1 Pastoral resources of Baringo and its neighbouring areas

describe below. In this way, communities engaged in cultivation absorbed people pushed out of pastoralism: at other times agricultural communities lost people to livestock production.

This movement is most clearly illustrated in Baringo in the example of Il Chamus, who in the nineteenth century were settled in fortified villages at the southern end of Lake Baringo and engaged in a sophisticated system of irrigation agriculture. This community, and other cultivating Maa-speaking communities like it up and down the Rift Valley, absorbed destitute pastoralists and then acted as a springboard for those who were able to accumulate sufficient livestock to move back into herding. Neighbouring pastoralists took care to keep open social networks with Il Chamus, through regular economic exchange, livestock bonding and inter-marriage. In times of warfare, drought or livestock epidemic, these became the networks of survival, with the destitute and displaced settling amongst Il Chamus villages as refugees. Always anticipating only a temporary stay, some of these people would settle permanently. Transitions of this kind from pastoralism to agriculture and from agriculture to pastoralism were a common and accepted strategy of survival in the Rift Valley: no group could afford to be isolationist, and the more adaptable a group was, the more successful it was likely to be.[5]

The second significant point for our understanding of East African history follows directly from this. It is important to recognize that the ethnic markers we now use to designate the peoples of the past have only a limited validity. Maa and Kalenjin oral histories are replete with the names of sections, clans and communities whose actual existence can only be determined in general terms and the definitions of which must remain vague. Family genealogies and clan histories reveal the close relationship of past identities to present communities, and these are crucial historical markers.[6] Thus, as we shall see in greater detail below, genealogies among Il Chamus clearly illustrate the arrival of several waves of refugees from defeated Maasai sections during the nineteenth century: people who were Toijo, Loosekelai or Laikipiak *became* Chamus. These same patterns of movement, of the fissuring of communities and the absorption of some by others, are a prominent feature of the oral histories of all the peoples living

---

[5] For fuller discussion, see David M. Anderson, 'Cultivating pastoralists: ecology and economy among Il Chamus of Baringo, 1840–1980', in Johnson & Anderson (eds), *Ecology of Survival*, 241–60; and David M. Anderson, 'Agriculture and irrigation technology at Lake Baringo in the nineteenth century', *Azania*, 24 (1989), 85–98. Elsewhere in the Rift Valley other groups of Maa-speaking agriculturalists fulfilled a similar role. For summaries and further references, see William M. Adams & David M. Anderson, 'Irrigation before develop-ment: indigenous and induced change in agricultural water management in East Africa', *African Affairs*, 87 (1988), 519–36; Richard D. Waller, 'Ecology, migration and expansion in East Africa', *African Affairs*, 84 (1985), 347–70; and Spear, *Mountain Farmers*, ch. 2.

[6] For a bold attempt to view these relationships in a regional perspective, see Gunther Schlee, *Identities on the Move* (Manchester, 1989); and his 'Interethnic clan identities among Cushitic-speaking pastoralists', *Africa*, 55 (1985), 17–38.

in and around the Rift Valley in the nineteenth century. We cannot always be precise about who was moving where or at exactly what time particular transformations occurred, but the oral histories do allow us to be sure of the sequence of events and of the processes involved.[7]

With these factors in mind, we can now turn to an outline of events in the nineteenth century. In the early part of the nineteenth century the Baringo plains had been occupied by a group of Maa-speaking herders known as Il Toijo. Closely connected with Samburu and also with Il Chamus Maasai at Lake Baringo, Il Toijo grazed their herds around Lakes Bogoria and Baringo and over the dry scrublands to the north and north-east. Beyond Bogoria, to the south, the Rift Valley was occupied seasonally by Maasai herders, whose movements took them through Baringo *en route* to the plateau grazing on Laikipia from the Rift Valley grasslands around Nakuru. This general territorial pattern began to be disrupted in the 1840s. The first pressures came with the gradual expansion of the Loosekelai Maasai out of the western Mau and into the Nakuru–Baringo area, then occupied by the large Purko section and other smaller Maasai sections. Initially accommodated by their closer Maa neighbours, Loosekelai expansion had greater immediate effect upon Il Toijo. The oral histories of the peoples of this region, first recorded by Dundas in the early 1900s, relate that competition over grazing and access to water led to the Loosekelai inflicting a series of heavy defeats on Il Toijo around the lakes, forcing them to retreat northwards to the inferior lands around Nginyang and Mount Pagaa. From there, Pokot and perhaps also Turkana pressure from the north and north-west pushed them further east. Histories collected among Samburu and other peoples to the south-east of Lake Turkana relate that, at some time during the 1850s, the advance of the Laikipiak Maasai on to the Leroghi Plateau again squeezed the unfortunate Toijo from the other side, forcing them further north. Due to this combination of pressures, over a period of perhaps 20 years, the Toijo were removed from the Baringo area by around 1860, whilst the Loosekelai Maasai had successfully expanded into the pastures of Nakuru and extended northwards through lowland Baringo.[8]

The Loosekelai were soon in competition with the numerous Il Purko section of Maasai for control of the strategically important Nakuru corridor – the narrow neck of the central Rift Valley around Lake Nakuru.[9] Control of the Nakuru corridor gave easier access to valuable grazing in the vicinity of Naivasha, whilst also opening up Kinangop, Solai and Laikipia to seasonal use. The oral histories of Tugen and Il Chamus agree that the

---

[7] To those sources already cited in footnote 2 above should be added David M. Anderson, 'Some thoughts on the nineteenth-century history of Il Chamus of Baringo', *Mila: Bulletin of the Institute of African Studies, Nairobi,* 7 (1984), 107–25.

[8] The dating here is supported by: Spencer, *Nomads in Alliance,* 152–3; Dundas, 'Notes on the tribes', 50–2; Sobania 'Historical traditions', ch. 2. Also BHT/CH/12; BHT/CH/16; and BHT/TG/3.

[9] The following passage draws heavily upon Waller, 'Lords of East Africa', *passim.*

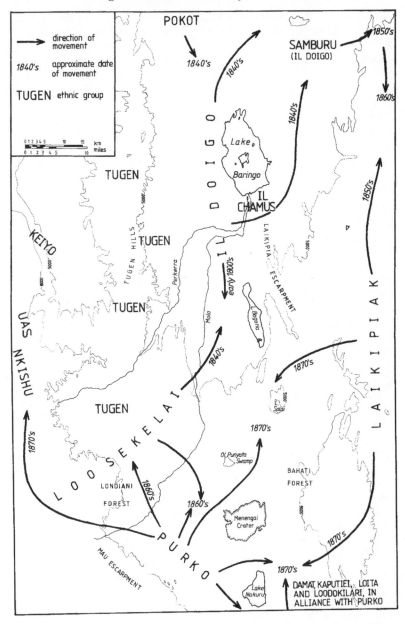

Map 1.2 Nineteenth-century movements in the northern Rift Valley

Loosekelai and Il Purko initially came into conflict not over the Nakuru area – where Waller has suggested they shared grazing and water rights – but over the exploitation of the more marginal grazing areas to the north, vacated by the Toijo.[10] However, as their conflict escalated in the Loosekelai War, cooperation around Nakuru disintegrated, and the Purko, in alliance with Keekonyukie, Damat and other Maasai sections, ultimately defeated the Loosekelai.[11]

With many of the defeated Loosekelai being absorbed by the victorious Purko, the latter now controlled the Baringo and Nakuru grazing areas. The only group capable of challenging this dominance was the Laikipiak Maasai, who then held all grazing across the Laikipia Plateau from Isiolo in the north-east to the Aberdares in the south-west. Their most obvious areas of conflict with the Purko were the pasturelands of Solai, Subukia and Kinangop, above the eastern wall of the Rift. As it was, the eventual struggle between the Laikipiak and Il Purko was precipitated by renewed Samburu pressure on the Laikipiak Maasai in the north, pushing their herds towards those of the Purko. The period of conflict between these two powerful sections lasted throughout the 1870s, with the Kaputiei, Damat, Loodokilari and Loita sections of the Maasai also being drawn into the spiralling conflict of raid and counter-raid. After initial Laikipiak success, including the occupancy of the Nakuru corridor for several years, an alliance of Maasai sections around the *loibon* Mbatiany resulted in the defeat of the Laikipiak in the Naivasha area, destroying their foothold in the Rift Valley.[12] The defeated Laikipiak retreated on to the plateau, where sporadic raiding against them lasted until around 1880. The surviving Laikipiak scattered, some being absorbed by other Maasai sections, some seeking refuge with Samburu and with Il Chamus at Lake Baringo. A small number of Laikipiak refugees even found their way as far west as the Tugen Hills.[13] During the 1870s, then, by which time the power of the Laikipiak had been broken, the Purko were strong enough to hold a fairly secure grip over the pastoral resources of the Nakuru corridor.

[10] BHT/CH/11; BHT/TG/52.

[11] Waller, 'Lords of East Africa', 384–6. For a general overview, see D.A. Low, 'The Northern Interior, 1840–84', in R. Oliver & G. Mathew (eds), *Oxford History of East Africa* (Oxford, 1963), i, 305–7.

[12] Waller, 'Lords of East Africa', 388–90; Neal Sobania, 'Defeat and dispersal: the Laikipiak and their neighbours at the end of the nineteenth century', in Spear & Waller (eds), *Being Maasai*, 105–19; Sobania, 'Historical traditions', ch. 2; Low, 'Northern interior', 306–9; Spencer, *Nomads in Alliance*, 153–4. For *loibonok* histories, see Berntsen, 'Pastoralism, raiding and prophets'; John L. Berntsen, 'Maasai age-sets and prophetic leadership, 1850–1912', *Africa*, 49 (1979), 134–45; and Richard D. Waller, 'Kidongoi's kin: prophecy and power in Maasailand', in Anderson & Johnson (eds), *Revealing Prophets*, 28–64.

[13] BHT/CH/9; BHT/CH/10; BHT/CH/27; and BHT/TG/47. The clans of Il Toimal and Loiborkishu among Il Chamus claim strong links with the Laikipiak Maasai, as well as with Il Doigo (Samburu). For further discussion of Chamus clans and their histories, see Spencer, *Pastoral Continuum*, chs 4 and 5.

The dominance of the Purko Maasai was further augmented in the early 1880s by the absorption of members of the disintegrating Uas Nkishu section, to the west of the Rift. Internal conflicts over grazing and water rights had by the 1860s fractured the Uas Nkishu into several rival segments. This was followed by pressure from Nandi, expanding on to the Uas Nkishu Plateau from the south from the 1870s. Purko bands were thus able to make a series of successful cattle raids against a Uas Nkishu community that by the early 1880s was already in rapid decline. As the cohesion of the section collapsed with the loss of livestock and grazing, remnants of the Uas Nkishu, like the Laikipiak before them, were dispersed among surrounding agricultural communities. During the early 1890s, one such small Uas Nkishu community was beginning to regroup in southern Lembus, near Eldama Ravine, where they were later to play a significant role as collaborators in the British colonial conquest of Baringo and the approaches to the Western Highlands.[14]

By the 1880s, then, Purko had come to control a vast tract of grazing, which their numbers made difficult to protect and impossible to fully occupy. The lands to the north of Nakuru, in particular, were now seriously underpopulated. The protracted period of Maasai internecine conflict that had brought about this situation revolved around competition for limited pastoral resources, in terms of stock, grazing and water. After 1880, all Maasai sections, but the Purko in particular, increasingly faced competition from other non-Maasai groups. Their dilemma and the transition that had brought it about have been neatly encapsulated by Richard Waller:

> There was a delicate balance between the amount of grazing needed for successful pastoralism and the number of men and animals available to exploit it effectively. Too little grazing led to congestion and conflict inside the pastoral community. Under-exploitation left the pastoral group in possession vulnerable to encroachment from outside. The Iloikop Wars, which had begun as a result of the former, ended with a shift towards the latter.[15]

The earliest references to the Iloikop Wars reached a European audience on the East African coast in the mid-nineteenth century, just as they began to learn something of the Baringo region. Swahili and Arab ivory traders were making visits to Baringo by 1840, and it was they who brought news of events and peoples in the interior. To the European missionaries who recorded these stories, the interior seemed a desperate and war-torn land,

[14] Matson, 'Early history of the Uasin Gishu'; Jackson to Lansdowne, 13 Sept. 1901, Intelligence Report, Uganda No. 4, App. A, 'Report on the Gwas Ngishu tribe', by Maj. E.H. Gorges, PRO FO2/804 (map at PRO MR 1013); *KLC:EM*, vol. II, 1795–7, provides a useful historical summary, repeated in *KLC:Report*, 247–8. For background, see Waller, 'Interaction and identity', 243–84. Also BHT/TG/52, BHT/TG/43 and BHT/TG/66, for Tugen oral histories on Uas Nkishu.

[15] Waller, 'Maasai and the British', 532.

but their first images of Baringo were of a peaceful sanctuary in the midst of savagery. 'Njemps', as Il Chamus and their fortified settlements at the southern end of Lake Baringo came to be known, was already by the 1850s an important resting place on the caravan trade routes that crossed the East African interior.[16] Baringo was an area rich in ivory, and the Chamus villages on the southern shores of the lake offered a suitable base for trade and hunting in the surrounding regions, as well as being an important source of food provisions for caravans pushing on to the north and west.[17] In the middle decades of the century Il Chamus expanded the production of their irrigation agriculture to meet the increasing demands of the caravan traders, and the area gained a reputation as a 'granary' in the midst of an arid and inhospitable land. Such did the fame of the district grow that the first European travellers to visit Baringo, Joseph Thomson (1883) and Count Teleki (1887), fixed upon 'Njemps' as a 'safe haven' from the outset of their explorations, sure that they would find a friendly welcome among Il Chamus and a ready supply of cereals to feed their caravan porters.[18]

Both these travellers found a friendly welcome, but Baringo was not the land of plenty they had supposed. By the last decades of the nineteenth century the irrigation system at Lake Baringo was already in slow decline; the ivory and trading frontier was moving beyond Baringo, and Il Chamus were no longer able to maintain a regular surplus of grains to supply passing caravans. The expansion of agricultural production had been driven by the demands of the caravan trade, but it had been made possible by the accumulation of population drawn to Lake Baringo as refugees from the Iloikop Wars between the 1850s and 1870s. The two fortified Il Chamus villages of Leabori (Njemps Mkubwa) and Lekeper (Njemps Ndogo) were situated on the banks of the Perkerra and Molo Rivers, respectively,[19] on the alluvial flats to the south of Lake Baringo and to the south-west of the swampy estuary at the confluence of these two rivers before they enter the

---

[16] The earliest references to Baringo in European sources are to be found in J. Ludwig Krapf, *Vocabulary of the Engutuk Eloikob* (Tubingen, 1854); L. des Avanchers, 'Esquisse géographique des Pays Oromo ou Galla, des Pays Soomali, et de la Côte Orientale d'Afrique', *Bulletin de la Société de géographie*, 17 (1859), 153–70; Wakefield, 'Routes of native caravans'; and Farler, 'Native routes'.

[17] The following description draws upon Anderson, 'Some thoughts'; Anderson, 'Agriculture and irrigation technology'; Anderson, 'Cultivating pastoralists'; and Spencer, *Pastoral Continuum*, 129–203. See also Little, *Elusive Granary.* For a brief description of the ivory trade at Baringo, see Frederick D. Lugard, *The Rise of Our East African Empire*, 2 vols (Edinburgh, 1893), i, 352–4.

[18] Joseph Thomson, *Through Masailand* (London, 1897); L. von Hohnel, *Discovery by Count Teleki of Lakes Rudolf and Stephanie*, 2 vols (London, 1894). For further accounts, see Carl Peters, *New Light on Darkest Africa* (London, 1891); and J.W. Gregory, *The Great Rift Valley* (London, 1896); H.H. Austin, 'From Njemps to Marish, Sowe, and Mumias (British East Africa)', *Geographical Journal*, 14 (1899), 307–10.

[19] Leabori, the 'Down-River Chamus', is named Lemeluat by Spencer, and Lekeper, 'Up-River Chamus', is named Lekenyuki: Spencer, *Pastoral Continuum*, 140–1.

lake. The cultivations of the larger village, Njemps Mkubwa, were more extensive, and it certainly supported the larger population. Von Hohnel reckoned the population of the smaller village, Njemps Ndogo, to be over 1,500 in 1887–8.[20] This may be an exaggeration, as in the final quarter of the nineteenth century the population of both villages fluctuated considerably.[21] It is also possible, as Spencer notes, that this estimate reflected the recent absorption of pastoralist refugees into the Chamus community.[22] Clan and family histories among Il Chamus provide evidence of the absorption of numbers of Il Toijo after their dispersal in the 1860s. Several Il Chamus clans claim descent from Il Toijo, and each still retains close links with their kin amongst Samburu. These same families, along with others, later gave refuge to remnants of the defeated Laikipiak and Uas Nkishu sections.[23] These influxes may have doubled the total population of the Il Chamus villages by the late 1870s and into the 1880s. By the time of von Hohnel's visit the population may once again have been on the point of decline. Each of the Europeans to visit Baringo in the later nineteenth century commented on this absorption of pastoralists among Il Chamus, and von Hohnel and Gregory both noted that some of these refugees later returned to herding.[24] The incoming population came to find food and shelter, of course, but they also contributed the labour that was needed to expand the area of land under irrigation and to hunt the elephants to gather ivory for exchange. Through these activities destitute pastoralists hoped to accumulate sufficient resources in livestock to move back to herding, and to this end their involvement in the ivory trade was crucial. By the end of the 1870s, a decade in which oral history testifies to the success of Il Chamus ivory hunting in the region, it seems likely that the Chamus villages were again losing labour as families moved back to herding, and that this worked to diminish the level of surplus production obtainable.[25]

Even though these movements of population are indicative of the rise and fall of nineteenth-century irrigation production, it is unlikely that the surplus produced at Baringo was ever as large or as reliable as Thomson and others had been led to believe. To be sure, Thomson was much impressed by the system of irrigation, which he described as 'wonderfully ingenious'. Brushwood and boulder dams were constructed across the rivers,

---

[20] von Hohnel, *Discovery*, ii, 5.

[21] Spencer, *Pastoral Continuum*, 140 n13, usefully surveys the data on Chamus demography. However, his assumption that an official estimate of three persons per hut in 1936 is a reliable basis for calculating the population before 1900 overlooks the likely impact of dramatic changes in settlement and production.

[22] Spencer, *Pastoral Continuum*, 158.

[23] Anderson, 'Some thoughts', but note also some important additional information in Spencer, *Pastoral Continuum*, 134–7, 145–8.

[24] Thomson, *Through Masailand*, 263; von Hohnel, *Discovery*, 4–6; Gregory, *Great Rift Valley*, 354–6.

[25] The dynamic of this is discussed in Anderson, 'Cultivating pastoralists', 87–9, and in Spencer, *Pastoral Continuum*, 157–8. We shall return to this matter in Chapter Nine below.

diverting the waters into 'artificial canals'. The field system was of 'enormous extent', being 'divided like a chessboard, into plots from three to four miles square.' These huge fields were then bisected by 'an intricate network of channels', to 'spread the precious fluid over a large area'.[26] But, all this said, when Thomson arrived at Njemps Mkubwa, in November 1883, the rivers were low and the fields were dry, and no rain had fallen by the time of his return in January 1884, the people by then being reduced to extensive gathering to obtain food.[27] The rains had also failed to materialize in November 1887, when the caravan led by Count Teleki and von Hohnel arrived at Lake Baringo. They found it impossible to purchase food from Il Chamus, whose grain stores were almost empty.[28] Gregory's experience was worst of all, arriving in 1893 in the midst of a famine. The rains of 1892 had failed completely, whilst those of 1893 had been so heavy that flooding had occurred and much of the crop had been washed away.[29] Alongside the impact of drought and deluge, other difficulties were evident. Von Hohnel observed that much of the field system was lying fallow in 1887, possibly for lack of labour, and reported that the people complained of serious damage to the crop from the predations of birds, wild game and rats.[30] Agriculture on the floor of the Rift Valley, even under irrigation, was evidently a precarious business. Lake Baringo was never the granary that some have supposed, although the system of irrigation agriculture practised by Il Chamus in the nineteenth century gave them a remarkable comparative advantage over their neighbours. But the myth, which so vastly exaggerated the extent and sustainability of Baringo's surplus production in the nineteenth century, was to last well into the twentieth century, becoming a key element in European perceptions of the district's environmental decay.[31]

In comparison with our fairly detailed knowledge of Il Chamus in the nineteenth century, we know much less about the conditions of Tugen society. Most Swahili caravans and European travellers approached Baringo either from the east, dropping down from the Laikipia escarpment, or from the south-east, entering the Rift Valley to the south of Lake Bogoria and passing through parts of lowland Baringo. But in these regions travellers passed through what were then still Maasai-held areas, not Tugen, and anyway the available accounts give us surprisingly little information on conditions in the lowlands of southern Baringo.[32] When food was scarce at

[26] Thomson, *Through Masailand*, 264; von Hohnel, *Discovery*, 5.

[27] Thomson, *Through Masailand*, 312.

[28] Von Hohnel, *Discovery*, 1–8.

[29] Gregory, *Great Rift Valley*, 118.

[30] Von Hohnel, *Discovery*, 5. See also Thomson, *Through Masailand*, 265, and Lugard, *East African Empire*, i, 354, for similar observations.

[31] Little, *Elusive Granary*, 30–8. Chapter Nine below offers a fuller discussion of this in the context of attempts to develop irrigation on the Perkerra in the 1950s.

[32] Thomson, *Through Masailand*, 263–72; von Hohnel, *Discovery*, i, 426–7, ii, 284; Peters, *New Light*, 264–83; Gregory, *Great Rift Valley*, 117–27.

'Njemps' some traders did send parties westwards into the notoriously more hostile Tugen Hills to purchase supplies, but this was seldom successful and no lasting trade links with Tugen appear to have been established.[33] It was not until the 1880s that European-led expeditions traversed the hills, *en route* to Buganda, and these were very few in number. The German explorer, Karl Peters, was the most notorious of these travellers, refusing to pay *hongo* – the payment demanded by Tugen of all trading caravans crossing their country – and battling his way across the hills from Lake Baringo toward Mumia's with 400 head of cattle in train.[34] Lugard made a less violent procession through the hills, commenting upon the extent of cultivation on the craggy landscape, but also noting the poverty of the people.[35] Where Lake Baringo had been a magnet of attraction to traders and travellers, the Tugen Hills were an area to be avoided, occupied by an apparently hostile people who had little surplus to trade.

By the 1880s, just as Europeans began to make journeys across the Rift Valley, the Iloikop Wars were coming to an end. Weakened by their internal struggles, the social and political cohesion of many sections seriously diminished, the Maasai were more scattered and less dominant than they had previously been in the Rift Valley. Over the next decade their vulnerability was to be greatly accentuated by the ravages of disease.[36] First came bovine pleuropneumonia, to be followed by the cattle plague, rinderpest, until then unknown to Maasai. Livestock disease was followed by human disease, as an epidemic of smallpox swept across eastern Africa. Bovine pleuropneumonia (*ol kipie*) was seen just to the north of Nakuru by Joseph Thomson, on his journey across Maasailand in October 1883. Spreading southwards in the following months, the disease was widely established throughout the Maasai herds by 1887. Its impact was mediated by restrictions placed upon movements of stock and by an improvised form of immunization. By these means Maasai herders coped with the outbreak. However, they were to be completely overwhelmed by rinderpest (*olodua*) some eight years later. The first reports of this outbreak emanated from a German military patrol moving through the Kilimanjaro area in February 1891, but it is likely that the disease may already have become recently prevalent in areas to the north.[37] Its rapid spread and virulence were quite unlike anything the Maasai had experienced before. Entire herds

---

[33] For an early reference to the hostility of Tugen, see Charles New, *Life, Wanderings and Labours in Eastern Africa* (London, 1971: 1st edn, 1873), 465.

[34] Peters, *New Light*, 279–80.

[35] Lugard, *East African Empire*, i, 354–7.

[36] The following account is drawn mainly from Richard D. Waller, 'Emutai: crisis and response in Maasailand 1883–1902', in Johnson & Anderson (eds), *Ecology of Survival*, 73–112.

[37] Ben Polak, 'Rinderpest and Kenya in the 1890s' (MA dissertation, Northwestern University, 1985), for the fullest account of the spread of the disease. Also, R.W.M. Mettam, 'A short history of rinderpest, with special reference to Africa', *Uganda Journal*, 1 (1937), 22–6.

succumbed within weeks as the infection spread from section to section, transmitted as infected cattle shared pastures or congregated at watering points or by the movements of raided cattle. The mortality rate was so devastating that even comparative wealth brought no security: the rich were as likely to be rendered destitute as were the poor. By end of 1891, Maasai losses had probably already risen to more than 80 per cent of the total herd. Faced with utter destitution and imminent famine, Maasai cattle raiding increased dramatically, but the devastation was so acute and so widespread that few cattle were available.

In the wake of the rinderpest, loyalties to section and community gave way in a desperate battle for survival itself. The raiding that resulted amounted to a complete civil war, the intensity and anarchy of which far outweighed the more strategic struggles of the Iloikop Wars. In this civil war there was no order, no honour, no notion of longer-term gain or security: only desperation and chaos. The impact throughout Maasailand was profound and unprecedented. Those Maasai without stock began to congregate in refugee communities around the fringes of the Rift Valley. Those Maasai who could moved closer to Kikuyuland, hoping to acquire food in trade with their Highland agricultural neighbours.[38] Several large camps formed in the vicinity of Ngong, drawing in refugees from the southern Rift. In the central region, people gathered around Naivasha; and in the north, other Purko and Keekonyukie moved toward the Kikuyu around Nyeri, whilst Il Dalalelkuyuk settled near Meru[39] and refugees again flowed into the Chamus villages at Lake Baringo.[40]

These movements had two effects, the first with longer-term implications, the second with a more immediate impact. First, large tracts of Maasailand were left vacant as the population moved to the fringes, a fact that was widely reported by European travellers who passed through the region during the early 1890s. This experience gave rise to the often quoted tales from this period of East Africa as an empty land ripe for future European settlement.[41] Secondly, and of more immediate significance for Maasai, the vulnerable refugee communities, undernourished and gathered in ramshackle settlements, fell victim to outbreaks of epidemic smallpox (*entidiai*). The first cases probably occurred in the middle of 1892. Over the next year all Maasai sections were affected. Smallpox was already well known to Maasai, who understood that the infection was carried over the land by the Swahili trading caravans from the coast; but they had never before experienced its impact so severely. It was those refugee communities settled close to Kikuyu and close to the caravan routes to the coast who

[38] Waller, 'Emutai', 92–101.

[39] Ibid., 78.

[40] Anderson, 'Cultivating pastoralists', 248.

[41] Elspeth Huxley's, *White Man's Country: Lord Delamere and the Making of Kenya*, 2 vols (London, 1935), is certainly the best known, although Charles Eliot, *The East African Protectorate* (London, 1905), was among the earliest exponents of the 'empty lands' argument.

suffered worst in the epidemic. In these areas there are reports of whole camps having been wiped out by smallpox.[42]

The combination of bovine and human disease epidemics accentuated the imbalances between land, labour and livestock among the Maasai. Some communities had suffered the loss of stock and of labour; others had lost stock, but had not been so severely stricken by smallpox; others had still managed to maintain small herds, but now had too little labour to effectively protect their property. The effects of smallpox thus gave further impetus to the pattern of intersectional raiding that had begun with the onset of the rinderpest. Those communities who could took the opportunity to replenish their stock at the expense of those who were weaker. Patterns of patronage and dependence were broken and remade anew in these struggles for survival. In this process, the broader authority of sectional loyalty was undermined as groups fragmented into smaller elements. Richard Waller has found evidence of this in the patterns of raiding following the rinderpest. From 1892 through to 1894, the sections remained fairly coherent, and a number of large-scale raids took place by one section on another. But by 1894, any semblance of order had given way to a chaotic pattern of small, opportunistic raiding, in which only the fittest would survive.[43]

Amongst all the sections, only the Loita and Purko retained any recognizable authority, gathered around the *loibons* Sentue and Olonana, respectively. From 1894 to 1898, these two sections fought a sporadic war, which saw the Loita and their allies the Damat retreat southwards, into territory that was to become part of German East Africa. Under attack from the Germans as well as neighbouring Africans, the cohesion of the Loita quickly crumbled. By June 1902, Sentue and his remaining followers came north to surrender to Olonana and the Purko. But, if ever there was a Pyrrhic victory beyond the shores of ancient Rome, this was surely it. Olonana and the Purko were by then the clients and dependents of the British. Drought had struck central Kenya in 1887, followed by severe famine in 1898–9. Bovine pleuropneumonia and then rinderpest again reappeared among the Purko cattle, Olonana himself being reported to have lost more than 1,000 head. The rinderpest raged to the west of Ngong until mid-1900. The very survival of Olonana and his followers in this second period of disease and famine was dependent upon the support of the British. Within two years of his 'victory' over Sentue and the Loita,

---

[42] Waller, 'Emutai', 79–81, who cites the relevant contemporary observations. See also, Marc H. Dawson, 'Smallpox in Kenya, 1880–1920', *Social Science and Medicine*, 13b (1979); and Marc H. Dawson, 'Disease and population decline of the Kikuyu, 1890–1925', in C. Fyfe & D. McMaster (eds) *African Historical Demography*, Vol. 2 (Edinburgh, 1981), 121–38. For the only contemporary source of any substance, see J. Christie, *Cholera Epidemics in East Africa* (London, 1876).

[43] Waller, 'Emutai', 80–93.

Olonana would sign the treaty with his British allies that would condemn the former 'Lords of East Africa' to life in a 'Native Reserve'.[44]

Thus far we have considered these events only from the perspective of Maasai history. But the trials of the Maasai and the ultimate erosion of their former power, brought opportunities to others. In Baringo the principal beneficiaries were to be the Kalenjin-speaking Tugen, who, during the nineteenth century, occupied the rugged hills running south to north through the district.[45] As a sedentary community, viewing pastoralists on the lowlands below them, Tugen oral histories of this period offer a valuable fixed point of reference in an otherwise seemingly constantly moving picture. Tugen traditions tend to portray themselves as having been locked within the fastness of their hillside refuge to escape the maelstrom of Toijo, Loosekelai and Purko predations during the nineteenth century.[46] Whilst it is surely true that Maasai sections placed constraints upon Tugen movements, a careful reading of family and clan histories reveals a more flexible social reality. Living on the middle and lower slopes of the hills and utilizing the grazing and forests of the hilltops and the narrow Kerio Valley to the west, Tugen families subsisted on a mixed economy involving the cultivation of cereals (sorghums and millets) along with the keeping of large numbers of sheep and goats, but with only small herds of cattle. Small stock and cereals could be traded with neighbouring pastoralists, and the oral histories of Il Chamus Maasai, for example, confirm close links with Tugen. Tugen women often worked as seasonal labourers on the irrigated fields of Il Chamus, being paid in grain.[47]

The lowlands of Baringo offered an attractive potential for expanding Tugen livestock husbandry, but until the very end of the century this was not an option the Tugen were ready or willing to take up. Although Tugen prized this lowland grazing, they could not enjoy permanent access to it because of the dominant position of Maa-speaking herders. They achieved

[44] Waller, 'Maasai and the British', 530–2; Waller, 'Emutai', 84–5; D. Anthony Low, 'British East Africa: the establishment of British rule, 1895–1912', in Harlow & Chilver (eds), *Oxford History of East Africa*, ii, 3–5; Thomson, *Through Masailand*, 563–5.

[45] For nineteenth-century history of the Tugen and their Kalenjin neighbours, see: Kipkulei, 'Origin, migration and settlement'; Tarus, 'Outline history of the Keiyo'; Sutton, 'The Kalenjin', in Ogot (ed.), *Kenya Before 1900* (Nairobi, 1976), 21–52; Ochieng, *Outline History of the Rift Valley*, 55–112; Sutton, *Archaeology of the Western Highlands*; C. Ehret, *Southern Nilotic History: Linguistic Approaches to the Study of the Past* (Evanston, 1971); Distefano, 'Lagokap Miot'; Kipkorir, *Marakwet of Kenya*.

[46] Kipkulei, 'Origin, migration and settlement'.

[47] This view is informed by the collection of Tugen oral histories undertaken as part of this research project, but evidence is also contained in several early European accounts, for example Thomson, *Through Masailand*, 270–2; Lugard, *East African Empire*, i, 354–6, in Kipkulei, 'Origin, migration and settlement'; and in more recent research reports: see B.L. Kettel, 'Time is money'; B.L. Kettel & D.W.W. Kettel, 'The Tugen of Kenya: a brief ethnographic report' (Institute of African Studies Library, Nairobi, 1971); Ott, 'Decisions and development'.

temporary access to this area from time to time, however. In many years Tugen herders might move their few cattle down into the lowlands along the western banks of the Perkerra River and, in some years, might manage to extend with their stock east as far as the Molo River. Tugen oral histories even assert that at times during the nineteenth century they were able to graze their animals in the Rift Valley to the east of the Molo River.[48] The spatial organization of Tugen communities within the hills reflects this movement between upland and lowland. Territoriality was structured upon loose groupings based on clan affinity, known as *pororosiek*. Each *pororosiek* held lands running from hilltop to valley bottom, allowing each to cultivate at different altitudes and to move their small herds of cattle between lowland and upland pastures.[49] Advances as far as the Molo River are acknowledged to have been of limited extent and would only have been seasonal in duration.[50] This aside, it remains the case that throughout much of the nineteenth century access to the Nakuru corridor and its adjacent grazing areas was governed by the movements of larger and more powerful bands of Maasai herders.[51]

With the gradual weakening of Maasai power in the northern Rift Valley towards the end of the century, Tugen expansion eastwards across the Perkerra River and towards the Molo River became a more regular feature of seasonal grazing patterns. Tugen were at this time well placed to take advantage of available grazing. Having retreated to the hilltops with their stock at the onset of the rinderpest plague of the early 1890s, mortality among Tugen cattle had been comparatively low. Losses to the disease are certainly recalled in Tugen oral histories, associated with the Kipkoimet age-set, but the Tugen consider themselves to have escaped very lightly.[52] Two other factors furthered·the beginning of the Tugen drift to the plains at this time – and 'drift', in a gradual and unsystematic sense, it most certainly was. First, population pressure in the hills had increased. From 1850 onwards, the Iloikop Wars had served to supply a small but

---

[48] BHT/TG/16; BHT/TG/52.

[49] Huntingford, *Southern Nilo-Hamites,* 32–5, gives an explanation of the significance of the *pororosiek* (s. *pororiet*) among the Nandi, this being broadly similar in the case of the Tugen.

[50] BHT/TG/16; BHT/TG/52; BHT/TG/68.

[51] A number of papers have been written by East African scholars on the broader history of Kalenjin settlement, although most remain unpublished: Gideon S. Were, 'The Maasai and Kalenjin factor in the settlement of Western Kenya: a study in ethnic interaction and evolution', *Journal of East African Research and Development,* 2 (1974); Kipkorir, 'The Kalenjin phenomenon'; Tarus, 'Outline history of the Keiyo'; Kipkulei, 'Origin, migration and settlement'. See also, J.M. Weatherby, 'Discussion on the Nandi-speaking peoples', (East Africa Institute of Social Research conference paper, Kampala, 1963), and J.E.G. Sutton, 'Some reflections on the early history of Western Kenya', in Ogot (ed.), *Hadith 2,* 17–29.

[52] BHT/TG/68; BHT/TG/37. Popular opinion among Tugen asserts that a subsequent outbreak of rinderpest in Endorois and Loboi, in the 1930s, was more serious: Langridge to PC/RVP, 19 Feb. 1935, KNA PC/RVP.6A/23/9; Wheeler to All Farmers Associations, 26 Feb. 1935, KNA PC/RVP.6A/23/9.

steady flow of refugee population into the Tugen Hills. As among the Chamus, this development can still be traced in clan lineages, which declare connections with Il Toijo, Loosekelai, Uas Nkishu and Laikipiak sections of Maasai.[53] While no precise demographic calculation can be made, it is likely that the Tugen Hills made a net gain in population at this time.[54]

Secondly, in common with much of the rest of Kenya, the Tugen Hills were affected by a serious period of drought and famine around 1897–9.[55] Well remembered in Tugen oral history, this famine is often simply referred to as the 'Hunger of Chemngal' – meaning that many Tugen sought assistance at this time from Nandi, moving south through Lembus and into Tindiret in the hope of finding supplies of grain or other foodstuffs. Tugen from the northern locations are said to have come south at this time, a pattern also reported during the drought of 1901–2.[56] During these periods of drought and famine some Tugen descended on to the lowlands with their few animals, and those who did so are remembered as having fared comparatively well. Moreover, failure of the grain harvest during the prolonged droughts and the consequent shortage of seed for the following planting season increased reliance upon livestock production and gathering in the short term. Commenting on the effect of drought in Baringo in the late 1890s, Harry Johnston observed that many Tugen had abandoned their plantations, 'taking instead to a pastoral life'.[57] This tantalizing and unembroidered comment is the only direct documentary observation we have that corroborates the oral histories of the Tugen themselves. In the period 1897 to 1902, those Tugen with cattle were seen to enjoy a marked economic advantage over those who remained in the hills to farm. Tugen were taking advantage of an opportunity. The settlement patterns of the northern Rift Valley were again changing. After 1900, the improving conditions in which it appeared they might sustain this advantage were to be almost entirely the product of colonial intervention.

[53] BHT/TG/3; BHT/TG/18; BHT/TG/47; BHT/TG/52. For further examples, see the interview transcripts accompanying Kipkulei, 'Origin, migration and settlement', deposited in the archive of the History Department, University of Nairobi.

[54] Lugard, *East African Empire*, i, 354–6, comments that the hills were densely populated in the early 1890s, although he does not substantiate this observation.

[55] BHT/TG/19; BHT/TG/2O; BHT/TG/68; and others. R.R. Kuczynski, *Demographic Survey of the British Colonial Empire* (London, 1949), 195–9; A.T. Matson, 'Famine in the Nineties', *Kenya Weekly News*, 18 Aug. 1961. For the wider regional impact, see: Munro, *Colonial Rule and the Kamba*, 46–69; Charles H. Ambler, *Kenyan Communities in the Age of Imperialism: the Central Region in the Late Nineteenth Century* (New Haven & London, 1988), 122–49; Greet Kershaw, *Mau Mau From Below* (Oxford, Nairobi & Athens, OH, 1997), 74–6.

[56] Johnston to Lansdowne, 9 May 1902, Uganda Intelligence Report, PRO FO2/804; Isaac to Johnston, 31 March 1902, ESA A/20. BHT/TG/37; BHT/TG/52.

[57] H.H. Johnston, *The Uganda Protectorate*, 2 vols (London, 1902), ii, 870–1.

The coming of colonialism

Tugen contact with the forces of European imperialism only intensified in the mid-1890s, with the arrival of the Imperial British East African Company (IBEAC), the chartered company established to open up trade between the coast and Buganda.[58] During 1894 the Company set up a fort at Eldama Ravine, in southern Baringo, one of several supply centres established to provision and protect its trading caravans. Eldama Ravine was located on a new, more southerly and shorter caravan route between Mombasa and Buganda, which was to become known, rather grandly, as Sclater's Road.[59] Prior to the construction of the Mombasa–Kisumu railway in 1901, Sclater's Road was the principal imperial highway in East Africa. The track ran through the southern edge of the Kikuyu country, before crossing the Rift Valley by way of Naivasha and Nakuru and then coming through the southern marches of Baringo, beginning the climb up the west escarpment of the Rift Valley above Nakuru and towards Eldama Ravine. Eldama Ravine was located on the southern fringe of the Lembus Forest, commanding an important strategic position, with excellent views to the north, south and east. To the west along Sclater's Road lay a further climb through the escarpment forests, over the Nandi Hills, and then down to the major fort at Mumia's and on to Buganda. Along this dirt track the Company's forts provided greater security for all traders and travellers, and the new route soon drew the majority of caravans away from the more northerly route through to Lake Baringo. This development accelerated the decline of 'Njemps' as a centre of trade, and by the end of the century it was reported that Il Chamus could no longer be relied upon by passing caravans for food supplies.[60]

With the declaration of a British protectorate over Uganda and East Africa in 1895, the administration of Eldama Ravine and the others forts along Sclater's Road passed from the IBEAC to the British government.[61] This act can be said to have formally initiated the colonial conquest of Baringo, although the Tugen around Eldama Ravine had already begun to feel the impact of the European presence. Chosen primarily for its secure and easily defensible position, the fort at Eldama Ravine experienced continual difficulties in obtaining sufficient food for its garrison and to supply passing caravans. The area had no established food markets in the 1890s, and so lacked the advantages that had drawn traders to 'Njemps'

---

[58] For documents relating to the charter and early operation of the IBEAC, see Gordon H. Mungeam, *Kenya: Select Historical Documents, 1884–1923* (Nairobi, 1978), 19–64.

[59] Named after Captain Bernard Sclater, the military engineer employed by the Company to survey the route between Kibwezi and Uganda: A.T. Matson, *Nandi Resistance to British Rule 1890–1906* (Nairobi, 1972), 194–206; Mervyn Hill, *Permanent Way: The Story of the Kenya and Uganda Railway*, 2 vols (Nairobi, 1961), i, 156.

[60] Anderson, 'Cultivating pastoralists', 252.

[61] Mungeam, *Kenya*, 65–74, for establishment of British administration.

and to other forts, such as Kitoto's, Mumia's and Fort Smith. In these places, densely settled African populations participated very actively in the newly enlarged market economy created by the imperial presence.[62] The African households scattered through the forests around Eldama Ravine cultivated cereals and kept small numbers of livestock, but produced only a relatively small marketable surplus. As the number of caravans moving along Sclater's Road increased, the vulnerability of supplies at Eldama Ravine became a greater problem. Much of the daily activity of the fort came to revolve around securing food.[63] Repeated attempts were made to persuade local Tugen to cooperate in the establishment of a market, but without success. In desperation, officials resorted to transporting foodstuffs from other forts, at an extremely high cost: government financial estimates for 1896–7 included the transport of 79,600 lb. of food to Ravine from Mumia's and Fort Smith.[64]

Faced by the almost complete lack of cooperation from the local population, Frederick Jackson sought a solution early in 1896 by encouraging a group of remnant Uas Nkishu Maasai families to settle close to the fort at Ravine, placing them under British protection and giving them grazing lands in return for their agreement to assist in supplying the garrison with foodstuffs.[65] The arrival of Uas Nkishu Maasai had done nothing to improve the supply of food to the fort before other, unanticipated consequences became apparent. The new settlers were quickly in open conflict with their Tugen neighbours. Within a few months of the settlement of the Maasai at Eldama Ravine, thefts of their cattle were being frequently reported to the fort. In all cases the local Tugen were blamed, and this drew the British garrison into actions to protect the interests of their 'friendlies', the Uas Nkishu Maasai. On 6 November 1896, the British mounted the first

[62] Godfrey Muriuki, 'Kikuyu reaction to traders and British administration, 1850–1904', in B.A. Ogot (ed), *Hadith 1* (Nairobi, 1968), 101–18; Peter Rogers, 'The British and the Kikuyu 1890–1905: a reassessment', *Journal of African History*, 20 (1979), 255–69; John M. Lonsdale, 'The politics of conquest in Western Kenya, 1894–1908', *Historical Journal*, 20 (1977), 841–70. An essential and stimulating survey of the process of conquest is to be found in Bruce Berman & John M. Lonsdale, *Unhappy Valley: Conflict in Kenya and Africa*, 2 vols (London, 1992), i, 13–44.

[63] Matson, *Nandi Resistance*, 116–17. Ravine Station Diary [RSD], various entries throughout 1896–1897. Thanks are due to the late A.T. Matson for access to his copy of the Ravine Station Diary. This is now deposited with the Matson Papers, at Rhodes House Library, Oxford; Mrs R.T. Lambert, 'A political history of Baringo and Eldama Ravine' (typescript 1947), 11–13, Lambert Papers, S1397 and S1398, Rhodes House Library, Oxford. BHT/TG/15; BHT/TG/90.

[64] Matson, *Nandi Resistance*, 116–18; Gordon H. Mungeam, *British Rule in Kenya, 1895–1912* (Oxford, 1967), 87–91.

[65] Jackson to Lansdowne, 13 Sept. 1901, App. A. 'Report on the Gwas Ngishu tribe', by Maj. Gorges, PRO FO2/8O4; RSD, entries for 2 and 7 July 1896; Matson, 'Early history'; *KLC:EM, vol. II*, 1795–7 contains an account of these events. A number of Uas Nkishu had already begun to regroup in South Lembus before the arrival of the British: BHT/TG/52. See also Waller, 'Interaction and identity'.

'punitive expedition' against the Tugen of southern Baringo, attacking 'the Elkakimor section', who were accused of the theft of Uas Nkishu cattle. The garrison from Eldama Ravine sallied forth, augmented by the spearmen of the Uas Nkishu. Along the line of march through the *pororosiek* of Lembus, Kakimor and Kamuruswa, Tugen were harried from their homes, and indiscriminately shot at as they made their escape into the forests. Grain stores were raided and livestock captured by the Uas Nkishu allies who accompanied the expedition, and huts and granaries were set alight. To its Tugen victims, this brief but brutal attack must surely have appeared as little more than a British-sponsored cattle raid, in which the Uas Nkishu fell upon Tugen livestock, protected by the superior fire-power of British guns.[66] With this assault, typical of many such incidents throughout the East African Protectorate between 1894 and 1908, the colonial conquest of Baringo began to take on a grim reality.

By the end of 1896 wider political considerations served to deepen British suspicions of Tugen intent around Ravine. The British were increasingly aware of the close cultural contacts between all the peoples of the western escarpment of the Rift Valley. The most numerous of these peoples, and the most threatening to British policies, were the Nandi, who occupied an area straddling Sclater's Road to the west of Eldama Ravine. The British came to fear that a Nandi ritual leader named Koitalel, one of their more prominent *orkoiik* (*s. orkoiyot*) and allegedly their war leader, might unite the Tugen, Elgeyo and Kipsigis (Lumbwa) with the Nandi in a concerted attack against them.[67] These anxieties were fuelled at Eldama Ravine during December 1896 by a mounting series of hostile actions by vengeful Tugen against the Uas Nkishu allies of the British.[68] On 3 December reports reached the fort that two Uas Nkishu warriors had been speared by Lembus Tugen, followed a few days later by news that six Maasai had been killed and fifty head of cattle had been stolen less than 2 miles from Ravine. On 23 December the *manyatta* of Mrombi, the Uas Nkishu elder whom the British had appointed headman at Ravine, was attacked within view of the fort and burnt to the ground. Mrombi claimed that two of his warriors had been speared and that two women and their children had been burned in the fires. In each of these incidents, information supplied by Uas Nkishu suggested that Lembus Tugen were assisted

---

[66] Jackson to Lansdowne, 21 Nov. 1901, App. B. 'Report on the Wa-Kamasia', by Capt. Gorges, PRO FO2/804, recounting the history of conflict; BHT/TG/52; BHT/TG/92. Matson, *Nandi Resistance*, 183, 224, reports that four guns were captured on this sortie.

[67] Matson, *Nandi Resistance*, 224–49; Anderson, 'Visions of the vanquished', 164–95. For other views of Koitalel and Nandi resistance: Mwanzi, 'Koitalel and Kipchomber'; arap Magut, 'Rise and fall'; arap Ng'eny, 'Nandi resistance'.

[68] Matson, *Nandi Resistance*, 224–5; Jackson to Lansdowne, 21 Nov. 1901, App. B. 'Report on the Wa-kamasia', by Capt. Gorges, PRO FO2/804. The oral record suggests that several Uas Nkishu and Tugen were keen to use the opportunity offered by the British to settle personal scores between them: BHT/TG/52; BHT/TG/92. See also, Gold, 'Nandi in transition', 91–3.

by Nandi, although it is unclear on what basis such claims were made.[69]

British fears of a Tugen–Nandi alliance, along with the desire to protect their Uas Nkishu allies and to 'encourage' the Tugen to be more cooperative in supplying grain to the garrison, thus provided motivation for a second, and more substantial, punitive expedition against the southern Tugen in May 1897. For this more formal campaign a much larger force assembled, consisting of five Europeans, 220 regular troops, 150 porters and over 200 Maasai auxiliaries. A Maxim-gun was carried, although in the event it was not used. Two columns swept through the areas north and east of Eldama Ravine, inhabited by the Lembus, Keben, Kakamor and Kamaruswo sections of the Tugen, inflicting (by their own reckoning) approximately 100 casualties. The Maasai levies assisted in the seizure of 307 head of cattle, and over 8,000 sheep and goats and the burning of the millet crop in the gardens and many of the grain stores.[70] Tugen oral histories recalling these events make an explicit connection between the British need to secure food supplies, the mischievousness of the Uas Nkishu Maasai and the general political circumstances of the time:

> The Europeans started the trouble. They began the war around Sigoro, after the Uas Nkishu Maasai had told the Europeans that we Tugen were boastful because of our large grain stores. They said the Tugen never had problems of droughts! But at this time there was a severe drought. There was no rain; the ground was bare. It was a time of *sarangach* [many disasters] ... The Kaplelach murran went to guard the grain stores in the hills, and everybody else fled with the cattle, to Keyo and to Nandi. But some of the Tugen cows were taken by the Uas Nkishu, before they departed with the Europeans. After that we faced the problem of the drought, some of our people even going as far as Chemngal [Nandi] in their search for grain.[71]

The larger portion of the Tugen stock, mostly goats and sheep, evaded capture by being run to the borderland areas with the Keyo and hidden in the valleys and caves in the upper reaches of the Kerio Valley. Despite this, the loss of the grain stores was felt severely and served to greatly accentuate the effects of drought in the region through 1897 and 1898.[72]

The attacks upon Tugen homesteads in the late 1890s were typical of the process by which colonial control was extended over much of what was to become central and western Kenya.[73] British authority only slowly extended its reach beyond the forts that protected the lines of communication, and the defence and support of African 'friendlies', such as the Uas

[69] Matson, *Nandi Resistance*, 224–7.

[70] BHT/TG/15; BHT/TG/20; Matson, *Nandi Resistance*, 259–61; H. Moyse-Bartlett, *The King's African Rifles* (Aldershot 1966), 66–8; MacKinnon to Berkeley, 7 June 1897, and Jackson to Berkeley, 10 August 1897, both ESA A/4/9.

[71] BHT/TG/52. For further details, see BHT/TG/15 and BHT/TG/20.

[72] BHT/TG/19; BHT/TG/68; BHT/TG/92.

[73] Lonsdale, 'Politics of conquest', *passim*.

Nkishu Maasai at Ravine, played a prominent role in determining the nature of conflict and its timing. The Tugen of Lembus and Kakamor locations, in closest proximity to Eldama Ravine and Sclater's Road, became further embroiled in struggles with the British during 1899–1900. A small punitive expedition was mounted against them in December 1899, capturing almost 100 of their cattle and 2,000 sheep and goats. Further troubles began in April 1900, precipitated by persistent rumour-mongering by Uas Nkishu that these Tugen sections were on the point of an alliance with Nandi against the British. Assisted by Maasai auxiliaries, the British again raided Tugen settlements, taking 300 cattle and 2,000 sheep and goats.[74] From a Tugen perspective, they saw themselves primarily as the victims of Uas Nkishu opportunism. This was to slowly change after 1900 as the demands of colonialism – taxation, labour and land alienation – took effect. While it could not be said that the punitive expeditions between 1896 and 1900 subdued the Tugen of southern Baringo, in the aftermath they were certainly more cautious in dealings with the British and more inclined to seek a compromise with the Uas Nkishu Maasai. Over the next five years, Tugen relations with Uas Nkishu improved markedly. By the time of the drought of 1901–2, Tugen, Uas Nkishu and Naivasha Maasai were all reported to be herding their stock in the vicinity of the Molo River, maintaining friendly relations.[75]

Other than protection of Sclater's Road, early British interest in Baringo was informed by concern about events to the far north of Lake Baringo, where Abyssinian imperialism was pushing into the lands around Lake Turkana. During his brief spell as Commissioner to Uganda, Sir Harry Johnston was keen to thwart Abyssinian ambitions by establishing British claims. In 1899, he authorized the establishment of a new government post at Lake Baringo, to serve as an intelligence base, and declared a Game Reserve over a vast area to the north of the lake, known as Suguta.[76] Situated first at Loiminangi, near the southern shore of the lake and close to the Chamus villages, the government post was later moved to Arabel and then to Mukutan, situated a few miles above the lake on its eastern

---

[74] Martin and Coles to Johnston, both 19 December 1899, ESA A/4/23; Martin to Johnston, 5 January 1900, ESA A/4/25; Bagnall to Johnston, 26 April 1900, ESA A/4/27; Bagnall to Johnston, 14 May 1900, ESA A21/1; RSD, 16 May 1900; Bagnall to Johnston, 15 June 1900, and Hyde-Baker to Johnston, 21 July 1900, both in ESA A/30. For a general impression of British perceptions of the Tugen at this time, see Frederick Jackson, *Early Days in East Africa* (London, 1930), 298.

[75] Jackson to Lansdowne, 3 Feb. 1902, PRO FO2/804.

[76] Johnston, *Uganda Protectorate*, gives an 'official' view of expansion to the north. For a fuller account of British imperial ambitions to the north-west of Baringo, see James P. Barber, *Imperial Frontier* (Nairobi, 1968); James P. Barber, 'The moving frontier of British imperialism in northern Uganda, 1898–1919', *Uganda Journal*, 29 (1965), 28–30. For a more specifically Baringo perspective, see Lambert, 'Political history', 20–23; J.B. Carson, *Pages from the Past – Kenya* (Braunton, 1990), 10–16; and David M. Anderson, 'Expansion or expediency: the British in Baringo to 1902' (unpublished typescript, 1979).

side.[77] The Foreign Office, fearing the potential costs of Johnston's aggressively expansionist policies, prevented any further extension of British control beyond the lake,[78] but not before the colonial power had suffered a serious setback. In January 1900, Johnston ordered that a government presence be established to the north in the Kerio Valley, an area where ivory hunters were known to be active. The Baringo District Collector, Hyde-Baker, was sent out from Loiminangi with some 50 Sudanese soldiers and established the post at Ribo, in the territory of the Japtuleil section of Marakwet to the east of the Kerio River. The local population opposed Hyde-Baker and refused to supply his force with food. When Hyde-Baker sent out 40 of his soldiers to gather food from the fields they were massacred, and the Japtuleil then attacked the government post. One of the Ribo garrison managed to escape back to Loiminangi, from where the Chamus came to Hyde-Baker's assistance. As a consequence of this dramatic setback – the worst defeat suffered by the British at any stage in the conquest of East Africa – the post at Ribo was withdrawn.[79]

One year later, in 1901, Il Chamus and Uas Nkishu warriors joined the British punitive expedition against the Japtuleil, burning huts and granaries and looting large numbers of cattle, sheep and goats. The officer commanding the patrol admitted that he could not be sure that the guilty people had been punished, but a 'lesson' had surely been administered. For Il Chamus, their employment as British allies brought significant rewards. They were given the 100 head of cattle officially captured in the attack, and looted many more on their own account – probably more than 250 head.[80] As a consequence many Chamus were able to reduce their commitment to agricultural production on the irrigated fields of Njemps Mkubwa and Njemps Ndogo and move back to herding. In the years after 1901 the drift of population away from the villages accelerated markedly, until by 1917 only the elderly and a handful of young families remained. When a flash-flood destroyed the main dam works on the Perkerra River in that year,

[77] Lambert, 'Political history', 21–2.

[78] A.T. Matson, 'Harry Johnston and Clement Hill', *Uganda Journal*, 23 (1959), 190–91, and A.T. Matson, 'Uganda's old Eastern Province and East Africa's federal capital', *Uganda Journal*, 22 (1958), 45; Jackson to Johnston, 2 Nov. 1900, ESA A8/1, and reply 29 Nov. 1900, ESA A9/1; Johnston to Lansdowne, 6 January and 15 March 1901, and minutes by Hill, PRO FO2/461.

[79] Hyde-Baker to Bagnall, 3 July 1900, and to Johnston, 21 July 1900, both ESA A4/30; Hyde-Baker to Johnston, 'Report on the attack on the Ribo Post by the Japtulail', 17 August 1901, ESA A/20; Johnston to Lansdowne, 15 March 1901, PRO FO2/461. Some of the key documents are reproduced in Lambert, 'Political history', 17–23. BHT/NB/1, for an oral history that recalls the death of the Sudanese askaris.

[80] BHT/CH/l; BHT/CH/4; BHT/CH/9; H. Moyse-Bartlett, *King's African Rifles*, 90–94; Johnston to Lansdowne, 15 March 1901, PRO FO2/461; Hyde-Baker to Bagnall, 28 October 1900, and Hyde-Baker to Johnston, 17 August 1901, in ESA A/20; Lambert, 'Political history', 16–21; Anderson, 'Expansion or expediency', 12–13; Anderson, 'Cultivating pastoralists', 253.

there was insufficient labour to undertake the reconstruction and the fields went dry.[81]

The once famous cultivators of Baringo were by then herding cattle on the surrounding lowlands, exploiting grasslands vacated by the Maasai. They were not alone. Moving rapidly out of the hills and on to the lowlands, Tugen herders now rivalled Il Chamus for access to and control of grazing.[82] The territorial patterns of settlement and land use in Baringo were already being utterly transformed under colonialism.

---

[81] Anderson, 'Cultivating pastoralists', 253–5.

[82] Jackson to Lansdowne, 3 February 1902, Uganda Intelligence Report no. 9, Capt. Wortham, 'Sketch showing the sub-divisions of the Kamasia tribe', PRO FO2/804, MR 1013(15). This map indicates that at least one section of Tugen had by the end of 1901 established permanent settlement on the east bank of the Molo.

Two

Lines on a Map
Moving Frontiers
c. 1900–1920

Over a period of no more than three decades, between the 1880s and 1910, the territorial patterns of settlement and land use that had prevailed in the Baringo lowlands for much of the nineteenth century underwent a major transformation. In these tumultuous years the dominance of the Maa-speaking herders who had seasonally grazed through the lowlands came to an end. Weakened by their own internal struggles over pasture, water and salt, and their prosperity then severely eroded by devastating epidemics of cattle disease, the Maa-speakers were finally to be undone by their encounter with colonialism. Signing away their rights to lands throughout the Rift Valley to the British in a treaty of 1904, the Maasai were legally confined to two 'reserves': one on the Laikipia escarpment (immediately above Baringo to the east), the other to the south of the railway that linked Lake Victoria with the Indian Ocean. In 1911 a further treaty, the legality of which some Maasai tried unsuccessfully to contest in the courts, removed those Maasai on Laikipia to the Southern reserve. Where a few scattered Maasai communities survived at all in the northern Rift Valley after 1910, it was because of their alliance with the forces of colonialism: the remnants of Uas Nkishu Maasai – a few hundred souls – held on to the pastures of Kabimoi and Kipsokon, between the trading centres of Eldama Ravine and Mogotio in southern Baringo; and around the southern and eastern fringes of Lake Baringo, a population of less than 4,000 Il Chamus Maasai held the rich swamp grazing lands, extending their territory to the Mukutan Gorge in the north-east and following the Arabel valley beyond Ngelesha to the south-east. Apart from these fragments, the power of the Maasai had by 1911 been utterly broken in the northern and central Rift Valley.

Even before the Maasai were removed from Laikipia, others were already

rushing to seize the vacated grazing lands. In Baringo, Tugen herders, moving down from the western escarpments of the Rift Valley with small herds of cattle and larger flocks of sheep and goats, poured across the low-lands to the east. By 1920, they had pushed their livestock to the well-watered pastures of Solai and Ol Punyata in the east, and to the south as far as Kiplombe Hill and Kampi-ya-Moto. In these better-watered, upland grazing areas the Tugen collided with others who were also keen to take advantage of the demise of the Maasai as a power in the land: European settlers.

From 1904, Europeans began to stake claims to farms in the uplands ringing the Baringo lowlands to the south and east. Just as Maa-speaking sections had fought one with another over seasonal grazing in and around Baringo in the nineteenth century, so too would Tugen herders and European farmers struggle to establish rights of access and ownership over that same land in the twentieth century. Although the territorial and cultural lines of this resource competition were new, the underlying issues of the control of key resources were remarkably familiar. In many ways the Tugen who expanded on to the Baringo lowlands after 1900 sought simply to establish a fluid form of land use similar to that of the Maasai, moving between upland and lowland grazing in a seasonal cycle. European farmers, on the other hand, were determined to break this cycle of movement by denying access to upland areas over which they claimed exclusive owner-ship. Two sets of immigrants therefore confronted one another, one seeking to continue an established system of land use, the other to impose their own notions of good land husbandry. This chapter examines the manner in which that confrontation took shape.

Expanding horizons

The frontier that beckoned in lowland Baringo had begun to open up with the weakening of Maasai authority in the last quarter of the nineteenth cen-tury. In the early years of the twentieth century colonialism set the seal on the decline of the Maasai in the northern Rift. In 1904, Olonana and other Maasai leaders signed a treaty with the British. This agreement split the Maasai sections between two 'reserves', one in the southern Rift Valley, the other on the Laikipia Plateau to the east of Baringo. Commissioner Charles Eliot, who pushed the treaty through, predicted the extinction of the Maasai: pastoralism was an archaic form of land use and an uncivilized mode of life. Eliot's intention was to clear lands for European settlers, who would come to Kenya, Eliot hoped, from Europe and southern Africa. Before the treaty was agreed, settlers were already arriving and the government had awarded large commercial concessions to land companies for development. There was no place for the pastoralist Maasai in Eliot's vision of a 'White man's country'.[1]

---

[1] Eliot's views, along with those of many other European administrators and settlers, are

In theory, the 1904 treaty should have cleared all Maasai herders out of the Baringo lowlands, but in practice the Laikipia Reserve was poorly administered. Its boundaries were not accepted by many of the Maasai, who continued to make use of the pastures below the escarpment at Solai, around the areas of Ngentalel and Ol Kokwe.[2] Tugen herders who moved toward this area in the early years of the century therefore did so cautiously. Speaking of this area in around 1910, one herder gave the following account:

> Kipnikue were murran when we came here. This land was the land of the Maasai. By then we were watering our cows and our sheep in a place called Emsos, near to Lake Bogoria. The Maasai gave us no trouble, because they only came here for a short time to water their animals, and then went back again to Laikipia. It was then that the Tugen *murran* [young men] began to come here slowly, and the *wazee* [old men] followed the *murran*. They [the Maasai] went away peacefully.[3]

The peaceful departure of the Maasai came between 1911 and 1913, when the British administration foisted a further treaty upon them, this one removing all Maasai sections from Laikipia to place them in an enlarged southern reserve. Once again, European land demands lay behind government action: Laikipia was to be opened to settler farmers. Many Maasai opposed the move from Laikipia and it took the government two years to complete the transfer of the people and their animals. By 1913 no other African herders stood in the way of Tugen and Il Chamus expansion. The frontier was open.[4]

As we have already suggested, a few Tugen herders had begun to cross the Molo River in search of seasonal pastures as early as 1900, and it is certain that, year by year thereafter, they were occupying the area between the Perkerra and Molo Rivers in ever greater numbers. This seasonal movement of Tugen may well be that indicated on a map compiled by an army intelligence officer in 1901 to illustrate the distribution of the 'Kamasia tribe', which shows a section of the Tugen as having crossed the Molo in the area between Lakes Bogoria and Baringo.[5] However, other than the odd fragment of information from colonial sources such as this,

---

[1 (cont.)] discussed in Joan Knowles & David Collett, 'Nature as myth, symbol and action: notes towards an historical understanding of development and conservation in Kenya Maasailand', *Africa*, 59 (1989), 433–60.

[2] M.P.K. Sorrenson, *The Origins of European Settlement in Kenya* (Oxford, 1967), 196–7; Mungeam, *British Rule*, 120–22; Robert L. Tignor, *The Colonial Transformation of Kenya* (Princeton 1976), 33–4; Low, 'British East Africa', 34–8; Norman Leys, *Kenya* (London, 1924), 114–19. For official correspondence on this, see KNA DC/Laik./1/1.

[3] BHT/TG/28.

[4] Low, 'British East Africa', 38–9; Sorrenson, *Origins of European Settlement*, 197–207; Mungeam, *British Rule*, 259–67; Leys, *Kenya*, 119–32.

[5] Jackson to Lansdowne, 3 February 1902, Uganda Intelligence Report No. 9, 'Sketch showing the sub-divisions of the Kamasia tribe', by Capt. Wortham. MR 1013(15), PRO FO2/804.

our understanding of the pattern and process of Tugen expansion derives exclusively from oral histories. The eastward advance was led by herders of the Kipkoimet and Kaplelach age-sets, but it was those of Kipnikue who began to 'settle' the lowlands in large numbers.[6] This process was analogous to a period of exploration, followed by initial exploitation, followed by colonization. Thus, it was during the time of Kipkoimet that the drift to the plains began and during the time of Kaplelach that Tugen herds grazed the plains in greater numbers, but not until the initiation of Kipnikue that Tugen were commonly to be found establishing homesteads in the lowlands.

However, this expansion was not a rapid gallop eastwards to exploit the rich pasture of Sipili and Solai and the glades of Marmanet and Bahati, but rather a gradual extension, in which the movement of the vanguard was most often determined by pressure from behind. Migration eastwards, out of the Tugen Hills, took place in a series of short steps, each step having as its goal the better exploitation of a particular resource, in a situation where *all* resources were scarce. The herders involved must be viewed as individuals making choices regarding their own available herding strategies in an effort to maximize the potential exploitation of certain key resources, these being pasture, water and salt.[7]

The moving of the homestead or the extension of the grazing pattern to incorporate an area of fresh pasture would be decided upon by each individual herder, and yet several indicators as to the bases upon which a decision was reached can be set down. The most crucial concerns the relationship between pasture and water. In his typical nineteenth-century grazing pattern the Tugen herder would have taken his animals to the lower slopes of the Tugen Hills in the wet season and retreated to the hilltops with the onset of the dry season. In the foothills grazing was limited, but larger herds could be kept and put to economic use by grazing them on the plains for whole seasons. This systematic use of external pastures demanded sophisticated standards of herd management, particularly when the distance between homestead and grazing land was greatest.[8] This development came to be increasingly the case for all Tugen herders as they moved further across the plains, with the result that, if the maximum mobility of the herd to exploit the resources of the plains was to be maintained, then the homestead had to be moved on to the plains and the traditional pattern of dry-season hilltop grazing adjusted. Mobility could be limited by the availability of herdsmen to manage the cattle, but with steady population growth up to 1920 this was not a factor that affected the pastoralists of

[6] BHT/TG/10; BHT/TG/15; BHT/TG/64.

[7] All Tugen oral records of the move eastwards across the plains stress the very gradual process, moving from one area to another. See, for example, BHT/TG/22, BHT/TG/33, BHT/TG/42.

[8] For discussion of herding practices, see Sutton, 'The Kalenjin', 30, and Maher, *Soil Erosion and Land Utilisation*, 6. BHT/TG/96; BHT/TG/98.

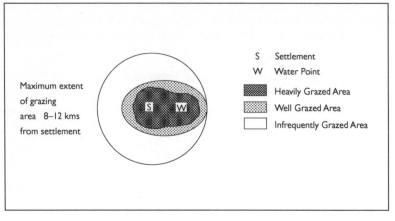

Figure 2.1 A model for the pattern of grazing of a lowland homestead
(From Paul Spencer, *Nomads in Alliance*, 1973, p. 15)

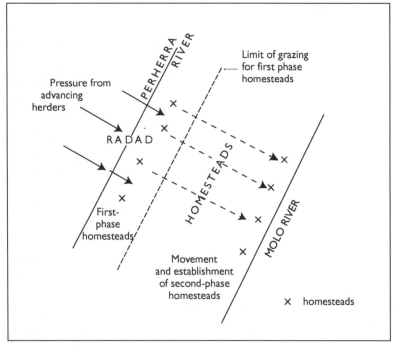

Figure 2.2 The mechanics of Tugen movement between Radad and Molo

Baringo to any noticeable extent.[9] More importantly, mobility was limited by the ability of the herd to travel between grazing and water. In common with most East African stock-keepers, Tugen herders will typically water cattle at least every second day.[10] Frequent watering is desirable and necessary, so the herd must be managed within a grazing radius that allows access to water.

Paul Spencer has put forward a model to explain the pattern of grazing, which we shall borrow and adapt to the Tugen circumstances. This model is illustrated in Figure 2.1. The outer limit of the grazing potential is half the distance that the cattle are capable of travelling in a day. In Baringo the outer limit of the potential grazing zone is therefore certainly no greater than 10 km from the homestead. The model supposes that there is only a single convenient watering point, at a distance of, say, 7 km from the homestead. If the herder wishes to water his herd he cannot then in the same day graze distant pasture in the opposite direction. This consideration alters his area of effective grazing from a circle to an ellipse and results in the area between homestead and water being heavily grazed, with the outer areas being rarely grazed. When the only good grazing remaining is too far from the settlement, the settlement must move. This pattern must be modified in practice by the presence of other settlements, environmental variations in the terrain, the alternative availability of water and human factors, such as the desire to live within easy porterage distance to facilitate water carrying for domestic use.[11] Taking these considerations into account, we can see that the Tugen movement was in fact a series of steps from one water source to another. For example, the movement from Radad on the east bank of the Perkerra to the banks of the Molo River some 8 km beyond was accomplished in a single step. Once grazing around Radad had been put under pressure by the arrival of more herders from the hills, groups settled on the east bank of the Perkerra found it increasingly difficult to efficiently balance the management of water and grazing. Going back westwards into the press of oncoming families would not ease the situation, so the only alternative for the herder was to move on to the next source of available water, the River Molo 8 km to the east. This is shown in Figure 2.2. A similar pattern repeated itself to provoke the move from Molo to Emsos, to the south of Lake Bogoria. This process was described by several herders resident in the Ol Kokwe and Kisanana areas. Many families in

[9] Bonnie Kettel ('Time is money', 56, 112) suggests that Tugen population declined early in this century, based upon her work among the Hill Tugen. She also points to a decline in population in north Baringo between 1918 and 1925. My data would indicate that these were not periods of overall decline, but of a shift of population from hill to plain.

[10] G. Williamson & W.J.A. Payne, *An Introduction to Animal Husbandry in the Tropics* (London, 2nd edn, 1965), 50. See also Gudrun Dahl & Anders Hjort, *Having Herds: Pastoral Herd Growth and Household Economy* (Stockholm, 1976), 238–41; BHT/TG/11; BHT/TG/25; and others.

[11] Spencer, *Nomads in Alliance*, 15−17. For a discussion of this model see Dahl & Hjort, *Having Herds*, 239–40.

these eastern areas originated from the foothills below Tenges, moving to their present homes via Radad, the Molo River and Emsos over a period of approximately ten years.[12]

For Tugen and Il Chamus herders the desire to minimize the distance between homestead and water source was, more often than not, the decisive factor in positioning the homestead. But as demographic pressure increased in the locality or as drought made good pasture more difficult to find in the dry season, the family herd might have to be subdivided. Goats and sheep, along with one or two milch cows – depending on the needs of the family and the local availability of fodder – formed a static herd which remained around the homestead throughout the dry season to provide a store of meat and milk for the family's consumption. The bulk of the cattle then formed a more mobile herd, which could be taken over greater distances to water and dry-season grazing zones. For example, before 1920 many herders then living around Emsos took their herds some 20 km to the highland at the head of the Arabel Valley north of Solai in the dry season. During the droughts of the interwar period the movement of stock from the west bank of the Molo River to the Solai border was common during every dry season.[13] This, in fact, is little more than a variation on the traditional pattern of Tugen transhumance grazing, previously described, of seasonal alteration between *soi* (lowland) and *masop* (hilltop).

Having described the mechanics of the expanding pastoralist frontier in Baringo, let us now turn to a fuller examination of the dynamics of that expansion. Other than a few isolated references in the government record to the Tugen and Il Chamus 'gradually becoming a pastoral people', and several comments in the evidence of the Kenya Land Commission regarding Tugen movement across the Molo, written data on the expansion of these peoples into the pastoral sector are almost completely lacking. The oral histories are therefore a crucial source. Tugen of Nyongi age-set had firsthand experience of these events, as did the most senior members of the Chumo age-set. Younger Chumo, born after 1920, were normally able to recount the chronology of their family's movements based upon information acquired from older relatives.[14] Among Il Chamus, expansion was geographically less extensive, but movements into new grazing areas were commonly recalled by the majority of members of the more senior age-sets. All these accounts, both Tugen and Il Chamus, are very particularistic in character, each family or group of families moving eastwards for their own

---

[12] See, for example, BHT/TG/22, BHT/TG/25 and BHT/TG/30.

[13] BHT/TG/12, BHT/TG/35, BHT/TG/37. For documentary corroboration, Rimington to DC/Eldama Ravine, 30 January 1932, KNA PC/ERD.6A/41/5.

[14] Those of Nyongi age-set were born between *c.* 1895 and *c.* 1915, and those of Chumo age-set between *c.* 1910 and *c.* 1925. See Appendix. It should be noted that the age-set list quoted by Lambert, 'A political history', 25, taken from the Eldama Ravine annual report of 1912, is inaccurate in several respects. Nandi and Tugen cycles have become conflated in this listing, with the inclusion of Maina and the omission of Chumo.

individual sets of reasons, the differences between them sometimes reflecting regional variations in their circumstances, but more often indicating the specific nature of the household being described.

Among the motives for and influences upon expansion, four major factors can be identified. First, Tugen and Il Chamus stress that the movement of the Maasai from the Baringo plains lessened competition for grazing and water, while also creating a more settled and safer herding environment: from 1900 onwards cattle raiding was much less prevalent than before. Secondly, land pressure had become more acute in the Tugen Hills towards the end of the nineteenth century. Tugen stock holdings also increased at this time, largely due to the better survival of their herds on the hilltops of the Tugen Hills during the rinderpest pandemic. Thirdly, expansion between 1900 and 1920 coincided with a climatically favourable period. Evidence of this is to be found in the traditions of the Tugen, the time of Kipnikue being generally held as an era of good rains and prosperity, and is also confirmed in the (rather limited) climatological data available. This consists of rainfall data for government stations within the Perkerra and Molo catchment areas (see Chapter Three, Fig. 3.3), indicating rains for the years 1904 to 1917 to be well above the long term average.[15] Finally, and perhaps most significantly, there were cultural influences. At the most general level, Tugen and Il Chamus now living on the lowlands invariably assert the superiority of herding above cultivation. It is presented as a choice that any household would make, given the opportunity. In the words of one Tugen herder, recalling the prosperity of the Kipnikue age-set:

> Everybody here had many cows. Here in Ol Kokwe people used to drink nothing but milk. That is why we had no need to cultivate shambas any more. And the murran were always able to slaughter big fat bulls for meat.[16]

Though exaggerated and idealized, such accounts are an important indication, applicable to the Il Chamus with as much force as it is to the Tugen, of the strong pastoralist cattle-keeping ethos of those individuals who were motivated to make the transition to the lowlands after 1900.[17] In

---

[15] BHT/TG/9; BHT/TG/15; BHT/TG/39; and others. Rainfall statistics have been compiled from the reports of the Meteorological Department, Nairobi, 1902-1928, consulted at the Ministry of Agriculture Library, Nairobi. See also Bille & Heemstra, 'Rainfall Patterns of Kenya'; and H.E. Carrick & A.E. Tetley, 'Report on the Perkerra River Irrigation Scheme', 25 June 1936, Annexure 3, KNA PC/RVP.6A111/26.

[16] BHT/TG/25.

[17] Cultural bias toward livestock husbandry is a feature of more recent reports on the development of the district: Peter D. Little, 'Pastoralism and strategies: socio-economic change in the pastoral sector of Baringo District, Kenya' (Institute of Development Studies, University of Nairobi, Working Paper No. 368, April 1980); Peter D. Little, 'The effects of increased crop production on livestock investments in a semi-arid area: some examples from Baringo District, Kenya' (Institute of Development Studies, University of Nairobi, Working Paper No. 386, August 1981); de Wilde et al., *Experiences with Agricultural Development*, ch. 5; Ott, 'Decisions and development'.

this idealization of cattle-keeping, the pastoral Maasai are commonly presented as a cultural model that both Il Chamus and Tugen herders sought to emulate. The new migrants sought to adopt the same patterns of herding as had the Maasai before them. More surprisingly, Tugen coming on to the lowlands appear also to have mimicked key elements of Maasai culture. The clearest example is the adoption of the custom of *murran* attending *manyatta* after initiation. It is certain that Tugen Nyongi initiates in the southern and eastern locations of Baringo attended what approximated to a *manyatta* around 1920, and oral histories suggest that some Kipnikue had done the same ten years previously. This may have developed as a direct consequence of their close proximity to the Uas Nkishu Maasai, but it is more likely to have represented a conscious attempt to imitate Maasai practice in the wake of the rapid shift towards cattle pastoralism.[18] Il Chamus herders also began the practice of attending manyatta for the first time in this period, the age-sets Irimpot and Il Kireo, *c.* 1914, being the first to do so. Il Chamus claim that, prior to this, they had not gone to *manyatta* simply because they did not have sufficient numbers of stock to make it worthwhile. Many Il Chamus witnessed the circumcision ceremonies of the Il Dareto Maasai age-set, held on the Laikipia Plateau before the second Maasai move in 1911, and some may even have taken part in these initiations.[19] Tugen and Il Chamus herders would not ultimately 'become' Maasai, but for some at least the move to the lowlands evidently implied more than a mere physical relocation.

With the motives for migration now in mind, let us look more specifically at the sequence of movements by which these herders moved to the lowlands, indicated on Map 2.1, beginning with Il Chamus. Before 1900, Il Chamus had operated their small herds and flocks in close proximity to their settlements at the south end of Lake Baringo. Nearby pastures at Meisore to the south-west of the lake and at Nosuguru to the south-east of the lake provided reserve grazing for dry-season use. With the greater accumulation of stock – which most Chamus attribute to their close alliance with the British from 1895 – they expanded into three new grazing zones. Each of these areas had probably been used periodically prior to 1900, but it proved impossible for Il Chamus to lay permanent claim to them in the face of competition from Il Toijo, Laikipiak and Loosekelai Maasai. The richest and most important of these areas was Ngelesha, control of which gave access to the Arabel Valley. This area of abundant grazing and easily available and plentiful water suffered the disadvantage of the presence of tsetse-fly. Despite the danger of stock losses within the fly belt, Il Chamus herders assert that the risks of infection were outweighed by the benefits of using the Ngelesha pastures. In fact Il Chamus cattle grazed Ngelesha only as a staging-post *en route* to the pastures of Sipili above the escarpment.

[18] Several informants acknowledged a strong Maasai influence on Tugen practice, especially in the southern locations: BHT/TG/19, BHT/TG/52 and BHT/TG/79.

[19] BHT/CH/4, BHT/CH/10 and BHT/CH/12.

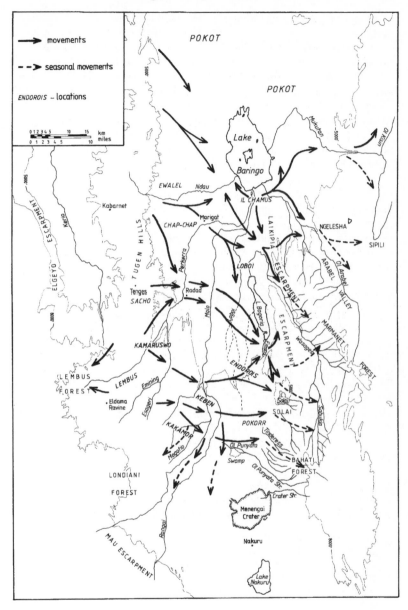

Map 2.1 Tugen and Il Chamus movements, 1900–1920

Consequently, very few homesteads were established in this area. When the government boma was moved from Loiminangi in 1904, they found that the new station beside the Arabel River on the edge of Ngelesha was in the midst of an unpopulated zone.[20] The second area of Il Chamus expansion was at Kailerr, to the south of the old 'Njemps' villages and adjacent to the swampy area around Loboi and Sandai. This area provided good grazing after the rains, but seems to have been less popular due to the brackish nature of the water near to the sulphurous Lake Bogoria and the unpalatability of some of the salty grass types in the swamp area.[21] The Mukutan Gorge was the third area of Il Chamus expansion, and here settlements were established in quite large numbers. A cattle track above Mukutun gave access to Ol Kisim Stream in the north and, beyond it, Churo, while to the south the Mukutan River flowed through Sipili. At Ol Kisim the Il Chamus encountered Pokot competition for water and pasture. From 1910 onwards the administration was frequently involved in attempting to arbitrate between the two sides, and indeed the threat of greater Pokot encroachment contributed to the decision to move the government *boma* from Arabel to Mukutan, to protect Il Chamus interests, in 1907.[22]

Up until the mid-1920s, most Il Chamus resettlement occurred within areas fairly close to the old villages of Lekeper and Leabori. With the exception of those who went to Mukutan, this expansion therefore involved movements on a much smaller scale than did Tugen migration from hills to lowland. Tugen migration was more expansive, more extensive and more rapid. Before 1910, Tugen from Arror, Ewalel and Chapchap were competing with Il Chamus for pastures in Ngelesha and Kailerr. The Arror Tugen were not rich in cattle, and their attempts to make fuller use of the northern Baringo pastures were then being challenged by the Pokot. By 1910 a small number of Arror herdsmen had crossed the Ndau River and were pushing towards Kailerr. Here they encountered herders from Chapchap and Ewalel, who had crossed the Molo before 1910 and moved into the region of Loboi-Sandai to the north of Lake Bogoria.[23] As early as 1904 several Tugen families were reported to be living close to Arabel; and, a few miles to the south, significant numbers of Tugen had crossed the Molo and entered the northern portion of Endorois by 1911. After 1920 the herds of both Tugen and Il Chamus were regularly to be found

[20] BHT/CH/10, BHT/CH/16 and BHT/CH/27; R. Edmundson, 'Forts of Baringo', unpublished typescript, held by Mrs Betty Roberts.

[21] BHT/CH/1; BHT/CH/3. On cattle fodder, see Dahl & Hjort, *Having Herds*, 244, 250.

[22] BHT/CH/10; BHT/CH/24; BHT/CH/27; Baringo Political Record Book [PRB], vol. I, 'Memo. on Mukutan Grazing', 8 January 1946, BAR/13, marks the most serious of almost annual troubles between Pokot and Il Chamus in this area, with two Il Chamus being murdered. It was noted that 'water has been the constant source of trouble here'.

[23] BHT/TG/3; BHT/TG/4; BHT/CH/5; BHT/CH/15. The issue of when exactly the Tugen began to encroach on Il Chamus grazing areas has been obscured by recent and highly politicized conflicts over land rights in the area.

trespassing on farms at Sipili, on the escarpment above Ngelesha.[24]

Other Ewalel and Chapchap Tugen crossed the Molo and moved into the lands around Maji Moto, along the western shores of Lake Bogoria. The Loboi and Sandai Rivers watering this area are both prone to run dry during the dry season. It is an area therefore long recognized by Tugen herders as being poor cattle country, and few herders care to linger long in this unfavourable zone. Two gathering points, one to the east and the other to the west of this zone, can be identified. To the west, on the banks of the Perkerra, Radad and Koiteran Hill became key settlement areas for Tugen emerging from the forested hillsides of Tenges and Kabarak. By around 1914, overcrowding became acute here, the drought of 1918 heralding a major movement eastwards. As early as 1911, the colonial Assistant District Commissioner had described this area as being 'heavily populated', where 'a good tax return' could be expected.[25] Movement eastwards from here brought people to the River Molo, and then to the southern end of Lake Bogoria, around the seasonal River Emsos. Vegetation in this area is salty in character, and the Tugen recall that their goat flocks did especially well here. Many Tugen established homesteads in the Emsos area between 1910 and 1920, and it was from this base that the *murran* of Kipnikue and Nyongi began to take their cattle herds across the ridges of Chepkereret and on to the upland pastures around Lake Solai. These movements and the gradual extension of grazing towards Solai are well summarized in Tugen oral histories:

> When we left the Perkerra Kipnikue were *murran*. After that my family moved slowly to this place, Ol Kokwe. First we came to the Molo River, then on to Emsos, and then slowly to this land here. Before crossing the Perkerra we had very little grass. So we moved to these other places looking for better grass. We followed the grass, and when we reached here Nyongi had become *murran*. When we were around the River Molo, that was the time when Nyongi were initiated.[26]

On reaching the Solai escarpment, these herders encountered Tugen who had originated from the hills to the south of Tenges and had come to Solai by a more southerly route. Generally richer in cattle than their northern counterparts, due to more extensive availability and higher quality of grazing prior to 1900, the southern Tugen of Kamaruswo, Keben, Kakimor, Lembus, Endorois and Pokorr locations were very well placed to occupy the pastures east of the Molo vacated by the Maasai. The plains lying between the Perkerra and Molo Rivers in this area are watered by the Esageri, Emining and Mogotio Rivers. With this advantage, livestock brought to this area did especially well. Yet, once these herders pushed beyond the eastern bank of the Molo, they encountered very serious

---

[24] Hobley to Lansdowne, 22 July 1904, PRO F02/838; Colvile to PC/RVP. 30 June 1939, and Lambert to DC/Rumuruti, 16 November 1942, both in KNA PC/RVP.6A/15/15.

[25] Baringo PRB, vol. I, Memo. by DC Bruce, 1911, BAR/13. BHT/TG/25 and BHT/TG/29.

[26] BHT/TG/25; see also BHT/TG/30; BHT/TG/32; BHT/TG/33.

difficulties; no reliable water source existed between the Molo and Rongai Rivers and Lake Solai and the Tinderess Stream at the foot of the escarpment, a distance of over 16 km. This dry region, known as Mugurin, was consequently crossed rapidly. It was *murran* of Kipnikue age-set who led this advance across the Molo before 1910, and it was they, along with those of Nyongi age-set, who established homesteads in the vicinity of the escarpment prior to 1920.[27] Despite later government attempts to provide water by digging boreholes and dams (see Chapter Six), the Mugurin area of Keben-Pokorr to the east of the Molo still today remains a notoriously dry area sparsely inhabited by an impoverished population. Conversely, the escarpment region provided herders with ready access to salt deposits at Ngentalel and Solai itself, abundant water above the escarpment, where the Subukia River was fed by numerous tributaries, and a variety of good grazing lands, including the Marmanet Forest to the north.[28]

The plains in the extreme south of Baringo were by 1910 stocked up by Tugen from Lembus and Kamaruswo, alongside the herds of the Uas Nkishu Maasai. Closer contact between the two brought a great deal of intermingling of stock on grazing areas, despite attempts by the administration to restrict the Uas Nkishu within their designated territory. In 1905, an area of some 18,000 acres to the east of Eldama Ravine was reserved exclusively for the use of the Uas Nkishu. Four years earlier a government intelligence report on the Uas Nkishu settled here noted that:

> they have prospered and increased … under the protection of the government officials … and they now inhabit a large tract of land in the Baringo District, extending from the Tigerish [*sic*] [Perkerra] to the Molo river.[29]

This prosperity continued, their numbers being augmented in 1906 by the addition of other Uas Nkishu sections from Nandi, to be followed in 1909 and 1910 by the purchase of four unoccupied farms on their behalf to ease congestion on their land. A land exchange before the outbreak of the First World War brought them a further 17,500 acres, previously belonging to a European settler named Grogan. Their population by 1920 was approximately l,500, their presence in Baringo representing something of an administrative anomaly. Efforts to remove them to join other Maasai sections in the Southern Reserve were generally opposed by the Uas Nkishu themselves. The opinion prevailed among government that they should remain where they were as a reward for their loyal service. Although a small number moved south during the early 1920s, it was not until after the Kenya Land Commission inquiry in 1932 that the majority of the Uas Nkishu joined up with the other Maasai sections in the Southern Reserve

[27] BHT/TG/24, BHT/TG/104 and BHT/TG/115.
[28] KNA PC/RVP.6A/11/18 contains papers concerned with efforts to solve the water problem in the area below the escarpment during the 1930s by constructing boreholes and dams.
[29] Jackson to Lansdowne, 13 September 1901, Intelligence Report, Uganda No. 4, App. A., 'Report on the Gwas Ngishu tribe', by Maj. E.H. Gorges, PRO F02/804.

at Kilgoris.[30] By 1920, the Uas Nkishu contributed to make this southern extreme of Baringo the most heavily populated portion of the plains. From here, herders moved on towards Solai and Ol Punyata to the east, crossed the Sclater Road to penetrate into Rongai and even moved west to infiltrate the glades of the Lembus Forest. Continuing movements of people into this southernmost part of Baringo, even after 1920, were to create serious land pressure and contribute greatly to the high level of trespass on the European farmlands that by then bordered Baringo.[31]

Closing frontiers

The alienation of lands for European settlement adjacent to the Baringo plains effectively halted the expansion of the Tugen and Il Chamus pastoralists. The higher and wetter margins of Baringo to the east and south were considered suitable for white settlement, the allocation of European farmlands being roughly contemporaneous to, and equally as rapid as, Tugen migration across the plains. Within a very few years of the removal of the Maasai from the Baringo periphery, the bottleneck of the Rift Valley, the Nakuru corridor, had once again been sealed up and the opportunity for the advancement of the African pastoral sector once again restricted. This process began in 1903, with the granting of a concession in the Lembus Forest to the west of Eldama Ravine to Messrs Lingham and Grogan. The lease of this forest area became a major political issue in Baringo after 1945 and was a continuing irritant to the government, as we shall see in fuller detail in Chapter Seven. Although grazing rights and other allowances were later made within this concession to Tugen and Okiek who could claim to have previously inhabited the forest, the original lease paid scant attention to African land rights, giving priority instead to the economic exploitation of the forest's timber reserves.[32] This was to be the pattern for much of the early settlement of Kenya, with prospective settlers being encouraged to select the better and potentially richer land areas.

The process of European settlement was rather haphazard. Applications from Europeans wishing to settle and farm in British East Africa had begun in earnest in 1903 and 1904, but with no surveyor available to work within the Land Office to delineate and allocate farms the situation quickly became

---

[30] BHT/TG/42, BHT/TG/52. No record of the movement of Uas Nkishu during the early 1920s survives in the archival files, but for the broader context, drawing upon Uas Nkishu oral accounts, see Waller, 'Interaction and identity'.

[31] Jackson to Lansdowne, PRO F02/804; *KLC: Report*, 247–9; Lambert 'Political history', 24; Sorrenson, *Origins of European Settlement*, 216–17.

[32] Lingham and Grogan intended to establish a timber industry in the area (see Chapter Eight below). Stewart to Lansdowne, 16 March 1905, PRO CO 533/1; Sorrenson, *Origins of European Settlement*, 71; Baringo PRB, Hyde-Clarke to PC/RVP, 28 July 1938, 'Memo: Lembus Forest: An Appreciation of the Position', BAR/13, gives a historical summary.

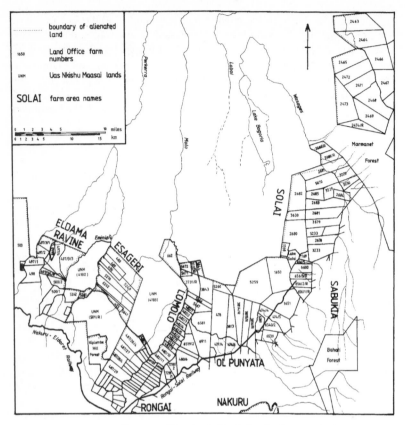

Map 2.2 European Farmlands Bordering Baringo c. 1930

chaotic. Prospective settlers quite literally went out and selected their own lands, laying claims on the Land Office desk on their return to Nairobi. On this basis the overworked and understaffed Land Office was prepared to issue certificates of occupancy, contingent upon a later examination of African rights on the land concerned. As Keith Sorrenson has so ably pointed out, investigations of African rights rarely took place, and there is no evidence that such claims were ever investigated along the Baringo borders. European land claims here were invariably ratified without any enquiry. Among the earliest settlers, pastoral land in the Rift Valley rivalled agricultural land in the Kikuyu country in popularity, and yet it was not until June 1906 that the subdivision survey of the Rift Valley was completed. Just over a year later the allotment of the first group of Rift Valley farms was made, forty-seven farms each of approximately 5,000 acres having been alienated, surveyed, and allocated to European claimants. These included farms running

from Eldama Ravine in the west, along Sclaters Road towards Kampi-ya-
Moto. From there the farms followed the River Molo northwards as far as
present-day Mogotio, the boundary then turning east, towards Ol Punyata
and Kisanana (see Map 2.2). These farms, sold at 6d an acre, came to mark
the boundary of Baringo and the limit of Tugen grazing to the south.[33]

The lands on the eastern edge of Baringo were allocated for European
settlement after 1915. Some of the plots had been claimed ten years earlier,
but no survey could be undertaken until after the completion of the second
Maasai move, in April 1913. At the northern extreme of this area the Arabel
block of farms in Laikipia District were settled as part of the Soldier
Settlement Scheme implemented in 1919. The zone of European settlement
was therefore finally defined along the Baringo boundary by 1920, and
some three years later the Baringo Native Reserves were created, under the
title Kerio Native Land Unit. This comprised the Kamasia Reserve, the
East Suk Reserve and the Njemps Reserve. The Uas Nkishu Reserve was
retained under the direct administration of Eldama Ravine.[34]

The African herders only slowly realized the actual effect of these land
divisions. The farm allotments, many of them 5,000 acres in extent, were
generally too large to be initially fully utilized by the European occupier,
and the boundaries with the African reserves were not fenced. African
herders therefore continued to enjoy the freedom to graze on the farms
pending the farmer's ability to exert adequate control over the movement
of African-owned stock. Some farmers in fact found it to their advantage
to allow African cattle to remain on their otherwise underutilized lands, the
grazing of African-owned livestock keeping bush encroachment to a minimum. Major Boyce, one of the earliest settlers at Subukia, was particularly
well remembered by Tugen in Endorois location for precisely this reason,
recalling that when he arrived 'he only had a very few cows, so he allowed
us to have the land'.[35] Even where a farmer wished to immediately restrict
African encroachment, control could be very difficult to effect. Where a
farm boundary ran along a river or an escarpment or was marked by
prominent features, these points of reference could be used to explain to
the herder where the boundary ran. But much of the eastern boundary,

---

[33] Sorrenson, *Origins of European Settlement*, 69–71, 100–101. On farm surveying and allotment
prior to 1914, see G.E. Smith, 'The Survey of British East Africa', *British East African
Agricultural Journal*, 1 (1908), 69–73; G.E. Smith & A.C. MacDonald, 'Rapid allotment of
farms in the Uasin-Gishu', *British East African Agricultural Journal*, 1 (1908), 103–114.

[34] Sorrenson, *Origins of European Settlement*, 102–103. The Baringo farm boundary is thoroughly
defined in Baringo PRB, Vol. I, Champion to PC/Kerio, 30 January 1929, BAR/13. Later
disputes over the exact delineation of the boundary are documented in KNA PC/RVP.6A/
14/31 and KNA PC/RVP.6A/14/36. See also J.H. Williams, 'Historical outline and analysis
of the work of the Survey Department, Kenya Colony, 1 April 1903 to 30 Sept. 1929'
(mimeo, Nairobi 1931), held by the Foreign and Commonwealth Office Library, London.

[35] BHT/TG/28. On the dangers of bush encroachment on underutilized pasture, see H.F.
Heady, *Range Management in East Africa* (Nairobi, 1960), 37–8; and D.J. Pratt & M.D.
Gwynne (eds), *Rangeland Management and Ecology in East Africa* (London 1977), 110–12.

from Ol Punyata to beyond Solai, lacked these invaluable aids. Under such circumstances it might take several years for the settler to convince his African neighbours that a boundary even existed.

The obvious solution was to fence the boundaries between European farmlands and African reserves, but this course was opposed by settlers on the grounds of expense. The debate over fencing had been opened up by Chief Veterinary Officer Stordy as early as 1904, in an effort to assist the Department's campaign to control the spread of East Coast fever to European herds. Stordy sought direct government action to compel settlers to fence their lands in order to prevent the mixing of stock, and further requested that the Veterinary Department be given the power to slaughter all infected animals without payment of compensation. While the Colonial Office agreed that these policies were in principle sound – with the noteworthy reservation that the slaughter of livestock without compensation would 'definitely risk trouble and disturbance' – they left the final decision up to the British East Africa administration, with the result that settler opinion against the enforcement of a fencing ordinance prevailed and the issue was left in abeyance, where it was to remain for the next half-century. Settlers wanted their lands protected, but were unwilling to pay to keep Africans out when they believed it to be the responsibility of government to keep Africans in.[36]

Owner-absenteeism on European farmlands was a further hindrance to attempts to make African herders aware of new boundaries. After the original allocation of Rift Valley farms in 1907, several farms had remained unoccupied until after 1916, their claimants being unable, or perhaps unwilling, to take them up. For example, at Eldama Ravine only seven of the area's twelve farmers were actually in occupation in 1912.[37] On unoccupied farmlands there was no form of control to prevent African herders from continuing to have a free run of the range. The administration expressed the justified fear that the high degree of absenteeism – perhaps as high as 30 per cent for the Protectorate as a whole in 1909 – was the direct result of land speculation. Accumulation of land for speculative purposes was frequently achieved in East Africa by disguising the owner's true identity through dummying – that is, the use of another's name on a claim or deed. The Colonial Office had issued a warning to the Protectorate administration to guard against this at the time of the initial allotment of Rift Valley farms but nothing was done to legislate against it, with the result that vast

---

[36] Stewart to Lansdowne, 4 October 1904, enclosure Stordy to Stewart, 6 September 1904, and Lyttleton to Stewart (draft), 23 December 1904, PRO CO 519/1. For the emergence of the debate on fencing and disease control, see: A. Theiler & J.M. Christy, 'The prevention and eradication of East Coast Fever', *British East African Agricultural Journal*, 4 (1911), 30–41; F.R. Brandt & R.E. Montgomery, 'East Coast Fever in the East Africa Protectorate', *British East African Agricultural Journal*, 4 (1912), 99-102; and R.N. Newland, 'Review of the cattle trade in BEA, 1904–08', *British East African Agricultural Journal*, 1 (1908), 264–8.

[37] Lambert, 'Political history', 24, RH MSS.Afr.s.1388; Anon, *The Brands Directory of British East Africa* (Agricultural Department, Nairobi, 1908).

tracts of land came to be accumulated by syndicates, families and individuals who had no intention of occupying them fully. Rising land prices in 1912 saw many of these larger units beginning to become fragmented as early settlers and speculators sold off portions of their farms to newcomers. With these subdivisions, farms changed hands rapidly, as there was a shortage of readily available Crown Land for settlement after 1919. The incentive to sell gradually became greater; by 1912 Rift Valley farms on the Baringo periphery were selling for 10s. per acre and only two years later at £1 per acre.[38]

Tugen and Il Chamus who had expanded into the lands claimed by Europeans therefore continued to exploit these areas for several years after the formal alienation of those lands as settler farms. Only in the early 1920s did the majority of European farmers along the Baringo boundary begin to exert firmer control over the movement of African cattle. The delay served to confuse the issue of boundaries and grazing rights in the eyes of the African herders. It was indeed difficult for the herder to accept that pasture he required and had made use of over several years and that was not visibly being used by anyone else could be denied him on the basis of a boundary having been created − a boundary he was unaware of and that was not physically marked on the land. Tugen bewilderment was increased by the apparent rejection by Europeans of their determined claim to have used the alienated lands prior to European intervention. As one Tugen elder rather bitterly expressed it:

> When the Europeans came we were pushed back from Solai, where we had previously been grazing our animals. They took our land and they made boundaries, and said we should not cross. And they even divided up their own lands, and kept each to his own part. All of Solai became theirs, so we were moved to this small area.[39]

This and other African accounts differ in substance from the settler view of the sequence of events. Settler opinion is best summarized in the evidence collected by the Kenya Land Commission in 1932. The settlers expressed the adamant opinion in 1932 that no Tugen herder had crossed the Molo prior to 1910 and therefore that, on the grounds of historical claim, a major guiding factor in the inquiry, the Tugen could advance no claim to any lands along the Baringo borders. Alongside this, several settlers had evidently laid claims to lands in the Solai area even before the removal of the Maasai. Surely, they argued, this must give them a prior historical claim? Against this, Tugen witnesses before the Commission drew attention to fluctuations in 'tribal' boundaries in the period before 1900, contesting that Tugen herders had made use of these so-called Maasai lands at periods throughout the nineteenth century.[40] This view sat uncomfortably with the

---

[38] Sorrenson, *Origins of European Settlement*, 105, 130; C.C. Wrigley, 'Kenya: the patterns of economic life, 1902−1945', in Harlow & Chilver (eds), *Oxford History of East Africa*, ii, 221−5.

[39] BHT/TG/26, and BHT/TG/11 for a similar account.

[40] *KLC:EM*, ii, 1800−1927, and also 1773−99.

prevailing European opinion regarding the set nature of African ethnic identity and group territoriality and without any more substantial evidence to give it support, was treated lightly by the Commission. Further confusion stemmed from differences in systems of land use and consequently attitudes towards occupancy and rights regarding land. For Tugen, the necessary seasonal use of a grazing area did not imply the establishment of Tugen dwellings and homesteads in that same area. Yet, by the terms under which the settler judged land to be occupied, the presence of homesteads was demanded; it seems that Europeans considered that without permanent dwellings there could be no permanent people. Of course, this position failed to acknowledge the importance of seasonal pasture and watering points within the African system of herd management. The conflicts of view exposed in the deliberations of the Kenya Land Commission will be fully examined in Chapter Five.

As can be seen by a comparison of Maps 1.1 and 2.2, the land alienated for European use effectively swallowed up the best grazing and the majority of the better-watered areas ringing the Baringo lowlands. Several important specific areas of future conflict between settler and herder should be pointed out at this stage. At Solai the incorporation of the lake and its adjoining salt-lick within the area of European settlement deprived herders in Endorois of their nearest reliable watering point. Unable to press east to the streams feeding Lake Solai and the Subukia River, these herders were faced with a trek of more than 10 km back westwards to the Rivers Rongai and Molo. The same was true in Pokorr to the immediate south, where Tinderess Stream and the Ol Punyata swamp were both well inside the settled area. If herders here were to retreat to the rivers to their west for water, they could only utilize those waters to the north of Mogotio, as the upper sections of both rivers flowed through lands designated as settled areas. If trespass on farmland was to be avoided, this greatly increased the distances that the herd had to be walked to water. In this respect farm L.0. 662 was to be a particular trouble spot, straddling as it did three rivers, the Mogotio, Molo and Rongai. River courses also marked farm boundaries further west, where the western boundary of the Esageri block of farms was marked by the Esageri River. This river crossed the Ravine to Kampi-ya-Moto road, where it became the eastern boundary of the southern block of Ravine farms. This left an arid portion of land below Kiplombe Hill free for African use, despite its being surrounded on three sides by well-watered farmland and on the fourth by a forest reserve. To the north of this section, the Esageri farms were allocated after the removal of African occupiers and, being surrounded on three sides by poorly watered African lands, naturally became a major area of friction as a result of persistent African stock

<hr>

[41] BHT/TG/20, BHT/TG/45, BHT/TG/48 and BHT/TG/64 discuss these specific blocks of land. See *KLC:EM*, ii, 1831–2, for a summary. The question of trespass will be discussed in Chapter Four.

trespass. Finally, the northern block of Ravine farms incorporated the Emining River and all of its tributaries. Each of these areas was valuable to the African pastoralists of Baringo, and access to each of them was denied.[41] By 1920 the frontier of African pastoralist expansion had been closed and, with its closure access to key watering points and grazing areas was denied to the herders on the lowlands.

The Baringo lowlands in 1920

An unusual conjuncture of events had thereby drawn Tugen and Il Chamus with livestock holdings toward a fuller use of grazing on the Baringo lowlands in the late 1890s and early 1900s.[42] The beginnings of movement had not initially implied permanent resettlement. The lands vacated by the Maasai offered an enticing opportunity for households seeking to maximize resources and spread risk. Moving to take advantage of this opportunity did not represent any radical innovation. Hill-dwellers had commonly utilized the plains for additional grazing when the opportunity arose, and the fluidity of relations between cultivation and herding was a central feature of life for most Rift Valley communities. On this occasion, however, the opportunity for expansion was made more permanent – or so it must have appeared before European farmlands began to close down the frontier.

What kind of communities had those Africans who had moved on to the lowlands established by 1920? Young males had been the first to come with cattle and goats, and by 1920 they still predominated in the Tugen population. The cattle they brought usually belonged to their fathers' herds, and close social and economic linkages were always maintained with those remaining in the hills through the exchange of livestock and the trading of grains. The men of Kipnikue and, more commonly, Nyongi age-sets were the first to bring wives and to establish proper homesteads, with small family gardens. The homesteads were scattered across the landscape, not clustered in villages, but invariably higher densities of settlement were to be found nearer to water sources. Even as these homesteads became established, the community remained demographically skewed. Very few elders were amongst the migrants, those of the more senior age-grades apparently preferring to remain in the Tugen Hills. The oral histories are silent on the process by which younger men detached themselves and their livestock from the households of the hills, but it would be reasonable to suppose that this may have sometimes been the source of generational tensions. Perhaps for this reason, Tugen imagery of the early years of settlement often characterizes the pioneer lowland communities as ill-disciplined, even hotheaded. Without elders to regulate disputes, it was said, fighting and reckless behaviour among the young men was more commonplace.[43] Even though

---

[42] BHT/TG/15; BHT/TG/37; BHT/TG/52.

[43] BHT/TG/16, BHT/TG/27.

these communities lacked elders, they appear to have quickly adopted political structures replicating those they had known in the hills. The Tugen territorial divisions, *pororosiek*, around which the politics of life revolved, were clan-based, but on the lowlands persons from different clans found themselves thrown together in close proximity. Again, the oral histories are silent as to the process by which this was reconciled, but by the 1920s each locality seems to have established its own territoriality, with numerically dominant clans taking the lead. The colonial division of the lowlands into locations, each under the nominal control of a government-appointed chief, surely helped to consolidate these new groupings. But these new communities retained their ties with those in the hills to the west, whose livestock they often cared for and whose grain and vegetables they bartered. The frontier was distinct, but it was not separate.[44]

The distinctiveness sharpened over time. Confrontation between African herders and their European neighbours was imminent by 1920. Over sixty farms lay along the Baringo border, and many more lay within easy reach of the herders then still pressing up to the boundary in ever greater numbers. As more and more herders came into these areas and as their livestock holdings increased, the pressures upon the available land mounted. Good rains, the exploitation of fresh pastures and the advantages initially enjoyed of a more settled pattern of herd management under colonial administration undoubtedly facilitated the rapid growth of Tugen and Il Chamus herds.[45] We have no reliable figures for Baringo's African population before 1915 but, using a range of estimates in the colonial records between 1915 and 1926, it seems likely that the lowlands of Baringo were inhabited by approximately 10,000 people by 1920.[46] To estimate the extent of their livestock holdings presents a more daunting problem. The earliest such estimate for the southern Tugen sections was made in 1911, suggesting a figure of 40,000 head of cattle, based upon a census accomplished over the course of the previous year.[47] This figure is surprisingly high in relation to the land/livestock ratio, implying a density greater than one beast to every 10 acres of grazing, but even this would amount to a relatively small household herd size of only four to five head of stock per person. The pressure exerted by these numbers was accentuated by the uneven distribution of the African population, the majority of which pushed hard up against the borders of Baringo to gain access to the water and better grazing on the uplands occupied by European farmers.

The efforts of European farmers to establish a firm boundary between their lands and the African reserves of Baringo began in earnest around 1920.

---

[44] BHT/TG/10, BHT/TG/27.

[45] BHT/TG/64, BHT/TG/67, BHT/TG/107, and others. For Chamus prosperity in the time of Il Kileku and Il Parakua age-sets, see BHT/CH/10 and BHT/CH/16.

[46] The estimate draws upon material in the Baringo PRB, 'Assessment of native population, 1936', BAR/13, and *KLC:EM*, ii, 1838–40, 1856–8.

[47] Lambert, 'Political history', 24, quoting from the Eldama Ravine AR for 1911.

The settler had by then acquired title to the lands he desired, and those lands were generally areas of better climate, more favourable soils, better pasture and plentiful water. In sharp contrast, the resources left to the herders of Baringo were inadequate to meet the demands of cattle pastoralism.[48] Without access to the dry-season pastures and rivers of Solai, Subukia, Rongai and Ravine, pastoralism on the Baringo lowlands became untenable. In allowing the alienation and settlement of these areas the colonial administration had failed to realize, or perhaps had chosen to ignore, the historical fact that the Baringo lowlands had always functioned as part of a wider pastoral system of grazing. To the nineteenth-century occupants of the Baringo plains, the Toijo, Purko, Laikipiak and Loosekelai, the area represented only a seasonal grazing zone.[49] By 1920, then, the herders of Baringo were restricted within an area that did not have the resources to support them. The plains were already heavily stocked, and stock density was still increasing, but the period of uninterrupted expansion for the Baringo pastoral sector had ended. To borrow a phrase from Forbes Munro, 'the demographic dynamic clashed with the inertia of colonial land policy'.[50] In the next chapter we shall look at the ecological and economic context in which this conflict took shape after 1920.

[48] Dahl & Hjort, *Having Herds*, 240–41, for a general discussion.

[49] BHT/CH/4; BHT/CH/9; BHT/TG/3; BHT/TG/74. Spencer, *Nomads in Alliance*, 152–3; Sobania, 'Historical traditions', ch. 2; and see also the maps in Waller, 'Lords of East Africa'.

[50] Munro, *Colonial Rule and the Kamba*, 190.

Three

Kiplel Kowo – 'The White Bones'
Drought & Depression
1917–39

The interwar years in Kenya were marked by sharp economic fluctuations and by ecological crisis, as the international depression of the 1930s descended and the Colony was forced to meet renewed economic and political challenges, just when it had seemed that the investment and endeavour of the European settler community were beginning to pay dividends. This was compounded by prolonged drought and locust invasions, adversely affecting the agricultural sector. Those European settlers with reserves of capital were able to survive independently, while the vast majority took advantage of emergency credit and long-term capital loans offered by the government; they borrowed to the hilt or went to the wall. Most African producers were as yet too marginal to the export economy to be much affected by a recession in international trade, and for some the setback to settler production was to prove an opportunity.[1] But for those more dependent upon livestock production the drought years between 1925 and 1935 brought the heaviest losses since the late nineteenth

---

[1] The best survey of the period remains E.A. Brett, *Colonialism and Underdevelopment in East Africa: The Politics of Economic Change, 1919–39* (London, 1973), 165–214. See also Anderson, 'Depression, dust bowl', 321–43; David M. Anderson & David Throup, 'The agrarian economy of Central Province, Kenya, 1918–39', in Ian Brown (ed.), *The Economies of Africa and Asia in the Interwar Depression* (London, 1989), 8–27; and David M. Anderson & David Throup, 'Africans and agricultural production in colonial Kenya: the myth of the war as a watershed', *Journal of African History*, 26 (1985), 327–45. For the politics of settler agriculture, Michael G. Redley, 'The politics of a predicament: the white community in Kenya, 1918 to 1932' (PhD thesis, University of Cambridge, 1976), esp. 215–25; and for a wider economic analysis, P. Mosley, *The Settler Economies: Studies in the Economic History of Kenya and Southern Rhodesia, 1900–1963* (Cambridge, 1983).

century. The small export market in hides and skins collapsed as prices fell, whilst within the domestic economy the exchange value of cattle plummeted. With harvest failures in the more arid reserves, such as Baringo, where cattle herding dominated, grain had to be purchased at high prices. Many people saw a dramatic decline in their household wealth. Some suffered famine.

Faced by these differing, but ultimately connected, crises, European settlers and African herders became locked in an antagonistic struggle. Government encouraged crop experimentation and diversification in the African reserves, but met with the opposition of European farmers, who demanded that restrictions be placed upon African development in order to protect settler production from competition. By 1930, with revenues in sharp decline, it was clear that the colonial state faced a huge challenge.[2]

This chapter will assess the impact of drought and economic depression on the peoples of Baringo, both African herders and European settlers. The opening section will chart the sequence of drought, infestation and epidemic that beset the rural economy between 1918 and 1939. This will be followed by a discussion of the responses of African herders, emphasizing the extent of their livestock losses and their strategies for household survival. The next section will examine the effects of these events upon the European farmers along the Baringo borders. Their sense of vulnerability led them to press for greater government support, in terms of financial assistance and of greater protection from the trespass of African herds upon their lands.

Catalogue of crisis

Drought and disease were recurrent experiences in Baringo during 'the doldrum years' of the interwar period.[3] A study of colonial reports between 1917 and 1940 reveals an almost annual catalogue of environmental difficulties, human and stock diseases and economic decline. The picture presented is of a district, even at the outset recognized as an 'economic backwater', experiencing a process of steady deterioration. To most European observers, this was perceived as a problem of land use. Year after year the descriptions of Baringo's decay took on an increasingly alarming tone, until by the 1940s, through repetition and reinforcement, the prevailing

---

[2] I.D. Talbott, *Agricultural Innovation in Colonial Africa: Kenya and the Great Depression* (Lewiston, NY, Queenstown and Lampeter, 1990). Bruce Berman, *Control and Crisis in Colonial Kenya: The Dialectic of Domination* (London, Athens, OH & Nairobi, 1990), ch. 4; Gavin Kitching, *Class and Economic Change in Kenya* (Yale University Press, 1980), esp. 101–107. Most important among government enquiries were: *Report of the Agricultural (Hall) Commission* (1929); *Report of the Financial Commissioner (Lord Moyne) on Certain Questions in Kenya* (1932); *The Kenya Land Commission (Carter) Report* (1934); *Report of the Economic Development Committee* (1935); *Report of the Commission Appointed to Enquire into and Report on the Financial Positions and System of Taxation in Kenya (Sir A. Pim)* (1935).

[3] The phrase is from Lambert, 'Political history', 38.

view had become ever more deeply entrenched. The report of the Soil Conservation Officer for 1945 is typical:

> By March the whole of southern Kamasia plains were as usual a grassless desert. There was not a blade of grass to be seen anywhere; even bark of certain thorn trees, on which the cattle habitually exist during the drought periods in these areas was in short supply. It is impossible to exaggerate the picture of utter desolation presented by these once good grasslands.[4]

African herders also recognized a deterioration of the quality of their lands as being central to their difficulties in these years. Yet they did not see these changes as indicating a permanent transformation. Periods of drought and disease had come before and would come again. These were struggles to be endured, and African accounts of these years lay stress on the day-to-day survival of their families and their herds. At the beginning of this period the Tugen Nyongi age-set had been initiated, and during it the Chumo age-set became *murran*. The durations of each are characterized in Tugen oral histories as times of hardship and great difficulties. Particularly severe years of drought were given graphically apt names by Tugen, and these recur in the oral histories recounted, being used to arrange the chronologies of families and individual lives:

> Nyongi were *murran* during the famine of *Kipngosia*. That was a drought which affected both cattle and people. We took our cows to Solai [the settler farms] at that time. Also there was *Kiplel kowo* – a very serious time for our herds. All the animals were dying, until the mounds of white bones of our dead cattle could be seen everywhere; that is how we came to name the drought. Everywhere throughout the Tugen area that drought was very severe, and everyone knows of it. A few Chumo had become *murran* by then. And even at the time of Chumo there was no real rest for us; always there were droughts. Even in the years when a little rain came it seemed we had problems.[5]

African memory and colonial documents record these years in some-times remarkably differing ways, each representing a distinctive appreciation of the cause and effect of the same events. In reconstructing the mounting catalogue of crisis we shall use both these sets of sources.

The period of crisis in Baringo was heralded in 1917 not by drought, but by deluge. The Baringo lowlands receives less than 30 inches of rain per year, but this average disguises dramatic spatial variability caused by the rain-shadow effects of the escarpments, and the incidence of torrential, often destructive storms. The rains fail completely perhaps one year in five, but over the same period a short deluge might do just as much damage in another year. In 1917, rainfall in both the Molo and the Perkerra catchments was heavily in excess of average, falling in such concentrations during April and May of 1917 that in many places the shallow planted seeds

[4] Soil Conservation Officer's Report, Baringo Annual Report, 1945, KNA PC/RVP.2/7/3.
[5] BHT/TG/12.

	Droughts	Crop Plagues	Stock Disease	Human Disease	Comments
1917					Deluge
1918	*KIPNGOSIA*				
1919			Rinderpest	Influenza	
1920					
1921	Drought				
1922				↓	
1923			Goat Mange		Good rains
1924	Drought			Cerebral Meningitis	
1925					
1926			Rinderpest		Fair rains
1927	*KIPLEL*	Locusts			
1929	*KOWO*				
1930					Late deluge Crops washed away
1931	*TALAMWEI*	Locusts			
1932		Locusts			Good rains but late in year
1933	*KIPKOIKOIO*		Sheep scab		
1934		Locusts	Rinderpest	Smallpox	
1935		Stalk-borer↓	↓		Good year
1936			Foot-and-Mouth ↓		
1937		Army worm			Good year
1938		Locusts	Rinderpest		
1939		Locusts	Rinderpest		

Figure 3.1 Chronology of crisis in Baringo, 1917–39

of millet and sorghum were simply washed away. After a brief respite during June, the deluge resumed in July, lasting until the end of October.[6] The most dramatic result was the flooding of the River Perkerra at Marigat, causing the river to alter its course and, in so doing, to leave the irrigated

---

[6] Meteorological Department ARs, 1902 to 1928. Also, Bille & Heemstra, 'Rainfall Patterns of Kenya'. For details of agricultural problems related to Baringo's unreliable and volatile rainfall regime, see de Wilde et al., *Experiences with Agricultural Development,* ii, 157–87.

fields of Il Chamus cultivators without any source of water. As we noted in Chapter One, irrigated cultivation had been in gradual decline amongst Chamus since the turn of the century, but it was the floods of 1917 that brought the cultivation system to an end. The flood resulted in the largest cultivated area, at Leabori near to present-day Ngambo, being disconnected from the existing network of canals and channels bringing water from the river. With the gradual loss of the majority of the young men to the pastoral sector over the preceding two decades, insufficient labour remained to undertake the reconstruction of a new canal system or to clear and prepare a new area for planting. This was the final catalyst in the Chamus shift towards pastoralism. By the time the Napunye age-set was initiated in 1926, both Chamus settlements of Nkang Leabori and Nkang Lekeper were almost completely deserted.[7]

Neighbouring Tugen suffered in the wider ramifications of this development. Those living in the hills to the west of Lake Baringo and in the areas of Kipcherere and Sabor lost their own crops. Normally in such circumstances they would have hoped to obtain grain from Il Chamus in exchange for small stock. Similarly, lowland Tugen, living to the south of Marigat, did not grow sufficient cereals to meet their own requirements and expected to trade with people in the hills and at Lake Baringo. Their predicament was deepened when deluge was followed in the 1918 growing season by drought. This drought, known to Tugen as *Kipngosia*, was severe and widespread. With no grain stored from the previous year, the effects of *Kipngosia* were quickly manifest. Those who could travelled across the Kerio Valley to the west and south-west into Nandi in search of grains to be exchanged.[8]

During the nineteenth century, such conditions could be partially offset by hunting and gathering. Substantial herds of game were then to be found in Baringo, notably large numbers antelope and zebra, but also of elephant and rhinoceros. By 1920, the larger animals were only rarely to be seen, having been 'shot out' by the demands of the ivory traders and European hunters, and only small and scattered herds of other animals remained to provide an alternative food supply.[9] However, gathering, the common

---

[7] Baringo AR 1917/18, KNA BAR/I. For reliable eyewitness accounts, see BHT/CH/1 and BHT/CH/3, and for discussion of wider implications, BHT/CH/10 and BHT/CH/16. For the historical background, Anderson, 'Some thoughts'; Anderson, 'Cultivating pastoralists'; and Anderson, 'Agriculture and technology'. For subsequent flash-floods and further changes to the river, Lambert, 'Political history', 34.

[8] BHT/TG/2, BHT/TG/6 and BHT/TG/39.

[9] On Chamus hunting: Anderson, 'Expansion and expediency', 6–11; Anderson, 'Cultivating pastoralists', 245–8; Spencer, *Pastoral Continuum*, ch. 4. For European accounts of nineteenth-century hunting, Thomson, *Through Masailand*, 317–32; Gregory, *Great Rift Valley*, 139–40; von Hohnel, *Discovery*, ii, 1–4; Johnston, *Uganda Protectorate*, 17–20. At the turn of the century, small fortunes could be made by ivory trading. Lord Delamere even went to the excesses of hunting elephant in Baringo with a Maxim-gun: see Johnston to Sclater, 6 March 1900, ESA A/7/6. The Tugen oral record contains valuable accounts of hunting methods, for example BHT/TG/37 and BHT/TG/92.

subsistence companion of hunting, remained important during the interwar period. The name *Kipngosia* was derived from the edible berries of the *Ngosiek* tree, which were widely consumed at the height of the drought. These fruits were gathered and boiled for several hours before the white flesh of the berry could be eaten. Other fruits, such as *Yaganiek, Chemoniek* and *Sumbaek*, the latter most commonly found in upland areas, were also gathered in large quantities and eaten.[10]

Kipngosia came to an end with above average rains during 1920, but with the rain came an outbreak of rinderpest. This affected herds along the eastern border of the district. Further droughts occurred in 1921–2, and again in 1924–5. Then, after a poor harvest in the hills in 1926, the complete failure of the rains of 1927 marked the beginning of the drought on the lowlands that became widely known as *Kiplel kowo*, 'the white bones'. In the early 1980s, *Kiplel kowo* was still spoken of as being the worst drought within living memory – sometimes referred to as *Sarangach* (a time of such hardship that is better not spoken of).[11] *Kiplel kowo* was widespread, prolonged and devastating. No rain fell in 1927 or in 1928. Light rains came to some locations in the middle months of 1929, but by then stock losses on the lowlands had been very heavy and famine was reported from the northern parts of the district. Large herds were decimated by starvation and exhaustion. No herder escaped unscathed. Each elder has a tale to tell of his own family's tribulations during *Kiplel kowo*, stories relating the piles of bones of dead cattle, the distances travelled to find grass, the generosity of kinsfolk and neighbours, the humbling of the wealthy and the 'stealing of grass from the *Wazungu* [Europeans]' through trespass on neighbouring farms.[12] The colonial record provides an account of these events that is more detached and impersonal, but European officials also conveyed a strong sense of the sheer depth of suffering in the district. These comments from 1928, in the midst of *Kiplel kowo*, are typical of many:

> along the route from Endorois to Lake Baringo there are many carcasses of stock dead from starvation. I moved back 98 herd of stock from Mr. Stanning's farm … last week, and 14 died on the road from sheer starvation.

> Since leaving Ravine [travelling towards Maji Moto] the country has been desert. The only grazing seen on the whole route was a small patch at Maji Moto camp, in East Endorois location. A great number of stock have died of starvation and more are dying every day.[13]

---

[10] BHT/TG/25, BHT/TG/26 and BHT/TG/71 all give explanations of the naming of the 1918–19 drought. In those areas where *Chemoniek* was more commonly found than *Ngosiek* the drought of 1918–19 was given the name *Chemonong*. Minor regional variations on drought names were common. The name *Kipngosia* is also sometimes used to denote an earlier drought, in the latter part of the nineteenth century.

[11] *Sarangach* is more commonly used to refer to events in the very distant past, of which few details are recalled: BHT/TG/12, BHT/TG/77 and BHT/TG/81.

[12] See, for example, BHT/TG/11; BHT/TG/21; BHT/TG/74.

[13] The first quote is from C. Lydekker to G. Osborne (PC/Kerio), 27 March 1928, quoted in

Stock mortality during *Kiplel kowo* probably reached over 70 per cent for Baringo as a whole.

The impact of drought was greatly intensified for herders by locust invasions. Like harbingers of doom, the swarms foreshadowed the failed rains in 1927, in 1928 and again in 1929. The huge swarms settled in many parts of the southern and central Baringo lowlands, devouring whatever pasture, crops and green foliage they could find. Areas of several square miles were utterly denuded of vegetation. Arable production in the hills was also badly hit, the cereal crops of 1927 and 1928 being almost completely lost. Locust damage also severely affected production in the neighbouring settler farming districts of Nakuru and Eldama Ravine. Mustering their farm labour as beaters, European farmers were often able to prevent swarms from settling in as large numbers as in the reserve, but some suffered badly all the same. With crops destroyed over such a wide area, the commercial traders in grain who had begun to travel through Baringo by the early 1920s also found supplies difficult to obtain. These traders, mostly Asian immigrants and Sudanese ex-soldiers based at Eldama Ravine and Mogotio, continued to trade, but their supplies were limited and the prices they demanded were very high.[14]

Although rains in the second half of 1929 brought some relief to the herders on the lowlands, the unpredictable nature of the rainfall regime again played havoc with cultivation during 1930. Good rains fell early in April, before most families had planted. With the early wet weather most households then hurried to take advantage of what promised to be a fine season. But after mid-April a long, dry period followed with little rain. A heavy deluge in October then did severe damage to the late crop. The bumper harvest forecast by colonial officials in early April therefore turned out to be a very poor one at the end of the year. The administration made free issues of seed for the planting season of 1931, financed from the funds of the Local Native Council – that is, paid for by African taxation. This eased the worsening situation in some areas, but could not prevent an acute grain shortage in central and northern Baringo in the early part of 1932 after yet

---

[13 (cont.)] *KLC:EM*, 1784. The second is from the Safari Diary of Carr, ADC Baringo, March 1928, quoted in *KLC:EM*, 1784.

[14] Reports on locust invasions and estimates of the stock mortality during droughts are to be found in the Baringo and Eldama Ravine Subdistrict Annual Reports for 1927, 1928 and 1929, KNA PC/RVP.2/7/2, and 'Diseases to Crops, Locusts 1929', KNA PC/RVP.6A/ ll/37. See also E. Harrison, *History and Activities of Locusts in Kenya and Relative Costs of Destruction* (Department of Agriculture, Nairobi, Bulletin No. 9, 1929). Oral records give accounts of the collapse of the local grain trade during *Kiplel kowo*: for example, BHT/TG/37 and BHT/TG/78. Traders were keen to exploit the shortfall in the reserve, but could not cope with demand. Donkey caravans leaving Eldama Ravine at this time loaded with *posho* would sometimes only get as far as Emining, where previously they would have proceeded to Marigat or beyond before selling out. See BHT/TG/38 for the testimony of a Tugen Muslim employed by Nubian traders at this time. PC Osborne was responsible for the decision to begin famine-relief measures: see Kerio Province AR, 1927, KNA PC/RVP.2/2/6.

another poor harvest.[15] The four years from 1931 to 1934 saw below-average rains and the return of the dreaded locust swarms, thicker and more wide-spread than before. The years 1931 and 1932 are remembered on the lowlands as the drought of *Talamwei* – the drought of the locusts – when flying swarms did considerably more damage to grazing than to crops. [16]

Talamwei came to an end with the good short rains of late 1932, these ironically coinciding with the visit to Baringo of the members of the Kenya Land Commission (KLC) to review the district's land problems and to make recommendations regarding the land requirements of the African population.[17] Had they come just a few months later they would have witnessed the return of severe drought, affecting both lowlands and hills. The failure of the rains of 1933 marked the beginnings of a drought named *Kipkoikoio* – the drought that never ends. The shortage of grain in 1933 and 1934 was worse than ever, prompting Rift Valley Provincial Commissioner Welby to request that famine-relief measures be introduced once again. By now the dynamics of Baringo's exchange economy and the consequences of its collapse were better understood by colonial officials, as Welby made clear in justifying his request for assistance:

> The reason for this is that, owing to the practically complete failure of the rains, those Kamasia who are in possession of food stocks and are in the habit of selling to the inhabitants of the more barren locations dare not deplete their stores further and moreover the goats and sheep are now so poor and weak that they are practically unsaleable, so that the purchase of food from traders is difficult. The price of hides and skins also is again very depressed, and the milk supply is practically non-existent.[18]

The three years 1935 to 1937 brought comparatively good rains and better harvests, only marred by an infestation of 'army worm' in 1937. These caterpillars invaded the entire district lying under 7,000 ft, doing consider-able damage to the millet and sorghum crops and seriously affecting the production of local beer. Flying swarms of locusts returned to southern Baringo in 1938, striking the farms of Ravine and Solai, where the battle to save crops and pasture lasted well into the following year. The interwar period in Baringo ended the way it had begun, the rainfall of 1939 being the lowest since that of 1918.[19]

[15] Baringo District AR, 1929, 1930, KNA PC/RVP.2/7/2. See also correspondence in KNA PC/RVP.6A/11/5 and PC/RVP.6A/11/6.

[16] BHT/TG/34; BHT/CH/11. Chamus refer to the drought of *Talamwei* as *Ngolong Omaati*. See also Baringo District AR, 1933, KNA BAR/2. Full accounts of the damage to pasture and crops are given in 'Damage to Crops; Locusts, 1931–1932', KNA PC/RVP.6A/11/9. For a wider survey of the 1931 locust invasion, see D.L. Blunt, *Report on the Locust Invasion of Kenya* (Department of Agriculture, Nairobi, Bulletin No. 21, 1931).

[17] See Chapter Five, below.

[18] Welby (PC/RVP) to CNC, 25 May 1933, KNA PC/RVP.6A/111/6.

[19] Baringo District ARs 1937, 1938 and 1939, KNA PC/RVP.2/7/3; Langridge to PC/RVP, various, late 1938 to early 1939, re locust campaign, KNA PC/RVP.6A/11/11.

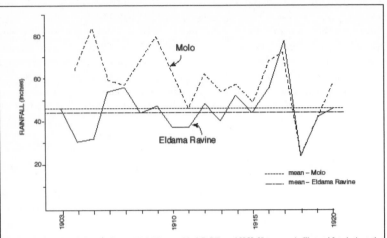

Mean calculated from long-term figures 1914–77, quoted in J.C. Bille and H.H. Heemstra, *An Illustrated Introduction to the Rainfall Patterns of Kenya* (ILCA Working Document No. 12, Nairobi 1979). Also, Meteorological Department, Nairobi, Annual Reports, 1903–20.

It should be noted that the Molo figure for 1905 is clearly inconsistent and probably represents the misuse or misreading of the rain gauge in that year. Rainfall readings at Molo were incomplete during 1919; hence the use of a different key to represent the Molo graph at that point.

Figure 3.2 Annual rainfall, Molo and Eldama Ravine, 1903–20

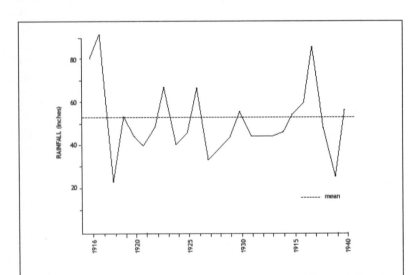

Mean calculated from long-term figures, 1914 to 1977, quoted in J.C. Bille and H.H. Heemstra, *An Illustrated Introduction to the Rainfall Patterns of Kenya* (ILCA Working Document No. 12, Nairobi 1979). Also, KNA, Rainfall Returns, Kabernet, 1914–40, Baringo District Annual Report 1939, PC/RVP.2/7/3.

Figure 3.3 Annual rainfall, Kabarnet, 1916–40

Heavy stock mortality over these years was not the total sum of the herders' woes; they also had to contend with the evils of stock disease. Rinderpest and bovine pleuropneumonia were endemic to the herds of Baringo throughout most of the 1920s and 1930s, sporadically occurring in more widespread outbreaks and taking a heavy toll of stock. Tugen know rinderpest by the name *kipkeita*; it is dreaded by all.[20] Only in 1933 did the colonial Veterinary Department begin to operate in Baringo with any regularity, and so there exists no administrative catalogue of disease outbreaks, other than occasional (and often imprecise) references in annual reports. However, four significant occurrences of rinderpest can be confidently identified. The first of these came in 1919, just after the drought of *Kipngosia*, when infected Tugen cattle carried the virus on to the farmlands of Ravine and Londiani, where it ran rampantly through settler dairy stock already weakened by the ravages of drought. A second outbreak occurred in 1926, lingering on in the reserve for many months.[21] Late in 1934 a third outbreak of rinderpest was confirmed in northern Baringo, spreading to herds then grazing in Loboi and Endorois. The Veterinary Department hurriedly implemented a double inoculation of stock in Baringo, to protect the dairy herds of Solai and Subukia, but this came too late to prevent high mortality among the African-owned cattle. Quarantine restrictions imposed at this time were still in force in 1936, when foot-and-mouth disease became evident among traders' cattle in the holding ground at Mogotio. At the same time, two isolated cases of rinderpest at Rongai and Njoro, in the vicinity of small-stock markets, raised the fear that goats being traded out of Baringo were carrying the disease into the settled area, and so the export of small stock from Baringo was also prohibited for a time. A fourth confirmed outbreak of rinderpest occurred in the Lembus Forest, early in 1939, gradually spreading through the southern locations. An outbreak of East Coast fever occurred in Pokorr at about this time, but this subsided without substantial loss of stock.[22] Veterinary officials thought that the high susceptibility of Baringo stock to disease was in large part attributable to the effects of prolonged droughts and the steady deterioration of the pastures in the district; but it seems more significant that the flow of livestock into the district from the north was completely uncontrolled, and that the movements of herds, taken in conjunction with the large numbers of animals traded into and through the district, created an environment in which transmission was relatively rapid.[23]

[20] BHT/TG/22 and BHT/TG/72 for accounts of this disease.

[21] Lambert, 'Political history', 28; W. Aubrey (Subukia) to C. Lydekker (DC/Baringo), 4 April 1928, quoted in *KLC:EM*, ii, 1785.

[22] BHT/TG/121 and BHT/TG/124. Baringo District AR, 1936, KNA PC/RVP. 2/7/3; Baringo District and Eldama Ravine ARs, 1939, KNA PC/RVP.2/7/3; Murphy (DC/Baringo) to DC/Nakuru, 17 January 1936, and Wyatt (Stock Inspector) to Veterinary Officer, Nakuru, 30 March 1935, both in KNA PC/RVP.6A/23/9.

[23] D.E. Faulkner, *Notes on Animal Health and Husbandry for Africans* (Government Printer, Nairobi,

Strategies for survival

Cattle pastoralism and hill cultivation have historically been well integrated throughout the East African Rift Valley. The networks of kinship, exchange and reciprocity, which link farmers and herders, are social and economic bonds providing insurance against risk in a precarious environment. These networks have particular importance when ill-fortune strikes a household, and especially when more widespread drought or disease affects a community.[24] We have already stressed that those Tugen who migrated on to the Baringo lowlands did not sever their ties with the kin they left behind in the hills. Indeed, the very dynamics of their movement undoubtedly depended upon those ties being maintained and even reinforced; herders needed to obtain grain through exchange, and hillfolk were likely to want their cattle herded on the lowlands. These relationships were often kin-based, but they were also common between persons of the same clan and same age grade. In Tugen custom, it is claimed that hospitality cannot be refused to an age-mate or clansman. In this way no member of society could be excluded from assistance in time of need, although some were more assiduous in cultivating networks than were others, and such persons increased their security and their options should troubles descend.[25]

Studies of the dynamics of these relationships in all parts of eastern Africa have emphasized the vulnerability of cattle-herding communities to drought, and have accordingly tended to present these ties as being primarily driven by the subsistence needs of pastoralists: Herders are seen as having a permanent and more immediate interest in ties of reciprocity in order to secure food, whereas agriculturalists make a longer-term invest-ment in the reproduction of loaned livestock.[26] This was certainly the normal, seasonal pattern in Baringo. Even in a year of average rains on the Baringo lowlands, most households would obtain a harvest from their gardens that was insufficient to see them through the dry season. Before the next planting a member of the household would expect to visit kinsmen in the hills, in the hope of finding them still with a grain surplus to exchange. Acquiring the grain in this way would most often be accomplished by the

---

23 (cont.) 1956), 31–108; Heady, *Range Management*, 99–101. For a broader discussion, see H.E. Jahnke, *Tsetse Flies and Livestock Development in East Africa: a Study in Environmental Economics* (Munich, 1976).

24 For an overview, Johnson & Anderson, *Ecology of Survival*, 4–11. For examples: Adams & Anderson, 'Irrigation before development'; Waller, 'Ecology, migration and expansion'; and Neal W. Sobania, 'Fisherman herders: subsistence, survival and cultural change in northern Kenya', *Journal of African History*, 29 (1988), 41–56.

25 For recent discussion of these points, see Anderson & Broch-Due, *The Poor Are Not Us*, esp. the introduction.

26 For example, Beverley Gartrell, 'Prelude to disaster: the case of Karamoja', in Johnson & Anderson, *Ecology of Survival*, 193–218.

exchange of goats or goat products – milk, meat or skins. But grain might also be freely handed over, on the common understanding that the donor would expect the favour to be reciprocated at some later date. By accepting this form of assistance the recipient was placed under strong social obligations to the donor family until the debt could be cancelled.[27] These were the ordinary transactions of everyday life.

The succession of droughts and harvest failures between 1917 and 1939 was so severe and so widespread in extent that it placed even these deeply rooted ties under strain. The migrations of the period 1900 to 1917 had been accomplished in the context of favourable environmental conditions, when production remained relatively secure. After 1917, the drift of people to the lowlands continued, but throughout the 1920s it was driven by the basic needs prompted by widespread shortage of grain in the hill regions rather than the aspiration to herd cattle. The rigours of *Kiplel kowo* were such in the hills that people recall having moved to the parched lowlands, 'where at least people could eat the meat of the dying cattle'.[28] It was a trend that district officials also noticed, as this comment from 1928 indicates:

> A notable result of 3 bad harvests has been the steady drift of the Hill Tugen down to the plains and their gradual transmutation from an agricultural to a pastoral people; this is readily understandable when one sees the pitiable shambas that they try to cultivate, and the almost complete lack of grazing up in the hills.[29]

Most newcomers to the lowlands during *Kiplel kowo* would have arrived in the knowledge that, at least in the short term, they could exploit the hospitality of relatives and friends. In this respect, strategies of survival were little different in the 1920s from previously, even if the pattern of seasonal dependency between hill and plain had temporarily shifted.

Herders on the lowlands dealt with their predicament in these years in several ways. Most obviously, herding strategies had to be modified to cope with drought. Herds became increasingly mobile, moving to pastures and watering points far distant from the normal grazing pattern. During each dry season and in time of drought, Tugen and Chamus herds were to be found on pastures beyond the Baringo boundary, such as at Churo, Il Kisim, Sipili, Waseges, the Arabel Valley, the Marmanet Forest and Subukia. As the shortage of grazing became more acute, so the herders became more desperate and more likely to take greater risks. Animals were held for longer periods in the tsetse-infested areas of Waseges and Arabel, for example. 'Why should we stay here and watch our cattle starve?' asked one Tugen herder: 'At least in Waseges we could have some hope.'[30] The same attitude

[27] BHT/TG/37 and BHT/TG/38.

[28] BHT/TG/78.

[29] Native Affairs Department, Annual Report 1928 (quoted from the Baringo District AR, 1928, KNA BAR/2).

[30] BHT/TG/25.

prevailed with regard to trespass on European-owned farms, which, as we shall see in Chapter Four, reached huge proportions by the early 1930s. Taking animals greater distances to pasture and into areas with such unusual attendant dangers placed greater demands upon herd management, particularly in terms of labour requirements. Every male in the family might accompany the stock on these movements, sometimes remaining away from the permanent homestead for two or three months. Close friends, age-mates or clansmen combined their herds for these trips, for safety and companionship. Extra labour was also demanded to find food for cattle when grazing was not available. Tree bark was commonly stripped and branches lopped to provide cattle with alternative fodder.[31]

The division of the herd as a form of risk spreading had always been a popular practice among Tugen and Chamus herders. The loaning of two or three head of cattle to a kinsman living in another part of the district, with a mutually beneficial arrangement regarding the division of the future progeny, brought advantage to both parties: the recipient gained a prospective source of milk, whilst perhaps establishing the basis for the future development of his own herd, and the donor could be reasonably assured of a long-term return on his investment.[32] But as livestock deaths from starvation increased, cancelling these bonds but leaving debts unsettled, the utility of such arrangements appeared less obvious.

Whilst herders struggled to maintain their cattle herds in the face of drought and disease, flocks of sheep and (especially) goats fared remarkably well. Where cattle and sheep could no longer find grazing, goats were able to browse on woody vegetation and less palatable grasses. During dry periods goats could survive reasonably well with less frequent watering. Outbreaks of sheep and goat diseases were comparatively rare, and their effects less destructive. Goat mange, known locally as *Simbirian*, is recalled as having been prevalent for a short while in the early 1920s, and minor outbreaks of sheep and goat scab are documented in the southern locations for 1933 and 1934 respectively.[33]

The resilience of the goat, an animal milked and also slaughtered for its meat, was a crucial factor in the survival of Baringo households during the 1920s and 1930s. Tugen view their goats as a reserve of wealth, both as a store of food and as items of exchange. As one herder explained:

> Goats are traditionally a food to us, as well as being a sort of money to us. If you wished to buy a cow from the Somali, or some grain from a neighbour, then you will give out your goats ... Goats were our store; goats were our food ... Goats are the reason most Tugen have survived. It is even how they have bought their cows.[34]

[31] BHT/TG/12, BHT/TG/35 and BHT/TG/40.
[32] BHT/TG/18 and BHT/TG/41.
[33] Baringo Annual Reports. 1933 and 1934, KNA BAR/2 and KNA PC/RVP.2/7/3, respectively. Also, BHT/TG/96 and BHT/TG/99.
[34] BHT/TG/25.

No scheme of stock management was usually applied to a family goat flock; rather, they browsed near the homestead, often tended by smaller children. By rapid breeding, any losses to the herd due to slaughter or exchange could be quickly recouped. This factor, above all else, reinforced the Tugen herders' conviction that the goat was the crucial element in the maintenance of households on the lowlands. During the interwar period, family herds of well over 100 goats were common, and in areas such as Emsos and Ngentalel, where the salty nature of soil and vegetation was a limiting factor on cattle-keeping, herds of more than 200 were not exceptional. So long as a regular supply of salt was available, goats could survive without water for up to a week, and still be expected to thrive.[35] Even during severe droughts, such as *Kiplel kowo*, Baringo's goat herds managed to eke out an existence on the thorny bush and acacias, whilst cattle were starving for want of grass. At times of prolonged drought, Tugen placed even greater reliance upon the goat as a means of subsistence and of longer-term household survival. The rebuilding of cattle herds in the wake of losses due to drought was dependent upon the exchange of goats for cattle. This was facilitated by itinerant stock traders, who brought cattle into Baringo from the north. These cattle were exchanged for goats, the traders then selling the goats on to butcheries to the south and east of Baringo. This trade had been a significant factor in the rapid build-up of Tugen and Chamus cattle holdings prior to 1918,[36] and during the droughts of the 1920s and 1930s Baringo's herders again used goat–cattle exchange as a means of replenishing their cattle herds.

As Baringo's apparent environmental decay became a subject of growing concern among Europeans, the prevalence of the goat was noted. In 1929, a visiting Agricultural Officer, Mr Lynn Wyatt, reported that:

> overstocking has depleted the vegetation to such an extent that erosion has set in and reduced the fertility so much that the recuperation of the natural grasses will be difficult; but although large numbers of cattle have died, goats have not been greatly affected.[37]

The point was repeated in the Native Affairs Department annual report of 1931:

> The recent privations have killed off the weaker cattle, but has unfortunately left the flocks of hardy but destructive goats almost untouched.[38]

Whilst African herders saw the increase in the goat population during these years as a rational response to drought conditions, European opinion came to see the goat as a causal factor in degradation. This view was most

---

[35] BHT/TG/25 and BHT/TG/32. Williamson & Payne, *Introduction to Animal Husbandry*, 275; Dahl & Hjort, *Having Herds*, 251.

[36]. BHT/NB/1 and BHT/SW/1. The trade will be discussed in more detail in Chapter Five.

[37] Native Affairs Dept. Annual Report, 1929.

[38] Native Affairs Dept. Annual Report, 1931.

vigorously argued by Colin Maher, a highly energetic and well-educated Agricultural Officer with a particular interest in the problems of soil erosion, who came to be recognized by the mid-1930s as the leader of what we may call Kenya's 'anti-goat lobby'.[39] Between 1932 and 1937, Maher conducted tours around several of the colony's African reserves, including those in Baringo, for the purpose of assessing the extent and seriousness of soil erosion, suggesting methods for its amelioration and giving instruction in the improvement of African agriculture. As he completed each of these detailed inspections, Maher became more and more convinced that the goat played a dangerous role in the process of pasture decay, especially in low-lying semi-arid areas such as lowland Baringo. The stark picture presented by Maher of Machakos and Baringo districts, in reports compiled between 1935 and 1937, offered an alarming analysis of rapid environmental degradation, in which the humble goat played a highly significant role.[40] The goat, according to Maher, was not a primary agent of erosion, but a major catalyst:

> When the grass has been destroyed by overgrazing and trampling by cattle, the goats begin to enter into their own. Goats can feed on very short grass by means of their mobile upper-lips and very prehensile tongues. This characteristic enables them to graze young grass ahead of the cattle which remain hungry while the goats fatten; or the goats can graze grass which has already been grazed too short for the cattle to make use of it … This close grazing results in the exposure of the grass roots to the burning sun and deterioration of the pasture.[41]

By the mid-1930s, popular opinion among Europeans in Kenya, officials and settlers alike, condemned the goat as an agent of erosion. Increased dependence upon the goat was seen as symptomatic of the severe limits within which African agrarian production functioned. The Africans of Baringo therefore found that the resource they considered most valuable at time of drought and famine was under attack as being a prime agent in the creation of those very same circumstances.[42]

---

[39] KNA Min. of Agri./1/580 contains numerous memos by Maher on 'the goat problem', including a questionnaire circulated by him to all District Commissioners. See also, Colin Maher, 'The goat: friend or foe?', *East African Agricultural Journal*, 11 (1945), 115–21.

[40] Maher, *Soil Erosion and Land Utilisation in the Kamasia*; Colin Maher, *Soil Erosion and Land Utilisation in the Ukamba (Kitui) Reserve, Pts I, II and III* (Nairobi 1937); Colin Maher, 'Land utilization as a national problem, with special reference to Kenya Colony', *East African Agricultural Journal*, 2 (1936), 133–44. Between 1930 and 1950 Maher published eighteen articles and pamphlets and numerous newspaper articles on aspects of his work, first as an Agricultural Officer concerned with maize development, and later as the Senior Officer in the Soil Conservation Service. Maher's personal file, KNA Min. of Agri./2/274 outlines his career.

[41] Maher, 'The goat', 118. See also, Maher, *Soil Erosion and Land Utilization*, 90–95. Later authorities on range management have adopted a similar view: Heady, *Range Management*, 78–80; Williamson & Payne, *Introduction to Animal Husbandry*, 287.

[42] Wolfe (Dir. of Agri.) to PC/Central Province, 24 March 1937, KNA Min. of Agri./1/580; Waters (Dir. of Agri.) to Chief Secretary, 22 June 1938, KNA Min. of Agri./1/588.

Wage employment in the colonial economy was a less attractive option in Baringo during the troubled years of the 1920s and 1930s than in many other parts of Kenya. Tugen and Chamus had largely resisted all attempts to draw them into waged labour prior to 1920. It was reported during 1914 that the 'labour concept' was as yet poorly understood among the Africans of Baringo, due to their having 'had insufficient contact with the administration'. Very few Tugen were therefore recruited for the Carrier Corps during the 1914–18 war.[43] In the early 1920s, Tugen and Chamus were recruited by the Railways Department to work on the construction of the Uas Nkishu and Solai branch lines, but the conditions of employment were notoriously bad, and the inexperienced Baringo labourers found the work difficult and heavy. Labourers from the Baringo lowlands were unpopular with recruiters, being 'straight from the Reserve and raw'. Employment on railway construction quickly came to be hated by the Tugen, and by 1925 the administration found it impossible to acquire labour for railway contractors without resort to coercion.[44] Less onerous work could be found on the European farms to the south and east of the reserve, and before 1910 Uas Nkishu Maasai and Tugen labourers were employed on the farms of Ravine. Throughout the 1920s and 1930s the numbers of Tugen taking up such employment slowly increased.[45] But many employers preferred to use Kikuyu or Luo labour, as labourers from Baringo were thought to be 'undernourished' and 'unfit for physically strenuous work'.[46]

Even if Tugen labour was not popular with European employers, labour shortages often meant they had to take whatever they could find. During

---

[42] (cont.) Experiments with goats as a control on bush encroachment provided results that in some respects contradicted Maher. See R.R. Staples, 'Bush control and deferred grazing as a measure to improve grazing', *East African Agricultural Journal*, 11 (1945), 93–6, and R.R. Staples, H.E. Hornby & R.M. Hornby, 'A study of the comparative effects of goats and cattle on a mixed grass-bush pasture', *East African Agricultural Journal*, 8 (1942), 62–70. For interesting comments on Maher's attitude from two officials who worked with him, see BHT/ES/1 and BHT/ES/3. Minutes on Maher's personal file, KNA, Min. of Agri./2/274, also show a strong division of opinion over the goat issue.

[43] Baringo District AR, 1914/15, KNA BAR/I. D.C. Savage & J. Forbes Munro, 'Carrier corps recruitment in the British East Africa Protectorate, 1914–18', *Journal of African History*, 7 (1966), 313–42. Informants BHT/TG/48 and BHT/TG/49 were among those Tugen recruited for service.

[44] BHT/TG/18 and BHT/TG/39. Osborne to all DCs, 9 February 1925, and Osborne to Resident Engineer, Solai Branch (Uganda Railway), 19 February 1925, both in KNA PC/ERD.6A/38/1. For a critical account of the Uas Nkishu railway project, see W. McGregor Ross, *Kenya From Within* (London, 1927), 238–55. Also, R.M. van Zwanenberg, *Colonial Capitalism and Labour in Kenya, 1919–1939* (Nairobi, 1975), gives a full account of labour conditions in the colony, with particular reference to methods of recruitment.

[45] BHT/TG/44 and BHT/TG/52. Baringo District AR, 1913/14, KNA BAR/I. On the early settlement of Ravine, see Lambert, 'Political history', 24–5.

[46] Rongai and Lower Molo Farmers' Association to DC/Nakuru, 22 August 1931, Dwen to DC/Nakuru, 7 November 1938, and Sabine to DC/Nakuru, 23 September 1931, all in KNA PC/RVP.6A/25/4.

1925 the shortage of labour on the Ravine and Lomolo farms became acute. Many farmers laid the blame on the District Commissioner, Osborne, who they claimed did too little to foster the work ethic among the Tugen. In his own defence, Osborne drew attention to the fact that 'the local Ravine farmers of any standing [had] kept themselves generally supplied with local labour'; it was those employers with a bad reputation among Africans who experienced the greatest difficulties in securing labour.[47] Moreover, farm wages along the Baringo boundary were amongst the lowest paid anywhere in East Africa. In the most developed parts of Nakuru and Naivasha, to the south, labourers wages were 12s. per month (plus *posho* ration) in 1926, compared with only 8s. per month on the farms bordering Baringo. During the depression of the early 1930s wages sank to 5s. per month and remained at that level until after 1935. Even by the standards of cash value within an economically peripheral district such as Baringo, these wage levels were generally unattractive, approximating to no more than the value of the sale of a goat or two.[48] During the interwar period the average number of men registered to leave the Baringo Reserves in search of employment was less than 1,000 annually. Only in 1931, when 1,500 men were registered for work and when demand for labour on the farms was lower due to the depression, were vacancies on local farms completely filled. Increases in the numbers of Tugen taking on such work in these years was purely a function of desperation in the face of drought and hunger, a short-term means of raising small amounts of cash to purchase stock or grain or to meet annual tax demands.[49]

In contrast to wage labour, squatting on European-owned farms became a far more popular option among Tugen. The squatter system 'depended on the fact that many Europeans owned large areas of surplus unused land' and 'required cheap easily available labour', whilst the Africans had too little land and so were prepared to meet the European's labour requirements in exchange for access to his land.[50] In Baringo, African herders faced acute grazing shortage within the reserve by the late 1920s, while the

[47] Osborne to Senior Comm./Kerio, 22 April 1925, KNA PC/ERD.6A/38/l. Most Tugen expressed their preferences with regard to European employers quite clearly; see, for example, BHT/TG/45 and BHT/TG/47.

[48] A survey of the labour recruitment is to be found in each annual report, with wage rates, but for especially detailed comments see the report for 1934, KNA PC/RVP.2/7/3. Also, 'Labour for Sir Francis Scott', 6 February 1925, KNA PC/ERD.6A/38/l.

[49] BHT/TG/45, BHT/TG/39, BHT/TG/16 and BHT/CH/10. Baringo District AR 1931, KNA PC/RVP.2/7/2. V.L. Liversage, 'Some observations on farming economics in Nakuru District', *East African Agricultural Journal*, 4 (1938), 195–204, and Colin Maher, 'African labour on the farm in Kenya Colony', *East African Agricultural Journal*, 7 (1942), 228–35. Farm labour was never popular with Tugen or Il Chamus; nor were they popular with prospective employers. Tugen registered as out to work never rose above 500 at this time; see Baringo District ARs, 1927, 1928, 1929 and 1930, KNA BAR/2 and KNA PC/RVP.2/7/2.

[50] van Zwanenberg, *Colonial Capitalism*, 211.

impoverished European farmers of Solai, Lomolo, Rongai and Ravine managed underutilized lands and suffered annual labour shortages at harvest time. By permitting African herders to graze stock on the farmlands in return for labour at a time when the settler most required it, during the harvest, both groups could benefit. The practice of squatting had gone on since the earliest days of white settlement in Kenya. Some settlers took 'Kaffir farming', as squatting was known, to extremes, leaving their farms un-occupied and undeveloped but opening them up to large numbers of rent-paying Africans. Such behaviour raised criticism from other Europeans, who feared that this increased the likelihood of livestock disease being transmitted from African-owned cattle to European dairy herds, or who argued that the opening of access to African use undermined the political integrity of the White Highlands as an area reserved solely for European ownership.[51] The Resident Native Labour Ordinance, framed in 1918, was partly designed to tackle this problem. By stating 'that no African should live on European land unless he had contracted to work for the proprietor for 180 days in the year', the Ordinance sought to regulate the terms upon which squatters resided on the farms, especially through specifying the number of cattle to be kept on the farm by the African and empowering the authorities to remove squatters who were found to be improperly regis-tered or to hold cattle in excess of the stipulated limit. European landowners could also be punished for failing to comply with the regulations.[52]

Yet squatter arrangements were such that little could be done to legislate for their effective control. The Labour Department did not run inspections at this time, and the police seldom entered European farms unless summoned by the owner.[53] The district administration left European farmers to themselves. Indeed, the lack of regulation was in large part responsible for the popularity of squatting among the Baringo herders. The squatter agreements were known to Tugen as 'Blue' – because of the need to certify the document with an ink thumbprint. The contracts normally allowed the herder to take up to ten head of cattle to graze on the European farm. By the late 1920s, every herder along the Baringo boundary endeavoured to take a 'Blue' with at least one European farmer. In payment for this right to graze cattle on the farm, the herder and his family would undertake labour for the farmer at stipulated times of the year. Members of a herder's family engaging in this labour were also likely to be paid in *posho* or be permitted to cultivate grain and vegetables on a small area of the farm. It was quite usual for Tugen squatters to greatly exceed the

[51] Ibid., ch. 8, gives a detailed account of the squatter issue. Also, see Wrigley, 'Patterns of economic life', 238–9.

[52] van Zwanenberg, *Colonial Capitalism*, 210–74.

[53] David M. Anderson, 'Policing the settler state: colonial hegemony in Kenya', in Dagmar Engels & Shula Marks (eds), *Contesting Colonial Hegemony: State and Society in Africa and India* (London, 1994), 248–66. For a survey of labour law, David M. Anderson, 'Master and servant in colonial Kenya', *Journal of African History*, 41 (2000), 459–85.

number of animals permitted by contract to graze; a squatter might keep thirty or forty additional head of stock on the farm without detection. Some herders managed to hold squatter contracts on more than one farm simultaneously, and others who did not have contracts loaned their stock to those who did.[54] Many settlers made unofficial agreements with herders, without formal contracts, demanding payments in livestock as a form of grazing fee.[55] 'Kaffir farming' of this type was illegal but very common along the Baringo border, becoming a crucial factor in African survival strategies throughout the interwar period.

Away from the farm boundary, people had fewer options as the effects of drought, disease and locust infestation multiplied. During *Kiplel kowo* the worst hardships were faced in the northern locations. Rumours of severe hunger and pending famine from this area prompted the colonial government to organize supplies of grain to be delivered to the district after the failure of the rains in 1928. *Posho* to the value of 19,406s. was purchased from the Kenya Farmers' Association and moved by lorry to distribution centres speedily established in the hills to the north of Kabarnet, in the Chamus area at Marigat and on the southern lowlands at Emining.[56] Although government officials described this action as a famine-relief measure, the cost of the grain in 1928 was actually met directly from the funds of the Baringo Local Native Councils. Further famine relief was issued in 1929 and again from 1931 to 1934, and in these years the government made loans to the Local Native Council account so that the necessary quantity of grain could be purchased. The loans were recouped over an extended period through the imposition of a local cess of an additional 1s. on the rate of hut tax payable throughout the district. The sum to be repaid therefore accumulated each year. When, in the early 1930s, some chiefs voiced complaints about the effects of an additional tax burden in such difficult times, the Council was merely advised to make savings in other categories of expenditure which might then be offset against the loan.[57] As can be seen in Table 3.1, the overall expenditure on famine relief was paltry in terms of government finance, but it did represent a significant

---

[54] The numbers of cattle permitted on each squatter contract was not at this time legally formalized, but was usually arrived at by common agreement of the local farmers' association. See for example, DC/Baringo to Manager, Estates and Investments Rongai, 1 September 1928, and Secretary, Ravine FA to DC/Eldama Ravine, 4 July 1929, both in KNA PC/ERD.6A/38/4.

[55] BHT/TG/19, BHT/TG/22, BHT/TG/45 and BHT/ES/3 all give accounts of such arrangements. From the late 1930s these irregular squatter 'contracts' came under closer administrative scrutiny. See the various cases raised in KNA PC/ERD.6A/38/3, KNA PC/ERD.6A/38/3, and in particular the Esageri case uncovered in 1942, Wolff to PC/RVP, 21 February 1942, KNA PC/RVP.6A/15/15.

[56] For an analysis of famine-relief expenditure, based on district files, see Maher, *Soil Erosion and Land Utilisation*, 73–4, and Appendix 8. For monthly accounts, see KNA, PC/RVP.6A/11/S–7.

[57] 'Baringo LNC's History', PRB vol. I, KNA BAR/13.

Table 3.1 Famine relief expenditure in Baringo, 1928–33

Year	Expenditure (shillings)
1928	19,406
1929	86,918
1930	Nil
1931	6,241 (borne entirely by LNC*)
1932	33,597
1933	40,000 (approx.)

Sources: KNA, PC/RVP.6A/ll/5, 6 and 7. Also C. Maher, *Soil Erosion and Land Utilisation in the Kamasia, Njemps and East Sink Reserves*, (Nairobi 1937), appendix 8.
*LNC Local Native Council.

slice of Local Native Council funds. Even when judged to be suffering from famine, it seemed that the peoples of Baringo were expected to help themselves.

Resentment among some chiefs over this question was deepened by the fact that not all locations were the recipients of food aid, although all paid the cess. Some thought they should not pay for relief which they did not receive; others argued that the system of distributing grain from 1931 meant that, in effect, families were being asked to pay twice over. These complaints were to some extent justified. Initially, local chiefs and headmen assisted in determining who was entitled to receive famine relief by drawing up lists of destitute families. But it soon became clear that such lists were somewhat arbitrary. Headmen tended to add as many families to the lists as possible, in order to increase the relief given to the people under their care.[58] The increased expenditure on relief in 1929 led the District Commissioner to suggest that grain had been handed out to all, without adequate controls. In 1930 famine relief was not supplied, but when it was again delivered in 1931 stricter controls were introduced at the distribution centres to try and determine who was and who was not destitute. The rules drawn up required the applicants for relief to prove the seriousness of their circumstances before the District Officer, thus placing the onus of responsibility on the individual. This measure was combined with the introduction of a goat levy to pay for the grain being given as relief: no family with surviving male livestock or more than two head of female stock could receive aid without payment.[59] These regulations dramatically reduced the number of applications for aid. Commenting upon the introduction of a goat-levy at Emining during 1933, District Commissioner Brown stated that 'when I announced

[58] Welby (PC/RVP) to CNC, 26 May 1932, KNA PC/RVP.6A/ll/5. BHT/TG/35 and BHT/TG/40.

[59] Welby (PC/RVP) to DC/Bar and DC/ER, 7 September 1931, and PC/RVP to CNC, 21 December 1931, both in KNA PC/RVP.6A/11/5; DC/BAR to PC/RVP, 12 June 1933, 'Rules for the Guidance of Officers having Applications for Famine Relief', KNA PC/RVP.6A/ll/6.

the order to local chiefs the effect was electrical: A large crowd of applicants outside the office melted away.'[60]

While the administration was determined to avoid the potential scandal of a famine in Baringo, officials were equally determined to target the recipients as carefully as possible. In 1931, suspicions were expressed that Tugen and Chamus had already come to 'view the free issue of posho by government as a natural course' in each dry season. If they were in a position to exploit its availability they would do so 'without compunction', the district commissioner asserted.[61] It was certainly true that Baringo's hard-pressed African population found it difficult to accept the validity of the criteria imposed by government to determine who was entitled to assistance and who was not.[62] What sense did it make for a family to sell their last remaining few goats to obtain grain? From where would they obtain adequate milk in the coming weeks with only two female goats remaining? Would they then be expected to rebuild their household herd on so fragile a basis when the rains returned? To the Africans of Baringo, the insistence that only those households without livestock holdings should receive food aid appeared an absurd and unwise condition.

It seems unlikely that widespread famine was imminent in Baringo in the late 1920s or early 1930s: if it had been the limited quantities of grain moved into the district by government would hardly have been sufficient to cope with needs. But it is certain that the distribution of grain at government centres brought welcome short-term relief to many families, especially in areas of lower livestock holdings. In evaluating the importance of this intervention in African life, the colonial government tended to overestimate the significance of its own role; just as government was fearful of adverse publicity concerning deaths from starvation in a British colony, there was much to be gained in propaganda terms from being able to claim to have saved lives by the prompt issue of relief.[63] The distribution of famine relief was presented as evidence that government was active in assisting the district – even if the grain was ultimately paid for by Africans themselves; but it also helped to reinforce the growing opinion amongst Europeans that Baringo was a land locked in a downward spiral of decay and increasing dependency.

Finally, we must ask what impact this catalogue of crisis over the 1920s and 1930s had upon human health and nutrition. The short answer is that we know too little about this aspect. In the area of health, as in other social-welfare respects, colonial intervention in Baringo was minimal. In 1929 the provision of government medical facilities amounted to a single dispensary at Eldama Ravine, which also dealt with the needs of those people living on

[60] DC Brown to Sabine (DO), 17 June 1933, KNA PC/RVP.6A/15/36. The incident is recalled in the oral record, BHT/TG/35.

[61] PC/RVP to CNC, 21 December 1931, KNA PC/RVP.6A/11/5.

[62] For comments to this effect, BHT/TG/3 and BHT/TG/17.

[63] Rimington (DC/BAR) to PC/RVP, 10 February 1932, and PC/RVP to CNC, 14 April 1932, both in KNA PC/RVP.6A/ll/5.

the nearby European farms. In that year the dispensary treated an average of only three patients per day, and most of those attended with very minor complaints. As one District Commissioner dryly noted, the facilities were somewhat 'primitive':

> There is one native dresser at Ravine who is flatteringly referred to as '*doctari*', and the Dispensary is a condemned native hut. I know nothing about the medicines supplied, but when the Deputy Director of Medical and Sanitary Services inspected the place he did not appear to be favourably impressed, and took a bottle of medicine away with him, possibly as a souvenir.[64]

There were improvements in provision in the 1930s, but they were not welcomed by the local population. Dispensaries were opened at Emining, Marigat and Nginyang in 1932, Mukutan in 1936 and Pokorr in 1939, but none were well attended. The twenty-bed hospital opened at Kabarnet in 1932 continued to be under used until after the Second World War. Local lack of interest was such that in 1933 the Medical Officer was withdrawn and replaced by a more junior Assistant Sub-Surgeon.[65] The Africans of Baringo preferred their own traditional cures and treatments, it seemed, rather than placing trust in unknown European methods.

In the circumstances of drought and harvest failure, we might expect the colonial record to make reference to the manifestations of malnutrition, but these are absent. In contrast, serious diseases and unusual illnesses causing fatalities, such as the influenza pandemic of 1918–19 and outbreaks of cerebral meningitis in 1924, 1935 and 1943 (the last taking 45 lives within the space of a few weeks), are discussed in some detail, perhaps because of their comparative rarity.[66] One conclusion to be drawn from this might be that malnutrition was absent, but other evidence suggests this could not have been the case. Although famine was avoided in south and central Baringo in these years, hunger was reported as commonplace. Tugen oral histories emphasize that people somehow managed, but they do especially stress the suffering of the elderly.[67] As we have seen, even the supposedly fitter young men, who left Baringo to take wage labour with the government or on European farms, were often described by their employers as undernourished and weak. For this reason some government departments would not recruit in the district. During the worst years of harvest failures, between 1929 and 1934, many people came to the government offices to receive famine-relief food and others signed on for food-for-work schemes. All these factors indicate that malnutrition was probably widespread in the

[64] Eldama Ravine subdistrict AR, 1929, KNA PC/RVP.2/7/2.

[65] Baringo and Eldama Ravine ARs, 1932, 1933, 1936, 1939, in KNA PC/RVP.2/7/2, KNA BAR/2, KNA PC/RVP.2/7/3.

[66] Lambert, 'Political history', 28–9. Baringo District ARs, 1924, 1935, 1940, KNA BAR/2, KNA PC/RVP.2/7/2 and KNA PC/RVP.2/7/3.

[67] Deaths due to famine may have occurred in the northern locations, where the effects of food shortage were more marked. See Kettel, 'Time is money'.

district for much of the interwar period. Its absence from the admittedly limited colonial medical records might therefore be more readily explained by the suggestion that malnutrition was simply not noted because it was so very prevalent: the commonplace was not worthy of comment.

The litany of disaster in Baringo had become all too familiar by the eve of the Second World War. Baringo had, by 1939, experienced two decades during which drought, disease and crop failure had been almost constant concerns. It is not surprising that some colonial officials had begun to dismiss the district as a hopeless case, a rural slum whose peoples were for ever condemned to poverty. A palpable tone of inevitability had come to dominate the correspondence of officials in the district, and to a great degree this reflected the prevailing mood among Baringo's herders. For the majority of the African population, it was surely a time of suffering, hopelessness and despair, when life seemed constantly beset with difficulties and when it must have appeared that good fortune had deserted them. The use of the term *Kipkoikoio* to name the drought of 1933–4 is perhaps indicative of the resignation and frustration felt by the African population.[68] But during these years the communities on the Baringo lowlands showed themselves to be remarkably adaptable and resilient – more so, indeed, than their European neighbours.

Depression & European farming

Drought began to have an impact upon the European settler farmlands neighbouring Baringo towards the end of the 1920s. Its impact, as witnessed by fluctuating yields and a hugely increased problem of trespass by African cattle from the neighbouring reserve, coincided with the onset of the Great Depression. This combination of drought and depression was to have a devastating effect upon those farmers who lacked capital or were most heavily mortgaged. Many Europeans along the Baringo borders were in this category. The economic depression of 1929 to 1935, following hard on the heels of the droughts and plagues of *Kiplel kowo*, glaringly revealed their enormous vulnerability.

To fully understand the impact upon these farmers, we must look at the wider context of the development of European agriculture in Kenya over the interwar years. The 1920s saw a very rapid development of the White Highlands. Between 1918 and 1929 the numbers of Europeans farming the land almost doubled, climbing to over 2,000 on the eve of the depression. Where farms had often lain dormant before 1918, their owners hoping to gain from land speculation rather than productive agriculture, rapid expansion of cultivation took place after 1920. By the end of the decade the total area of the White Highlands under cultivation had multiplied more than threefold. Coffee, sisal and cereals, mainly maize and wheat, were the

[68] BHT/TG/11, BHT/TG/15 and BHT/TG/22.

basis of this expansion. Coffee led the way. By 1921 over 30,000 acres were already under coffee, by 1929 over 90,000 acres. By 1935 more than half of Kenya's white farmers were growing coffee, with the major estates in the Central Highlands accounting for two-thirds of the total acreage.[69] Many fewer settlers grew sisal, but the increase in cultivation was comparably dramatic: from 30,396 acres in 1920 to over 100,000 acres in 1929, from which 15,000 tons were produced for export. But the most startling developments were in cereal production. For the majority of Kenya's white farmers, cereals rapidly became the mainstay of their prosperity in the 1920s. European farmers grew only 32,167 acres of maize in 1920. By 1930 that figure had climbed above 200,000 acres, from which 1.8 million bags were produced, mostly intended for export.[70]

The farms ringing Baringo, in Eldama Ravine and Nakuru Districts, were very much at the centre of this boom. White settlement in the Rift Valley had originally been envisaged along European models of stock rearing, with exotic stock being introduced for cross-breeding with indigenous stock to provide the basis for the development of beef and dairy herds. But few of the early settlers had sufficient reserves of capital to make this expensive proposition viable. The difficulty of controlling stock diseases, particularly East Coast fever, had been seriously underestimated. Infection played havoc with settlers' attempts to maintain and cross-breed exotic stock.[71] Prior to 1920 in the Rift Valley, settlers searched for alternative farm products on which to base their economy. Most farmers experimented with coffee, but it did less well here than on the higher, wetter farms of the Central Highlands. Sisal fared better in drier areas, and major plantations were developed by 1920 along the Baringo boundary at Lomolo and Ol Punyata. But sisal required investment in machinery for processing and was not suitable for the majority of undercapitalized and inexperienced farmers who came into the Eldama Ravine and Nakuru Districts. The Bowring Committee, appointed at the beginning of the 1920s to study the economic and financial position of the colony, stressed the need:

> to foster and develop, by every possible means, and with the least possible delay, an export trade in some easily produced local bulk commodity for which there was a steady and virtually unlimited demand in the markets of the world.[72]

[69] Figures from: Kenya Colony Agricultural Censuses, 1920–29, summarized in Anderson & Throup, 'Agrarian economy', 27; John D. Overton, 'War and economic development: settlers in Kenya, 1914–18', *Journal of African History*, 27 (1986), 91–7; 'Register of Coffee Estates, 1 January 1936', KNA Ag. Dept 85/935.

[70] Figures from the Kenya Colony Agricultural Censuses, 1920–30.

[71] M.E. Luckham, 'The early history of the Kenya Department of Agriculture', *East African Agricultural Journal*, 25 (1959), 97–105; L. Winston Cone & J.F. Lipscomb (eds), *The History of Kenya Agriculture* (Nairobi, 1972), 40–50.

[72] *Final Report of the Economic and Financial (Bowring) Committee, 1922–23*, (Nairobi, 1923), quoted in Wrigley, 'Patterns of economic life', 235. The general thrust of policy put forward by

Table 3.2 European maize harvests, 1919–40

Year	European maize (acres harvested)
1919–20	32,167
1920–21	30,846
1921–2	57,131
1922–3	74,747
1923–4	108,556
1924–5	129,647
1925–6	155,751
1926–7	177,987
1927–8	177,009
1928–9	204,945
1929–30	233,973
1930–31	200,926
1931–2	160,546
1932–3	164,018
1933–4	112,949
1934–5	*
1935–6	117,848
1936–7	*
1937–8	113,103
1938–9	*
1939–40	93,517

* No census figures available.
Source: Food Shortage Commission of Inquiry Report, 1943 (Government Printer, Nairobi, 1943), p. 8. Quoted in M. Miracle, *Maize in Tropical Africa* (Madison: Wisconsin University Press, 1966), pp. 139–40.

The report advocated that this commodity ought to be maize.

As can be seen from the statistics in Table 3.2, Kenya's white farmers produced increasing quantities of maize from 1923. Yet, although maize yields were comparatively high in Kenya – perhaps double those of South Africa, where maize cultivation was also being developed as a way of affording relief to struggling farmers – the margin of profit on production was in many parts of Kenya small. As Mosley has pointed out, the development of infrastructure was the crucial factor; 'the high cost of ox-wagon transport caused the national maize market to be fragmented into a cluster of regional sub-markets each with a different ruling price for maize'.[73] To even out these regional variables the government followed the advice

[72 (cont.)] the Bowring Committee was that of high tariff protection for agriculture, reflecting the fact that among its members were only two officials, as against six non-officials. Few of its proposals were accepted. See G. Bennett, 'Settlers and politics in Kenya up to 1945', in Harlow & Chilver (eds), *Oxford History of East Africa*, ii, 296–7.

[73] Mosley, *Settler Economies*, 184.

of Bowring and sought to assist maize farmers by reducing railway freight charges on the crop to a flat rate of 1s. per 200 lb. bag. This allowed farmers distant from the railhead to defray some of their heavy transport costs. For farmers in outlying parts of Nakuru, at Lomolo, Ol Punyata and Solai, expanding production was given further impetus by the construction of a new branch railway line from Rongai to Solai. With improved access to the rail system and with subsidized freight charges, in only three years from 1922 to 1924 the acreage under maize on the European farmlands bordering Baringo was already dramatically increasing. This development provided the majority of undercapitalized and less efficient farmers with what seemed a stable living: stable, that was, so long as the export markets remained strong.[74]

Inefficiencies in settler production, notably fluctuating and poor cereal yields in areas like northern Nakuru and Eldama Ravine, were disguised between 1924 and 1929 by the generally high prices received for the colony's exports. Market prices for coffee, which represented almost half the total value of all agricultural exports from the White Highlands, remained high throughout the 1920s. Coffee exports realized an average of £951,585 per annum between 1924 and 1930, and in 1928 the average export price was over £5 per cwt. Sisal planters, who needed a price of above £25 per ton to produce at a profit, were realizing £39 15s. per ton in the early months of 1929.[75] But it was the high prices obtained for exported cereals that brought unaccustomed economic confidence to the great majority of Kenya's settlers. In the mixed arable and stock farms of Nakuru District, occupied by some 300 European farmers, only 10 per cent of the land had been under cultivation in 1922; by 1929 this had doubled to 20 per cent. Cereals, mostly maize, accounted for more than 70 per cent of the total acreage under crops in the district at the end of the decade. The same pattern was evident in the much smaller and more marginal farming district of Eldama Ravine. Here there were only some forty farms, and the level of development was more modest, but the acreage of maize cultivated climbed steadily through the 1920s, doubling from 1923 to 1929, the peak year.[76] Confidence was high towards the end of the 1920s, and many farmers had extended their credit at the banks to further develop and mechanize their farms. With maize fetching over 13 Kenya shillings per bag, f.o.b. Mombasa, in 1929, the future looked very bright indeed.[77] Despite this apparent prosperity, vast fluctuations in yield from year to year suggested that the basis of production was not secure in either district. Ravine farmers

[74] Marvin P. Miracle, *Maize in Tropical Africa* (Madison, 1966), 137–9.

[75] Kenya Colony ARs, 1926, 1927, 1929 and 1930, pp. 17–21, 36–8, 28–37 and 17 respectively, summarized in Anderson & Throup, 'Agrarian economy', 27. Nicholas J. Westcott, 'The East African sisal industry, 1929–49: the marketing of a colonial commodity during depression and war', *Journal of African History*, 25 (1984), 445–61.

[76] Figures abstracted from the Kenya Colony Agricultural Censuses, 1920–29.

[77] Mosley, *Settler Economies*, table 3.6b, 94–5.

achieved an average of 11.28 bags of maize per acre in 1926, only to see this plummet to 1.7 bags per acre in the disastrous drought-affected harvest of 1929. Ironically, yields in 1930 were the highest ever experienced in both districts, an astonishing 12.17 bags per acre being achieved in Eldama Ravine. By then the recession was already beginning to bite and the profit margins of Kenya's maize farmers were falling fast.[78]

The impact of the 1929 slump was devastating. Export prices for maize rapidly spiralled downwards, reaching 8s. per bag in 1931 and less than 7s. per bag in 1933.[79] In 1929 maize accounted for 12 per cent of Kenya's domestic exports by value, and probably more than 80 per cent of the Ravine and Nakuru farms depended upon it for their livelihood. At 1931 prices these farmers could not realize a profit on the crop. Sisal growers at Lomolo and Ol Punyata were hit just as badly. In January 1930 sisal prices began to slide and, by December, had fallen to £21 10s. per ton, substantially below the Kenya planters' profit threshold. The fall continued in 1931, the year's average declared values on shipment from Mombasa being only £14 10s. 10d. per ton.[80] The fall in the export value of coffee was equally spectacular. Kenya coffee was selling at £6 4s per cwt early in 1930, but had slumped to £2 14s by July. A partial recovery to £3 19s 11d per cwt in 1932 was followed by further falls in 1933 and 1934. The total value of sisal, coffee and maize exports had reached a peak of approximately £2.5 million in 1930. In 1934 the combined value of these principal settler exports was less than £1 million.[81]

For the majority of farmers throughout Ravine and Nakuru the depression was a catastrophe. During the early 1920s many settlers had already borrowed to the absolute limit of their capacity, the commercial banks being encouraged to lend by the upturn in the maize and sisal markets and by the prospects for opening up the economy of farming areas with the extension of the railway network. Although steady, the small turnover of profit from maize cultivation was inadequate to allow farmers to repay any significant proportion of these debts. By 1930, with yearly profits wiped out, this problem was indeed a serious one. The attitude of the banks naturally changed. Restrictions were placed on the overdraft and forward-financing facilities afforded on the value of crops, particularly to those farmers already heavily in debt. As Redley has concluded, 'many farmers

---

[78] Kenya Colony Agricultural Censuses, 1920–29.

[79] Mosley, *Settler Economies*, table 3.6b, 94–5; V. Liversage, 'Official economic management in Kenya 1930–45', Rhodes House Library, Oxford, MSS.Afr.s.510.

[80] Figures from, Anderson & Throup, 'Agrarian economy', 27; Wrigley, 'Patterns of economic life', 239–47; Cone & Lipscomb, *Kenya Agriculture*, 71–3; Brett, *Colonialism and Underdevelopment*, 184–6. For personal accounts of farmers' difficulties in Solai and Lomolo at this time, see BHT/ES/2 and BHT/ES/3. For sisal prices, see Kenya Colony AR, 1930 and 1931, 17 and 30 respectively.

[81] For coffee prices, Kenya Colony ARs, 1930, 1931 and 1934, 16, 30 and 26 respectively. Total export values calculated from the Kenya Colony Agricultural Censuses for 1930 and 1934.

were left without the means to harvest and plant for the next season'.[82]

Farmers struggled to cut the costs of production. Farm labourers' wages had dropped to 5s. per month by the harvest season of 1931, but even this could not restore profit when there was no export market for the crop.[83] Many farmers reduced their activity to simple care and maintenance levels, but this brought its own problems. Undermanning contributed to a serious outbreak of maize stalk-borer on the Solai and north Nakuru farms in 1935 and 1936, their inability to exert controls on its spread greatly irritating the Department of Agriculture.[84] Some farmers sought other forms of income to tide them over. Several European farmers began trading in the African reserves, transporting their maize into the African areas by bullock-cart and exchanging it for livestock or for hides and skins. A fall of over 50 per cent in the prices of hides and skins at this time and the low values of livestock due to prolonged drought made this type of venture barely profitable. Two Solai farmers found profit in trading donkeys from Samburu and north Baringo.[85] Others left for the gold-fields of Kakamega, where some 600 Europeans found meagre employment at the peak of production in 1935, although fewer than half this number are likely to have been settlers.[86] Like the herders of Baringo, European farmers were adopting novel strategies of survival in these difficult years.

Levels of absenteeism soared as farmers seached for alternative sources of income, and yet very few gave up the struggle completely. Although fewer than 300 farmers were permanently forced off the land by the depression, many more were forced to abandon their farms temporarily during the worst years. Cereal farmers in marginal areas were most prominent amongst these absentees: of the thirty-nine European farms occupied in Eldama Ravine in 1929, only nineteen were being actively farmed in 1934.[87] Had they been in a position to do so, it is certain that many more farmers would have sold up and left. But for the most part their assets were

---

[82] Redley, 'Politics of a predicament', 26, 218. For firsthand commentary, BHT/ES/2 and BHT/ES/3. On the economics of maize cultivation in the 1930s, see V. Liversage to Dir. of Agri., n.d. [1935], KNA CNC/10/4; and Liversage, 'Farming economics in Nakuru District', 195–204.

[83] On farm wages, see Baringo District ARs 1925 and 1931, KNA BAR/2, and KNA PC/RVP.2/7/2.

[84] Dir. of Agri. to All Farmers' Associations, RVP, 20 April 1937, KNA PC/RVP.6A/ll/12.

[85] BHT/ES/2, BHT/ES/3 and BHT/CH/13 each give accounts of settlers entering Baringo to sell grain. Falls in the price received for hides and skins are recorded monthly at this time in KNA, Min. of Agri./4/361. One of the two Solai farmers involved in donkey trading, Jack Barrah, was able to use this experience to gain a job with Livestock Control during the Second World War. See Ian R.G. Spencer, 'Settler dominance, agricultural production and the Second World War in Kenya', *Journal of African History*, 21 (1980), 511, fn. 81.

[86] Hugh Fearn, 'The gold-mining era in Kenya Colony', *Journal of Tropical Geography*, 11 (1958), 43–58, and Andrew D. Roberts, 'The gold boom of the 1930s in eastern Africa', *African Affairs*, 85 (1986), 545–62.

[87] Kenya Colony Agricultural Censuses, 1930 and 1934; Lambert, 'Political history', 25.

not realizable. Banks and other creditors could see no advantage in foreclosing farms at a time when new buyers or tenants would be unlikely to come forward. As one Lomolo settler put it, 'What else could we do: we dug our heels in and got on with it'.[88]

Drought conditions and annual locust visitations worsened the farmers' plight from 1930 to 1934. Many, especially those along the Baringo border, greatly extended their 'Kaffir-farming' practices in these years, encouraging an increased number of squatter cattle on to their farms and living off the rent. Unoccupied European-owned farmlands were quickly invaded by African cattle from the drought-stricken reserves. These farms were then often used as convenient 'outspans' from which African herders could trespass into other, more distant European farms. Absenteeism and the extended 'Kaffir farming' to which poorer European landowners resorted therefore generated vociferous complaints from neighbouring farmers, who suffered the attendant consequence of increased trespass.[89] The depression exposed the economic divisions among the settler community between efficient and better-capitalized farmers, who were better placed to cope with economic setback, and the less efficient or those occupying more marginal lands. For these people, the alternatives were meagre because their resources were meagre, and this in turn was why so many of them had been content to rely upon cereal monoculture. This vicious circle confronted all small settlers bordering Baringo: lack of means dictated that they live hand to mouth. The problem of developing European systems of farming in Kenya appeared to be economically beyond them. Although this had been realized in the early days of settlement, the political ideals that dictated the establishment of another 'White Colony' allowed ill-equipped and underfinanced settlers to come to Kenya and government policies permitted them to remain there. The attractions of lifestyle, favourable climate, abundant land and, above all, elevated social status were strong positive forces. The farmlands around Baringo were not among the best in Kenya – those at Esageri and Lomolo were possibly among the worst – and yet European land-owners were a racially and socially distinct group whatever the quality of their lands or the details of their personal means. The differences between African and European were much more than colour of skin; in Kenya the white man organized and supervised, whilst the black man laboured with his hands. In essence, the vast majority of settlers farming near the Baringo boundary were men of limited means, who saw in Kenya a country where they could enjoy a lifestyle and a status that they would have been very unlikely to obtain in Europe. Having invested in Kenya, most European immigrants had little choice but to endure a period of austerity once it had been pushed upon them.[90] In this

[88] BHT/ES/2. An example of one settler who did give up completely was Simpson of Thompson Falls. He did so by absconding without paying the wages of his labourers or settling other debts. See KNA PC/RVP.6A/25/2 for the full details of this case.

[89] BHT/ES/2, BHT/ES/3, BHT/TG/25 and BHT/TG/45.

[90] Wrigley, 'Patterns of economic life', 215–21.

respect, at least, the European settlers and the African herders who had migrated on to the Baringo lowlands had something in common.

The survival of European settlers, however, was supported by the state in ways that were not available to African herders. Reluctant though the state surely was to increase its own budget deficit in order to bail out failing farmers, the importance of settler exports to the revenues and the simple immediacy of the predicament compelled action. In the short term, at least, the Kenya government intervened to provide the settler economy with the crutch it so badly needed. Cereal farmers, whose plight was the most serious, received refunds on grading, inspection and storage charges for their crop and further rebates on railway freight charges. Loan subsidies were granted on the 1930 cereals crop, and an Agricultural Advances Ordinance was rushed through in May 1930, releasing £100,000 for loan to the most needy farmers.[91] In a more far-reaching move, the government established a Land Bank, which began operations in July 1931 with an initial capital of £240,000. During the first full year of its operations the Land Bank prioritized those farmers in the deepest trouble, and 39 percent of all loans awarded were specifically towards the discharge of existing mortgages.[92] Applications for loans during the first year of the Land Bank's operation totalled more than twenty-two times the initial capital of £240,000.[93] The Bank accordingly adopted the general policy of spreading its capital as widely as possible, initially setting a ceiling of only £3,000 per loan. This was raised in 1936 to £5,000, giving better facility to the higher capital needs of sisal and coffee planters.[94] In 1933 a further £500,000 was added to the Bank's capital, and in 1936 another £250,000. These monies were loaned to farmers at an interest rate of 6.5 per cent per annum (as compared with 8 per cent then charged by commercial banks). Many of the loans were made contingent upon the borrower moving away from cereal monoculture and towards a regime of mixed farming, usually including dairying. This condition was applied to all the loans given to farmers along the Baringo border, who accepted the terms with only muted enthusiasm.[95] By the end of 1936 the Land Bank had assisted one in four of Kenya's settler farmers, with loans totalling £631,260.[96] The Land Bank undoubtedly saved many

[91] Kenya Colony Annual Report, 1930, 6–8; Wrigley, 'Patterns of economic life', 247–9; Mosley, *Settler Economies,* 170–94; Brett, *Colonialism and Underdevelopment,* 145–8.

[92] Mosley, *Settler Economies,* 185, citing figures from the *Annual Report of the Land and Agriculture Bank* (1932), 10.

[93] Mosley, *Settler Economies,* 185–6; Brett, *Colonialism and Underdevelopment,* 196; Redley, 'Politics of a predicament', 20–21, presenting analysis of loans to a sample of farms in Naivasha and Trans Nzoia, indicating that the Land Bank very rapidly replaced commercial-bank loans, and 219–220, for figures on the capital of the Land Bank.

[94] Mosley, *Settler Economies,* 185–6.

[95] BHT/ES/1, BHT/ES/2 and BHT/ES/3. Liversage to Dir. of Agri. n.d.[1936], KNA CNC/10/4.

[96] Kenya Colony Annual Report, 1936, 44; Mosley, *Settler Economies,* 178–85.

farms from ruin, especially along the Baringo border, where it seems that more than 70 per cent of all landowners relied upon assistance from the Bank to see them through.[97]

These measures kept European settlers in business, but the restructuring of settler agriculture that Land Bank conditionality sought to impose took longer to effect. By 1936 settler maize growers were still unable to make the crop pay, and yet another subsidy was sought, bringing the price of a bag of maize to 4s. 50 per bag with free rail freight. The Standing Board of Economic Development in London accepted the proposal, though not without strong reservations:

> The period during which maize fetched high prices between 1920 and 1930 is really the only period of high prices for the last 50 years ... I fully recognize the importance of the maize industry to Kenya and the precarious position of the maize growers, who have been struggling against adverse circumstances for 5 years ... [But] ... it must be faced that maize in Kenya is an uneconomic crop, that is, it cannot be produced for export except at a loss.[98]

This cold blast of realism was accepted by the Kenya government's agricultural economist, Liversage, a long-standing critic of 'maize-mining', but even he was moved to ask what single alternative crop would lend itself to large-scale intensive cultivation of the type Kenya maize farmers were capable of. There was no obvious answer to this question.[99]

Of course, the subsidy achieved in 1936 was essentially political, intended to keep afloat the majority of inefficient producers until they could re-establish themselves on a firmer agricultural footing. But debate over the subsidy split the settlers, those who were able to produce efficiently claiming that their advantage was being eroded by government intervention to support less able producers. Few, if any, of the settlers around Baringo objected to the subsidy; they were among the inefficient producers and needed the subsidy to remain competitive. Through subsidies, rebates, loans and other forms of protection, the government had done enough to 'shelter the inefficient' farmers along the Baringo borders.[100] But there was to be no shelter for Baringo's African herders.

---

[97] The figure is an estimate, based upon the various sources on Land Bank loans given above.

[98] J.H. Thomas (Sec. of State) to Chief Secretary, 4 January 1936, KNA CNC/10/4.

[99] Liversage to Dir. of Agri., n.d. [1936], KNA CNC/1O/4.

[100] On the division of settler opinion on the question of the maize subsidy, see Mosley, *Settler Economies*, 186–9, and Redley, 'Politics of a predicament', 210, 222–8. Redley points out that the policy and support of the Kenya Farmers Association (KFA) aided the smaller producers; 90% of all European maize farmers were members of the KFA, but this accounted for only 85% of the total crop. After 1930 the KFA intervened directly in the Kenya maize market in an effort to force European maize on to the African market at a higher price than was being realized for African maize, a measure prompted by the inability of many inefficient European maize producers to keep up with the export market. This was yet another form of protection, although as Kitching points out, its total effect remains somewhat obscure: Kitching, *Class and Economic Change in Kenya*, 59–61.

Four

The Baringo Range War
1918–48

At the time of the alienation of lands for European settlement in the northern Rift Valley it was generally believed by Europeans that the removal of Maasai herders had freed the land from African occupation. This assumption was unfounded. All along the boundary of the White Highlands, and for several kilometres inside it at Subukia, Solai and Ravine, Tugen herders had already established themselves as seasonal graziers and some were beginning to settle their homesteads permanently. At Ravine, for example, the farms lying to the north of Sclater's Road had been heavily populated by Tugen, who had to be forcibly moved back to allow settlement and who thereafter constantly drifted back on to the farms purchased by Collier, Smith, Pearson and their neighbours.[1] To the east, more and more Tugen families were still crossing the Molo and pouring towards Solai and Subukia after 1912, even before the majority of the farms intended for Europeans had been occupied. Tugen herders were already established on land some 12 kilometres inside the European settled area at Subukia by 1912 – this before the movement of the Maasai out of that area had been completed.[2]

Baringo's African herders were at first unaware that their right to graze and water their animals on these lands would be contested. With high absenteeism among European farmers in the early days of settlement and with many farms being held for speculation rather than development, it was not until after 1914 that settlers began to complain of African 'trespass'. 'Trespass' was not a concept easily understood by Chamus or Tugen

---

[1] *KLC:EM*, ii, 1831–2; BHT/TG/49 and BHT/TG/52.
[2] *KLC:EM*, ii, 1784.

herders. European notions of individual title in land for exclusive use had no parallel among the African peoples of Baringo, for whom property in land was a matter of access rather than ownership. Moreover, rights of access to land were negotiable, mediated by circumstance and need, though ultimately brokered by power and authority. For much of the nineteenth century, the power and authority of Maasai herders had dominated the pastures of Solai; but this did not prevent Tugen herders making occasional forays into that area. Under colonialism, negotiation and flexibility gave way to fixed ideas of ownership of and property in land. The impact of this upon African herders was only gradually appreciated. As the farm boundary hardened after 1914, the number of African cattle pressing to the east continued to increase. Confrontations became increasingly common as European farmers sought to prevent African herders gaining access to the lands to which they had acquired title. By the end of the 1920s, in the drought of *Kiplel kowo,* the crisis reached a peak as herders ignored the farm boundaries in their search for water and grazing for their starving cattle. The herders' desperation matched that of the European settlers. Confrontation and violence erupted along the boundary as European settlers battled to protect their property from what they saw as an African invasion.

Tugen oral histories speak of this time as 'the war we fought with the Europeans'.[3] The terminology is apt. Baringo's range war was a desperate struggle for survival, revolving around the contested meaning of land ownership and access to resources. For the European settler, it was simply a matter of upholding the rule of law. Facing financial ruin because of recession and drought, his very future depended upon the protection of his property from encroachment. For the African herder, this was irrelevant. His choice was equally stark: either he remained in the reserve and watched his cattle die or he crossed the boundary to take advantage of better pasture. Even when confronted by the threat of arrest and fining or imprisonment, the majority of herders were willing to take the risk. This chapter will explore the history of trespass along the Baringo border from 1918 to the late 1940s, dealing both with the mechanics of how trespass was successfully accomplished and the measures settlers and government employed to prevent it.

Trespass: 'a little place on the scene'

Though settlers most often complained of the loss of grass to trespassing cattle or expressed anxiety about the spread of livestock diseases, it was more often the need for water that drew African herders on to European-owned lands. During the dry season of 1926, Major Smith of Ravine, whose farm lay along the Emining River, bordering the Uas Nkishu Maasai lands to the east and adjacent to the Tugen Reserve to the north, became so desperate as to ask for a land exchange. One of the earliest settlers at

---

[3] BHT/TG/25 and BHT/TG/32. Many settlers also likened the trespass issue to a war – for example BHT/ES/1 and BHT/ES/3.

Ravine, having arrived in the district before 1908, he wrote to the Commissioner of Lands:

> It is impossible to keep the Kamasia from trespassing. This tribe is notoriously short of grazing for their stock, and this causes them to run their cattle on the farms on every possible occasion.[4]

The Smith farm, LO497/3/3, was a major trouble spot. Jutting out into the reserve, with African-occupied lands on two sides, Smith's farm contained the only available water for several miles.

On the eastern edge of the Baringo lowlands, below Solai, the situation was, if anything, worse. Here the widespread seasonal shortage of surface water was acknowledged as the most common reason for trespass. After the failure of the late rains in 1926, Tugen living in the eastern section of Pokorr sought government permission to take their stock on to the farm of Colonel Lean to obtain access to water, an act they had been committing regularly without such permission for many years.[5] As Lean himself complained to the district administration,

> The Kamasia Reserve is not merely overstocked, but is waterless, and warnings and fines will not prevent native stockowners of starving cattle disregarding orders, they being of the opinion that it is better to pay a fine than to lose all their cattle. As a brother stockowner I sympathise with their point of view; as a landowner I must combat it.[6]

In this case combating it was easier said than done. Cattle feeding at the eastern extreme of Pokorr had to leave their grazing grounds by midnight in order to traverse the distance to the Molo River, the nearest source of water in the reserve, by early the next morning. As the dry season set in and the condition of the cattle became poorer, deaths of large numbers of the weaker animals were to be expected on these lengthy journeys. Given these circumstances it is hardly surprising that the African herder opted to accept the risks of trespass and walk his animals the mere 3 or 4 kilometres to watering points in the settled area. So desperate did herders become in this area in the worst months of *Kiplel kowo* that some even offered to buy water from European farmers.[7]

The examples of Smith and Lean are typical of many others that could be cited. Settlers were not unsympathetic to the dilemma of the African herder in the early 1920s, many of them believing, as another Solai settler, Caleb Kerby, phrased it, 'that they ought to have a little place on the scene just as much as we'.[8] However, that 'place' was certainly *not* on the Euro-

[4] *KLC:EM,* ii, 1783. Land exchanges were requested on similar grounds by Dwen (LO4103) in 1931, and Baillie (LO5259) in 1932: Perreau to PC/RVP, 27 November 1931, and Baillie to Comm. Lands & Settlement, 17 August 1932, both in KNA PC/ERD.6A/41/6.

[5] *KLC:EM,* ii, 1784.

[6] Ibid., 1783.

[7] Ibid., 1786–7.

[8] Kerby to PC/RVP, 25 July 1933, KNA PC/RVP.6A/ll/18. Other farmers with particularly

pean farmlands; like his African neighbour, the European settler ultimately had to give priority to his own survival. During the 1930s, as the trespass problem continued unabated and as one measure after another was tried and found to be inadequate for its prevention, the tone of the many complaints pouring into the District Commissioner's Office became less tolerant and considerably more irate. By then, Baringo's range war was at its height and both sides had evolved a variety of sophisticated tactics in their struggle for survival.

From the early 1920s onwards most farmers close to the reserve boundary employed grazing guards to patrol their land. The guards would be sent out with the farm's herdboys. Their job was not to capture trespassing stock, but rather to ensure that the farmer's herd did not come into contact with trespassing cattle and to raise the alarm at the farmhouse should trespassing stock be encountered. To any settler with a dairy or beef herd the prevention of the spread of disease to his stock was of greater immediate importance than the protection of his pasture. For this reason, attempts to apprehend and detain trespassing were rare during the early years of the range war. But, while grazing guards might protect salt-licks or watercourses reasonably well, their presence was only a minor deterrent to trespass. They were particularly ineffective on large farms where trespassing herds could easily be kept away from areas being grazed by European-owned stock.[9] By the late 1920s most farmers had taken further steps to protect their property, employing guards to patrol the farm borders and to apprehend and detain the stock of any African herder found illegally on the farm. So well used were some of the points of entry into the settled area that cattle tracks leading across the farms were clearly visible.[10] All the same, many of the farms were between 4,000 and 5,000 acres in extent, so that even a regular boundary patrol could not expect to be completely successful in preventing trespass.

Tugen and Chamus herders were quick to adopt tactics that undermined the limited protection offered by both grazing guards and border patrols. Extra family members would be sent along with the usual herders when European lands were to be entered, acting as outriders and scouts, keeping an eye on the movements of the grazing guards and ready to sound the alarm should the need arise for a speedy retreat. Many herders even went to the lengths of spying out particular pastures and watering points, gathering and sharing intelligence on the pattern of movements of grazing

[8 (cont.)] serious problems were Dwen (LO662), Stanning (LO5260, 3732 and 3844), Poestkoke (LO6600), Simpson (LO2680), Cornegliano (LO5681/1 and 5681/2). Unoccupied farms where trespass was serious included LO1168, 1651 and 474/1/R.

[9] Poestkoke to PC/RVP, 18 April 1932, KNA PC/RVP.6A/151/15; Welby (PC/RVP) to Colonial Secretary, 20 September 1934, KNA PC/RVP.6A/24/6; BHT/ES/3 and BHT/TG/11.

[10] BHT/TG/11 and BHT/TG/60; Kerby to PC/RVP, 13 March 1935 and 23 September 1939, KNA PC/RVP.6A/15/15.

guards. Herders occupying the eastern portions of Pokorr and Endorois locations were those most frequently to be found on the European farms, and so were quick to adopt these strategies to avoid detection. As one herder recalled:

> In the Solai area we were always struggling to avoid the grazing guards employed by the Europeans. When they saw us coming onto the farm with our cows they would quickly try to chase us away. We did not really want to fight, so when you were seen you just had to flee back to the Reserve. I would trespass with my cows, maybe 40 or 50 in the herd, but that was a small number compared to others who took as many as 200. We would go in a group of up to 4 murran together, although once on the farm each herder would graze his animals alone. From where one herder was he could usually see the herd of the other herder just a little way from his own herd. We murran had to keep a look-out to see that no one was coming. If you grazed at night you could proceed more freely, and you might even go alone … It was only rarely that I took my animals to steal grass during the daytime, and on these occasions I took some of my older children along with me to herd the animals while I spied out the land.[11]

Even on farms where trespass was evidently taking place the susceptibility of the grazing guards to bribery more or less guaranteed that the interlopers would not be apprehended. Farmers were not entirely ignorant of this danger, and most learned that it was unwise to employ local Tugen or Chamus as guards. Samburu, Kipsigis and Kikuyu were believed to be less open to bribery and by the 1930s dominated the ranks of the grazing guards. But ethnicity appears to have presented only a minor inconvenience to herders intent on obtaining unhampered access to grazing:

> The guards were from all different tribes, yes, but it is true that we could bribe them. Well, if they caught you maybe you could talk with them, and offer to give them some small thing. Maybe it would be a goat, or perhaps a little money. In this way you would get to know the guards, and eventually they might tell you the safest time for you to come and graze, and where was best to go. So, we could continue bribing them for this information. It would all depend upon the individual you were dealing with; if you could make a good friend of the guard then stealing became easy. It was the people who were unable to give the guards anything who were always being caught. It was not cheap to bribe.[12]

Many herders enjoyed long-standing 'arrangements' with guards of the sort described above. Although settlers were aware of this corruption among their employees, they could do little to eradicate it completely. The rotation of grazing guards between various parts of the border seems to have disrupted the patterns of bribery for only a very short time.[13]

[11] BHT/TG/26 and BHT/TG/25; for similar accounts referring to the Chamus, see BHT/CH/10.
[12] BHT/TG/25.
[13] BHT/TG/11 and BHT/TG/45.

What these payments may have cost the herder in exchange or financial terms is not easy to assess. In recalling such transactions herders are understandably coy; bargains were struck on an individual basis and were considered to be a personal matter, not to be disclosed or even discussed with others. Whatever the cost, it was deeply resented. Cash payments of a few shillings at a time appear to have been the norm, but larger sums were handed over in respect of longer-term arrangements. Although on occasion a goat or sheep did change hands to effect a bribe, the exchange of stock was not as popular as one might have thought; livestock represented a very tangible form of evidence, explanations being required for their acquisition or disappearance. Unless a guard could quickly get a goat to market or was willing to slaughter and consume it on the spot, accepting it as a bribe could become something of a liability. Livestock products could more easily be used to bribe. The handing over of hides or skins was common, as were arrangements whereby the guard received a regular calabash of milk from the herder's family. Where hard cash was necessary for a bribe, it could be raised by the sale of hides and skins to visiting traders or by sale of small stock. Somali or Nubian traders could always be found in Baringo for exchanges of this kind. Other Tugen recalled, with conscious irony, having sold a few head of cattle to a European farmer in order to obtain the money with which to bribe guards who were protecting the lands of the same settler.[14]

As drought descended and competition for very limited grazing resources became ever keener, intelligence regarding the movements of guards and patrols came to be at a premium. In contrast to the public sentiment among both Tugen and Chamus herders that at time of drought resources should be openly shared amongst those in need, the issue of trespass gave rise to a private attitude of individualism motivated by self-preservation. The secrecy of stock movements was maintained within a well-established unit of friends and kinsmen. Whilst no group would deliberately seek to obstruct another in the exploitation of pastoral resources, the group with the most efficient information-gathering network and the more skilful herdsmen was likely to manage its stock better.[15] Conditions of severe drought therefore generated a certain degree of social tension within the Tugen and Chamus communities adjacent to the farm boundary.

It was common for a group of herders to regularly trespass together, the cattle being used to moving quietly and the extra labour allowing for a sharper lookout to be kept. Herds of over 200 head were commonly reported on the farms, this being the combined herd of perhaps three or

[14] BHT/ES/3, BHT/TG/19, BHT/TG/32, BHT/TG/60 and others: Poestkoke to CNC, 8 April 1933; Kerby to PC/RVP, 13 March, 1935; Harries to DC/Ravine, 24 May 1944; Wolff (PC/RVP) to DC/Kabarnet, 22 July 1944, all in KNA PC/RVP.6A/15/15. Hickson-Mahoney (DC/Baringo) to PC/RVP, 15 July 1948, PC/RVP.6A/ll/34.

[15] BHT/TG/32 and BHT/TG/37; Kerby to PC/RVP, 27 March 1935, KNA PC/RVP.6A/15/15.

four families.[16] It was found that trespass with such large herds was easier under cover of darkness. This very radical strategy began to be regularly employed in the mid-1920s. Grazing guards rarely worked after dark, and there was little chance of encountering a patrol or of coming across the farmer out inspecting his land. The herd would be led on to the farm shortly after dark. In places where wire fences had been erected in an effort to prevent encroachment the wire was simply freed from the posts and lifted up by a strong tree branch to allow the cattle to pass underneath. The cattle would be grazed on the range for a few hours before being taken to the most convenient watering point on the farm, and then herded back to the reserve before daybreak. In the daytime the herd would be rested and the whole process repeated the following night.[17]

Those Tugen living permanently adjacent to the settled area, especially along the Solai and Subukia borders, were most closely involved in the networks of bribery and adopted the most sophisticated approaches to trespass. During periods of drought herders from locations lying to the west also crowded along the border, intending to trespass on to the farms. Between 1926 and 1935 these movements took place annually and were very extensive. Less experienced in the arts of trespass, these herders often became embroiled in confrontations with grazing guards and even with local Tugen herders on whose 'territory' they were impinging. During the dry season of 1932, for example, trespass was especially bad from the East Endorois location. Local Tugen leaders defended themselves against government criticism over this by asserting that it was herders from other locations, and not they, who were the cause of the trouble. Investigations by DC Rimington revealed seventy-eight herders from other locations in East Endorois, approximately 75 per cent of them originating from the Ewalel and Chapchap locations to the west of the Molo River. Others had come from even further afield. Their total stock was estimated at over 1,200 head of cattle and more than 3,000 goats. As Rimington admitted, this was likely to be but a portion of the true numbers of animals moved into the location during the dry season.[18] By the 1930s, such temporary migrants were as much of a nuisance to the hard-pressed Tugen of East Endorois as they were to the European farmers on whose land they intended to trespass.

---

[16] Kerby to PC/RVP, 13 March 1935, KNA PC/RVP.6A/15/15; BHT/TG/12, BHT/TG/ 40 and BHT/CH/9.

[17] Poestkoke to CVO, 6 October 1931, and PC/RVP to CNC, 19 January 1932, both in KNA PC/RVP.6A/15/15; BHT/TG/11, BHT/TG/19 and BHT/ES/3.

[18] Rimington (DC/Baringo) to DO/Eldama Ravine, 30 January 1932, KNA PC/ERD.6A/ 41/5. The stock counted by the DC was found to come from six different locations; thirty-one herders from Chap-Chap, with a total of 543 head of cattle and 2015 goats; twenty-one herders from Ewalel, with 365 head of cattle and 340 goats; sixteen herders from Kapropita East, with 165 cattle and 660 goats; eight herders from Kapturin with 140 cattle and 100 goats; one herder from Kapteberwa with only ten cattle; and one herder from Ngorora with fifty head of cattle.

Trespass was a game of hide-and-seek. If spotted on a farm, herders would run their stock as hard as they could back to the safety of the reserve. Herders learned to be highly skilled in controlling the movements of their animals, and most herds were trained to respond to specific sounds and to swiftly stampede towards the boundary. As one rather surprised European police officer reported:

> In the past it has been found that it is comparatively easy to seize cattle on this border but exceptionally difficult to retain them because the Kamasia have their cattle trained to come when called by their names, and if they hear two sticks knocked together they invariably stampede and follow the sound, and it must be seen to be believed.[19]

Farmers and their workers attempting to intercept this flight were sometimes bowled over and injured, an ignominy suffered by Stanning and Dwen at Lomolo and Poestkoke at Solai.[20] Another common tactic was to send children with trespassing stock and, in the event of capture, for the adult herders to flee leaving the child with the animals. This placed the guard in something of a social dilemma; he was likely to be ridiculed for being heartless enough to arrest a small child, and in a society where favours were customarily reciprocated was perhaps in danger of making himself a long-standing enemy. As one erstwhile trespasser delicately expressed it:

> Had the guard's salary been deducted because my children had stolen the grass? It had not. When he becomes older, can he not see that my boys will then help him? Did he not see that he would never be without water? It was better for him to say and do nothing, or else he may find that when these boys become men he will suffer the consequences.[21]

But, if cattle were caught, herders were not opposed to using violence to retrieve their property. One such incident was reported during 1931 by Gordon Stanning, the part-owner of farm LO5260. Having spotted a large herd of Tugen cattle on his land one evening, Stanning took some of his employees and attempted to round up the trespassing animals:

> Immediately the Kamasia [Tugen] realised that their cattle were being rounded up noises were made and moran came running to their assistance from the Reserve. One Kamasia was coming over the boundary with a drawn sword and evidently meant to use it on my boys who had some cattle rounded up. I had to threaten him twice with my rifle before he stopped.[22]

---

[19] Davies (Supt. Police) to Supt. Police/Naivasha, 14 November 1942, KNA PC/RVP.6A/15/16. Having personally been present when a Tugen herder was forced to stampede a herd of over sixty cattle across a road in a matter of seconds, thus avoiding collision with a bus, I can sympathize with the somewhat astonished tone of Supt. Davies.

[20] Stanning, Dwen and Poestkoke each reported independently on incidents of this sort, all in KNA PC/RVP.6A/15/15.

[21] BHT/TG/59.

[22] Stanning to DC/Nakuru, 11 March 1931, KNA PC/RVP.6A/15/15.

On this occasion Stanning succeeded in rounding up only nineteen head of a herd of approximately 200. Even when a trespassing herd was successfully confiscated, attempts were frequently made to release the cattle. A notable case of this kind occurred after a police raid in the Arabel area, when a large herd of Chamus and Tugen stock was captured by a police patrol. On the next day the African herders made three attempts to regain their stock on the road between Arabel and Rumuruti, their persistence forcing the police patrol to mount a round-the-clock watch on the stock and ultimately resulting in the arrest of two of the herders.[23] The use of the term 'war' to describe the struggles along the Baringo borders is by no means a misnomer.

By 1930 it was clear that the settlers were ill-equipped to control the trespass problem themselves, and so they increasingly directed their protests and complaints to government. Dairy farmers were under the greatest threat from trespass, and so were in the forefront of the campaign for government action. Their claim that trespassing stock presented a disease threat was easily demonstrable; before 1933 Caleb Kerby at Solai had suffered the loss of three dairy herds, each attributed to disease conveyed to his cows by Tugen stock, and his neighbour, the South African settler Poestkoke, had experienced outbreaks of rinderpest and East Coast fever among his cattle, each episode apparently connected with trespassing cattle.[24] In addition to the direct loss of stock as a result of trespass, the damage to pasture was immense. Rotational grazing systems and reserved fallow pastures were often completely disrupted by encroachment, and it is perhaps not surprising that settlers filed extensive claims for monetary compensation against Tugen as a result of this. This extract from a letter of complaint written by a Solai settler in 1932 is typical of many:

> My grazing, which is my living, has been demolished, some 100 acres of beans which I planted have been eaten and trodden out, channels I have made at great expense to conserve water to help my grazing have been stamped out, and whereas I was recently advertising for another 300 head of cattle I now have nothing like enough grazing for the cattle I already have … It must be realised that my life's work and savings are involved in this.[25]

This settler claimed compensation of 1,000s. as the result of a single night's trespass, small in comparison with the 8,000s. damages claimed by Stanning against trespass on his farms LO5260, 3844 and 3732 in 1931. In a single week of trespass, Stanning claimed that 600 acres of pastureland had been denuded and a further 100 acres of reserved grazing destroyed.[26] Virtually

---

[23] Davies (Supt. Police) to Supt. Police/Naivasha, 14 November 1942, KNA PC/RVP.6A/15/16.

[24] Kerby to Welby (PC/RVP), 25 July 1933, KNA PC/RVP.6A/ll/18; Poestkoke to PC/RVP, 25 March 1932, KNA PC/RVP.6A/15/15.

[25] Poestkoke to PC/RVP, 18 April 1932, KNA PC/RVP.6A/15/15.

[26] Stanning to DC/Nakuru, 11 March 1931, KNA PC/RVP.6A/15/15.

every farmer along the boundary had a story of similar proportions to relate. The administration, fearing lest they be inundated with requests for compensation, refused to acknowledge any liability for the payment of compensation for trespass.

Without assistance of some sort, many farmers could see trespass being their absolute ruin. This can be illustrated by the example of John Wallace, the owner of farms LO2461 and 2464 in the Arabel Valley, adjacent to grazing areas of both Tugen and Il Chamus. Up until 1931 Wallace had made his living from maize cultivation, but after the locust plagues of the late 1920s had ruined successive crops and the depression had brought the price down below his profit threshold, Wallace heeded 'the best official advice' and switched to dairying and ranching. This required the enlargement of his herd and, having only £500 in capital, he sought the help of the Land Bank. Before deciding on awarding Wallace a loan, the Bank made enquiries into the local conditions and risks of his situation, and noted that no real trespass problem should exist because an area of unalienated Crown Land lay between his farm and the reserve. Imagining government controls over encroachment into unalienated Crown Lands to be adequate, the Bank declined to make any provision for financial assistance with fencing the Wallace farm, but granted him £1,000, against a charge over his farm, for the development of his dairy herd. Early in 1932, after Wallace had bought fresh stock, extensive trespass by Chamus (and also Pokot) cattle introduced East Coast fever among his dairy herd. By the end of 1933, Wallace had lost 150 dairy cows to disease and had accordingly suffered a 'staggering' decrease in earnings, to the extent that he was unable to meet the provisions of the Land Bank loan or fulfil other financial commitments.[27] The difference here between the theory and principle of government controls and their actual reality is all too clear. Far from acting as a 'buffer zone' between the reserve and the settled area, the portion of unalienated Crown Land to the north of the Arabel Valley farms was in fact a jumping-off point for trespassing stock.[28] It had actually *facilitated* trespass on to the Wallace farm, rather than acting as an impediment. In making its loan to Wallace, the Land Bank had assumed that the letter of the law was observed and that Wallace's farm was suitably protected from encroachment. For their part, the administration, while sympathetic to Wallace's situation, would not accept any responsibility. Wallace was advised that a civil action against the individual herders concerned with the act of trespass was the only possible course of action, but one that was very unlikely to be successful. At each turn, it seemed, the settler was frustrated by the failings of the administration.[29]

---

[27] R. Russell (Solicitor) to PC/RVP, 11 November 1933, KNA PC/RVP.6A/23/7.

[28] *KLC:EM,* ii, evidence of C.H. Adams (AgPC/RVP), 1898–1908. Many items of settler correspondence lamented the lack of government control over unalienated Crown Land, especially at Ngelesha: KNA PC/RVP.6A/15/47.

[29] PC/RVP to CNC, 15 November 1933, KNA PC/RVP.6A/23/7.

Lack of confidence in the ability of the government to exercise adequate control was a major reason for settler opposition to several schemes designed to relieve grazing pressure within the reserve, and so indirectly ease the trespass problem. Settlers vigorously opposed the creation of stock routes for the export of Baringo's cattle on these very grounds and urged the tighter control of stock export from the African areas.[30] Settlers also opposed plans to give Tugen cattle access to Lake Solai and its adjacent salt-lick and to a complicated scheme to pipe water from the Solai–Subukia area to a portion of unalienated Crown Land adjacent to the reserve. In 1930, the owner of farm LO1168 was forced to give Tugen stock access to the salt-lick beside Lake Solai. The farm was unoccupied and had long been illegally used by Tugen. Settlers in Solai were appalled by this concession, pointing out that the farm was already used as a staging-post for stock trespassing further into the settled area. The regularization of Tugen presence there, they argued, could only result in a greater level of trespass. Moreover, access to the farm from the reserve entailed walking cattle down a fairly steep escarpment, which in times of drought they were often too weak to climb back up again. Livestock using the farm were therefore very likely to end up trespassing on neighbouring farms once they had become stranded on the wrong side of the escarpment. The wire fence around the salt-lick was a completely inadequate deterrent, as the Solai Farmers Association protested to the administration in 1931. The neighbouring farms, notably LO6600 owned by Poestkoke, were constantly grazed over by stock emanating from the salt-lick.[31] On visits to the salt-lick in 1932 and 1933 the government's Reconditioning Officer, Langridge, commented that the wire fence was almost completely wrecked and that the grazing on the farm was rapidly deteriorating.[32]

Fencing was a continual bone of contention between government and settlers. Only a handful of farmers near the Baringo boundary had estab-lished any type of fencing prior to 1930. Costs of fencing were high and, although lines of sisal plants were in places used to mark the boundary, these did not serve to keep out trespassing stock. Many settlers cherished the thought that government would ultimately take up the cost by fencing the Native Reserve to keep Africans in; government held the view that it was the responsibility of the landowner to fence his own land if he wished to keep Africans out. Requests to assist farmers at Lomolo and Solai with fencing costs were rejected.[33] An alternative suggestion that farmers should

[30] PC/RVP to CVO, 4 February 1932, KNA PC/RVP.6A/23/5; Wheeler (District VO) to CVO, 26 November 1934, KNA PC/RVP.6A/23/9.

[31] Kerby to PC/RVP, 25 July 1933, KNA PC/RVP.6A/ll/17; Welby (PC/RVP) to DC/Ravine, 2 October 1931, and Poestkoke to CVO, 6 October 1931, both in KNA PC/RVP.6A/15/15; PC/RVP to CNC, 17 August 1933, KNA PC/RVP.6A/ll/18.

[32] Langridge (RO) to PC/RVP, 7 January 1935 and 9 May 1935, both in KNA PC/RVP.6A/ll/25.

[33] Fencing had been considered crucially important by the Veterinary Department in the

cooperate with the Local Native Council (LNC) in fencing mutual boundaries – the farmer providing materials and the LNC labour – was attempted at Lomolo, but the wire fence erected completely failed to reduce the incidence of trespass.[34]

Despite the obvious indications that fencing around farm LO1168 had no effect upon trespass, the administration alarmed local settlers by giving serious consideration to a scheme to pipe water on to the farm to provide a water-supply for the herders of Pokorr and Endorois locations. This proposal suggested the construction of a pipeline from the Nyeria Stream, running into Lake Solai from the south-east. The project had been prompted by the tendency for Lake Solai to dry up in the portion that bordered on LO1168 during the dry season, which the administration claimed led to greater trespass in search of alternative water sources.[35] But to the settlers living nearby it was all too obvious that trespass was just as likely to occur whether Lake Solai became dry or not, simply due to the geographical position of the farm and the generally poor condition of the reserve. 'Even given all the good will in the world you will not stop trespass there,' claimed one settler.[36] European farmers in the area were relieved when the scheme was abandoned in 1933 on the grounds of expense, but the conflict the suggestion had raised illustrated very clearly the increasingly defensive posture being adopted by European farmers in the face of incessant trespass.[37]

The frustration with the lack of support from government led some to take the law into their own hands against trespassers. Some settlers took to patrolling the borders of their farms in person and for the most part they went armed, intent upon confiscating any trespassing cattle and arresting the herders. Police and government officials feared that such actions would cause the conflict on the border to escalate. The instructions issued by the Superintendent of Police to his patrols in 1932 were far more cautious:

> Cattle are not to be seized, but driven back over the boundary. Owners or herders are not to be charged, but brought directly to the police station, where all particulars will be recorded, the person be released, and a report sent to the DC by runner at once ... The question of ill-feeling between

[33] (cont.) earliest days of settlement: see Agriculture Department AR 1908–1909, PRO CO 544/1. For later discussion, H.R. Bisschop, *The Improvement of Livestock in Kenya* (East Africa Pamphlet No. 42, Nairobi, 1949). Among settlers who pressed for aid with fencing during the 1930s and 1940s were Stanning and Dwen (at Lomolo), and Kerby, Poestkoke and Harries (at Solai): 'Loose papers, undated and unsigned, re Trespass at Lomolo' (*c.* 1931), Poestkoke to CVO, 6 October 1931; Capt. Harries to DC/Ravine, 24 May 1944; Solai Association to PC/RVP, 1 July 1944; all in KNA PC/RVP.6A/15/15.

[34] 'Loose papers, undated and unsigned, re Trespass at Lomolo' (*c.* 1931); and Perreau (DC/Baringo) to PC/RVP, 11 July 1931, both KNA PC/RVP.6A/15/15.

[35] Welby (PC/RVP) to Kerby, 31 July 1933; PC/RVP to CNC, 17 August and 7 September 1933, all in KNA PC/RVP.6A/11/18.

[36] Kerby to Hopkins (DC/Baringo), 30 April 1939, KNA PC/RVP.6A/15/15.

[37] PC/RVP to CNC, 17 August 1933, PC/RVP.6A/11/18.

Kamasia and farmers must not be lost sight of. There is a likelihood of some hot-headed natives making a threatening gesture with a spear.[38]

Of course, the Superintendent was diplomatic enough not to mention the equally likely occurrence of a hot-headed settler making a threatening gesture with a rifle.

On the Lomolo boundary two such incidents occurred within a month of each other in 1931. In the first Gordon Stanning attempted to confiscate a herd of some 120 head of trespassing stock, with the following result.

> I rode up to the two Kamasia who were herding them … one was a murran … he immediately raised his spear and threatened me with it and said that if I did not let the cattle go he would kill me; he was quite calm about it and evidently meant what he said … He gave his sword to the youth with him and the latter drove off the cattle back into the Reserve, and the murran waited behind facing me and my boys until the cattle had gone. He then roundly abused my boys and finally departed.[39]

The second incident involved Stanning's neighbour, the sisal farmer Dwen. After Dwen and his herdboys had apprehended and rounded up a small herd of trespassing stock, the owners of the herd returned to the farm and by shouting at the stock from a distance succeeded in turning them and making them stampede towards the boundary. In the ensuing panic Dwen was knocked over by the cattle and was lucky to escape serious injury.[40]

Such events only rarely came to the notice of officials and, when they did so, it was invariably because the African herder had got the better of the situation. There were many other confrontations, as Tugen herders readily recall, in which settlers simply seized trespassing cattle at gunpoint, keeping the cattle as compensation for the loss of grazing. Herders who were caught trespassing were beaten, sometimes very savagely. It is even alleged that acts of murder were committed, although there is no independent evidence to support such claims. Certainly, herders saw little point in reporting their confrontations with settlers to the authorities.[41] An incident that came to the official notice of the police, however, gives us an indication of the intensity of the struggles along the farm border. This incident concerns John Wallace of Arabel and his farm manager, Ryan, and took place during Wallace's ill-fated attempts to develop dairying on his farm. The two Europeans encountered a group of Pokot trespassers on the farm and attempted to arrest them and impound their cattle. When the herders attempted to lead the animals away, a fracas ensued, ending with three of the Pokot sustaining gunshot wounds. Enquiries into the event indicated that tempers had frayed on both sides, Wallace candidly

---

[38] Kearney (Supt. of Police) to PC/RVP, 25 January 1932, KNA PC/RVP.6A/15/15.

[39] Stanning to Supt. of Police/Nakuru, 7 April 1931, KNA PC/RVP.6A/15/15.

[40] Perreau (DC/Baringo) to PC/RVP, 11 July 1931, PC/RVP.6A/15/15.

[41] BHT/ES/2, BHT/ES/3, BHT/TG/24, BHT/TG/39 and others. Tugen and Chamus informants gave numerous accounts of violent incidents concerned with trespass.

admitting that he was 'completely exasperated' and at his 'wits end over the business of trespass'.[42]

During the early months of 1932, with Baringo's herders experiencing the drought of *Talamwei*, complaints from farmers and from their local associations reached a peak. After six years in which the incidence of trespass had been steadily increasing all along the border, the locust infestations of 1932 had done serious damage to grazing on the farms as well as in the reserves. With many farmers recently in receipt of loans from the Land Bank and most using the money to improve and increase their own herds, they feared that disaster loomed if the expected rains failed again. In what was certainly an orchestrated assault, partly inspired by the imminent arrival of the Land Commission, Farmers' Associations from Ravine, Lower Molo, Rongai, Solai and Subukia bombarded the adminis- tration with stern and doom-laden letters of complaint. The Provincial Commissioner, doubtless also with his eye on the forthcoming Land Commission investigations, summoned settler representatives to Nakuru for a meeting to discuss the problem of trespass. With Provincial Commissioner Welby in the chair and the Nakuru District Commissioner in attendance, the settlers took full advantage of the opportunity to give vent to their feelings. The farmers expressed deep dissatisfaction with the inconsistencies in government policies, which they attributed to the rapid turnover in administrative staff in the area. The present officials 'were only birds of passage', observed Milton of Solai: 'there were no guarantees that original policy would be maintained when they left'.[43] Between 1910 and 1940 Baringo District had over thirty changes of District Commissioner, more than any other district in Kenya. The settler delegation demanded that an experienced official be left in the district for several years.[44] After listening to the catalogue of settler complaints, heavily laced with criticism of government lassitude, the Provincial Commissioner was quick to rise to the bait. Welby gave his view that the solution to trespass lay not in getting government to do what settlers wanted, but in improving conditions within the African reserves. Government policy should therefore focus on the improvement of the African lands in Baringo through the reconditioning of pasture, improving facilities for the marketing of stock and providing access for African cattle to additional sources of water. Matters became rather heated as this sharp division of interest became apparent: this was not what the European farmers wished to hear. Their demands emphasized what government ought to be doing to *protect* the property of legal land-

---

[42] Welby (PC/RVP) to CNC, 29 May 1933, KNA PC/RVP.6A/15/36.

[43] DC/Nakuru, 'Minutes of meeting with Settlers re trespass', 17 March 1932, KNA PC/RVP.6A/15/15. The following settlers were present: Duncan Stanning and Dwen (Lower Molo & Rongai), A.E. Smith and S.O. Crowther (Ravine), Capt. H.A. Stringer and Maj. Boyce (Subukia), J.H. Milton and Count Cornegliano (Solai Association).

[44] For complaints regarding this policy, see Lambert, 'Political history', 33–4; PC/RVP to Chief Secretary, 20 February 1939, KNA PC/RVP.6A/23/13.

holders from illegal trespass: they stressed the need for fencing and for increased policing of the boundary, to be paid for by government or by the African. The meeting, which Welby had intended to 'clear the air', served only to entrench settler distrust of government: if government thought they could only help the settler by helping the African, then it seemed that the settler must help himself.

Policing, punishment & public opinion

One demand regularly made by European farmers was that government should take fuller responsibility for the policing of the farm boundary. This issue was a constant bone of contention throughout the 1930s. Administrative officers in Nakuru and Baringo quarrelled over whose responsibility the matter should be. Neither district had adequate resources to deal with the matter effectively, and in the stringent days of the early 1930s there was even less room for manoeuvre on expenditure of this sort. Moreover, the arrangement of policing authorities only accentuated the difficulty. The Kenya Police, a properly trained force of European officers and Asian and African rank and file, held jurisdiction over the White Highlands. But this body had no authority within the Native Reserves, where the district administration recruited Tribal Police from the local community. These recruits received no formal training in police duties, being employed as general retainers by the District Commissioner and often assigned to the authority of a particular chief. The standard of recruitment to the Tribal Police was notoriously low, and they were seldom used in an investigative capacity. However, the Kenya Police constables were sometimes seconded to African districts such as Baringo, but only to assist with specific criminal investigations: in 1933 there were nine African constables in Baringo, rising to fourteen in 1935.[45]

Who, then, should police the border? The Kenya Police in Nakuru District had to cover the expanding Nakuru township and some 300 farms throughout what was a large district. The incidence of reported crime in Nakuru rose sharply over the 1930s, as the township expanded. The Nakuru branch of the Kenya Police was one of the busiest in the country, but its establishment had not expanded to cope with the increased workload. In 1933, Nakuru Police District was staffed by five European officers with one Asian Sub-Inspector and ninety-six African other ranks. In the following year financial cuts reduced this number by ten. In Baringo District the logistical problems of effective policing were even more striking: this vast district had only twenty Tribal Police in the 1920s, most of whom were based at the district headquarters of Kabarnet in the Tugen Hills, far

---

[45] Welby (PC/RVP) to CNC, 7 June 1933, and Comm. of Police to Colonial Secretary, 21 November 1933, both in KNA PC/RVP.6A/15/36.

distant from the major trouble spots on the reserve boundary. By the mid-1930s the numbers of Tribal Police had been increased to around thirty, but even this was inadequate for so large a district.[46] These Tribal Police were used for border-patrol duties on the reserve side of the boundary from the early 1930s, but with minimal effect. Baringo's Tribal Police were all local to the district, and all were themselves stock-owners who shared a great sympathy for the trespassers. On more than one occasion members of the Tribal Police were found to be directly complicit in acts of trespass.

In 1932, a force of eighteen special African police were recruited by the District Commissioner in Nakuru specifically for border-patrol work, to augment the work of the Tribal Police already deployed at trouble spots on the reserve side of the boundary. These special recruits were drawn from outside the district, in the hope of lessening their susceptability to influence and bribery. They were divided into four patrols, each allocated a portion of the farm boundary to police. They carried with them a 'Farm Patrol Book', which was signed by the farmer on each farm they patrolled, and in which he was invited to comment upon any recent incident of trespass or theft. Though the settlers welcomed this innovation, it proved utterly ineffective. Crimes involving stock theft and trespass actually increased markedly throughout 1932 and 1933 in the very areas in which the patrols worked. A number of apparent 'oversights' on the part of the special patrols led several settlers to openly suggest that the police had accepted bribes from Tugen herders.[47] The Nakuru District Commissioner at first robustly defended his patrols, but the truth of settler accusations soon became apparent. On more than one occasion whole patrols had to be sacked *in toto* because of corruption. As far as the Tugen herders were concerned, all African police patrols were as open to bribery as the grazing guards employed privately by the settlers, regardless of considerations of ethnicity.[48] The dilemma was rooted in their sense of social responsibility. As one Tugen herder explained, when asked how corruption of this sort could have been so pervasive: 'It was easy. After all, they [the African police] understood our problems.'[49]

Other local African agents of the colonial state were no more effective as foils against trespass. In 1932, the administration attempted to persuade the Baringo Local Native Council to divert some of its accumulated funds to assisting with the financing of additional border patrols, but the suggestion

---

[46] Asst. Insp. of Police to Supt. of Police/Nakuru, 8 April 1931, KNA PC/RVP.6A/15/15; Pritchard-Brown (Comm. of Police) to Colonial Secretary, 7 September 1934, KNA PC/RVP.6A/24/6.

[47] DC/Baringo to PC/RVP, 23 July 1931, KNA PC/RVP.6A/19/2; PC/RVP to CNC, 19 January 1932, KNA PC/RVP.6A/15/15; Vincent (Supt. of Police/Nakuru) to Comm. of Police/Nairobi, 27 April 1937, KNA PC/RVP.6A/24/6.

[48] PC/RVP to Colonial Secretary, 26 January 1934, KNA PC/RVP.6A/15/15; various items of correspondence, KNA DO/ER/2/24/13.

[49] BHT/TG/19 and BHT/TG/22.

was vigorously opposed. The matter was not raised again. The hostility of the council to this suggestion was in no small part due to the heavy involvement of several members of the council in trespass. Cattle owned by these government-appointed officials were frequently found among confiscated trespassing stock, and a number of chiefs were known to openly encourage the people under their charge to trespass. And, of course, these same chiefs supervised the actions of the Tribal Police along the farm boundary. For example, Chief Chesire of Pokorr was heavily implicated in several cases of corruption involving Tribal Police and grazing guards, and it was also proved that he had used his position to secure an illegal grazing agreement with a European farmer. The complicity of the settler in this case and a lack of hard evidence on the other charges prevented Chesire from being dismissed, despite strong protests from farmers in the Lomolo area. While the government expected better behaviour from its appointees, among the Tugen it was recognized that the need to seek water and grazing for the herd was no different for a chief than for any other herder. Indeed, by the nature of his position, it was almost inevitable that the chief would benefit from his contacts and opportunities; he was a fool if he did not.[50] These realities of survival pervaded all levels of Tugen and Chamus society, making it impossible for the administration to elicit African support in their efforts to control trespass. African public opinion was completely in support of the trespassers.

Faced by determined opposition even among African officials, settlers pressed for closer European supervision of all border patrols. A Kenya Police contingent from Nakuru was assigned to patrol the Solai border in February 1931, led by a European officer, and this became a regular feature of every dry season until 1939. The patrol had only a very limited impact and made only a handful of arrests. Advance news of its arrival usually reached Tugen herders as the patrol was making its way north from Nakuru: herds were simply moved back across the reserve boundary until the police patrol had passed. The annual patrol was more of a political gesture aimed at settler public opinion than an effective deterrent. With expenditure cuts in 1933, the police station at Solai and the police post at Kampi-ya-Moto were shut down, leaving the Kenya Police officer at Ravine as the only European stationed anywhere along the entire boundary.[51] Farms to the north of Marmanet, policed from Rumuruti, also lost regular patrols at this time. The increase of trespass and of stock theft along the Lomolo and Solai borders in 1934 was dramatic, the Solai–Subukia area accounting for nearly 50 per cent of all reported crime in the

---

[50] PC/RVP to CNC, 28 January 1932, KNA PC/RVP.6A/15/15. Also, various items of correspondence in KNA DO/ER/2/24/13. For a similar set of circumstances among Kamba, see Stannar, 'Kitui Kamba', 4–8.

[51] PC/RVP to Colonial Secretary, 26 January 1934, KNA PC/RVP.6A/15/15; Pritchard-Brown (Comm. of Police) to Colonial Secretary, 7 September 1934, KNA PC/RVP.6A/24/6.

Table 4.1 Prosecution and punishment of trespass, Kenya Colony, 1932–8

YEAR	PUNISHMENT											
	Fine	Detention or prison in default	Fine with detention or prison	Detention or prison	Whipping	Bound over	Other convictions	Committed to house detention	Bailed	Total convictions	Total acquittals	Total discharges
1932	638	550	–	94	–	–	156	–	212	1650	27	28
1933	470	676	–	75	1	1	185	1	147	1556	28	25
1934	619	1216	3	163	9	–	345	2	140	2497	19	66
1935	693	840	2	217	1	–	487	–	313	2553	62	63
1936	781	787	–	84	1	1	389	2	44	2089	72	56
1937	701	444	–	24	–	–	333	–	33	1535	24	33
1938	512	359	–	49	1	2	115	–	14	1052	30	83

Source: Judicial Department Annual Reports, 1932–38. PRO CO/544/38–55

Nakuru Police District. The European-led Kenya Police patrol on the Solai border seemed an expensive luxury in this context, given its conspicuous lack of success, and the provincial administration joined the local settlers in campaigning for the reopening of Solai police station; but it was not until 1938 that funds were found to allow this.[52]

Unable to afford regular, effective policing, the various authorities on either side of the border began, in the late 1930s, to organize surprise raids on specific groups of farms. This tactic was only used sporadically, but it met with considerably greater success in terms of arrests and the confiscation of stock. During the 1940s, such raids were mounted more frequently, as a consequence of which the numbers of trespass cases being prosecuted in the local courts rose sharply.[53]

Herders caught trespassing were prosecuted under the Trespass Ordinance. The majority of cases originating from Baringo were heard before the Resident Magistrate at Nakuru. Fewer cases came before the Class II courts in Eldama Ravine and Kabarnet, presided over by the District Commissioners in their capacity as magistrates.[54] Records of Kenya's subordinate courts do not survive, but it is possible to extract figures on prosecutions for trespass from aggregate court returns to the Judicial Department for some years. These figures only tell us about those cases which came before the courts, representing but a very small proportion of actual offences committed, and the limited information must restrict our commentary to the pattern of punishments administered. Table 4.1 presents figures for the prosecution of trespass cases for the whole colony from 1932 to 1938, with details of the nature of punishment. Trespass occurred in very many areas of the White Highlands, but as far as we can tell the offence was treated fairly consistently in the Resident Magistrate's courts, where the vast majority of all cases were heard.[55] We can therefore be reasonably confident that the pattern of punishments issued by all courts was reflected in the Nakuru cases.

---

[52] PC/RVP to Colonial Secretary, 26 January 1934, KNA PC/RVP.6A/15/15; Nakuru Police Unit, AR 1939, KNA PC/RVP.6A/24/l; Pritchard-Brown to Colonial Secretary, 7 September 1934; Blundell (Solai Association) to Colonial Secretary, 25 August 1934; Vincent (Supt. of Police/Nakuru) to Comm. of Police/Nairobi, 27 April 1937, all in KNA PC/RVP.6A/24/6.

[53] Harries to DC/Ravine, 24 May 1944, and DO/Baringo to DC/Baringo, 22 July 1944, both in KNA DO/ER/2/24/13.

[54] 'The Trespass Ordinance', *The Laws of Kenya 1948* (Nairobi, 1948), 8 vols, iv, 2256–7. Judicial Department, AR 1931, 3, PRO CO 544/34, for details of jurisdictions of differing levels of courts.

[55] Little has been written on punishment and the courts in colonial Kenya, but for an introductory discussion see David M. Anderson, 'Policing, prosecution and the law in colonial Kenya, *c.* 1905–39', in David M. Anderson & David Killingray (eds), *Policing the Empire: Government, Authority and Control, 1830–1940* (Manchester, 1991), 183–201, and, for a broader view, H.F. Morris & James S. Read, *Indirect Rule and the Search for Justice: Essays in East African Legal History* (Oxford, 1972).

The punishments prescribed on conviction for trespass appear comparatively trivial by Kenyan standards. Although magistrates held wide discretionary powers on sentencing convicts, custodial sentences were rare, these apparently being reserved for persistent offenders. The vast majority of those convicted received a fine. The level of fine was determined as a multiple of the number of cattle impounded at the time of the offence. In the 1920s fines were set at 5s. per head of cattle; in 1931 this was raised to 10s. per head, and doubled again to 20s. per head in 1945.[56] However, a very significant proportion of those fined defaulted on payment – 38 per cent of all convicts over the seven-year period. These persons were consequently sentenced to periods of imprisonment. The worst year in this respect was 1934, with 49 per cent of those convicted ultimately imprisoned as a result of defaulting on the payment of fines. The run of figures available here is too short to draw any very significant conclusions about trends, but it is notable that default on fines became more prevalent from 1933 to 1936, coinciding with the culmination of several successive years of drought and the worst years of economic depression. Numbers of prosecutions also show a sharp rise over these years.

The aggregate statistics of punishments for trespass for the colony over these few years broadly corresponds with the pattern we might expect from a closer examination of the Baringo records. More detailed information on the prosecution of cases is occasionally revealed in other, non-judicial sources to corroborate this and from which we can extend the analysis in other directions. The longest set of returns available was located in the files of the Eldama Ravine District office, and deal with cases arising in the dry season of 1932, from the beginning of January until mid-March. During this period, cases from Ravine, Esageri and Rongai were heard at Eldama Ravine, with those from Solai, Subukia and Lomolo going before the magistrate at Nakuru. Over this period twenty cases of trespass were prosecuted by the Resident Magistrate resulting from arrests made on seven blocks of farms, among them the farms of Simpson, Poestkoke and Rutherford at Solai, and a block of unoccupied land at Subukia. A total of over 5,700s. was administered in fines by the magistrates, amounting to an average fine of 300s. per herder.[57] The average herd size of only thirty animals suggested by these figures would seem rather small, but it must be remembered that a trespassing herd would often comprise animals from parts of several herds and that a herder would seldom trespass with his entire herd at one time. Also, the total amount of fine pertains only to the number of animals actually impounded at the time of the offence: when apprehended many herders were able to detach at least part of their herd

[56] Wolff (DC/Baringo) to PC/RVP, 22 April 1945, KNA PC/RVP.6A/15/15.

[57] 'Loose papers, undated and unsigned' (1929–32); Perreau (DC/Baringo) to PC/RVP, 4 February 1932; and PC/RVP to CNC, 5 February 1932, all in KNA PC/RVP.6A/15/15; Resident Magistrate/Nakuru to DC/Baringo, 10 February 1932, KNA PC/RVP.6A/23/5.

and run it back across the boundary. As the size of fines was increased in the later 1930s and again in the 1940s, individuals often found themselves liable to pay sums exceeding 1,000s.[58]

In recalling these punishments, most Tugen herders proudly claim to have paid the fines without hesitation.[59] The documentary evidence suggests otherwise. To herders with no regular source of cash income a fine of even 300s. was a very substantial sum, the equivalent of more than three years' wages for an African farm labourer even before the drop in wage levels in the early 1930s. Sheep and goats could be sold to raise cash, but for such a large sum this would make a considerable dent in the holdings of any Tugen household. Cattle sales would realize the sum more readily: this was clearly an undesirable option, although the sale of three or four head to meet the fine if the action of trespass had saved thirty from starvation was surely a rational choice and one that many herders made. The inefficiencies of the administration might allow some to avoid, or at least delay, the payment of fines. For example, in late 1931 a series of twenty-four convictions of Tugen and Uas Nkishu Maasai were made at Nakuru and Ravine, totalling 6,470s. in fines. By February 1932, the Provincial Commissioner reported with some annoyance to the Chief Native Commissioner that only 190s. of this sum had been collected (part of this being a payment due from the people of Keben under a separate prosecution under the Collective Punishment Ordinance).[60] Compulsory sale of impounded livestock by court order became the norm during the 1930s, thus ensuring that fines were collected and meeting settler demands that confiscated cattle should not simply be handed back to the herder. Cattle sales became a regular feature of court sessions at Nakuru and Ravine from the early 1930s, and by the end of the decade the courts were ordering the sale of impounded cattle whether or not the herder was able to meet the fine. To the herder, this was a most unwelcome innovation. Prices realized at these sales were invariably low as the only buyers were local butchers, veterinary restrictions normally preventing the movement of purchased cattle out of the district.[61] Trespass was a gamble in which the African herder calculated the risk and weighed this carefully against the advantages to be gained; to be prosecuted and have one's cattle sold at a low price to meet the fine was surely the worst of all possible outcomes.

Despite the obvious loss that conviction brought to the herder, there is no significant evidence during the 1920s and 1930s to indicate that increasing levels of punishment had any impact on the incidence or severity of trespass. District administrators continued to push responsibility on to the

---

[58] BHT/TG/11 and BHT/TG/19; Resident Magistrate's Court, Nakuru, Return of Criminal Cases, February and March 1932; and Poestkoke to PC/RVP, 18 April 1932, all in KNA PC/RVP.6A/15/15.

[59] For example, BHT/TG/19.

[60] PC/RVP to CNC, 5 February 1932, KNA PC/RVP.6A/15/15.

[61] BHT/TG/ll; BHT/TG/12; BHT/TG/32.

courts, seeking to pressurize the Resident Magistrate at Nakuru to impose harsher fines on individual offenders: Perreau suggested that higher fines might be imposed in 1932, and Hodge repeated the plea in 1937.[62] Such meddling was not welcomed by court officers, and in 1948 Hickson-Mahoney had his knuckles soundly rapped by the presiding Resident Magistrate for seeking to 'interfere' in a similar manner in the workings of the court.[63]

In the settler view, the fault lay with *both* the law and the district administration; the law simply did not go far enough and the district administration was too feeble in imposing what powers it possessed. Inevitably, settlers persistently demanded ever more stringent punishments. They were especially keen that the Collective Punishment Ordinance should be applied against those Tugen communities who were most regularly responsible for trespass. This Ordinance allowed a District Commissioner, acting as magistrate, to apply a fine to an entire community, rather than an individual. It was most often used to cover the costs of special police or army patrols after local disturbances, or in cases of persistent stock thefts when it was judged that the community at large were shielding the offenders by refusing to provide information that would permit an arrest. The parallels between the provisions of this legislation in relation to stock theft and trespass were clear enough, but officials were reluctant to extend the application of a piece of legislation that required the approval of the Governor in every case and which was viewed with great suspicion by the Colonial Office in London. After considerable debate in 1931, a decision was taken to apply the Collective Punishment Ordinance against the Tugen of Keben location, it being decided that they had offended against the Ordinance by failing to hand over a known trespass offender who had threatened a European settler with a spear. To the warm approval of local settlers, a fine of 2,000s. was imposed: but the District Commissioner, who all along had expressed his fears that such indiscriminate methods of punishment would utterly alienate African cooperation, dallied over the collection of the fine and only 630s. was finally paid.[64] The Collective Punishment Ordinance was not again applied to trespass cases in Baringo.

The reluctance of government to impose collective punishments was deeply frustrating to the settlers farming the Baringo borders. Trespass was, in their view, a form of theft. African herders might openly admit that they 'stole the Europeans' grass', and yet within the moral communities of Tugen

[62] Perreau (DC/Baringo) to PC/RVP, 18 January 1932; Resident Magistrate Court, Nakuru, Returns for February 1932; and Kerby to PC/RVP, 27 March 1935, all in KNA PC/RVP.6A/15/15.

[63] Hickson-Mahoney (DO/Baringo) to Resident Magistrate/Nakuru, 2 June 1948, and reply 10 June 1948, both in KNA DO/ER/2/24/13.

[64] Ibid. Also, 'Loose papers, undated and unsigned' (1929–32), KNA PC/RVP.6A/15/15. Baringo was one of the first districts where the administration attempted to utilize the Collective Punishment Ordinance in this manner.

and Chamus this was not considered a reprehensible act. To the herders of Baringo, it was a case of necessity, and the European settler had no right to deny access to grazing and water.[65] European officials hoped to cultivate African public opinion against trespass, but there was no evidence to indicate that such a development was likely. The assertion of Solai settler Caleb Kerby, 'We need protection, they need direction; and both need a sympathetic understanding of the problems involved,' was a plea to government for greater action.[66]

Many settlers suspected that officials were reluctant to assist European farmers, openly accusing them of being too 'sympathetic to the Kamasia [Tugen]'.[67] Welby, Hodge and others argued the case for helping Tugen herders with greater vigour than they were willing to defend European settlers. This was no doubt rooted in a proper sense of duty – as District Officers they were primarily responsible for protecting the interests of Africans, not Europeans – but it was an attitude that was also informed by their suspicions of settler actions and motives. While, on the one hand, settlers put pressure on government to uphold the law, on the other they were not above breaking the law when it suited them. As we have seen, illegal squatter arrangements between farmers and herders – 'Kaffir farming' – were common along the Baringo borders. This practice *encouraged* African herders to enter the settled area *with* livestock. At Solai one settler admitted that the practice was widespread, arguing that it was 'simply a realization of the existing situation'.[68] Given that trespass could not be controlled, making a charge on the trespasser for use of the land was one way by which the settler could recoup some of his loss. The same imperatives led many settlers to invoke their own regime of fines against trespassers, independent of the courts. Herders caught trespassing were often able to negotiate with the settler, coming to an agreement of benefit to both; in one case a herder recalled handing over two oxen, and then being allowed to leave the farm with the rest of his herd.[69] The herder was saved from a fine much greater than the value of the oxen, and the settler received a return for the use of his land that would otherwise have gone directly into the coffers of the government. Such bartering over the 'cost' of trespass undoubtedly reduced the force of any government legislation and blurred the whole question of the illegality of trespass in European terms in the view

---

[65] BHT/TG/25, BHT/TG/32 and BHT/TG/59. Some parallels are to be found with E.P. Thompson's *Whigs and Hunters* (Pelican, 1976). Attitudes to land, and its resources as property lie at the root of the conflict discussed by Thompson, just as they lie at the root of the conflict between herder and settler in Baringo.

[66] BHT/TG/11, BHT/TG/19 and BHT/TG/25. Kerby to PC/RVP, 25 July 1933, KNA PC/RVP.6A/ll/18.

[67] BHT/ES/2 and BHT/ES/3; 'Minutes of meeting at Nakuru re Tugen trespass', 17 March 1932, and Kerby to Hopkins (AgPC/RVP), 30 April 1939, both KNA PC/RVP.6A/ 15/15.

[68] Harries to DC/Baringo, 10 December 1943, KNA DO/ER/2/24/13.

[69] BHT/TG/22 and BHT/TG/28.

of the herder. Being able to pay off the farmer and avoid prosecution became just another factor in the gamble.

By the end of the 1930s it is probably fair to say that a majority of European farmers were no longer prepared to tolerate the 'Kaffir farming' of their less responsible neighbours. In 1941, information from a settler farmer led to the discovery of a long-standing series of illegal grazing arrangements on the Esageri block of farms, near Eldama Ravine.[70] After a dawn raid, in which over 500 head of trespassing stock were rounded up, interrogation of the herders revealed a complicated arrangement involving local settlers Crowther and Collier, who between them had at least a part share in all but one of the Esageri farms. The District Officer's report summed up the situation:

> All [nineteen trespassers] were Tugen; none were apparently on squatter agreements, and none had an endorsement of employment from Mr. Collier. Though the fiction was that these natives were each 'permitted to graze 25 head of cattle on Collier's farm in return for preventing Tugen trespass', in fact each man said he paid Mr. Collier one ox per annum for the right to graze 25 head of cattle there. Apart from this being a blatant case of Kaffir farming, it would seem that Mr. Collier has been a party to flagrant breaches of the Diseases of Animals Rules.[71]

A further case came to light two years later. When investigating a long-standing dispute over a boundary marker at Solai in 1943, the Nakuru District Commissioner, Wolff, discovered that large numbers of Tugen herders from the reserve were regularly and freely moving cattle to and from the farm of Captain Harries. When confronted to explain the situation, Harries admitted that he allowed the regular grazing of his land by Tugen cattle for payment of a fixed rent. In all, Harries had sanctioned the grazing of some 900 head of Tugen cattle on his farms LO1650 and 1651, for which the herders from the neighbouring reserve had paid a sum of 8,000s. over a period of four months. Harries had even accepted a number of Tugen cattle as security against the arrangement.[72] As Harries himself described the situation:

> When I took over the farms ... from the National Bank of India ... they had been lying almost derelict for 20 years, and this is what I consider to be at the bottom of the whole trouble. The Tugen had occupied the whole of the western side of these farms up to the railway line, which they considered their boundary, and had occupied it so long that they did not wish to relinquish the grazing ... [I]t was only with the greatest difficulty that I could get them to move out at all.[73]

---

[70] R.N. Edmondson to PC/RVP, 26 January 1942, KNA PC/RVP.6A/15/15. See also BHT/ES/3. (This informant is the same Mr Edmondson.)

[71] Wolff (DC/Baringo) to PC/RVP, 21 February 1942, KNA PC/RVP.6A/15/15.

[72] Harries to DC/Baringo, 10 December 1943; and Wolff (DC/Baringo) to Labour Officer/ Nakuru, 28 January 1944, both in KNA DO/ER/2/24/13.

[73] Hickson-Mahoney (DC/Baringo) to DC/Kabarnet, 18 August 1947, KNA DO/ER/2/24/13, quotes Harries's evidence.

It is clear that the 'arrangement' arrived at between the two parties was in their mutual interest.[74] His curiosity now roused, Wolff set the Nakuru police to extend enquiries to neighbouring farms. They uncovered similar illegalities all along the border. Caleb Kerby was found to have an arrangement of the same type as Harries, while Poestkoke allowed a herd of a hundred Tugen milch cows on to his farm, taking a quantity of the milk each day to make cream in exchange for the grazing. Tugen herders had even allowed Poestkoke to brand their cattle in order to protect himself from prosecution. This particular ruse had been organized with the active participation of the local government-appointed Chief.[75]

The Resident Native Labour Ordinance of 1918 had sought to outlaw practices of this sort by setting down that no consideration other than labour should be exacted or accepted regarding residency rights and that no African should inhabit European land unless he had contracted to work for the proprietor for at least 180 days of the year.[76] The safeguarding of African interests had been held up as a reason for this legislation, but the wider political need of assuring and preserving European rights to land within the legal structure was more significant. Yet illegal squatter practices persisted so long as there existed a mutual need.[77] Herders were willingly complicit. 'Kaffir farming' arrangements involved African herders in considerable expense, to be sure, but they were less costly than paying fines to the courts and having impounded stock sold for a pittance. In terms of their fragile economic predicament, especially in the difficult years of the 1930s, many of the Europeans farming along the Baringo borders had more in common with the African living in the neighbouring reserve than they cared to admit. Baringo's range war was fought out between African herders and European settlers over access to critical resources, but it was also a struggle for survival in which each party might sometimes have reason to negotiate – even collaborate – with the other.

---

[74] Hodge (PC/RVP) to Chief Secretary, 5 August 1944, KNA PC/RVP.6A/15/15. Harries was found guilty of twenty-five charges under Section 19 of the Resident Native Labourers Ordinance.

[75] Insp. of Police/Solai to Insp. of Police/Nakuru, 2 August 1945, KNA DO/ER/2/24/13.

[76] Wrigley, 'Patterns of economic life', 238–9.

[77] For a wider discussion of resident native labour, see van Zwanenberg, *Colonial Capitalism*, ch. 8.

Five

Grazing, Goats
& Responsible Government
The Kenya Land Commission
1932–4

As the range war raged along the Baringo boundary in the wake of the locust infestation of 1932, the commissioners appointed to sit on the Kenya Land Commission arrived in the colony. Their brief was to examine the land needs of the African population, and they were empowered to make recommendations for the adjustment of boundaries and the redistribution of lands between the races and between various 'tribes'. Among the better informed of Kenya's African communities, their arrival was eagerly awaited. In the Central Province the Kikuyu Central Association had been actively mobilizing the local landholding lineage groups (*mbari*) to prepare claims for the return of lands lost to European settlers. Expectations were high that past injustices might be put to rights. At the very least it was hoped that compensation would at last be paid for the lands taken. In Baringo, distant from the politics of Nairobi and lacking the Christian missions, schools and churches through which news of such affairs commonly circulated in Central Province, the importance of the Land Commission was not so widely appreciated – at least, not among the African community. The settlers living along Baringo's borders, like all others in Kenya, were all too well aware of the significance of the coming inquiry. For settlers, the Land Commission was looked upon with fear and trepidation. Here was a commission with the potential to undo the sanctuary of the White Highlands, to undermine the security of tenure that settlers had struggled so hard to establish for themselves. The commission had to be persuaded of the worth of the settler enterprise, and to that end settler politicians worked as hard as did their counterparts in the Kikuyu Central Association to ensure that the views and claims of their group were made with as much force and clarity as possible. The Land Commission was a political

battleground upon which the future of white settlement would be fought for.

The Land Commission's investigations in Baringo and the implications of their findings will be examined in this chapter. More than any other single body of evidence, it was the published findings of the Commission that entrenched a particular view of Baringo's environmental decay and its causes. The decisions reached by the commissioners favoured the European settler's interpretation of Baringo's ills, stressing that the land had become heavily overstocked due to the irrationality of African herders and that, moreover, their singular reluctance to treat their livestock as an economic asset threatened the future productivity of the neighbouring settler-owned farms as well as the African reserves. The first part of the chapter will consider the evidence presented before the commission. We shall then move on to look in more detail at the broader implications of the commissioners' views on the overstocking controversy and on livestock marketing in Baringo, contrasting the European settlers' account of Baringo's economy and ecology with the reality experienced by African herders.

The Land Commission, 1932–4

The Kenya Land Commission was ensnared in political manoeuvrings from its very inception. The idea for an inquiry of this kind had initially emerged out of the representations made to the Colonial Office by Jomo Kenyatta in 1929 and 1930. Kenyatta was at that time in London to represent the Kikuyu Central Association, and with the assistance of McGregor Ross and other Fabians he was able to get the ear of the Labour Party's Drummond Shiels at the Colonial Office.[1] The Labour government, which had come to power in Britain in 1929, was far from sympathetic to Kenya's settlers. Moreover, since 1926 Colonial Office staff had grown increasingly alarmed by the enthusiasm with which Kenya's governor, Sir Edward Grigg, advocated the settler cause, even pressing for more white settlement after the onset of the Great Depression and the collapse of the colony's export markets. Made aware of African land grievances, and especially those of the Kikuyu, and worried by settler political belligerence, in March 1931 Shiels made the tentative suggestion that a proper inquiry into the adequacy of the African reserves in Kenya should be launched.[2] Before the end of the month a Colonial Office memorandum had given the idea substance and, with the approval of the Labour Secretary of State, Lord Passfield, the Kenya administration was instructed to draw up a commission of inquiry 'to examine African land questions'.[3]

---

[1] Kenyatta to Sec. of State, 15 April 1930, and related correspondence, PRO CO 533/395, and Passfield to Grigg, 2 January 1930, and related correspondence, PRO CO 533/403.

[2] Minute by Shiels, 4 March 1931, PRO CO 533/495.

[3] 'Memorandum on Native rights to and need for, land outside Reserves', by C.G. Eastwood, 23 March 1931; and Passfield to Byrne, 30 April 1931, both in PRO CO 533/403.

Governor Byrne, who replaced Grigg later in 1931, did not welcome the interference. He worried that settlers would react adversely to what was so obviously a threat to their future position and that Africans would have false hopes raised. Byrne was to be proved right on both counts; but in the meantime he negotiated with the Colonial Office over the membership of the commission to try to diminish its immediate impact.[4] His cause was assisted by the fall of the Labour government, bringing a National Coalition to power and a new Secretary of State, Phillip Cunliffe-Lister, to the Colonial Office. A Conservative with distinctly pro-settler tendencies, Cunliffe-Lister did not sweep the Land Commission aside altogether, but he agreed to an alteration of its terms of reference. Where the initial brief had been to take a broad look at African land grievances, the emphasis was now shifted to establishing the extent of lands over which the European community might continue to exercise exclusive rights. Although the Colonial Office insisted that an assessment of the adequacy of the African reserves should still be retained within the terms, the commission was now to be principally concerned with defining European claims rather than reasserting African rights.[5]

The members now selected to serve on the commission gave further security of mind to the settler community. Sir Morris Carter's credentials as chairman of the inquiry appeared impeccable. He had served in the judiciary in Uganda from 1902 to 1920, starting out as Registrar and reaching the rank of Chief Justice in 1912. From 1920 to 1924 he held the same high office in Tanganyika, during which time he was also President of the Court of Appeal for Eastern Africa. He also had considerable specific experience in matters relating to African land tenure. In 1906 he had been a prominent member of a commission of inquiry into land tenure in Uganda, and in 1911 he had become chairman of Uganda's Native Land Settlement Committee. Most relevant of all, in 1925, a year after his retirement, he presided over the Southern Rhodesian Land Commission. This inquiry had come out strongly in support of the segregation of lands between the races, in order, it was argued, to give security of tenure to both African and European. Though Southern Rhodesia's Land Apportionment Act of 1930 was not of Morris Carter's making, the findings of his Land Commission had made it possible. Having bolstered white settlement in Rhodesia by legitimating land segregation, Carter was unlikely to do otherwise in Kenya.[6]

Morris Carter's fellow commissioners were to be Rupert Hemsted and

---

[4] Byrne to Bottomley, 15 June 1931, PRO CO 533/416.

[5] For a brief account of this, see Rita M. Breen, 'The politics of land: the Kenya Land Commission, 1932–3, and its effects upon land policy in Kenya' (PhD thesis, Michigan State University, 1976), 47–50.

[6] For Carter's role in Rhodesia and Uganda, see Robin Palmer, *Land and Racial Domination in Rhodesia* (London, 1977), and H.F. Morris & J.S. Read, *Indirect Rule and the Search for Justice: Essays in East African Legal History* (Oxford, 1972).

Frank O'Brien Wilson. Both were surprisingly obscure choices for so important an enquiry. Hemsted had served as a colonial officer in Kenya from 1904, rising to Provincial Commissioner in 1924. Much of his time had been spent in the Maasai districts, and he had a particular interest in livestock questions. He had retired at the end of the 1920s to take up fruit farming at Ngong. Wilson was the authentic 'settler voice' on the commission. He had come to Kenya in 1910, taking up a dairy farm in the drylands of Ulu, and was renowned as an industrious and skilled stockman. He was also politically active, having served on the executive of the Convention of Associations. He had deputized for Lord Francis Scott on Legislative Council in 1926 and 1931 and had also experience on the Central Native Land Trust Board. Yet, by the standards of colonial Kenya, Wilson was regarded locally as a liberal, and this made him unpopular with a substantial and vocal body of settlers whose views were a good deal more extreme. Immediately prior to his appointment to the commission, Wilson was unsuccessful in an attempt to win election to the Legislative Council.[7]

It seemed unlikely that so toothless a commission would challenge the status quo, but Kenya's settlers left nothing to chance. Besides, there was much to play for in ensuring that rights within the White Highlands were fully endorsed and that any threat that Africans might be awarded lands currently occupied by Europeans be vigorously combated. The settlers around Baringo were particularly worried that additional land grants might be made to the hard-pressed herders of the lowlands. The Land Commission considered three sets of proposals affecting the herders of lowland Baringo, and each held the prospect of land being returned to African occupancy. The first proposal was that an area of 50,000 acres of Crown Land on the Laikipia escarpment should be opened to Chamus grazing; the second, and most important, that a series of lands along the eastern and southern boundaries of Baringo should be added to the Kamasia Reserve for the use of Tugen herders; and the third, that the Uas Nkishu Maasai settled in Baringo should be removed from the district and resettled at Kilgoris, in the main Maasai Reserve. Approaching each of these proposals from the premiss that the Baringo lowlands were overcrowded, the commissioners sought to establish the historical claims that each community could make for the award of additional lands. The history of settlement and occupancy was therefore to be a key issue in the debate.[8]

When the commissioners assembled at Nakuru on the morning of 26 August 1932 to hear their first evidence relating to the northern Rift Valley

---

[7] Breen, 'Politics of land', 58. Mary Gillett, *Tribute to Pioneers* (privately published, Oxford, 1986). Byrne to Cunliffe-Lister, 19 January 1932 and 1 April 1932, both PRO CO 533/416.

[8] The secretary to the commission, S.H. Fazan, played a crucial role in defining the issues to be addressed. It was he, assisted by J.G. Troughton, who drafted the initial summaries of the land claims to be addressed by the commission in each district.

they were confronted by a well-prepared and determined body of European plaintiffs from the Solai and Subukia areas. Michael Blundell, James Eames and Count di Cornegliano represented the Solai Farmers' Association, and Major Boyce delivered a memorandum from the Subukia farmers. In addition, four settlers whose lands had been subject to persistent trespass by Tugen herders gave evidence from the floor – Milton, Stanning, Dwen and Lean. Blundell vigorously led the attack, giving the commissioners his pithy (and apparently well-rehearsed) account of Baringo's history and the causes of its current problems. The Tugen had never crossed the Molo River before 1910, he claimed: 'The land at present occupied by them, adjoining the settled areas of the Solai valley was never theirs, therefore, by right of tenure.'[9] Tugen herders had turned lush pasture into desert: 'the Reserve twenty years ago contained some of the very finest grazing in this country, and at the moment you can go for miles and there is very little grazing – in fact, there is none'.[10] Overstocking had 'persisted since 1923', and what was needed was a scheme to reduce the numbers of cattle, especially female stock. If the government could provide an outlet for livestock, with compulsory purchase at a set price, then the money accumulated from the sales could be set against the costs of properly fencing the reserve boundary. Giving Tugen herders more land was no solution, argued Blundell, for they would continue to exhaust the new land as well as the old and so the problem would only get worse.[11]

Blundell's evidence set the tone for all that followed throughout the day. Settler collective memory was invoked time and again to reiterate the point that Tugen herders had destroyed the land: 'Old residents in our district can remember when the Kamasia [Tugen] Reserve was excellent grazing country and they know that the present state of affairs in that Reserve is entirely due to the large number of sheep and goats which are kept,' stated Major Boyce.[12] Henry Stanning had farmed sisal at Lomolo since 1910, and could speak from personal experience: 'When I first came down there there were a few Kamasia [Tugen] across the Molo River and a few Uasin Gishu Masai,' but these families were only allowed to the east of the Molo by permission of the District Commissioner, he claimed. At that time 'It was the finest grazing in Africa.' Since then the grazing had steadily deteriorated over the whole district: '[Y]ou could ride straight across to Ravine [in 1910]; you can't do it today, it is solid bush.'[13] The prevalence of unpalatable bushes

[9] *KLC:EM*, ii, evidence of Blundell, 1803.

[10] Ibid., 1805.

[11] *KLC:EM*, ii, 'Memoranda from the Solai Association', 1803–5. Michael Blundell emerged as a prominent political leader in the 1950s. There are two autobiographies: *So Rough a Wind: the Kenya Memoirs of Sir Michael Blundell* (London, 1964), and *A Love Affair with the Sun: a Memoir of Seventy Years in Kenya* (Nairobi, 1994). Blundell died on 1 February 1993, so did not live to see the second book in print.

[12] *KLC:EM*, ii, evidence of Boyce, 1816.

[13] *KLC:EM*, ii, evidence of Stanning, 1820.

was presented as a vivid indication of land degradation, but it was the inability to burn off the bush seasonally that caused this change. Stanning recalled that up until 1920 African herders lit grass fires on the lowlands every year, endangering his sisal stands and forcing him 'to put on large fire-guards'.[14] The practice had been deterred by the administration, and was anyway now impossible since the land was dotted with African homesteads.

Colonel A.T. Lean was also able to speak with the authority of long experience. From 1917 until January 1932 he had owned the Lake Solai Estate, a block of three farms (LO474/1, LO657 and LO658) on the eastern boundary of Baringo. Every dry season his land had been subject to heavy trespass. Trespassing cattle introduced East Coast fever among Lean's herds; in one year alone he lost 543 head of cattle to disease, the next year 157. Unable to make a success of it in the depression, the farms were now in the possession of his mortgagers, the National Bank of India. Recounting his story, Lean stressed that the same dangers confronted all of the settlers along the boundary so long as Tugen trespass was allowed to continue. Lean, like every speaker before him, urged the government to intervene to protect settler interests.[15]

Two further written memoranda, submitted two months later in response to direct enquiries from the commissioners, rammed home the central points of the settler argument. Dermot Fawcus had farmed at Solai from 1906, and from then until 1914 made annual journeys through Baringo to shoot and trade. He recalled that:

> In 1906 there were no Kamasia at all anywhere east of the Molo River. The piece of country east of the Molo river and south of Lake Hannington was not permanently inhabited by any natives, but was definitely looked upon by the Masai as their country, and was spasmodically occupied by them, particularly in wet cold weather, when they came down from the Laikipia Escarpment. They looked upon the grazing as being particularly good there at those times. They usually came down in fairly large numbers as soon as the big rains broke in March, and generally left about June, coming down again, but not in large numbers, towards the end of October and leaving in December … The Kamasia then stuck religiously to the west side of the Molo River, and their country was then in very good condition. I never saw it really short of grazing even in the dry seasons … After the Masai move in 1911, the Kamasia gradually began to drift across the Molo River, and in 1914 there were a few villages to the east of the river.[16]

Frank Baillie had also hunted on the Baringo lowlands in the early years of the century. From 1904 to 1907 he and his brother had taken annual safaris through the area to the east of the Molo. He, like Fawcus, was adamant that no Tugen had crossed the Molo by that time.[17]

[14] Ibid., 1822–3.
[15] *KLC:EM*, ii, evidence of Lean, 1824–5.
[16] *KLC:EM*, ii, Fawcus memorandum, 1827–8.
[17] *KLC:EM*, ii, Baillie memoranda, 1828–9.

The settlers along the southern boundary took their turn before the commission at Eldama Ravine on 5 September. Here the tone was much as before, but the emphasis was upon the proposal to evict the Uasin Gishu Maasai from southern Baringo. The settlers were determined that any land given to Tugen as a consequence of this move should be rigorously controlled to prevent an escalation of trespass on to neighbouring farms. Their views were strongly endorsed by Baringo's Reconditioning Officer, W.H. Langridge, who told the commissioners that the use of the Uasin Gishu Maasai areas as a holding ground for stock held the key to the rehabilitation of the entire district.[18] Along the southern boundary, as in the east, the settler strategy was to avoid the sacrifice of lands to African occupation at all costs *and* to insist upon government taking more responsibility for controlling the Tugen herders and limiting the overstocking of the lowlands.[19]

Whereas the printed evidence and memoranda of the Land Commission represent a very full embodiment of settler oral tradition – a Domesday Book and Settler's Charter all rolled into one – the papers give us a comparatively thin account of African opinion, and for Baringo the paucity of African views is especially disappointing. In part this was a product of the assumption that district officials would represent the views of Africans. In Baringo, as we shall see below, some district officials did at least seek to offer a corrective to the highly self-interested and well-coordinated interpretations put forward by settlers. But in larger part it reflects the focus of the commission upon the firmer definition of European rights. Tugen from southern Baringo were not invited to give evidence before the commission at Eldama Ravine, as might have seemed logical if accessibility and openness had been deemed to be important. Instead, six elders who had been selected through the Local Native Council, under the guidance of the District Commissioner, made the journey northwards to the district capital, Kabarnet, in the Tugen Hills. They gathered there on 30 August, along with representatives of the northern sections of Tugen, the Pokot and Il Chamus. When it came to the turn of the southern Tugen to give evidence, Cherono arap Keino, chief of the Keben location, acted as their spokesman. He briefly addressed the commissioners on the difficulties the drought and locust plague had brought to his people and asked for government assistance. Cherono arap Chepkiyen, from Lembus, was more outspoken: he complained that land had been taken from the people of Lembus, first to be given to the Uasin Gishu Maasai and then to European settlers. He admitted to having been fined for trespass many times himself, but questioned how it had come about that the Tugen could be denied access to their own lands. His father had lived beyond Kiplombe Hill, now well within the settled area, and he could recall when the Uasin Gishu Maasai had been brought down to Ravine to help the government before

[18] *KLC:EM*, ii, Langridge evidence, 1872–5.
[19] *KLC:EM*, ii, evidence of Perreau, 1849.

1900. 'I see that the government has filled up the land with strangers,' ended Chepkiyen. Cheron arap Chemchor, from Kakamor, took up the theme. His family had lived on the land now occupied by the settlers Dwen and Garland at Lomolo before sisal had been grown there to the east of the river. It was evident that the Tugen witnesses did not share the Europeans' view that they had settled upon 'empty lands'.[20]

The same point was elaborated by Perreau, the District Commissioner at Ravine, who was summoned to give evidence on 5 September. All district officers had submitted memoranda to the Commission dealing with matters of 'fact' relating to local systems of land tenure and the history of specific land claims. Before the commissioners they were asked questions about these submissions and invited to comment upon other issues that might have arisen in evidence. Perreau lost no opportunity to advocate that the Tugen had legitimate claims to additional lands. He argued that the assertions of the Solai and Subukia settlers 'were almost certainly incorrect on historical grounds'. In his view, the Tugen had grazed to the east of the Molo on a seasonal basis prior to the arrival of Europeans and had certainly occupied all the lands given up to settlement and to the Uasin Gishu Maasai to the east of Ravine. They should now be given all three blocks of land held by the Uasin Gishu Maasai, along with the adjacent Esageri block of settler farms. In addition, as many farms as possible along the Solai boundary – certainly seven and perhaps as many as ten – should be opened to the Tugen herders. But Perreau's generosity came with a condition: it was that these lands should be managed by the government as holding grounds so as to allow an extension of the programme for reconditioning the degraded parts of the reserve.[21] It was a proposal that did not satisfy African demands but effected a compromise that European settlers could accept. It was to be very close to the solution that the Land Commission would ultimately recommend.

Perreau was not the first official to have taken up the cudgel on behalf of the southern Tugen. Writing in 1929, in the worst months of the *Kiplel kowo* drought, Provincial Commissioner Crewe-Read gave a lengthy and sympathetic account of the herders' hardships, an account that was extensively quoted in the précis of the Baringo evidence before the Land Commission:

> A dispassionate enquiry into the whole question can lead to but one conclusion, and it is safe to say that any European who knows that part of the country, be he official or settler will agree to that conclusion. It is that when the present Kamasia Native Reserve was demarcated, and when the adjoining European land was alienated, sufficient thought or enquiry was not taken for the needs of the native people. The facts must be stated quite plainly – not necessarily with any bitterness or acrimony: but they must be stated or else there is a danger they may be obscured. All the good land,

[20] *KLC:EM*, ii, evidence of Tugen witnesses, 1830–32.
[21] *KLC:EM*, ii, Perreau's evidence, 1854–9.

all the water, most of the grazing, was taken for European occupation; all barren, rocky, waterless land was left for the natives.

He commented with astonishment that in the dry season of 1929 the Tugen herders adjacent to the Solai boundary had asked to buy water from the Europeans. 'The passion for alienating land for European occupation was so great' in this area that settlers found themselves in possession of land that was useless for cultivation, and which Crewe-Read claimed many of them would gladly now rid themselves of. Who was to blame for this situation? Crewe-Read was unequivocal: The fault lay not with the settlers or with the African herders, but with government:

> There is one principle which should here be affirmed before considering what solutions may be sought: It is that Government has been responsible for the mistake and that the cost, whatever it may be, of providing sufficient land and water for the natives concerned ought and must be provided by Government. It has been suggested, as an example, that the natives might buy back some of the farms; or it might be suggested that the natives should pay the cost of obtaining water. Such proposals have no justice in them.[22]

Morris Carter and his colleagues on the Land Commission were less concerned with high principles of justice than with finding a solution that would compromise neither settler political sensibilities nor the strictures of an underfunded administration. It was not their job to apportion blame to government. In concluding that the African reserves of Baringo were grossly overstocked and that measures needed to be urgently implemented to relieve the situation and to protect neighbouring European farmers from encroachment, they studiously avoided any criticism of government. On the contrary, the herders of Baringo had a responsibility to respect the rule of law; trespass was not the fault of government, it was the fault of the stock-owner. They recommended that additional lands should be made available to African herders along the Baringo borders, but that these lands should be managed by government as controlled areas, linked to a scheme for the reconditioning of pastures. The largest area would be that vacated by the removal of the Uasin Gishu Maasai, and the government should also utilize vacated farms along the Solai boundary for the same purpose. Perreau's scheme for buying up a larger group of farms was rejected, and the commissioners made it plain that no settler should be compelled to transfer his lands against his expressed wishes. It might not have been a just solution in Crewe-Read's terms, but it at least appeared to be a workable one – assuming, that was, that the degraded lowlands could be 'reconditioned'.

Before we go on in the next chapter to test that assumption with a closer look at the implementation of the reconditioning policies in the 1930s, we must first examine in more detail two of the essential premises of the recommendations made by the Land Commission. The first of these was the acceptance that lowland Baringo was 'overstocked'; the second and

[22] *KLC:EM*, ii, Secretary's précis, 1786.

related point was that African herders refused to trade in livestock. Both premisses raise awkward and revealing questions about the perspective from which European officials and settlers alike viewed African land use. Their importance lies in their continued pervasiveness in policy decisions affecting Baringo over the three decades following the Land Commission.

The overstocking debate

In all the many pages of printed evidence and commentary contained in the proceedings of the Kenya Land Commission, the question of overstocking emerges as a dominating theme. This was most especially so for areas where livestock producers were in the majority. For the Kamba districts of Machakos and Kitui, the Maasai districts of the Rift Valley, the Nandi Hills, and even the more sparsely settled regions of Turkana and the Northern Frontier Province, as well as for Baringo, the evidence of overstocking was presented in compelling terms. Many European witnesses before the commission, both settler and official, advocated schemes for destocking, some favouring the provision of market incentives, others promoting outright compulsion. They frequently drew upon South African examples to support their case, citing the Drought Commission of 1921 and the reports on the Native Economic Commission of 1930–32 at length.[23] Kenya's own Agricultural Commission, sitting under the chairmanship of Sir Daniel Hall in 1929, had also given long consideration to overstocking, the report stressing the urgency of the problem and the need for a government scheme of destocking.[24] Kenya's settlers told the same tale to the Land Commission as they had to the Agricultural Commission, lamenting the economic waste of African herders who kept unproductive animals in excessive numbers. The Chief Veterinary Officer, Major Brassey-Edwards, and his deputy, Captain Mulligan, were among many commentators who emphasized the need to realize an economic return from African-owned cattle, possibly through the establishment of a meat factory capable of dealing with lower-quality animals. They wanted the revenue from culling to be put back into the development of the pastoral lands.[25]

If African herd management was uneconomic, virtually every witness before the commission agreed that the reason lay in the irrationality of African attitudes toward the accumulation of cattle. Supposedly untroubled by the constraints of ecology and unmoved by the economic considerations

---

[23] For examples, all from *KLC:EM*, iii: 'Memorandum from the Chief Native Commissioner', 3087–91; 'Report of the Board of Agriculture on overstocking', 3091–7; 'Memo: Overstocking in Native reserves', S.H. La Fontaine, 3101–3; evidence of H.H. Brassey-Edwards (Chief Veterinary Officer), 3103–13; and memo by Brasset-Edwards & E.J. Mulligan, 'Overstocking of Native reserves and disposal of Native stock', 3114–19.

[24] *Report of the Agricultural (Hall) Commission* (Nairobi, 1929).

[25] *KLC:EM*, iii, evidence of Mulligan, 3119–26.

that would determine stock management on a European model, the African herder was portrayed as driven only by cultural beliefs and social practices. Livestock ownership, and especially cattle ownership, was equated with wealth and prestige, and was particularly important in relation to the acquisition of wives through the payment of bride-price. (In the case of southern Baringo the Land Commissioners took some convincing that bride-price was not normally paid by Tugen.) This stereotype of the African herder was given academic credibility in the mid-1920s with the publication of Herskovit's influential series of articles on 'The cattle complex' in East Africa.[26] In many ways Herskovits' merely provided a scholarly gloss on what was already a widely accepted European explanation for apparently aberrant behaviour: the accumulation of too many cattle was symptomatic of the backwardness of African society, of their adherence to 'custom' and 'tradition', of their innate conservatism. These were the views that informed European opinion, and they were repeated before the Land Commissioners time after time.

Two of the three commissioners were reputed to hold similar views themselves. As a stock farmer and resident in an area bordering African rangelands that were reputed to be even more grossly overstocked than southern Baringo, Frank Wilson took more than a passing interest in the question. It was he who wrote the parts of the commission's final report dealing with overstocking, and his enthusiasm for pursuing ideas to reduce African livestock holdings can be seen in his questioning of witnesses throughout the commission's proceedings. Rupert Hemsted was less inclined to methods amounting to coercion to bring about destocking, but he too was convinced of the need to induce a more 'economic' approach to livestock husbandry among African herders. As a District Officer in Maasailand he had frequently been frustrated in his attempts to encourage the Maasai to be more 'progressive' in their attitudes towards cattle. For Hemsted, the future economic development of rangeland areas depended upon such a change.

Their own prejudices notwithstanding, the Land Commissioners did attempt to assemble empirical evidence to demonstrate the extent of overstocking, both in general terms and in relation to specific districts. All the statistics gathered proved highly problematic, not least those relating to Baringo. At the nub of the overstocking debate was the relationship of livestock numbers to land availability and human population, but the basic statistics for such calculations were not available for very many parts of Kenya. The first reasonably reliable population census was not conducted in the colony until 1948. Up until that year all demographic estimates were drawn from tax returns, a notoriously unreliable source. Livestock numbers were counted with less regularity and certainly even less accuracy; African stock-owners were openly suspicious of any interest taken by the

[26] M.J. Herskovits, 'The cattle complex in East Africa', *American Anthropologist*, 28 (1926), 230–72, 361–88, 494–528, 633–64.

government in their livestock, and even by the 1950s government officials still found it difficult to persuade herders to cooperate with censuses.[27] Population figures before 1948 and all colonial livestock figures for southern Baringo must therefore be treated with the greatest caution. Although such figures may suggest general trends, especially where those indications can be corroborated from other kinds of evidence, there are great dangers in using them as absolutes. The many officials reporting to the Land Commission do appear to have been aware of these limitations, but that did not always stop them drawing fairly substantive and precise conclusions from highly dubious statistics. We shall try to avoid the same temptation in the discussion of the statistics for Baringo that follows.

Table 5.1 Southern Baringo, gross estimates of population and livestock numbers, selected years 1916–39

Year	Population	Tugen		Il Chamus	
		Cattle	Shoats	Cattle	Shoats
1916	25,000	84,406	382,613	9,444	22,178
1926	34,000	n/a	n/a	n/a	n/a
1930	40,000	85,370	371,408	18,464	47,715
1932	38,000	58,958	349,486	12,202	31,829
1936	30,000	29,456	188,227	5,498	27,800
1939	33,000	79,030	121,269	12,170	12,980

Sources: Statistics adapted from the following sources. For 1916: Baringo District AR, 1915-16, KNA DC/BAR11. For 1930: W.M. McKay 'Survey of Native Reserves of Baringo District', 18 November 1930, KNA PC/RVP.6A/23/1 (based upon district tax returns). For 1932: KLC:EM, ii, 1781–7. For 1936: Maher, *Soil Erosion and Land Utilization*. For 1939: Baringo District AR 1939, KNA PC/RVP.2/7/3.

Let us begin with an indication of longer-term trends. Table 5.1 shows gross estimates for Tugen and Chamus population and stock numbers for a selection of years between 1916 and 1939. It is extremely difficult to draw firm conclusions from such tables, but a few general observations can be made. The figures for 1916 are based on returns for the northern Tugen locations, that is, those administered from Kabarnet – plus an estimated figure for the southern locations based on a percentage of stock found in those locations in later years where the data provide a breakdown. Overall the southern-plains locations, those south of Lake Baringo and Kabarnet and including all of Lembus, account for approximately 70 per cent of total cattle and 55 per cent of the small-stock figure. Given what is known about the incidence and sequence of drought, we might expect to see livestock

[27] BHT/CH/9, BHT/TG/12 and BHT/TG/19. BHT/ES/2 gives the testimony of a European administrative officer involved in the collection of stock statistics in Baringo. See also Rimington (DC/Baringo) to PC/RVP, 2 April 1931, KNA PC/RVP.6A/23/1; McClure (Stock Inspector) to PC/RVP, 17 September 1936, 'An analysis of the 1936 stock census, in relation to the land and the people', KNA PC/RVP.6A/23/10.

numbers, especially cattle numbers, peaking in the mid-1920s, prior to the onset of *Kiplel kowo*. This hypothesis is supported both by the oral histories recounted by herders and the evidence offered to the Land Commission in 1932.[28] Unfortunately, no census of any kind was recorded after 1916 until 1930, by which time the figures almost certainly reflect the first phase of decline as a consequence of the severe drought of *Kiplel kowo*. European officials in Baringo during this drought suggested a mortality rate among the African herds of over 50 per cent, whilst an acceptance of the estimates given in the accounts of herders themselves would place it as high as 70 per cent.[29] Estimated livestock losses to drought in Baringo during the 1980s have been above 70 per cent, so there is no reason to dismiss the oral record as an exaggeration.[30] Therefore, even allowing for the fact that herders might offset cattle losses at this time by acquiring fresh stock through trade or exchange, it would seem reasonable to estimate a peak stocking level in 1925 of over 130,000 head of cattle.[31]

To take our hypothetical projections to the next stage, further losses of around 30 per cent between 1930 and 1932 and of 40 per cent between 1932 and 1936 might be explained as the compound results of several consecutive periods of drought and locust plague during the early 1930s. Once again, both oral and documentary evidence corroborate the broad trends shown in the figures.[32] With reduced pressure on pasture from 1936 and with more favourable environmental conditions, grazing was partially restored and the Baringo livestock levels appear to have recovered rapidly.[33] This recovery was in part achieved through very active stock trading, exchanging numbers of sheep and goats to acquire cattle, especially reproductive cows. The steady decline in the sheep and goat population between 1932 and 1939 can in large part be attributed to this pattern of exchange, as we shall discuss more fully in the next section.[34] In the mid-1930s, at the tail-end of the drought period, cattle represented only 15 per cent of Baringo's total domestic stock, whereas by 1939 the process of conversion and the rapid recovery rate of the cattle herds had raised this proportion to more than 30 per cent.[35]

---

[28] For example, BHT/TG/36 and BHT/CH/9; *KLC:EM*, ii, evidence of Tugen witnesses, 1830–32.

[29] Baringo District ARs, 1927 to 1932, KNA BAR/2 and PC/RVP.2/7/2.

[30] Homewood & Lewis, 'Impact of drought'.

[31] Leslie Brown asserts that 'disease or drought can cause 70% mortality', Pratt & Gwynne, *Rangeland Management*, 38. See also the projected herd growth rate tables given in Dahl & Hjort, *Having Herds*, 275–94.

[32] BHT/TG/34 and BHT/TG/37; Baringo District ARs, 1932 and 1934, KNA BAR/2; Langridge to PC/RVP, 30 November 1932, KNA PC/RVP.6A/ll/25.

[33] Rapid recovery of this kind is not uncommon. For examples see: Paul Spencer, 'Drought and the commitment to growth', *African Affairs*, 73 (1974), 419–27; Pratt & Gwynne, *Rangeland Management*, 34–40; Theodore Monod, *Pastoralism in Tropical Africa* (Oxford, 1975), 113–21.

[34] BHT/TG/29, BHT/TG/38 and BHT/NB/l.

[35] Baringo District AR 1936, KNA BAR/2.

However, whilst the estimated stocking levels in 1939 remained well below those pertaining prior to *Kiplel kowo*, by even the most conservative estimate human population had remained at approximately the 1926 level. As a result of the environmental traumas of the period, Baringo's Tugen and Chamus herders therefore had many fewer animals per head of population by the end of the 1930s than they had in the early 1920s. If anything, the available estimates from the period tend to underestimate their losses. In economic and nutritional terms, they had become considerably poorer. Whilst the trends implied in these figures neatly matched the chronology described in the evidence of European settlers, their implications were not seriously addressed by the Land Commission.

Throughout the lengthy proceedings of the Land Commission, over-stocking was discussed as an absolute, scientific term that could be precisely defined through relating livestock numbers to the supposed quality of the land: thus, Baringo was said to have become overstocked 'by 1922', and subsequent landscape change was interpreted as an incremental conse-quence of that continued situation.[36] This reflected the prevailing ecological models that would dominate land-use planning in Africa from the 1930s to the 1970s, mostly derived from North American research and South African reports (but later to be greatly influenced by emerging ideas about landscape change on the desert fringes of West Africa), which highlighted processes of gradual degradation in 'mismanaged' lands. The model was 'static', in the sense that it was based upon the principle that each land area had a fixed 'carrying capacity' that could be sustained by good manage-ment. This 'stable equilibrium' was desirable ecologically, and therefore the economics of land use had to be defined around it. With increased inputs and constructive management – manuring, rotational paddocking to allow extended fallows, the provision of additional water sources and so on – carrying capacity could be improved. But if the carrying capacity was exceeded, then degradation would soon be visible and, if not checked, might become irreversible. Degrading lands, like those of lowland Baringo, were widely believed to be 'deserts in the making'.[37]

The reality of erosion, of degradation and of desiccation was apparent in many African-occupied lands throughout Kenya, but the Land Commission treated each example as if it were the same as the next: short-

[36] *KLC:EM*, ii, 1781–7.

[37] R. Ward, *Deserts in the Making: A Study of the Causes and Effects of Soil Erosion* (Nairobi, 1937), provides a good example of a popular local statement on the problem. For the 'official' view, see: V.A. Beckley, *Soil Deterioration in Kenya* (Nairobi, 1930); V.A. Beckley, *Soil Erosion* (Nairobi, 1936); and the various reports of Colin Maher, including his *Soil Conservation and Land Utilisation*. Local anxieties were informed by a wider colonial literature. For example, G.C. Watson, 'Erosion and the Empire', *East African Agricultural Journal*, 1 (1936), 305–8, and H.C. Sampson, 'Soil erosion in tropical Africa', *Rhodesian Agricultural Journal*, 33 (1936), 197–205. For an analysis of these and other influences, see Anderson, 'Depression, dust bowl', 321–43.

term and long-term changes were not distinguished from one another, and too little was known about soils or pastures to make any meaningful evaluation of the likely recovery of apparently degrading landscapes. Most important of all, in the deliberations of the commission the terms 'overstocking' and 'carrying capacity', along with 'degradation' and 'desiccation' and other descriptions of specific processes, escaped from their scientific confines, and were bandied about by amateur and professional alike, often being used as an accepted and empowering jargon with which to describe the perceptions and beliefs of the speaker. 'Science' was being invoked to expose the dangers of African land husbandry and to give force to the arguments for intervention. In short, a generalized narrative of long-term, incremental decay was adopted without sufficient attention being given to the ecological specifics of each situation.[38]

This narrow and essentially politically motivated view had human as well as ecological limitations. Whilst lowland Baringo undoubtedly held too many livestock for the available land, it was doubtful whether the herding families were overstocked in terms of subsistence. We can see this more clearly if we look at estimates for household livestock holdings. Based upon calculations in 1929 from the four lowland locations of East Endorois, Pokorr, Keben and Kakamor, Crewe-Read had acknowledged that there was overstocking in terms of the sustainability of the grazing, but pointed out that the livestock then held by the Tugen herders were barely adequate to meet their subsistence requirements. He estimated an average Tugen family of five to hold stock amounting to approximately twelve head of cattle and between fifty-five and sixty goats. These figures were only marginally above the working estimates of the Kenya Department of Agriculture that a family of this size, leading a pastoralist lifestyle, augmented by the cultivation of a small amount of grain, required a herd of ten cattle and forty to fifty goats. Even by the government of the day's own standards, therefore, southern Tugen families could 'hardly be said to have more stock than they needed' for their subsistence requirements.[39] And by 1932 they held fewer stock than they had in 1929. The implication was that the African herder's apparent overexploitation of his habitat was not the product of the irrational accumulation of livestock based upon cultural bias or an adherence to primitive economics, but was driven by the fundamental necessities of household survival.

Mobility was the key feature in the African herders' survival strategies, and colonial officials tended to grossly underestimate the extent of stock movements. A clue to this error was presented to the Land Commission in

[38] Anderson, 'Depression, dust bowl', 342–3. For other examples, see Ian Scoones, 'Range management science and policy: politics, polemics and pasture in southern Africa', and William Beinart, 'Soil erosion, animals and pasture over the longer-term: environmental destruction in southern Africa', both in Leach & Mearns (eds), *Lie of the Land*, 34–53 and 54–72 respectively.

[39] *KLC:EM*, ii, 1785–7.

Table 5.2 Statistics for southern Baringo, 1932 (Perreau, KLC:EM)

Location	Population (p)	Area (a)	Cattle (c)	Shoats (s)	c/p	s/p	a/c	a/s
Lembus	2,791	40	9,705	15,414	3	5	2.5	1.5
E. Endorois	1,544	200	7,137	31,758	5	20	18	4
Pokorr	1,692	40	5,676	16,031	3	8	4.5	1.5
Keben	2,030	75	4,604	16,562	2.3	8	10	3
Kakamor	1,096	60	2,396	9,027	2	10	16	4
Kamaruswa	628	32	1,180	2,936	2	5	16	7
Emom	661	30	1,390	3,383	2	5	13	6
Chepkeror	367	20	797	7,667	2	20	16	1.75
W. Endorois	996	100	2,037	36,772	2	36	32	1.8
Total	11,804	597	34,629	139,514	3	12	11	2.5
N. Tugen	20,000		24,000	200,000	1	10	25	3
Il Chamus	2,250		12,000	30,000	5	15	15	6

c/p, cattle per population; s/p, shoats per population; a/c, acres per cow; a/s acres per shoat.

Table 5.3 Population and livestock figures for southern Baringo, 1929 (from KLC:EM, p.1785. Crewe-Read's estimates)

Location	Area (sq. mls)	Population	Cattle	Shoats
East Endorois	191	1,885	4,750	
Pokorr	86	1,759	5,510	
Keben	51	2,259	4,880	82,000
Kakamor	43	1,172	1,920	
Total	371	7,075	17,060	82,000

the disaggregated locational statistics gathered by District Commissioner Perreau. These figures, reproduced in Table 5.2, show vast differences in the size of cattle and goat herds from place to place through the lowlands in 1932. Although these estimates need to be treated with caution, they indicate that Tugen, surveyed by Crewe-Read (Table 5.3) in the southern most locations during 1929, probably owned even fewer livestock than he supposed. Disparities in the locational distribution of small stock are especially glaring in the 1932 figures. Of the estimated 139,000 sheep and goats held in the southern locations at this time, more than 25 per cent were to be found in one location, West Endorois, with a similar proportion in neighbouring East Endorois. These two locations also had the lowest density of cattle in the district, and were accordingly areas where goat herding predominated. Both had particular environmental characteristics

141

that help to explain this. West Endorois was made up of the southern portions of the Tugen Hills, a rugged and poorly watered area where few people lived and where cattle fared badly. East Endorois was notoriously dry and, although local herders knew the area to be relatively unattractive for cattle, there were several localities that were said to be especially good for goat rearing. Goat flocks were brought into these areas to breed and to fatten. But East Endorois bordered the European settled area of Solai, and it was the prospect of trespass that drew larger numbers of cattle and many 'temporary' Tugen residents into the location. Therefore, although the density of cattle was low, the holdings per herder were higher than in any other Baringo location. With such large numbers of stock in the location – five cattle and twenty sheep and goats per person – it appeared as if the Tugen of East Endorois were the wealthiest in the district. This was far from true. Many cattle 'held' by residents of East Endorois actually belonged to herders who lived in other locations; and many goat herds were brought into the location to take advantage of the perceived advantages and to lessen pressure on better cattle pastures elsewhere. With an open range across the southern lowlands, such movement was easily accomplished. Of course, locational figures for only one year can tell us little about movement of animals from one area to another, but other evidence already surveyed with regard to trespass supports the view that large numbers of livestock were regularly brought into the locations adjacent to the European-owned farmlands. Welby told the Land Commission that 'cattle from all over the district are driven down in search of grazing to any location which may be slightly better off than the others'.[40] Disparities in herd sizes between locations, and especially the distribution of goats, thus reflected currently prevailing environmental conditions rather than substantive material differences between the resident populations.

Crewe-Read's analysis of the situation in southern Baringo in 1929 was therefore close to the reality of the herder's predicament, but made the situation appear rather more rosy than it was. The conclusion to be drawn was inescapable: African herders required more, not fewer cattle: subsistence and nutritional requirements would drive the herders to restore stocking levels to those of the mid-1920s. Moreover, the predicament of achieving the maximum level of subsistence from the minimal number of animals moves the herder towards the accumulation of a higher proportion of female stock. Before around 1920, in the period when the Kipnikue age-set were *murran*, Tugen oral histories suggest that herders on the lowlands were rapidly acquiring greater numbers of cows to increase the milk production of their herds.[41] As a consequence, they achieved rapid rates of increase in herd size, particularly because there were as yet few restrictions on the utilization of pasture and water. In this situation it is quite possible

---

[40] *KLC:EM*, ii, evidence of Welby, 1787.
[41] BHT/TG/37 and BHT/TG/39.

for the total herd on the Baringo lowlands to have doubled in size in a period of no more than four or five years. This period of growth, running through the 1910s to the mid-1920s, coincided with a relatively humid climatic period, to be followed by the droughts of 1926 to the mid-1930s. The appearance of overstocking with the onset of drought was accordingly alarmingly rapid and visually dramatic. Decline had not been gradual, but had come as a crash. Degradation appeared to have set in before starvation began to reduce the herd to a more appropriate size during and after *Kiplel kowo*.[42] Stocking rates in lowland Baringo bore a closer relationship to human population numbers than to environmental limitations or cultural idiosyncrasy.

Seen in these terms, Baringo's overstocking and the degradation it caused was interpreted by the Land Commission as what we would now recognize as a classic example of the 'tragedy of the commons', to adopt Hardin's now famous phrase.[43] Communal land tenure was identified as the key determinant in herders' decisions, allowing each household to accumulate livestock beyond the capacity of the rangeland, every herder seeking to maximize resource use. Many commentators argued that if communal tenure were allowed to persist, then a reduction of livestock numbers would only bring short-term respite. The solution, strongly advanced by the Chief Native Commissioner and many others, was to move as rapidly as possible towards a system of individual tenure. Though beyond the scope of the Land Commission's specific recommendations, the inevitability of this dramatic intervention in African land use was heavily implicit in the conclusions reached with regard to Baringo (and other supposedly overstocked areas). In the words of Captain H.F. Ward, a leading settler spokesman on agricultural development, 'the present need of the native peoples ... is not for more land, but that better and more scientific use be made of the land' already in their possession.[44] It was a view strongly endorsed by the Land Commission, whose report marked the beginning of the assault upon African communal land tenure in Kenya.

Trading on 'the goat standard'

In the European critique of African land husbandry, communal land tenure was not the only evil to be purged. In any discussion of land degradation, and lowland Baringo was no exception, the goat loomed large as a principal villain. Several witnesses before the Land Commission passed comment upon the large and seemingly increasing numbers of goats to be seen in Baringo. The memorandum from the Subukia Farmers' Association

---

[42] For discussion of this, see Leslie Brown, The biology of pastoral man as a factor in conservation', *Biological Conservation*, 3 (1971), 97–8.

[43] G. Hardin, 'The tragedy of the commons', *Science*, 162 (1968), 1243.

[44] *KLC:EM*, iii, evidence of Capt. H.F. Ward, 3300.

claimed that 'the current state of affairs' in Baringo was 'entirely due to the large numbers of sheep and goats', and called for their complete eradication.[45] Frank Baillie was another who emphasized the goat as an agent of degradation: 'They do not run well together with cattle,' he claimed, '[t]he country is eaten down far too closely, and any rain simply drains off at once.'[46] The district's Reconditioning Officer was even more explicit: 'simply the chief cause of the deterioration is the overstocking of goats; I do not think the cattle matter'. Goats, he claimed, had only been seen on the lowlands in large numbers over the past ten years.[47] This apparent blossoming of Baringo's goat flocks was interpreted as an indication of environmental decay, the marker of a system of livestock production in decline. Where the wealth of Baringo's herders had once been measured in cattle, by the early 1930s prosperity was more commonly measured in goats. The currency of African pastoralism had been devalued: Baringo had slipped on to 'the goat standard'.

Here, as with so much else, it is not immediately clear that the evidence presented before the Land Commission supported the claims being made. Aggregate livestock numbers for the district as a whole showed that small-stock numbers had been remarkably stable over nearly two decades up to 1932, estimated at around 350,000 head. But this figure was hardly a reliable indicator, given the lack of proper census counts. The impression that Baringo was becoming 'a goat country' in the early 1930s might have had more to do with the relative balance between cattle and small stock. Tugen and Chamus herders typically acquired additional cattle through exchanging them for goats. Goats survived periods of drought better than did cattle. In the wake of *Kiplel kowo*, many herders who had suffered heavy cattle losses sought to speedily build up their goats herds, both as a means of improving the immediate subsistence of the household and as a longer-term strategy of 'trading up' for cattle. Livestock trading would therefore normally increase after a drought, as herders restocked. In this process, goats were the crucial medium of exchange. To the African herder, a goat herd was more than a necessity of subsistence: it was an insurance policy against a drought that killed his cattle. Between the mid-1920s and the early 1930s the proportion of goats to cattle on the southern Baringo lowlands therefore increased, as cattle died and goat herds were built up. Baringo's herders had always traded on 'the goat standard', and their apparent shift toward greater holdings of goats at this time was *relative*, not absolute.

Livestock trading held the key to recovery after drought, and goats played a crucial role in this. But the livestock trade, or to be more precise, Africans' supposed aversion to it, was also a highly contentious issue in relation to the overstocking debate. Witnesses before the Land Commission

---

[45] *KLC:EM*, ii, 1818–19.

[46] *KLC:EM*, ii, 1828.

[47] *KLC:EM*, ii, 1872–3.

could not find agreement when it came to explaining the apparent reluctance of Africans to trade their livestock. The majority, including virtually ever settler who gave evidence, trotted out the convenient shibboleth that African herders simply would not market their animals no matter what the price: irrationality and cultural values prevented them behaving in an economically sensible manner.[48] Others, including many senior officials, among them the Rift Valley Provincial Commissioner H.E. Welby, highlighted the importance of government-imposed quarantines which 'locked up' the African reserves like 'little tin-boxes', preventing the legal export of animals.[49] In truth, for much of the time most African herders could not legally sell livestock for export from their reserve even if they wanted to. Overstocking was, at least in part, the product of the policy of quarantines, Welby contested. He wanted quarantines lifted and stock routes established so that an outlet could be provided for African stock. Only then, he argued, could an effective programme of destocking be implemented, whether compulsory or voluntary. European settlers vehemently opposed this, and they were supported by the Veterinary Department whose officers defended the quarantines as the only means of preventing the spread of disease.

The efficacy of the 'tin-box' policy had in fact been debated periodically since the early 1920s, with those who wished to see the development of the African reserves arguing for a change and those wishing to protect settler dairy and beef producers seeking to maintain the status quo.[50] Even amongst the veterinarians there were those who doubted the value of quarantines without accompanying disease eradication programmes. These arguments were once again rehearsed before the Land Commissioners between August 1932 and May 1933.[51] Among the commissioners themselves there was dispute over the matter, Wilson (taking the settler 'firm line') clearly favouring the maintenance of quarantine controls and compulsory culling, even if uneconomic, while Hemsted (reflecting his administration background) supporting the need to develop markets for African stock. The argument was ultimately won by Wilson, who took responsibility for the drafting of the parts of the final report dealing with overstocking. Here, as with their recommendations on land transfers, the commissioners again came down on the side of protecting settler economic interests: the quarantines were needed, it was concluded, but steps should be taken to establish a factory for the processing of low-quality African cattle

[48] For example, *KLC:EM*, ii, comments of Stanning, Dwen and Lean, 1820–8.
[49] *KLC:EM*, iii, evidence of Welby, 3142–7.
[50] For the background to this, see Ian R.G. Spencer, 'Pastoralism and colonial policy in Kenya, 1895–1929', in Rotberg, *Imperialism, Colonialism and Hunger*, 113–40; and Philip L. Raikes, *Livestock Development and Policy in East Africa* (Uppsala, 1981), 19–22.
[51] For the most relevant comments by veterinary officers: *KLC:EM*, iii, evidence of Brassey–Edwards, 3103–14; evidence of Brassey-Edwards & Mulligan, 3114–9; evidence of Mulligan, 3119–26; evidence of McCall, 3167–74.

that might be acquired through controlled culling measures.[52] Behind this conclusion, which repeated a recommendation of the Agricultural Commission of 1929, lay the basic assumption that Africans would not willingly market livestock and that, even if they could be persuaded to do so, it would be only the poorest stock that would be offered for sale.

This was a fair reflection of the balance of European opinion in Kenya at the time, but a closer examination of Baringo's livestock economy suggests a more complex reality. Studies of livestock marketing from many parts of East Africa now show that African herders tend to market cattle irregularly, but that at times this trade can be vigorous.[53] In Baringo, widespread livestock trading by Tugen and Chamus had been an important factor in the development of their herds up to the early 1920s, and after that was a crucial element in efforts to rebuild and reconstruct herds in the wake of drought. Even before 1910, itinerant Somali livestock traders were a common sight throughout the district, as cattle bought cheaply in the north were moved south to take advantage of better prices. European settlement gave a stimulus to this trade. During the First World War the government encouraged an increase in itinerant livestock trading as a means of securing a meat supply for the military and, throughout the 1914–18 war, Somali traders supplied government buyers at Nakuru with animals, many of them bought in Baringo.[54] Alongside Somali traders, many of whom were based at Mogotio close to the Uasin Gishu Maasai Reserves, Nubian ex-government askaris from Eldama Ravine, having developed a good knowledge of Baringo's trading conditions during periods of service at government stations at Ribo, Loiminangi and Mukutan, also played a significant role in the early development of stock trading in Baringo. After 1918, Nubians retired from military service and settled in the substantial Nubian Village at Eldama Ravine greatly swelled the number of traders involved.[55]

Government quarantine regulations increasingly influenced the pattern of stock trading in Baringo from 1918. The need to control the spread of rinderpest, bovine pleuropneumonia and other cattle diseases placed an

[52] *KLC: Report*, recommendations.

[53] Raikes, *Livestock Development*, esp. 191–204, is the most comprehensive study. See also Carol Kerven, *Customary Commerce: A Historical Reassessment of Pastoral Livestock Marketing in Africa* (London, 1992). For historical discussion of the issue in eastern Africa, see E. Harrison, *The Native Cattle Problem* (Agricultural Department Pamphlet, Nairobi 1929); Bisschop, *Improvement of Livestock*; T.J. Aldington & F.A. Wilson, 'The marketing of beef in Kenya' (seminar paper, Institute of Development Studies, University of Nairobi, 1968); and Michael D. Quam, 'Cattle-marketing and pastoral conservatism: Karamoja District, Uganda, 1948–1970"; *African Studies Review*, 21 (1978), 49–71.

[54] Baringo District ARs, 1914–15 and 1918–19, KNA BAR/I; BHT/TG/38, BHT/NB/1 and BHT/SW/1; Peter Dalleo, 'The economic factor in the history of the Somali of Kenya' (unpublished seminar paper, History Department, University of Nairobi, 1972).

[55] BHT/NB/l, BHT/SW/l, BHT/TG/9 and BHT/CH/l. More generally, see Ian R.G. Spencer, 'The development of production and trade in the Reserve areas of Kenya, 1895–1929' (PhD thesis, Simon Fraser University, 1975).

almost permanent prohibition on the legal movement of cattle out of Baringo through the settler farmlands. However, the quarantines imposed did not prevent the movement of potentially diseased stock into Baringo from the north, nor did they restrict the movement of sheep or goats.[56] Handsome profits could be made from buying goats in Baringo and selling them on to areas such as Kikuyuland, where good prices were paid for meat. Alternatively, the traders could realize a greater commercial advantage through a simple but highly remunerative sequence of exchanges involving cattle and goats. To the north, the remote Pokot and Turkana districts lay distant from the immediate orbit of the Kenya economy, and here livestock could be acquired at a significantly lower cost than elsewhere. Nubian and Somali traders became 'principally employed in sending out expeditions' into these northern areas 'where piece goods and specie were exchanged for stock'.[57] It is difficult to establish the exact economics of this trade, especially where goods were bartered rather than cash being paid. But the oral evidence of both traders and herders suggests that the trade could be lucrative. Cattle could be purchased in the north for around one-third of the equivalent cost in the southern Tugen areas. During the early 1920s, a trader might purchase a heifer in Turkana for the equivalent of about 15s.[58] This animal would then be trekked south, into Baringo, where it would be exchanged for goats. Tugen, Chamus and Nubian traders are all in agreement that before 1930 a trader might expect to receive as many as thirty decent-sized goats in exchange for a single heifer. After 1930, this figure gradually decreased, falling to around twenty by 1939.[59] In the next stage of this sequence of exchanges the trader would leave Baringo with his goats, taking them to one of the several nearby goat markets in the settled areas of Rongai, Njoro, Nakuru and Subukia. At these markets the trader could expect to receive 3s. to 5s. per goat from Kikuyu traders who were purchasing meat for the butcheries of Nakuru and Nairobi. The heifer purchased for 15s. in Turkana had therefore realised perhaps over 100s.[60] Given that on each trading expedition twenty or more head of cattle would have been exchanged and that overheads, such as the wages of assistant buyers and herdboys, were low, it will be seen that profits could be considerable. By the 1930s, a few enterprising Tugen had joined the traders, some travelling north to purchase cattle in the Pokot country, others buying goats in Baringo to sell on at Kikuyu markets to the east.[61] As one elderly Nubian

[56] Occasional quarantine rules briefly halted the export of goats, such as that of 1936 when Baringo goats were suspected of transmitting rinderpest to settler-owned stock at Njoro: Murphy (DC/Baringo) to DC/Nakuru, 17 January 1936, KNA PC/RVP.6A/23/9.

[57] Baringo District AR, 1913–14, KNA BAR/1, giving an early account of this trade.

[58] BHT/NB/1 and BHT/SW/1, both of whom were retired livestock traders.

[59] BHT/NB/1, BHT/NB/2, BHT/TG/38, BHT/TG/15, BHT/CH/10, and others.

[60] BHT/NB/1, BHT/NB/2, BHT/SW/1, BHT/ES/3, BHT/CH/23, BHT/TG/41 and others. For livestock prices recorded by colonial officials, see: Baringo District AR, 1914–15, KNA BAR/1, and DC/Eldoret to PC/RVP, 8 May 1937, KNA PC/NKU/2/34/21.

[61] BHT/TG/27.

trader tactfully replied to an enquiry about the money to be made in stock trading during the interwar period:

> Profit, bwana? Yes, in all trade there must of course be some profit. For us it was enough to put a little food in our stomachs, that is all.[62]

Traders like Haji Adam Halijab had reason to be circumspect in discussing their business. Although the colonial government was keen to foster trade in the African reserves, the Somalis and Nubians who dominated the itinerant livestock trade were viewed with suspicion on several grounds. First, as 'aliens' they were distrusted by many officials, who assumed they would be likely to 'fix' the market by setting price rings against African rivals and to the disadvantage of their African customers. Secondly, the Veterinary Department worried that their unsupervised and largely unregulated activities would facilitate the spread of diseases. And, thirdly, some suspected them of conniving in the disposal of livestock stolen from European farms. The Stock Traders Licensing Ordinance, placed on the statute books in 1921, was intended to assert a greater degree of control over their activities. The law compelled every trader to purchase a licence yearly or half-yearly, at a cost of 100s. and 50s. respectively. Undesirable traders could be denied a licence at the discretion of the Provincial or District Commissioner, and any administrative officer had the right to ask for the production of the licence as proof of a trader's legality.[63] In practice, it proved very difficult for the administration to ensure that all traders were properly licensed. The traders themselves immediately exploited a loophole in the regulations by operating in groups of half a dozen or so, only one trader purchasing a licence while the others claimed to be his employees. As District Commissioner Brown commented in 1932:

> It is almost certain that an increased amount of trading without licences is going on, but it is very difficult to prove the offence against anyone, and it certainly helps the natives to get rid of their numerous sheep and goats and to obtain money for taxes.[64]

This practice rendered the statistics on the numbers of trading licences issued in Baringo virtually useless as an indicator of the extent of trading activity. It is unlikely that more than 25 per cent of the traders operating in Baringo did so under licence in any year, with the numbers of unregistered dealers probably growing during the less profitable drought years between 1929 and the mid-1930s.[65] Although the records before 1928 are incomplete, it seems that itinerant livestock trading reached a peak in

[62] BHT/NB/1.

[63] 'The Stock-Traders Licensing Ordinance', 31 December 1921, *Laws of Kenya*, Ch. 498.

[64] Baringo District AR 1932, KNA PC/RVP.2/7/2.

[65] BHT/NB/l, BHT/NB/2 and BHT/TG/37. Official notification of permits issued were published in the *Official Gazette*. For discussion of the problem, and for examples on the grounds upon which a licence might be refused, see KNA PC/RVP.6A/1/7/l and Maher, *Soil Erosion and Land Utilisation*, 41.

Baringo in the early to mid-1920s, becoming more sporadic thereafter and eventually giving way in the late 1930s to the competition of more sedentary traders based at the district's formally gazetted trading centres. Up to 1934 there were only five gazetted trading centres within the reserve boundaries, these being at Kabarnet, Sibillio, Marigat, Radad and Mukutan. In 1934, a further nineteen centres were gazetted and, although they were initially unpopular with the livestock traders, by 1940 the itinerant trade had withered away.[66]

Table 5.4 Livestock trade licensing in Baringo, 1928–35

	1928	1929	1930	1931	1932	1933	1934	1935
Annual licence, @ 100s.	31	65	24	7	1	NIL	9	NIL
Half-yearly licence, @ 50s.	10	9	44	64	52	34	15	26

The decline of itinerant trade was hastened by government design. In a deliberate attempt to foster the emergence of local African traders and to diminish the role of the Somalis, five trading centres in Baringo were specifically designated as goat markets from 1934. At these places – Tangulbei, Emining, Mukuyoni, Mugurin and Sibillio – local small-stock traders were encourage to gather to buy and sell goats. At the same time, the District Commissioner secured an informal arrangement with a group of leading traders – mostly Nubian – persuading them to insist upon a security bond from any new 'alien' trader seeking to work in the district. This initiative followed a series of complaints regarding itinerant Somali traders allegedly 'cheating and robbing' Tugen herders, and it was intended that well-established traders should act in their own interests as well as those of the government 'to keep out the undesirable Somalis'.[67] These moves naturally had the effect of favouring the Nubian trader against the Somali, the former being much closer to government through their established connections of government service. At the goat markets and by the 'bonding' system, the Nubian traders were able to cartelize trade for a few years after 1934, squeezing the Somali out whilst influencing prices to their own advantage.[68]

---

[66] Baringo District AR, 1934, KNA PC/RVP.2/7/3; KNA PC/NKU/2/34/2 gives a variety of correspondence on the applications of traders to obtain plots at gazetted trading centres. For the demise of itinerant trade, BHT/NB/2 and BHT/TG/38.

[67] Wheeler to all Farmers' Associations, 4 April 1932, KNA PC/RVP.6A/23/4; Harrison-Lowder to PC/Central Province, 12 May 1934, KNA PC/NKU/2/34/2; Baringo District AR, 1934, KNA PC/RVP.2/7/3.

[68] BHT/SW/1, BHT/TG/22 and BHT/TG/35. DC/Baringo to Welby (PC/RVP), 9 June 1934, and Welby to DC/Baringo, 13 Aug. 1935, both in KNA PC/NKU/2/34/2.

The goat also came to be common currency in the grain trade, which developed during the 1920s. Herders on the lowlands maintained close links with their Tugen kin in the hills to the west, and the exchange of goats for grain, especially during periods of drought, was an important element of these relationships. By the early 1920s these local exchanges were augmented by traders who brought milled *posho* (maize meal) into the lowlands to exchange for goats. Nubians based at Ravine were again very prominent in this trade, as were Asian shopkeepers from Eldama Ravine. With the collapse of the export market in maize during the depression of the early 1930s, several European settlers also became involved in grain trading in the lowlands.[69] These itinerant traders, both European and African, would buy *posho* from the mills around Eldama Ravine, Kampi-y-Moto and Mogotio, taking the bagged flour into the reserve by donkey caravan. These caravans varied in size, but were generally between six and twenty donkeys strong, with each animal carrying approximately 120 lb of *posho*. Routes through the district followed by these caravans were well established by 1930, with several traders operating a monthly safari that took them from Ravine to Emining, then east to Mugurin, before turning north to Maji Moto and Radad, and finally on to Marigat to supply Il Chamus. Larger caravans are reported to have continued to Kipcherere in the Tugen foothills west of Marigat and further north to Kampi-ya-Samaki and Nginyang. With two or three goats being exchanged for a sack of *posho* – depending, of course, upon the size of the goats – this trade expanded dramatically in the early 1930s, as hunger on the Tugen lowlands increased demand at a time when economic recession had made maize virtually uneconomic in any other market. With maize priced at under 4s. a sack, profits could be doubled by exchanging the maize for goats within the reserve. The grain trade is remembered as having played an important role in providing the Tugen with a food alternative during the droughts of 1926 to 1934.[70]

Hides and skins were also used to barter for grain from travelling merchants. Hides and skins remained Baringo's most consistent commodity trade up to the end of the 1930s, the extent of trade peaking in drought years.[71] But the market for Baringo hides and skins was a volatile one, with

---

[69] BHT/NB/1 and BHT/ES/3. Asian shopkeepers based at Eldama Ravine financed many of these grain caravans, most notable among them being Juma Hajee who established his own mill. Half a dozen other mills to the south of the reserve also engaged traders on this basis. The description of this trade which follows is largely based upon the testimony of BHT/TG/38, a Tugen who had worked for a well-known Nubian trader at Eldama Ravine, and BHT/SW/1, who had been personally involved in the trade since the mid-1920s. On the general position of the Asian trading community, see Ian R.G. Spencer, 'The first assault on Indian ascendancy: Indian traders in the Kenyan Reserves, 1895–1929', *African Affairs*, 80 (1981), 327–43.

[70] BHT/TG/20, BHT/TG/40 and BHT/CH/10.

[71] Native Affairs Department, AR 1937, gives figures for overall trade in Kenya's reserves, showing that hides and skins remained the most consistently valuable product throughout the 1930s, rising from K£15,896 in 1931, to K£192,590 in 1934, to K£302,459 in 1937.

prices varying enormously. In 1937, for example, the price of goatskins went from 1s. 50 cents each early in the year to as little as 20 cents by the year's close as the market was glutted.[72] Figures for the export of hides and skins were not systematically recorded, but it is clear from the scattered returns presented in Table 5.5 that the trade fluctuated dramatically from year to year. The development of a stable export market was hindered by the unwillingness of Baringo's herders to shade-dry, rather than sun-dry, the hides. Constant government badgering and the erection of several shade-drying *bandas* at the expense of the LNC in an effort to encourage improvements overlooked the fundamental point that itinerant traders, who monopolized the trade, refused to pay any premium on shade-dried skins.[73]

Table 5.5 Baringo official hides and skins exports, 1932–39

		1933	1935	1937	1938	1939
Hides (shade-dried)	} fras.	64	70	72	45	
		11,616				
Hides (sun-dried)	}		902	845	300	2,272
Skins (scores)		5,746	875	8,153	7,345	4,500

Source: These figures were presented by the Field Administration as estimates. Real totals would have been much larger. For other years overall Provincial figures are given, but with no breakdown by district. Baringo District ARs, 1933–9, KNA PC/RVP.2/7/3; 'Trading in Baringo Reserves', 1931–42, KNA PC/RVP.6A/7/16.

Whilst it is clear that there was a lively trade in livestock and livestock products, it is very difficult to specify what numbers of stock were annually exchanged within the Baringo Reserves. Government figures for sheep and goats officially leaving Baringo under export permit vary dramatically between peaks of over 80,000 head during the First World War to lows of just over 10,000 per annum during the drought of *Kiplel kowo* and *Kipkoikoio*. However, these figures include animals 'in transit' from Turkana, Pokot and Samburu, amounting to perhaps 60 or 70 per cent of the totals in some years.[74] It seems certain that the official government figures represent only a small portion of the actual export trade, and that there was a considerable amount of internal trade that never came to official notice. Willingness on the part of Tugen to market their livestock was indicated by an astonishing discovery during the rinderpest inoculations being conducted at Emining during 1936. Tugen herders had made a copy of the Veterinary Department's 'AM' branding iron, which had been widely used to brand their stock, thereby clearing them for movement out of the reserve. So extensively had this brand been used by local herders that the Veterinary Department

---

[72] Baringo District AR 1937, KNA PC/RVP.2/7/3.
[73] See papers in 'Hides and Skins, 1933–1941', KNA Min. of Agri. 4/361.
[74] For estimated figures, see Baringo District ARs for 1913–14, KNA BAR/I; for 1935, PC/RVP.2/7/3; and for 1938, KNA PC/RVP.2/7/3.

felt compelled to produce a new brand with a more distinctive mark and rebrand all inoculated stock.[75]

It is difficult to believe that the many settlers who argued before the Land Commission that African herders refused to trade in livestock were unaware of these activities. European settlers were themselves involved in stock trading in Baringo. Some took out licences to trade in the reserve, especially after 1929. Others traded covertly, purchasing a few head of stock from Nubian or Somali traders or (more commonly) dealing directly with the African herder.[76] Such purchases did not contravene the Stock Traders Licensing Ordinance, as farmers did not require a licence to trade; but they did involve the flouting of quarantine regulations – ironically, those very same regulations that were established primarily to protect European farmers from the risks of stock diseases being carried into their herds. At least one farmer at Solai owed his livelihood to the regular illegal purchase of Tugen oxen, which he then trained as plough animals for sale on to other settlers.[77]

The poverty and hardship of the depression years of the 1930s perhaps led some of the European settlers bordering Baringo to argue that government was protecting the African herder from grim economic realities. The common chorus before the Land Commission was that Tugen herders should be made to pay for the damage they caused by trespass and should be made also to pay for the development and improvement of their own lands within the reserve. Accordingly, the call for a cattle or goat tax was a popular cry.[78] This would be a sure way of making African herders reduce their livestock holdings and contribute something to the coffers of the state, it was argued. Already by 1932, what officials liked to think of as a 'progressive' tax system pertained in Kenya, with African herders generally paying higher levels of tax than did Africans living in agricultural districts, on the grounds that their cattle holdings made them wealthier. In colonial terms, tax was a payment for government services rendered, but African contributions to government coffers in Baringo in fact greatly exceeded their return throughout the interwar years. Indeed, this was a point of great frustration to the district's administrative officers. Surveying the year 1932, Perreau made some rough but revealing estimates:

> The Kamasia [Tugen] will this year have spent 18,000s. on their famine relief (a year's LNC revenue including cess of the combined Councils is

[75] Murray (Stock Inspector) to DC/Baringo, 29 January 1936, and CVO to All Officers and Staff, 19 February 1936, both in KNA PC/RVP.6A/23/9.

[76] BHT/ES/l, BHT/ES/2, BHT/ES/3, BHT/TG/29 and BHT/CH/13.

[77] BHT/ES/3, BHT/TG/21 and BHT/TG/24. The administration were aware that settlers purchased cattle directly from the reserve: Baringo District AR, 1935, KNA PC/RVP.2/7/3, giving a figure of over 600 head of cattle bought by settlers in that year; and comments on similar figures in the AR of 1936, KNA PC/RVP.2/7/3, that 'It appears common knowledge that considerably more cattle did go out.'

[78] For example, *KLC:EM*, iii, evidence of Troughton, 3137–41.

under 20,000s.), and I do consider that they have done all that can be expected of them … The Kamasia pay in revenue about 160,000s., and the only service they receive from Government are Medical and an allocation of 8,000s. from the Public Works Department for road making, and 510s. from the Agricultural Department.[79]

Tax revenue in Baringo for 1932 was, in fact, only 122,477s. but this still vastly exceeded government expediture on services. As Table 5.6 indicates, tax returns for the district were unpredictable. In the early years of colonial administration tax collection was only slowly extended over the more remote regions of Baringo and tax-avoidance was comparatively easy. A more relentless officer could well increase tax collection figures dramatically above those of a more lethargic predecessor, and this in part explains the fluctuations in collection figures. However, it is notable that the highest revenues were gathered during some of the worst years of drought between 1926 and 1934: more Africans had paid greater sums of tax at precisely the time they could least afford it.[80]

Table 5.6 Baringo District taxation revenue, 1902–36

1902–1903	2,659 Rupees	1921	40,123 Florins
1903–1904	2,424	1922	114,520 Shillings
1904–1905	3,499	1923	117,276
1905–1906	8,992	1924	107,748
1906–1907	8,804	1925	99,360
1907–1908	8,920	1926	194,916
1908–1909	8,311	1927	197,284
1909–10	9,539	1928	80,920
1910–11	12,081	1929	124,910
1911–12	11,706	1930	220,464
1912–13	9,519	1931	163,092
1913–14	19,104	1932	122,447
1914–15	23,832	1933	124,000
1915–16	30,167	1934	113,173
1916–17	n/a	1935	82,907
1917–18	35,600	1936	81,254
1918–19	46,610		
1919–20	46,920		
1920–21	64,592		

Source: Figures compiled from annual reports, and Native Affairs Department reports. But many of the early reports from Eldama Ravine are missing, and so the returns are incomplete. Up to 1925 the figures given do not include taxes collected from the southern Tugen at Eldama Ravine. Between 1917 and 1921 the taxes of the Il Chamus were not included in the returns. The figure given for 1933 is an estimate, based on the population returns, as in this year some adjustments in the administrative functions between Nakuru and Eldama Ravine led to confusion in the presentation of tax figures. The drop in tax after 1933 is partly explained by the Uas Nkishu Maasai having left the district. See also Maher, *Soil Erosion and Land Utilisation*, appendix 9.

[79] Perreau to PC/RVP. 9 May 1932, KNA PC/RVP.6A/ll/5.

[80] For comments on this, Maher, *Soil Erosion and Land Utilisation*, 73–4, and Memo. by Hyde-Clarke (DC/Baringo), 'Baringo District Rehabilitation Scheme', January 1939, KNA PC/RVP.6A/ll/23.

Table 5.7 European ideals and African realities in herd management

European ideals	African realities
1. Pasture control. Pasture should be a controlled resource, fenced wherever possible. Rotational systems of grazing should be employed to preserve pastures, and the number of livestock utilizing any area should be strictly controlled	Grazing and water were not 'owned' and although access might be mediated by negotiation it could not be denied. Seasonal movement of stock from lowland plains to higher, wetter and forested areas was disrupted by European settlement: access had been obstructed
2. Water management. Access to water must also be effectively managed. Each grazing zone must have more than one source of water to avoid the overgrazing of stock around the water source	Watering points within the lowlands were inadequate, forcing herders to congest around them and leading to the acute deterioration of pasture in the vicinity of all rivers, dams and boreholes
3. Sustainability. Stocking levels must be kept within limits that allow for the continued maintenance of pasture quality even in a year of poor rains	Prevailing stocking levels by the 1930s were not adequate to meet the subsistence requirements of a herding family. Especially in a period of drought, when there were fewer subsistence alternatives, household requirements alone compelled each herder to maintain as many animals as possible
4. Marketing. Access to a reliable marketing system is critical to provide a regular income	Marketing of cattle from Baringo was prevented by quarantine regulations imposed throughout much of the inter-war period. Baringo's herders were formally denied access to an external livestock market
5. Culling. Where commercial markets may be temporarily closed, stock should be regularly culled to preserve the carrying capacity of the land	Unless the herder requires the meat from the carcass, there is no incentive to cull. Greater security lay in maximizing cattle numbers within the limits of labour resources and, where possible, spreading risk by loaning out cattle to others

6. Breeding. The breeding standards and production qualities of the herd should be periodically reviewed, and new stock regularly introduced to ensure improvement	The herder will endeavour to improve his stock, particularly with regard to their milk-producing capacity, but he is severely constrained by environmental factors. In periods of recovery and expansion new stock was bought in from the north
7. Disease. To control the spread of disease among livestock all necessary inoculations should be undertaken, and regular dipping should be enforced	No permanent facilities existed to provide for the inoculation of African-owned stock. No Veterinary Officer was posted to Baringo until 1937
8. Economic Rationale. It is the prime aim of the stock farmer to market, and not to consume, the produce of his herds, therefore the herd will only be an indirect source of subsistence	The herd was the direct source of subsistence, supplemented by grains and vegetables grown or traded by the household. Through stock loaning animals carried a social as well as an economic value, giving potential access to other resources and building the strategies of future survival

European ideals, African realities

The impact of the Kenya Land Commission's findings upon future government policy in Baringo was to be profound. In practical terms, some lands were returned to African use. Chamus herders gained access to an area of unoccupied Crown Lands to the north of Solai, and along the Solai border two unoccupied farms were opened up to Tugen stock. Along the southern border the removal of the Uas Nkishu Maasai cleared three further blocks of land. But these areas would not be formally added to the reserves. Instead, it was proposed that they be administered as 'controlled areas' under local ordinances, so that the numbers of livestock gaining access could be regulated within the estimated carrying capacities. For Baringo's African herders, these recommendations confirmed that government had failed to recognize their claims. For the European settlers along the Baringo boundary it was a significant victory.[81] The Land Commission confirmed their security of tenure, in effect creating a 'European tribal

---

[81] *KLC: Report.*

reserve',[82] from which it was impossible to transfer lands to African use without settler consent. The longer-term implications of this were immense. No matter what their future demographic profile might be, African communities would have to make do with the land they now held. The settlers had argued that the Africans' problem was not land shortage but bad land husbandry, and the Land Commission firmly endorsed this view in its findings.

To make their case, the settlers bordering Baringo had constructed a compelling master narrative of African backwardness, ignorance and incompetence in land husbandry. Fearing that their own tenure would be challenged on political grounds, they had successfully attacked African tenure for its wasteful and uneconomic practices. Europeans were the guardians of sound land management, the defenders of future productivity and economic well-being: Africans were a threat to the very soil itself, responsible for erosion, degradation and the collapse of rural production. The model they constructed for Baringo and other pastoral areas was an ideal of intensive, commercial livestock production, in which land was managed to effect regular yields, in which markets were open and stable and in which capital was available for investment and improvement. It was not a model any African herder would have recognized as even remotely achievable. The contrast between this European ideal and the African reality is set out in Table 5.7.

The general intention of the Land Commission's recommendations was plain enough: Africans must transform their husbandry or perish. This was a charter for the imposition of 'scientific agriculture', and its main elements would be the ending of communal tenure and the reduction of African livestock holdings, by compulsion if necessary. But it was to be a revolution within limits. European settlers did not intend to modernize African production so that it could compete with their own: the 'development' of the African areas was primarily seen as ameliorative and protectionist, to allow Africans to sustain a level of productivity that would satisfy their own subsistence and thereby prevent the need for them to be given any further lands. These broad conclusions were to shape colonial policies in Baringo for the three decades following the Land Commission. Having eroded the commons of the Baringo lowlands through the alienation of lands in the early part of the century, the colonial state was now to embark upon a further erosion of the commons by challenging the very basis of communal tenure.

---

[82] The phrase is Wrigley's, 'Patterns of economic life', 260.

Six

Reconditioning the Range
The Emerging Politics of Ecology
1929–1940s

> Development programmes are in existence for all districts and are added to or modified as experience dictates, and as it is seen on what lines the inhabitants respond most readily to the efforts to promote development ... An encouraging feature is that applications are now being received from locations not yet touched for operations to be commenced there.[1]

This glowing testimony to the progressive and modernizing influences of colonial programmes for rural development was written by Kenya's Chief Native Commissioner in his annual report for the year 1934. The inspiration for these fine words and high praise came almost exclusively from Baringo District, where the administration was then engaged in an extensive and pioneering experiment in land rehabilitation. Large acreages had been closed to African herders for reseeding, and it was hoped that the reconditioned land would then permit increased numbers of livestock to be grazed without further deterioration of the quality of grazing. The capacity of an eroding land would thus not simply be restored, but enhanced. The campaign was still in its early stages, but the Chief Native Commissioner was not alone in heralding its success. The reports of the Provincial Commissioner, the Agricultural Department and other administrators all emphasized the rapid progress that was being made, avidly calculating the acres improved and the numbers of herders and livestock that would reap the benefit. The solution to Baringo's problems had, it seemed, been found, and many, like the Chief Native Commissioner, hoped soon to apply the same successful methods in other districts:

[1] Native Affairs Dept., AR 1934.

reconditioning of pasture was to be the saviour of Baringo and of Kenya's other semi-arid areas also.[2]

But these paeans of praise were to prove premature. By the end of the 1930s the attempts to rehabilitate lands in Baringo were recognized as an embarrassing failure, poorly planned, only partially implemented and perpetuated in the face of a complete lack of cooperation from the local population. Stern critics of government programmes pointed to a combination of bad science and maladministration as the causes of failure, arguing that the measures employed were woefully inadequate to meet the nature and extent of the problem. If Baringo's decay was to be halted, other, more draconian measures were needed, and such measures would inevitably be more costly. The failures of the 1930s were to give greater authority to those who wished to adopt these more interventionist policies, resulting in renewed debates from 1938 about the need for compulsory culling of African stock. This chapter will examine the history of Baringo's failed experiments between 1929 and 1940, the experience of which was to lay the basis for subsequent colonial development projects in the district.

Rhetoric & reality

The decision to embark upon a programme of land rehabilitation in Baringo was taken by Provincial Commissioner Crewe-Read in the early months of 1929, during the drought of *Kiplel kowo*. By the time the Kenya Land Commission held its hearings in Baringo three years later, the reconditioning schemes Crewe-Read had inaugurated were presented as part of the government's response to the difficulties faced by the African herder: a positive means of improving African land and land husbandry. This answer appears to have impressed the Land Commissioners, and was probably a fair reflection of how officials had by then come to view the schemes; but Crewe-Read's first priority in appointing a Reconditioning Officer had been 'to stop the encroachment onto the European farms of Tugen in search of grazing'.[3] From its outset, the reconditioning of pasture in Baringo was closely connected with the politics of the European settler community.[4] The connection only became blurred as successive District and Provincial Commissioners held up the various reconditioning projects as tangible evidence of their own efforts towards improving the welfare of the African population under their care. The reconditioning programme thus quickly came to have a dual political utility for the colonial administration. The rhetoric of Baringo's successful development programme therefore filled government reports; the reality was rather different.

[2] Hennings, *African Morning*, 94–6, sums up this optimistic view.
[3] Hyde Clarke to PC/RVP, 13 January 1939, KNA PC/RVP.6A/ll/23; Maher, *Soil Erosion and Land Utilisation*, 54–5, both making reference to correspondence from Crewe-Read.
[4] Anderson, 'Depression, dust bowl', *passim*.

Mr W.A. Langridge began his work as Baringo Reconditioning Officer in June 1930, his appointment to the post having been delayed by one year owing to his activities as Locust Officer in the destruction campaign in southern Baringo. As his job title implied, his principal task was to be the improvement of pastures in the district. No guidelines existed as to how this could be accomplished, and no written instructions appear to have been issued to Langridge.[5] Though a farmer and skilled general handyman, he had no specific training for the job. His appointment was made directly by Crewe-Read and, in keeping with that officer's habit, there was no consultation with other officials.[6] Until 1938, the post of Reconditioning Officer remained under the direct guidance of the Provincial Commissioner, which meant, in effect, that Langridge worked unsupervised and undirected. He reported annually to the Provincial Commissioner, who gladly accepted accounts as evidence of the progress made in reconditioning for that year.

In many respects, the reconditioning programme designed by Langridge was informed by the most fashionable ideas on pastureland conservation and rehabilitation then available. Working from the principle of carrying capacity, Langridge attempted to calculate rates of overstocking and to reduce herd sizes to levels that would allow for the sustainability of pastures. Like others who advocated destocking as a means of improving the condition of African lands, as was discussed in Chapter Five, Langridge accepted that the physical appearance of the Baringo lowlands in the early 1930s was the product of overstocking. His work was driven by the conviction that a reduction in stocking rates was the only means of conserving the land against exponential rates of degradation. This principle was underpinned in Kenya by the ideology of settler dominance. As we have seen, the basic premise was that Africans must make do with the land they had, a view given official sanction – if any were really needed – with the publication of the Land Commission's findings in 1934. The problem was the methods of African land use, not African land shortage. It became the central tenet of settler politics in Kenya that no land from the White Highlands should be given back to Africans. Therefore, in the words of Forbes Munro, reconditioning would offer a treatment only of the symptoms and not of the disease itself;[7] and the methods adopted by Langridge were thought to be the best treatment available.

Ideas on soil conservation also formed an important element in Langridge's programme of work, and here again his intentions appear to have been well informed by the standards of the day. While southern Africa was the inspiration for many ideas on rangeland management, North

---

[5] Maher, *Soil Erosion and Land Utilisation*, 54–5; 'Reports of Locust Officers, Kerio Province', 1929, KNA PC/RVP.6A/ll/37.

[6] Hyde-Clarke (DC/BAR) to PC/RVP, 13 January 1939, KNA PC/RVP.6A/11/23, reports these matters from a discussion with Langridge.

[7] Munro, *Colonial Rule and the Kamba*, 215.

American research and writing led the way in the field of soil conservation. As early as 1911, the United States Department of Agriculture had begun to identify the processes of soil erosion as a serious hazard on farm and rangelands and, during the 1920s, a substantial education programme had been inaugurated to inform American farmers of these dangers. In 1928, soil erosion became a national issue in the United States with the allocation of central government funds to the investigation of erosion-control measures.[8] By this time, American publications had found their way on to Agricultural Department desks throughout colonial Africa, and Agricultural Officers in South Africa and the Rhodesias, as well as Kenya, had been quick to identify similar problems of land degradation in their own areas, especially where African populations were increasing rapidly or where the compression of colonial boundaries had reduced the land available to existing populations.[9] Settler communities in Kenya, especially those neighbouring areas such as Baringo and Kitui, which had been so badly hit by drought in the years after 1925, witnessed the rapid deterioration of African lands and attributed the visible degradation to permanent processes of soil erosion. By the end of the 1920s a popular consensus had already grown up amongst many colonial officials and settler farmers alike in East Africa that the processes of erosion were most dramatic where overstocking of rangeland was occurring. As images of the North American dust bowl became more widely disseminated in the 1930s, alarmist reactions reinforced the view that steps had to be taken to prevent African husbandry practices from threatening the livelihood of European settler farmers.[10] As the 1930s moved on, Langridge's activities in Baringo therefore came to seem increasingly pertinent. And, for the Kenya administration, it was surely satisfying to be able to point to a programme of work in this area that had been inaugurated so early and was already, apparently, bringing results.[11]

Reconditioning methods employed in Baringo appeared remarkably straightforward, the aim being to reseed and restore denuded pastureland.[12]

---

[8] H.H. Bennett, *Soil Conservation* (New York, 1939), pp. vii–x; H.H. Bennett & W.R. Chapline, *Soil Erosion: A National Menace* (Washington, 1928); P. Bonnifield, *The Dust Bowl: Men, Dirt, and Depression* (Albuquerque, NM, 1979).

[9] Bennett, *Soil Conservation*, 922–7; A.M. Champion, 'Soil erosion in Africa', *Geographical Journal*, 82 (1933), 130–39; *Report of the Native Economic Commission, 1930–32* (Pretoria, 1932); G. Kay, *Changing Patterns of Settlement and Land Use in the Eastern Province of Northern Rhodesia* (Hull, 1965), 16–25.

[10] Anderson, 'Depression, dust bowl'. For southern African parallels, Beinart, 'Soil erosion, conservationism', 52–82, and Phimister, 'Discourse and the discipline', 263–75.

[11] The Kenya Arbor Society, founded at Nakuru in April 1929, acted as the most significant pressure group influencing the Department of Agriculture. The records of the Society are held in the microfilm collection of the Seeley Library, Cambridge: Redley, 'The politics of a predicament', 212–13.

[12] Similar procedures were adopted in the Kamba areas of Machakos and Kitui: Munro, *Colonial Rule and the Kamba*, pp. 215–16; Stanner, 'Kitui Kamba', 84–8; Colin Maher, *Soil Erosion and Land Utilisation in the Ukamba (Kitui) Reserve*, Parts I, II and III (Nairobi, 1937), 233.

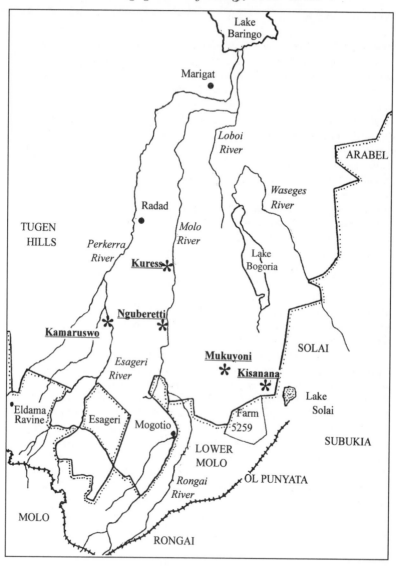

Map 6.1 Reconditioned grazing blocks, southern Baringo, 1929–39

Areas selected for this treatment were cleared of people and livestock for between eighteen and twenty-four months, this allowing enough time for planting to be completed and pasture to regenerate by the natural seeding of the grasses after two rainy seasons. In preparation for planting the land was trenched to a depth of 6 inches to prevent run-off and, before the onset of the rains, the grasses were planted by hand. The good-quality star-grasses recommended for replanted pastures were not available in the district, and so they were brought in by lorry from the neighbouring settled areas. To break the crusty cap formed on the soils throughout much of the region by sheet erosion, most reconditioned lands had to be disc-harrowed before planting. When sufficient quantities of manure were available or when this could be brought in from the settled area, it was applied to the reseeded land. Once the grass had begun to come up, thorn bushes that might have prevented grass development were cut back, and the regeneration of vegetation was allowed selectively. Finally, when the pasture had seeded naturally, the original inhabitants were permitted to return to the area, on the condition that they only grazed a restricted number of animals on the reconditioned pasture, the use of which would initially be supervised and permanently controlled through the branding of livestock.[13]

Prior to 1940, these basic methods had been applied to approximately 18,000 acres of land in the southern locations of Baringo. The six blocks of treated land all lay adjacent to roads, and most were close to the farm boundary – a group of Tugen herders at Kisanana joked that the reconditioned areas had to be near roads so that officials from Nakuru could come to inspect them without the inconvenience of having to leave their cars.[14] The 3,000-acre block in Pokorr, just to the north of Kisanana, was clearly visible from the farms above Lake Solai, while a few miles further west in the same location the Mukuyoni Reconditioned Area of more than 2,000 acres bordered on the Dwen and Stanning farms at the north end of Lomolo. A larger block of 4,000 acres lay between the Emining–Ravine and Molo–Marigat roads in Lembus location, bordering the Esageri and Ravine farms. Immediately to the north of the Lembus area, lying between the Emining–Ravine road and the Narozoia River, was the smallest of the six zones, the 1,500-acre Kamaruswo Reconditioned Area. To the west of the same river lay the Kakimor–Keben zone, some 2,500 acres in extent. Finally, further north at Kuress, in Keben location, was an area of 4,000 acres of reconditioned land.[15]

---

[13] This description is based upon the summary in Maher, *Soil Erosion and Land Utilisation*, 55–60, and the testimony of BHT/TG/60. This informant worked for over ten years with Langridge in Baringo, and later supervised controlled grazing schemes under Edmondson (District Range Officer). For further information on technical aspects of the schemes: Heady, *Range Management*, 81–5; Pratt & Gwynne, *Rangeland Management*, 121–7.

[14] DC/BAR to PC/RVP, 22 January 1940, KNA PC/RVP.6A/ll/23; BHT/TG/21 and BHT/TG/22.

[15] Maher, *Soil Erosion and Land Utilisation*, 64–9; Langridge to PC/RVP, 27 July 1936, KNA PC/RVP.6A/ll/25.

The circumstances under which reseeding and anti-erosion methods were applied in Baringo were radically different from those prevailing in North America or South Africa. In the former the education of farmers and the strict supervision of all stages of reconditioning by trained agricultural staff were considered to be essential for even small-scale projects of under 500 acres; and in the latter the sweeping powers of government assured a ready supply of labour for anti-erosion work and compulsion in the movement and destocking of herds.[16] Such measures required trained staff, adequate powers to implement policy and, above all, sufficient finance. Langridge possessed none of these essential elements.

The Reconditioning Officer occupied an anomalous position within the administration, being assigned to Baringo District and yet working under the direction of the Provincial Commissioner, not the District Commissioner. However, those Provincial Commissioners following Crewe-Read took little direct interest in Langridge's activities and, partly also as a consequence of the unspecified nature of his duties, successive officials were able to divert his energies into any number and variety of tasks that needed doing in the district from time to time. Langridge came to represent an extra pair of hands to a short-staffed and overworked district office. Having quickly become recognized as the local 'jack of all trades', the overworked but enthusiastic Langridge was at times endeavouring to single-handedly complete a series of tasks worthy of a complete district administration. With no Agricultural Officer appointed to Baringo until after 1940, Langridge established and supervised demonstration plots at Loboi and Mukuyoni and distributed loads of government seed as part of campaigns to increase agricultural production on the plains. When famine relief was delivered to Baringo, he assisted in its distribution.[17] With the outbreak of rinderpest in 1935–6, Langridge assisted with the campaign of inoculations and kept a general watch on the veterinary position in Baringo until the appointment of a regular Veterinary Officer in 1938, visiting areas where outbreaks of disease were suspected and reporting to the Veterinary Department.[18] He was also responsible for the issue of stock permits for the movement of branded cattle out of the district.[19] Finally, Langridge's duties embraced the work of a locust control officer, a function that took up virtually all of his time during the several major infestations of the early 1930s.[20]

---

[16] Bennett, *Soil Conservation,* 378–93 and 436–9; H.H. Bennett, 'Land and the Union of South Africa', *Soil Conservation Magazine,* 11 (1945) 12–14; V.G. Carter & T. Dale, *Topsoil and Civilisation* (Oklahoma, 1st edn. 1955, reprinted 1974), 249–56; Colin Maher, *A Visit to the United States to Study Soil Conservation* (Agricultural Department pamphlet, Nairobi, 1940).

[17] Langridge to PC/RVP, 30 November 1932 and 29 April 1933, both KNA PC/RVP.6A/11/25.

[18] Langridge to PC/RVP, 7 January and 12 April 1935, and 27 July 1936, all in KNA PC/RVP.6A/11/25.

[19] Welby (PC/RVP) to DC/BAR, 18 September 1935, KNA PC/RVP.6A/11/25.

[20] Langridge's 'Weekly Locust Reports, 1932', KNA PC/RVP.6A/11/9: Acting Locust

The work diary in Table 6.1, which is compiled from Langridge's reports and correspondence during March 1933, indicates his many and disparate activities in a fairly average month, when no major crises developed to divert his energies into other areas. At this time Langridge was concerned with encouraging the Tugen to cultivate larger acreages, so as to reduce their dependency upon livestock, and was distributing seed throughout the district in time for the April rains. He was also endeavouring to complete a long-standing project to construct two earth dams in the Uas Nkishu Maasai Reserve on Baringo's southern margins, in the hope that this would reduce trespass on to neighbouring European farms.[21] That Langridge was able to achieve any results at all in connection with the rehabilitation of pasture with so much else heaped upon him must be considered something of a triumph. On the other hand, it may also be taken to indicate that the colonial administration was, in practice, less committed to Baringo's reconditioning programme than the rhetoric of the annual reports would suggest.

The low level of financing provided for reconditioning work must throw further doubt upon the intentions of the colonial government. In the first year of reconditioning work, 1930, an allocation of £1,250 was made, out of which only £966 was actually spent. The balance of £284 was carried into the following year, total expenditure for 1931 amounting to £1,080. The general cutbacks in administrative expenditure in 1932 saw the reconditioning vote pegged back to £600. It remained at this annual figure until 1940. These paltry sums were the limit of the government's contribution. From 1935 onwards, the Baringo Local Native Councils were reluctantly persuaded to make annual contributions to reconditioning expenditure. With no noticeable sense of irony, it was argued that the reduction in famine-relief expenditure after 1934 had 'released' Local Native Council funds for use in reconditioning. By 1937, the Councils were meeting over 40 per cent of the total expenditure on reconditioning. Expressed as a proportion of the African hut and poll tax collected in the district each year over this period (see Table 5.6), expenditure on reconditioning in Baringo never exceeded 20 per cent of annual tax revenues. Baringo's reconditioning programme, trumpeted as a tremendous government initiative, was beginning to look more like a self-help project, and a poorly funded one at that.[22]

The greatest portion of reconditioning expenditure went towards reseeding of pasture, with smaller sums being expended on the construction of small earth dams and the establishment of experimental agricultural plots. Over the period 1930 to 1939, a total of £8,419 was spent on the

---

[20] (cont.) Control Officer to Blunt (Agri.Dept.), 11 August 1932, KNA PC/RVP.6A/11/10.

[21] This diary was submitted by Langridge in note form. Langridge to PC/RVP, 31 March 1933, KNA PC/RVP.6A/11/25. Other items of correspondence from the same file have been used to broaden out the original diary and produce the version given in Table 6.1.

[22] The figures are given in Table 6.2. For a discussion of expenditure, see Maher, *Soil Erosion and Land Utilisation*, 55, 62–3.

Table 6.1 Langridge's reconditioning work diary, March 1933

1	Travelled to Nakuru to pick up labourers' wages and returned to Mukuyoni to issue February's pay
2	At Mukuyoni. Paperwork and accounts brought up to date
3	Arranged for labourers to build fresh barrages for dams
4	Started work on barrages. Began clearing land and planting fresh seeds in the nurseries at Mukuyoni.* Visited the Uas Nkishu Maasai Reserve to inspect the dams
6/7	Moving seeds from Kampi-ya-Moto railhead to Mukuyoni
8	Delivered 13 sacks of seed to Eldama Ravine government post, for issue amongst Tugen of Lembus, Kamaruswo and Emon
9/10	Visit the Annual Nakuru Agricultural Show (with permission of PC)
11	Inspected grazing at Uas Nkishu Maasai Reserve dam, then visited the Public Works Dept. at Nakuru
12	Had to cart water to the labourers working on the barrages at the Uas Nkishu Maasai Reserve dam. Inspected new African shamba areas in Lembus, Kakamor, Kurgess, and Mukuyoni
14	Delivered seed to Maji Moto for distribution among people of East Endorois. Then delivered new tools to Loboi Agricultural Experimental Plot
15	Recruited 15 labourers, with Tribal Policeman in charge, to construct water furrow to Experimental Plot at Loboi. Marked out 3-acre plot for planting. Severe sandstorms hampered work all day
16	Supervised labour on furrow. Target of 100 ft per day to be dug
17	To Maji Moto and Mukuyoni to check on issue of seed
20	Issued seed at Eldama Ravine
21	Labour finished at first Uas Nkishu dam, so moved them to dam No. 2
22	Issued seed at Emining. Near Lower Molo saw a large herd of Tugen and Uas Nkishu cattle trespassing on a European farm. Reported to police at Kampi-ya-Moto, while picking up 8 bags of bean seed
23	Issued seed at Mukuyoni to Tugen from Keben, Kakamor, and Pokorr
24	Measured and pegged out the second dam in the Uas Nkishu Maasai Reserve
25	Picked up mail from Kampi-ya-Moto, and gave a formal statement of evidence to District Officer Sabine, at the Police Post, regarding last week's trespass incident
27	Completed seed issues in W. Lembus and W. Endorois
28/29	Started ploughing the closed area at Mukuyoni in preparation for planting grass. Several labourers employed digging holes for tree planting
30	Inspected work of new African ploughs on shambas at Kurgess
31	Inspected planting progress on 25 shambas in Lembus. Visited the Uas Nkishu Reserve dam to issue water to labourers. No rain at all this month, although there has been a good response from the natives to plant early. Bad sandstorms and high winds all month

---

* These nurseries were for experimentation with drought resistant grasses and trees: Langridge to PC/RVP, 29 April 1933, KNA PC/RVP.6A/11/25. Langridge became increasingly involved in the control of stock trespass, in 1935 being made responsible, briefly, for supervision of the Tribal Police Border Patrol: Langridge to PC/RVP, 9 November 1935, KNA PC/RVP.6A/11/25.

reconditioning of 18,000 acres of land under programmes of reseeding and controlled grazing.[23] Those surviving accounts kept by Langridge are incomplete and rather confused, so a detailed breakdown is not possible. However, fairly lengthy runs of labour returns allow us to estimate that approximately 10 to 15 per cent of the annual budget was spent on labour costs, a relatively small sum. Langridge's salary accounted for a further 665s. per month from the reconditioning vote. This, along with his transport costs and personal expenses amounted to a further 25 per cent of the total budget. The remaining monies were allocated to items such as seed, fencing and building materials, tools and other items of equipment.[24] Even if it was ultimately to have a significant impact upon the lives of many Tugen herders, this was, in every other sense, a small-scale operation run on a shoestring budget.

Table 6.2 Baringo reconditioning schemes: expenditure 1930–39

Year	Govt. votes (£)	LNC Contribution (£)	Total (£)
1930	966		966
1931	1,080		1,080
1932	600		600
1933	600		600
1934	600		600
1935	600	60	660
1936	600	73	673
1937	600	440	1,040
1938	600	500	1,100
1939	600	500	1,100
Totals	£6,846	£1,573	£8,419

Sources: KNA, Sweatman (DC/Baringo) to PC/RVP, 22 January 1940, PC/RVP.6A/11/23; C. Maher, *Soil Erosion and Land Utilisation in the Kamasia, Njemps, and East Suk Reserves* (Nairobi, 1937), Appendix 6.

The Local Native Council contribution to reconditioning was financed by a continuation of the annual cess of 1s. per person that had originally been introduced to defray the costs of famine relief. This cess had been unpopular from the outset, but many Tugen chiefs serving on the council were especially angered by its use to fund reconditioning. Langridge's reconditioning schemes were not evenly distributed throughout the district, but were concentrated in only four southern locations. The representatives of Chamus and of those Tugen living further north argued that they should not contribute to work undertaken elsewhere, whilst the the majority of chiefs in the southern locations were bitterly opposed to the schemes already

---

[23] Sweatman (DC/BAR) to PC/RVP, 22 January 1940, KNA PC/RVP.6A/11/23.

[24] KNA PC/RVP.6A/11/16 contains most of Langridge's accounts. Wages paid out to labourers came to 1,261s. in 1936, and 2,394s. in 1937.

introduced on their lands.[25] Chaired by the District Commissioner, the Local Native Council was by no means a democratic body, and this measure, like so many others in the 1930s, had been foisted upon a reluctant, impotent and, for the most part, mute council. As we shall see, their opposition to the reconditioning schemes was later to manifest itself in more direct ways.

African opposition to reconditioning work was immediately apparent in the grave difficulties experienced in recruiting labour for the work. In the early stages, during 1930 and 1931, unpaid communal labour had been raised through the chiefs and headmen, the men often coming out to work only after threats and coercion. These rough-and-ready methods were halted early in 1932, following a circular from the office of the Chief Native Commissioner, declaring the practice to be 'no longer in accordance with the ideas of modern civilisation'.[26] After this directive Langridge found it increasingly difficult to recruit any labour at all, even though he was offering a wage and *posho*. Although one or two headmen seemed able to persuade labourers to come forward, notably the formidable Cherono arap Kaino of Keben, most endeavoured to avoid Langridge's demands. The heavy nature of much of the reconditioning work and rates of pay below those offered on the farms acted as disincentives, but it is clear that opposition to the work itself played an important part in discouraging labour.[27] Only during periods of drought and grain scarcity, when labour quotas were tied to the issue of famine relief in 'food-for-work' schemes, was Langridge able to secure a reasonable supply of labour.[28] Langridge found it impossible to adequately supervise the reseeding of several large areas of pasture simultaneously, and his labour problems only compounded these difficulties. The only permanent staff he employed were a group of about a dozen local Tugen, who had been taught the basics of the reconditioning process as they worked alongside Langridge. Their training was rudimentary, to say the least, although Langridge had no choice but to leave these workers to supervise general reconditioning work. With such haphazard control and inadequate training of labour, reconditioning work fell well below acceptable standards. On inspecting reconditioned areas in Baringo in the later 1930s, it was commonly found that areas of trenching were inadequately constructed, that bush encroachment had been permitted and that the regeneration of the vegetation had been allowed too freely.[29]

[25] BHT/TG/18, BHT/TG/29 and BHT/TG/60.

[26] CNC, Circular No. 16, 18 March 1932, and Welby (PC/RVP) to CNC, 31 March 1932, both in KNA PC/RVP.6A/1/12/1.

[27] BHT/TG/41 and BHT/TG/60; Baringo PRB, 'New Locations and Headmen', 18 April 1934, KNA(m) BAR/13.

[28] KNA PC/RVP.6A/11/16 gives details of reconditioning labour returns for the period 1934 to 1937.

[29] BHT/TG/60 and BHT/ES/3; Maher, *Soil Erosion and Land Utilisation*, 64–70; DC/Baringo to PC/RVP, 22 January 1940, KNA PC/RVP.6A/11/23.

The provision of watering points in connection with the reconditioning work was an area where Langridge's inexperience and the poor planning of the programme became only too apparent. By the end of 1931 two bore-holes had been successfully sunk in connection with reconditioning work on the eastern boundary of Baringo, one in East Endorois and the other in Pokorr. It was hoped that this watersupply would ease the level of stock trespass in the Solai, Subukia and Lomolo settled areas, but difficulties with maintaining the pumps in good working order restricted their value.[30] The holes were too deep to be efficiently operated by hand-pump and, even with the installation of oxen at both pumps in 1936 their supply could not meet demand.[31] With over 1,300 head of cattle estimated to be grazing in Pokorr at the start of the 1936 dry season, requiring approximately 7,500 gallons of water per day, the capacity of the pump, calculated at 6,000 gallons for a ten-hour working day operating at a maximum stroke, could not cope. The requirements of the human population for drinking-water added still further to this deficiency. The pump was grossly overworked and eventually suffered mechanical damage as a consequence. It took several months to obtain and fit a replacement part, during which time no water was available.[32]

In other respects also, the boreholes can be seen to have created greater problems than they solved. Far from easing trespass on neighbouring farms, it was soon realized that the pumps attracted greater numbers of livestock than ever before into the area, placing local grazing resources under even greater pressure and resulting in vastly increased trespass on neighbouring farms. Later efforts to establish boreholes in East Lembus and at Nguberetti, further back from the farm boundary, were even less of a success, supplies at both being intermittent and insufficient to meet even the estimated requirements of locally resident herders.[33] Wherever boreholes were constructed, more cattle were drawn in and local overgrazing was seen to increase. As an alternative to the expensive construction of boreholes, from 1933 Langridge embarked upon a programme of earth-dam construction. Similar problems developed around the dams. Seven dams were completed by 1940, three in Pokorr, one at Noiwe, one at Kabimoi and two in the Uas Nkishu Maasai area. Each attracted over 1,000 head of cattle to them during the dry season, more than three times their intended maximum capacity. Grazing within a 3- or 4-mile radius of each dam therefore became dramatically degraded by the additional numbers of livestock

---

[30] Director/PWD to PC/RVP, 17 June 1933, KNA PC/RVP.6A/11/18.

[31] Acting Executive Engineer/PWD to PC/RVP, 15 December 1936; Langridge to PC/RVP, 30 January 1937, both in KNA PC/RVP.6A/11/17.

[32] Welby to Colonial Secretary, 28 April 1931, KNA PC/RVP.6A/11/18; Welby to Executive Engineer/PWD, 16 March 1934, and Shirtlift to Director/PWD, 5 December 1936, both in KNA PC/RVP.6A/11/17.

[33] Welby to Executive Engineer/PWD, 16 March 1934, KNA PC/RVP.6A/11/17; O'Hagan (DO/Kabarnet) to DC/Baringo, 30 April 1934, KNA PC/RVP.6A/11/17.

watering at the dams each day. Lack of coordination between schemes for reseeding pasture and schemes for water provision ultimately did more harm than good, particularly where the measures enacted were inadequate to deal with prevailing numbers of livestock.[34]

The most fundamental stumbling-block in Langridge's work proved to be his utter failure to properly control the numbers of livestock readmitted to reconditioned areas. Here, as in so much else, the Reconditioning Officer was hampered by the lack of support from government and by active Tugen opposition. From 1930 to 1934 no land was provided for the relocation of livestock removed from an area to allow reseeding to take place. This meant that, while one area was being reseeded, the grazing pressure on neighbouring areas was dramatically increased. The removal of the Uas Nkishu Maasai from lands on the southern edge of the district after 1934, on the recommendation of the Land Commission, did provide an area to be used as a holding ground, but this block of land was also soon judged to be in need of rehabilitation.[35] Local settlers successfully blocked several other proposals to use unoccupied Crown Land and unoccupied farms as holding grounds.[36] Without adequate land to accommodate displaced livestock, Langridge was not able to properly control the process of reconditioning. The lists of herders and their stock holdings, compiled with the help of local headmen, were far from accurate. To avoid the threat of having ultimately to reduce livestock numbers, herders in areas scheduled for reconditioning scattered their animals amongst friends and kin throughout the reserve. Branding was introduced only toward the end of the 1930s, and then only to regulate stock readmitted to reconditioned pastures, so there was no independent means of establishing the ownership of cattle. The greatest problems emerged when cattle were to be readmitted to reconditioned lands. Langridge made his own assessment of the carrying capacity of reseeded areas. Having set the overall stocking level, the number of cattle permitted to each herder was then determined by the number of herders with a prior claim to grazing in that zone. No account was taken of household subsistence requirements; nor was any attempt made to link the use of the reconditioned land to offtake levels. Typically, each herder was restricted

---

[34] Long delays were experienced by Tugen herders waiting to water animals at these dams, and they became unpopular for this reason. BHT/TG/21; BHT/TG/60. Langridge to PC/RVP. 9 November 1935, KNA PC/RVP.6A/11/25; Maher, *Soil Erosion and Land Utilisation,* 52–3; Heady, *Range Management,* 85–7, suggests figures relating watering points to carrying capacity which emphasize the acute water problem faced in Baringo.

[35] This followed the removal of the Uas Nkishu Maasai to the Maasai Reserve, see KNA PC/RVP.6A/1/2/1 and PC/RVP.6A/15/32.

[36] *KLC:EM,* ii, in particular 'Memo. on Conditions in the Kamasia Reserve', by the Solai Farmers' Association, 1803–5; the evidence of Mr M. Blundell (Subukia Association), 1806–11; and the evidence of Langridge, 1872–6. Langridge argued for the acquisition of settler farms for African use. See also Langridge to PC/RVP, 6 August 1932, and 27 July 1936, KNA PC/RVP.6A/11/25.

to no more than ten head of cattle within the reconditioned area. All sheep and goats were banished.[37] The problem of what was to be done with the herders' small stock and his residual cattle was never confronted. Indeed, this crucial question was largely ignored. This oversight, more than any other, heralded disaster for Baringo's reconditioning schemes. Livestock not permitted back into the reconditioned areas were simply loaned out to friends and kinsmen in neighbouring parts of the district, thereby shifting the relative burden of overstocking from one area to another, without ever solving the overall problem that the programme of reconditioning had been intended to address.[38]

The attitude of individual Tugen herders towards the reconditioning schemes largely depended upon their personal success in exploiting the alternatives they offered. Most herders now reflect upon the schemes favourably, stating that the reseeding of pasture was a good thing and that 'Bwana Chemonge [Langridge] did good work.' But the same herders admit that they vigorously opposed reconditioning at the time, seeing the movement of their stock from one place to another as government inter-ference and the restricted use of pasture as the denial of their right to their own land.[39] This ambiguity may well reflect the intensity of government campaigning for land-use reform in the district since the 1930s, but it also suggests that the early reconditioning schemes introduced new divisions among Tugen herders. Under normal circumstances, although notions of common land were modified by factors such as residence and community, Tugen herders would not deny access to water or grazing to neighbours or friends, especially where these resources appeared to be abundant. Reconditioning schemes created an apparent abundance of pasture, but in circumstances that compelled the participating herder to protect the pasture from outside encroachment, rather than open it up to common use. Efforts to foster a strategy of exclusion amongst those given grazing rights on reconditioned lands were undermined by the predicament faced by participating herders who could not graze their entire herd within the reconditioned area. Whilst only a small portion of the herder's stock grazed inside the reconditioned pasture and the majority remained in the neighbouring areas of lower pasture quality, his prime aim was to obtain greater access for the rest of his herd to the reconditioned area. Therefore, although the reconditioning programme introduced the idea of exclusion, it did so in an ambiguous way: herders sought to exclude others from the improved lands, but were quite prepared to exceed the prescribed stocking limits with additional stock in their own care.[40] Later development projects

---

[37] BHT/TG/60; Langridge to PC/RVP, 15 September 1939, KNA PC/RVP.6A/11/25; Maher, *Soil Erosion and Land Utilisation*, 86–7.
[38] BHT/TG/24, BHT/TG/35 and BHT/TG/60; Hyde-Clarke, 'Baringo District Rehabili-tation Scheme', January 1939, KNA PC/RVP.6A/11/23.
[39] BHT/TG/18, BHT/TG/24 and BHT/TG/60.
[40] BHT/TG/25, BHT/TG/42 and BHT/TG/60.

in Baringo, after 1945, were to take this all much further, as we shall see in the next chapter, but Langridge's schemes did mark a first step on the path toward individual tenure and land registration.

By the later 1930s, trespass on reconditioned lands within the reserve had become as great a problem as it was on European farmlands along the Baringo border. In the midst of the reserve, where the land in question was recognized to belong to the Tugen people and was surrounded by other, less well-favoured Tugen lands, conflict of interests between those with access to the reconditioned areas and those excluded soon became apparent. Trespass was serious on each of the reconditioned areas, but let us take the Nguberetti grazing scheme in Keben as a typical example. When this area was closed in 1937, over 2,500 head of cattle were removed from the land. Once reseeding was completed some eighteen months later, it was decided that only 1,300 head were to be allowed to return. Even this much reduced figure still exceeding the estimated carrying capacity of the land after improvement, but was seen by Langridge as a fair compromise, which might be accepted by the herders.[41] With no trading outlet for livestock from the reserve and no marketing system incorporated within the reconditioning programme, the remaining 1,200 head of cattle denied readmission to Nguberetti were simply left 'in already deteriorated areas to their further detriment'.[42] At Nguberetti, as was usual elsewhere, each herder was limited to only ten head of cattle, so each herder was likely to have the majority of his herd grazing outside the reconditioned area. The incentive for participants in the Nguburetti grazing scheme to themselves trespass was therefore very high, and it was very easily accomplished.[43] Cattle exceeding the declared stocking limit and owned by participants in the scheme flooded Nguberetti soon after it was reopened. Along with these locally owned trespassing cattle came herds from other parts of Keben and also from Endorois and Kakamor. Competition for access to Nguberetti became acute, and conflict flared between various groups of herders, with herders resident in Keben increasingly striving to preserve Nguburetti for their own use. These strategies of exclusion were already creating a great deal of ill-feeling and strife among southern Tugen communities by the end of the 1930s.[44] Where trespass was comparatively easy, as apparently at Nguberetti, it was more difficult to exclude other herders and conflict was likely to be more pronounced. R.O. Hennings, a District Officer, gave this account of a tour of inspection of Nguberetti grazing scheme, conducted during the late 1930s:

> I found that a large part of the work to be done concerned grazing control…
> There was a flush of new grass after a few local showers, but elsewhere there

[41] Maher, *Soil Erosion and Land Utilisation*, 64.

[42] Hyde-Clarke, 'Baringo District Rehabilitation Scheme', January 1939, and Sweatman to PC/RVP, 22 January 1940, both in KNA PC/RVP.6A/11/23.

[43] BHT/TG/19, BHT/TG/26 and BHT/TG/60.

[44] BHT/TG/24, BHT/TG/28, BHT/TG/60 and BHT/ES/3.

had been little rain, and the grass was already short; which was the reason for the large number of convictions for bringing cattle into the closed area without permission. I was particularly concerned to check each herd of cattle that we saw, to see whether they were all properly branded stock, legally entitled to be in the area. Sure enough, in the second herd we inspected there were twenty-six cattle without the requisite brand. When I enquired who they belonged to, nobody knew. This was quite usual, but it did not matter, for when the cattle were removed into police custody at the camp, the owner would turn up soon enough to claim his property and pay his fine.[45]

The administration attempted to control trespass on reconditioned areas by appointing patrols of grazing guards to supervise each one, and introduced a series of fines under local by-laws and overseen by the Native Court.[46] These guards proved even more susceptible to bribery than their counterparts employed along the farm boundary, perhaps because they were simply offered greater opportunity. By all accounts, trespass was widespread and surprisingly overt.[47] Many Tugen headmen played a prominent role in organizing trespass, allowing unrestricted access to local herders whilst threatening to report those from other locations. In this way, headmen whom Langridge set to supervise the reconditioned areas in fact became the guardians of local interests.[48] The headman's popular support was dependent upon a high degree of political duplicity; what the administration suspected as the traits of a 'bad headman' Tugen applauded as the functions of a 'good headman'.[49] During the 1930s, Chebei arap Kiburet of East Endorois location and Cherono arap Kaino of Keben location were among the more successful exploiters of their posts in this way, both being suspected of involvement in the bribery of guards to facilitate trespass by the people of their own locations. To the Tugen herder the ease of trespass was in some way seen as a necessary compensation for the drastic reduction in the official stocking levels on the reconditioned pastures.[50]

The experience of Baringo in the 1930s as we have so far described it might well have been in Harold Heady's mind as he wrote this passage, published in his guide to rangeland management in East Africa, long a classic work and much used by veterinary staff since the late 1950s:

To force a grazing scheme on to a community of Africans without control

[45] Hennings, *African Morning*, 96.
[46] Magistrates' court records do not survive from this period.
[47] BHT/TG/11, BHT/TG/12 and BHT/TG/60. Also Langridge to PC/RVP, 19 January 1937, KNA PC/RVP.6A/11/25.
[48] BHT/TG/15, BHT/TG/16 and BHT/TG/22; Langridge to PC/RVP, 16 and 25 March 1935, KNA PC/RVP.6A/11/25.
[49] Stanner, 'Kitui Kamba', 9–11, suggests a similar contrasting set of values among the Kamba. See also John Tosh, *Clan Leaders and Colonial Chiefs in Lango* (Oxford, 1978), *passim*.
[50] BHT/TG/12, BHT/TG/19, BHT/TG/37, BHT/TG/60 and BHT/ES/3; Langridge to PC/RVP, 25 March 1935, KNA PC/RVP.6A/11/25.

over their entire programme may lead to improvement within the scheme but it will undoubtedly cause damage outside it. This is because the African areas are overstocked. When the area used for the scheme is destocked to the proper stocking rate the excess animals usually go to the land not in the scheme, which is already over-used. Perhaps they appear in court later as trespass stock.[51]

Crewe-Read had initiated reconditioning primarily in an effort to reduce trespass on European farmlands and, although successive officials had been happy to present the programme of work as an important initiative in African rural development, none had troubled to seriously scrutinize the work being undertaken. Reconditioning had been proudly presented to the Land Commissioners as evidence of the progressive policy of government and had played its part in convincing them that Africans did not require additional lands if those they had could be so improved; and the activities of Langridge at least deflected some of the criticism of settlers against the administration in Baringo. For these reasons, Baringo's reconditioning schemes received a glowing press. Officials came to believe their own propaganda and, when repeated often enough, this grew into a powerful, self-perpetuating rhetoric of successful development. The reality was rather different.

Reconditioning reassessed

Despite the generally positive impression given of Langridge's successes during the early 1930s, some officers in Baringo were then already expressing their 'serious doubts' as to the longer-term impact of the reconditioning programme. District Commissioners Perreau and Brown were among these critics, but neither had been prepared to interfere in the main work of an officer who reported directly to the Provincial Commissioner. Their critical comments remained buried in the files of the district office.[52] The first full, independent review of reconditioning policy was conducted by Colin Maher, then an Agricultural Officer but soon after to be put in charge of the colony's fledgling Soil Conservation Service, who made a visit to the district early in 1937 to report on the general problems of soil erosion. Maher toured the reserve and visited each of the reseeded zones. When his very detailed report was made available, it was all too clear that things were going badly amiss. The methods of reconditioning and the failures of implementation were both savagely criticized by Maher. A second detailed survey was carried out after the appointment of Hyde-Clarke as District Commissioner in 1938, and this added weight to Maher's comments. Suspicious that Langridge's claims of success were exaggerated, Hyde-

---

[51] Heady, *Range Management,* 44–5.

[52] See Hyde-Clarke's correspondence on the question of previous reconditioning policy, in KNA PC/NKU/2/2/45.

Clarke prevailed upon the Local Native Council to fund the salary of a new Development Officer to assist Langridge. The man appointed, Kirk, was then ordered by Hyde-Clarke to compile a full report on the work at each of the reconditioned areas.[53] Kirk remained in the district only a few months before he was called away for military service on the outbreak of war, but his investigations 'revealed the futility of existing reconditioning policy'.[54] The surveys of Maher and Kirk together indicated that a major crisis was growing within the reconditioned areas, as Langridge failed to maintain control of stocking levels and failed to compensate for the gradual processes of deterioration which set in again even after rehabilitation work.[55] By 1940 the government conceded that Baringo's reconditioning programme had deteriorated into 'an alarming state of affairs'.[56]

The sequence of events at Mukuyoni Reconditioned Area was typical. Bordering on the settled area to the north of Lomolo, Mukuyoni had been closed to stock and reseeded in 1931 and 1932, but four years later Maher estimated that over one-third of the pasture was again suffering heavy sheet erosion and that gullying was evident over wide areas where the land had even the most gradual slope. This was partly attributed to the complete breakdown of grazing control in 1936 and the consequent trespass of large numbers of goats. More pertinently, the area had been heavily overgrazed in January and February of 1935, when over 3,000 head of cattle had been held there awaiting rinderpest inoculation, after a serious outbreak had threatened to spread to European stock.[57] In 1936 over 300 head of cattle were branded to graze on Mukuyoni, slightly more than the area's carrying capacity according to the Reconditioning Officer's calculations. This produced a stocking density of one beast to every 6 to 8 acres, approximately equivalent to the level that might have been found on a well-managed rotational grazing scheme on a European farm in the White Highlands. By Maher's estimate, the actual carrying capacity of the area was fewer than 150 cattle, at a stocking density of no more than one beast to every 15 acres.[58] Langridge's tendency to overstock reconditioned areas was a common theme in the reports of both Maher and Kirk.

Carrying more than 600 head of cattle in 1939, the reconditioned zone

[53] DC/Baringo to PC/RVP, 4 September 1939, enclosing minutes of the LNC meeting of 14 August 1939, where the Council agreed to the appointment of Kirk as a Development Officer, 'so that Mr. Langridge can concentrate on reconditioning work', KNA PC/RVP.6A/11/23.

[54] DC/BAR to PC/RVP, 11 November 1939, KNA PC/NKU/2/2/45.

[55] Maher, *Soil Erosion and Land Utilisation*, *passim*; DC/BAR to PC/RVP, 'Report on Reconditioning Progress in Baringo', 8 May 1939, KNA PC/RVP.6A/23/13.

[56] Sweatman (DC/BAR) to PC/RVP, 22 January 1940, KNA PC/RVP.6A/11/23.

[57] Langridge to PC/RVP, 20 August 1935, and Langridge to PC/RVP, 15 September 1936, both in KNA PC/RVP.6A/11/25.

[58] Maher, *Soil Erosion and Land Utilisation*, 64–5.

at Kuress, in Keben, was similarly overstocked. Although Maher had observed the vegetational cover to be bare in patches during his inspection in 1936, the pasture that had been closed for reseeding in 1932 and 1933 was still in fairly good condition. However, during 1938 it was decided to recondition the south-east portion for a second time due to its state of decay.[59] The situation in the neighbouring location of Pokorr was markedly worse and, by 1939, the grazing on this scheme was more degraded than before work had begun on its improvement in 1934. Trespass here had been very frequent, due to the influx of stock passing through the area *en route* to watering at the Pokorr borehole, with the result that severe overgrazing had again taken place. Control on cattle numbers here was virtually non-existent. In 1936, Langridge reported the area to be carrying 1,039 head of stock immediately after it had been reopened for 'controlled grazing'.[60] In an area of only 3,000 acres this represented one beast per 3 acres, which, in Maher's words 'could only be described as ridiculous'.[61]

The reconditioned block in Kamaruswo had only recently been reopened to cattle when Maher toured the area in early 1937, having been reseeded and rested between March 1935 and December 1936. Conditions were more favourable for the control of stock numbers here. The serious locust invasions of 1927 and 1933 had resulted in much of the pasture being eaten out and this had apparently contributed to a natural reduction in the stock population, as cattle were moved away in search of grass. Maher attributed the relatively good conditions in Kamaruswo at the time of his visit to be a consequence of these events. But by 1939, when Kirk reported, the area had experienced heavy encroachment and was said to be 'virtually indistinguishable from the surrounding untreated areas'.[62]

In another project managed by Langridge to the north of Lake Bogoria at Loboi, a water furrow had been constructed in 1932 to lead water from the Sandai River over the flat plains to restore and improve the grazing. A fodder crop of lucerne had been planted and the local farmers encouraged to experiment with a number of crops, among them cassava, beans and bananas, using water from the furrow for irrigation. Maher described conditions here as being uncharacteristically favourable, compared with the rest of the plains area. But the good progress witnessed by Maher was no longer in evidence when Kirk reported on Loboi in 1939; the scheme had fallen apart and, 'due to neglect, had largely reverted to its former barren condition'.[63]

But it was the astonishing mismanagement of the block of land formerly occupied by the Uas Nkishu Maasai, farms LO4103, LO4102 and

[59] Ibid., 69; DC/BAR to PC/RVP, 8 May 1939, KNA PC/RVP.6A/23/13.
[60] Langridge to PC/RVP, 19 January 1937, KNA PC/RVP.6A/11/25; DC/BAR to PC/RVP, 8 May 1939, KNA PC/RVP.6A/23/13.
[61] Maher, *Soil Erosion and Land Utilisation*, 60.
[62] Ibid., 68–9; DC/BAR to PC/RVP, 8 May 1939, KNA PC/RVP.6A/23/13.
[63] BHT/TG/120 and BHT/TG/121; Maher, *Soil Erosion and Land Utilisation*, 70; DC/BAR to PC/RVP, 8 May 1939, KNA PC/RVP.6A/23/13.

LO501/R, that caused greatest embarrassment to government. At the time of the Kenya Land Commission, the presence of the Uas Nkishu Maasai in southern Baringo was a glaring administrative anomaly. It was recommended that this should be solved by removing the Uas Nkishu to join other Maasai in the Maasai Native Reserve, to the south.[64] This argument was given further support by Rift Valley officials, who made a strong case for utilizing the three blocks of land comprising the Uas Nkishu Reserve as a holding ground for cattle being removed from areas in Baringo to be reconditioned.[65] Or, to put matters another way, it had proved easier to argue for the removal of the Uas Nkishu for this purpose than to fight the settlers for access to the many unoccupied farms along the reserve boundary. In 1934 and 1935, the long-standing intention to transfer the Uas Nkishu and their stock to Kilgoris in the Southern Reserve was therefore finally carried out.[66] The vacated lands were by no means lush pastures, but it was estimated in 1932 that the area could comfortably support 3,000 head of cattle.[67] The figure of 3,000 head of cattle ought, then, to have marked the maximum potential of the reconditioning programme in Baringo, in that only areas holding a total of not more than 3,000 head of cattle could be cleared for rehabilitation at any time. But Langridge found it impossible to work within this limit. When herders were to be moved into the holding ground to allow reconditioning, Langridge invariably found that they brought many more animals than he had provisionally estimated them to own. What was happening was in fact very simple; on hearing that people of an area were to be removed to allow reconditioning, friends and kinsmen from neighbouring locations would bring cattle to offload on to those who were to move to the better grazing in the holding ground.[68] This reached farcical proportions in 1937, when Langridge prepared to move Tugen sections from West Lembus into the holding ground. It had been calculated that the households involved owned no more than 3,000 head of cattle and yet, when they were moved in, Langridge discovered to his horror that they brought with them 7,463 head of cattle and 2,416 sheep. 'Something is very wrong,' reported a frustrated and bewildered Langridge:

---

[64] On Uas Nkishu attitudes to the move: BHT/TG/19, BHT/TG/43, BHT/TG/47 and BHT/TG/66; Eldama Ravine ARs 1929, 1930 and 1932, KNA PC/RVP.2/7/2. Some Uas Nkishu Maasai did leave Baringo in 1922: see Suk-Kamasia Reserve AR, 1922, KNA PC/RVP.2/2/1. For a fuller account of the history of the Uas Nkishu in Baringo, see *KLC:EM*, ii, 1794–5, and especially evidence of the Uas Nkishu Maasai, 1866–8. Also Waller, 'Interaction and identity', 243–84.

[65] *KLC:EM*, ii, evidence of Acting PC Adams, 1899–1900; evidence of Welby (PC/RVP), 1909–25; evidence of Perreau (DC/Ravine), 1849–56; evidence of Langridge, 1872–6.

[66] BHT/TG/42, BHT/TG/43 and BHT/TG/59; Rift Valley Province AR, 1935, KNA PC/RVP.2/3/1; Baringo AR, 1935, KNA PC/RVP.2/7/3. Papers on the movement of the Uas Nkishu Maasai can be found in KNA PC/RVP.6A/1/2/1 and PC/RVP.6A/15/32; Waller, 'Interaction and identity'.

[67] *KLC:EM*, ii, Secretary's précis, 1795–9.

[68] BHT/TG/24, BHT/TG/43, BHT/TG/44 and BHT/ES/3.

These people have been getting cattle and sheep from East Lembus for months in hopes of getting them in, and they are in! I can plainly see in two years the Uas Nkishu Reserve will be barren of all grazing. According to Mr. Murray's [stock] census the whole stock population of East and West Lembus and Kamaruswo is only 6,408 head of cattle. Therefore it seems we have put all the animals from 3 locations into one small area.[69]

Langridge's fears for the fate of the grazing in the holding ground if subjected to this incredible level of overstocking were completely justified. By 1939 the largest of the three blocks of the holding ground, LO4103, some 24,000 acres in size, had become so severely overgrazed that it had to be closed, awaiting reconditioning. This left a capacity for only 1,200 head of cattle in the remaining area, restricting the amount of reconditioning that could be undertaken in the reserve further still.[70]

Of the 18,000 acres the administration had proudly claimed to have reconditioned by 1939, it was admitted that only 50 per cent contained any decent grazing. These 9,000 acres had therefore cost £8,419, at a rate of just under £1 per acre.[71] The provincial budget had met part of the cost, the unfortunate herders of Baringo the rest. Who was to blame for the failures? Many of Maher and Kirk's criticisms were directed at the unfortunate Langridge and, perhaps inevitably, others seized upon the opportunity to blame the most junior officer. The Provincial Commissioner was especially keen to wash his hands of the matter, writing to the Chief Secretary:

reports on reconditioning have been based mainly on Mr. Langridge's statements and not on the personal investigation or knowledge of the Administration. Information has come to hand from time to time which aroused my suspicions that reports in regard to reconditioning were perhaps over-optimistic and that the best use was not being made of funds. I, therefore, gradually put more responsibility on the DC and instructed Mr. Langridge to consult him instead of me on a number of occasions.

Having neglected to mention the appallingly low level of funding Langridge received or to detail the numerous tasks he was encumbered with by the demands of other officers, the report went on to conclude:

it is, I fear, quite obvious that while Langridge has definitely proved that grass can be grown on sheet eroded semi-desert country, he was very definitely been dressing his windows on the knowledge that PC's have not

[69] Langridge to PC/RVP, 19 January 1937, KNA PC/RVP.6A/11/25.

[70] Sweatman to PC/RVP, 22 January 1940, KNA PC/RVP.6A/11/23; Langridge to PC/RVP, 27 July 1936 and 19 January 1937, both in KNA PC/RVP.6A/11/25. Other smaller grants of land were made to ease land pressure in southern Baringo, but all suffered a similar fate. Farm LO1168, granted to give access to the salt-lick adjacent to Lake Solai was among these, as was the Simpson farm, LO5259. *KLC:EM*, ii, 1787–9; Perreau to PC/RVP, 27 November 1931; F.W. Baillie to Commissioner of Lands and Settlement, 17 August 1932; and Perreau to PC/RVP, 19 August 1932, all in KNA PC/ERD.6A/41/6.

[71] DC/BAR to PC/RVP, 22 January 1940, KNA PC/RVP.6A/11/23.

the time to spend investigating the extent of work done in places difficult of access, and will only drive along the roads that in most cases bound the reconditioned areas.[72]

Criticism of the Reconditioning Officer was justified to some extent, and yet this should not be allowed to disguise the responsibility that must be borne by the provincial administration in Nakuru for year after year reallocating funds without reviewing progress. It had suited the government to present reconditioning as a success, not least before the Kenya Land Commission, both to placate settler complaints and to demonstrate its progressive policies to a wider constituency. Senior government officials were as guilty of window-dressing as was Langridge.[73]

Colin Maher was critical of Langridge, to be sure, but he looked to government for the solution. Lamenting 'the almost complete lack of economic or social progress, as far as can be seen during the last 40 years of British rule' in Baringo, he suggested that the administration had a clear responsibility to meet in preserving the land of the African reserves as a viable resource. He elaborated a detailed scheme that would make the reconditioning and future protection of Baringo's lands possible.[74] But this was not to be cheap: Maher advocated the expenditure in one single year of more than the administration had thus far been willing to part with over a decade. An initial outlay of over £3,000 would be required, plus recurrent expenditure of more than £7,000 per annum over a period of 20 to 30 years. Where one European officer had been employed, Maher claimed three were required, one Assistant Agricultural Officer, one Reconditioning Officer and one Stock Inspector. Below these would work an Assistant Forester, a Head Clerk, twelve Agricultural Assistants, a welter of other specialized African postings and a permanent squad of over 500 labourers.[75] Not surprisingly, Maher's recommendations were considered to be beyond the financial resources of the colony, and his proposals were quietly shelved.[76]

Maher's was not the only voice in Kenya calling for a more intensive government response to the problems of African land use. The Kenya Arbor Society, which had been founded in 1934, took up the issue with a campaign to encourage the government to seek financial support to prevent land deterioration. A booklet, *Deserts in the Making: A Study of the Causes and Effects of Soil Erosion*, authored by the Society's president, was printed in 1937, making the case for the need to urgently introduce measures for soil

---

[72] PC/RVP to Chief Secretary, June 1939, KNA PC/RVP.6A/23/13; BHT/TG/24 and BHT/TG/45.

[73] The Colonial Office would not entirely accept the innocence of the provincial administration. See MacDonald (S of S), Despatch no.810, 11 December 1939, KNA PC/RVP.6A/11/23, for an indication of London's attitude.

[74] Maher, *Soil Erosion and Land Utilisation*, 74.

[75] Ibid., 73–102.

[76] Hyde-Clarke to PC/RVP, 13 January 1939, KNA PC/RVP.6A/11/23.

conservation in Kenya.[77] That same year the Society's general meeting passed a resolution demanding sterner government action in those districts where erosion was believed to be most severe:

> This meeting considers that the speedy and complete reconditioning of the Kamba [Machakos and Kitui] and Kamasia Reserves [Baringo], and other badly eroded areas, is of vital importance to the welfare of Kenya, and it urges the Government to apply for a grant sufficient for this purpose, as it is considered that the financial resources of the Colony are inadequate to deal with it.[78]

On the same October day, the Kenya government met the challenge with the announcement that a Soil Conservation Service – with Colin Maher at its head – was to be established under the Department of Agriculture, its aim being to assist farmers in the White Highlands to protect themselves against the spread of the erosion menace.[79] Here, once again, the government had entwined the solution to the problems of African land husbandry with those of the European farmer, inevitably to the advantage of the latter.

The critique of failure in Baringo was linked to broader trends that were apparent by the later 1930s. By this time, colonial policy on African land use in Kenya was also being stirred by deeper currents,[80] emanating from far beyond the colony. It was these external pressures that would ultimately propel the government into bolder attempts to reform African husbandry. Colin Maher's fact-finding tours around Kenya's African reserves during the mid-1930s to investigate the extent of soil erosion[81] were but one indication of a trend toward broader, larger-scale programmes of intervention. Maher was already sharply aware of the potential dangers of 'the erosion menace' before his posting to Kenya. Like the majority of colonial agricultural officers employed in Africa during the 1930s, Maher had completed his training at the Imperial College of Tropical Agriculture in Trinidad.[82] Opened in 1922 and given its Royal Charter in 1926, the college quickly became recognized as an international centre for research; its postgraduate Diploma in Tropical Agriculture, involving a year spent in Cambridge followed by a year in Trinidad, was widely recognized as a highly prestigious qualification. The problems of land management in the tropical environment, including the evils of soil erosion – which were well known in the Caribbean – were the bread and butter of the Trinidad

---

[77] Ward, *Deserts in the Making*. A copy can be found in PRO CO 533/483/6. See also the *Annual Report of the Kenya Arbor Society, 1936 and 1937*, in KNA PC/RVP.6A/11/26.

[78] Kenya Arbor Society AR, 1937, PC/RVP.6A/11/26.

[79] Brooke-Popham to Ormsby-Gore, 18 September 1937, and MacDonald (S of S), Despatch no. 810, 11 October 1939, both in KNA PC/RVP.6A/11/23.

[80] The following paragraphs draw upon Anderson, 'Depression, dust bowl', *passim*.

[81] Maher, *Soil Erosion and Land Utilisation*; Maher, *Soil Erosion, Ukamba*.

[82] KNA Min of Agri. 2/274, 'Personal, C. Maher', contains detailed correspondence covering his career in Kenya.

syllabus.[83] Drawing heavily upon the wealth of research then under way through the United States Department of Agriculture's Soil Conservation Service, trainee colonial officers were made aware of the latest methods of erosion prevention and soil conservation. As Maher's generation of Trinidad graduates began to infiltrate colonial agricultural departments throughout British Africa, the technical aspects of land-use management, including soil-conservation measures, were given increasing prominence.[84]

Greater awareness of soil erosion was evident in East Africa over the 1930s as a number of research initiatives were launched to investigate local processes of land degradation. In Kenya, emphasis was initially given to the impact of excessive livestock numbers, as we have already discussed in Chapter Five, and further research findings were published in this field in the later 1930s. After 1935, Maher's work was important in forging a direct link between these concerns and contemporary scientific approaches to soil erosion.[85] In neighbouring Tanganyika, the regional Agricultural Research Station at Amani had been reopened in the 1920s, and over the next decade its research came to be focused increasingly upon the question of soil erosion. In 1932, Amani hosted a conference of soil chemists from all over East and Central Africa, and thereafter pushed ahead with work towards compiling a soil map of East Africa. Amongst other important work at Amani was research on overstocking and pasture degradation.[86] More extensive research of a similar nature was carried out in the late 1930s by staff of the Agricultural Department of Northern Rhodesia, in collaboration with the Rhodes–Livingstone Institute, giving emphasis to land-use planning models in the assessment of carrying capacities.[87] All of this activity in colonial Africa was ultimately concerned with protecting and sustaining African rural production, and so it brought together the latest scientific

---

[83] G.B. Masefield, *A History of the Colonial Agricultural Service* (Oxford, 1972), 37–43; 'Tropical Agriculture: the work of the Trinidad College', *East African Standard*, 5 April 1930.

[84] By 1948, almost half of the field staff and more than half of the technical staff of the Kenya Agricultural Department were Trinidad trained: *Colonial Office Lists, 1929 to 1948* (HMSO, London, 1929 to 1948).

[85] Alongside Maher's official reports, he also published many pamphlets and articles. Among the most important were *Peasantry or Prosperity?* (Nairobi, 1940) – a pamphlet published by the *East African Standard* – and 'The people and the land: some problems', *East African Agricultural Journal*, 7 (1942–3), pp. 63–9, 146–51.

[86] H.H. Storey, *Basic Research in Agriculture: A Brief History of Research at Amani, 1928–1947* (Nairobi, n.d. [1950?]); *Technical Conferences of the East African Dependencies: Proceedings of a Conference of East African Soil Chemists held at the Agricultural Research Station, Amani* (Nairobi, 1932), and the connected papers in PRO CO/822/47/3; G. Milne, *A Provisional Soil Map of East Africa* (Amani Institute, 1936); H.E. Hornby, 'Overstocking in Tanganyika Territory', *East African Agricultural Journal*, 1 (1935–6), 353–60; Staples, Hornby & Hornby, 'A study of the comparative effects', 62–70.

[87] C.G. Trapnell & J.M. Clothier, *The Soils, Vegetation and Agricultural Systems of North-West Rhodesia* (Lusaka, 1937). Though published much later, William Allan's *African Land Usage* also reports research from this period.

research on land degradation with governmental concerns about demographic pressure on the available land.

In the mounting climate of scientific and official concern over soil erosion in the 1930s, research in one territory tended to feed anxieties in another. Colonial research on such matters in East Africa was influenced by studies from other parts of the world.[88] The alarm triggered by images of North America's dust bowl contributed to increased government involvement in campaigns against the processes of land degradation in Australia and South Africa[89] and new investigations of desert encroachment in West Africa and overstocking in India.[90] Popular publications presented apocalyptic scenarios of fertility loss and the decline of agricultural production, Jacks and Whyte's *Rape of the Earth* being the most celebrated.[91] Even in more scholarly works, the effects of erosion were often generalized from specific cases to suggest a massive threat to the land's productivity. Several articles of this type appeared in colonial publications, which presented soil erosion as a major imperial problem, some of the most important being authored by senior colonial agricultural officers.[92]

The most influential colonial official in promoting government policies for the prevention of erosion was undoubtedly Frank Stockdale. As Agricultural Adviser to the Colonial Office, from as early as 1930 Stockdale had encouraged the view that soil erosion was an issue common to all British colonies.[93] On a tour of Kenya in 1930 he had taken particular interest in the effects of overstocking and the impact of drought.[94] As the decade wore

---

[88] For evidence of American influence: Beckley, *Soil Deterioration*, and Beckley, *Soil Erosion*. Maher was sent to the USA to study soil conservation methods in 1940: Maher, *A Visit to the United States*.

[89] For South Africa, Bennett, 'Land and the Union'; J.C. Ross, *Land Utilisation and Soil Conservation in the Union of South Africa* (Pretoria, 1947); Beinart, 'Soil erosion, conservationism'; For Australia, J.M. Holmes, *Soil Erosion in Australia and New Zealand* (Sidney, 1946); K.O. Campbell, 'The development of soil conservation programmes in Australia', *Land Economics*, 24 (1948).

[90] On West Africa, E.P. Stebbing, 'The encroaching Sahara: the threat to the West African colonies', *Geographical Journal*, 85 (1935), 506–24; B. Jones, 'Desiccation and the West African colonies', *Geographical Journal*, 91 (1938), 401–23; and L.D. Stamp, 'The southern margin of the Sahara: comments on some recent studies on the question of desiccation in West Africa', *Geographical Review*, 30 (1940), 297–300. On India, R.K. Mukerji, 'The relations between human and bovine population pressure in India', *Indian Journal of Economics*, 17 (1937).

[91] G.V. Jacks & R.O Whyte, *The Rape of the Earth: A World Survey of Soil Erosion* (London, 1939). For later works in a similar vein, see P.B. Sears, *Deserts on the March* (Norman, 1935) and Carter & Dale, *Topsoil and Civilisation*.

[92] Watson, 'Erosion and the Empire', 305–8; Sampson, 'Soil erosion in tropical Africa', 197–205; H.A. Tempany, H.A. Roddan & L. Lord, 'Soil erosion and soil conservation in the colonial empire', *Empire Forestry*, 23 (1944), 142–59.

[93] Minute by Stockdale, 29 January 1930, PRO CO 822/26/9.

[94] F.A. Stockdale, *Report on His Visit to South and East Africa, Seychelles, The Sudan, Egypt and Cyprus, 1930–31* (London, 1931).

on Stockdale became increasingly impatient with the tardiness of the Kenya administration in tackling these problems, which in his view contributed substantially to accelerating rates of soil erosion in the African reserves. Reviewing progress with soil-conservation measures in East Africa by 1937, Stockdale commented that government efforts, including Baringo's reconditioning programme, were 'about as effective as attempting to build a bridge across Sydney harbour with a Meccano set'.[95] A visit to the United States to see the devastation of the dust bowl at first hand and close contact with the work of Hugh Bennett and other leading soil conservation experts in North America[96] convinced Stockdale that the colonial state needed to be more ambitious in its measures to combat erosion and to commit greater expenditure to the cause. South Africa's greater willingness to dictate agrarian policy to African farmers also made its impression, and the damning report emanating from a visit to Kenya in 1938 by the prominent South African agrarian expert, I.B. Pole-Evans, only reinforced the view that Kenya's government was shirking its responsibilities.[97] At Stockdale's urging, the East African Governors discussed the problem of soil erosion at their conference in 1938, and he was instrumental in the papers on proposed conservation strategies later being printed in full and circulated to other colonies.[98] Stockdale was deeply committed to direct government action to enforce better land husbandry on often reluctant farmers and herders, and by the later 1930s he had convinced administrators in East Africa and officials in London that the reforms needed were certain to be profound and pervasive. Compulsion was never desirable, but it might none the less be necessary.[99]

---

[95] Minute by Stockdale, 9 June 1937, PRO CO 533/483/6.

[96] 'Notes on Soil Conservation work in America', by Sir F. Stockdale, 17 November 1937; Stockdale to J.H Reisner (US SCS), 26 October 1937, and reply 9 November 1937, all in PRO CO 533/483/7; Minute by Stockdale, 9 June 1937, PRO CO 533/483/6; Bennett to Reisner, 6 December 1937, PRO CO 533/483/8. Among Bennett's many important publications are these: H.H. Bennett & W.R. Chapline, *Soil Erosion, A National Menace* (USA Department of Agriculture, Washington, 1928); Bennett, *Soil Conservation*; H.H. Bennett & R.C. Pryor, *This Land We Defend* (New York, 1942); H.H. Bennett, *Our American Land: The Story of its Abuse and Conservation* (USA Department of Agriculture, Washington, 1946). For a biography of Bennett, W. Brink, *Big Hugh* (New York, 1951).

[97] I.B. Pole-Evans, *Report on a Visit to Kenya* (Nairobi, 1939).

[98] 'Papers concerning the conference of governors of British East Africa, June 1938', PRO CO 822/88/6, published as *Soil Erosion, Memoranda by the Governments of Uganda, Kenya and Tanganyika* (Nairobi, 1938).

[99] 'Soil conservation in the Tropics', memo. by Frank Stockdale, June 1939, PRO CO 852/249/17; Wade to Ormsby-Gore, 17 March 1937, and reply 23 June 1937; Minute by Stockwell, 9 June 1937, all in PRO CO 533/483/6; Brooke-Popham to Ormsby-Gore, 18 September 1937, and related papers, in PRO CO 533/483/7. For a more accessible statement of Stockdale's position, see F. Stockdale, 'Soil erosion in the colonial empire', *Empire Journal of Experimental Agriculture*, 5 (1937), 1–19. However, it should be noted that Stockdale was not in favour of the heavily mechanized programme of land amelioration

Compulsory culling

In Frank Stockdale's view, no progress could be made in Kenya's rural development until the livestock kept by Africans were dramatically reduced by culling. The need for a cull of African-owned livestock had been vigorously debated within Kenya over a good many years. Before the First World War there had been proposals to introduce a cattle tax in the Maasai districts, and during the war the government had investigated the possibility of establishing a meat-canning factory to dispose of the livestock.[100] The proposal resurfaced on several occasions in the 1920s, most notably in 1927, when local officials put forward a scheme for the compulsory culling of cattle in the Machakos Reserve. Although energetically supported by Governor Grigg, the idea was squashed by the Colonial Office, 'which feared Kamba unrest and favoured a more gradual approach'.[101] The need for culling was taken up with greater vigour by the Agricultural Commission of 1929, and a canning or processing plant was again mooted.[102] But the Commission's report was untimely: no commercial company had been prepared to make the investment without substantial government subsidy in the 1920s, and as the recession of the early 1930s bit deeper the likelihood of action receded still further. As we have already seen in our discussion of the overstocking debate in Chapter Five, the Land Commission revived the idea of a meat-processing and canning plant, but their pessimism about the low quality of the African-owned stock likely to be offered for sale led the Commissioners to advocate the establishment of a fertilizer factory as a more appropriate means of disposing of the surplus cattle. A proposal to build such a factory at Eldalat was consequently put up to the Colonial Development Fund and received a grant of £23,590 in 1936.[103] However, the Eldalat scheme was linked to the idea of progressively educating the African herder as to the need to rid himself of poor-quality stock, and not to any predetermined programme of culling.

Kenya's new Director of Veterinary Services, Daubney, had by then grander ambitions for the development of the colony's livestock industry. Daubney wished to see a livestock factory capable both of freezing good-quality meat from European settler producers for export and of processing

---

[99 (cont.)] followed in the United States, arguing that African lands could not carry the costs of so expensive an undertaking and that local labour should be used in constructing conservation works such as terraces and contour ridges. See Anderson, 'Depression, dust bowl', 342.

[100] See the report by Ainsworth of 26 April 1915, in PRO CO 533/154, and the memorandum by Hemsted of 30 June 1918, enclosed with Bowring to Long, 13 March 1918, PRO CO 533/194.

[101] Munro, *Colonial Rule and the Kamba*, 220, citing correspondence and minutes in PRO CO 533/372/10510.

[102] *Report of the Agricultural (Hall) Commission, passim.*

[103] Eldalat grant.

low-quality African-owned scrub stock for extracts and meal. This would serve each side of the industry without bringing them into competition with one another. In 1934, such an operation had been established in Southern Rhodesia by the Liebig's Company, and Daubney saw this as a good model for Kenya's development. He opened negotiations with Liebig's, and in June 1936 visited their Rhodesian plant himself. Before the month was out a senior representative of the Liebig's Company was in Kenya to assess the market opportunities and, by August 1936 draft terms and conditions for a proposed factory on the railway at Athi River were under discussion.[104]

The somewhat comic débâcle that ensued was to prove deeply embarrassing to Daubney and the Kenya administration, but its repercussions established the framework for the marketing of African livestock that would facilitate postwar rural development in the pastoral reserves.[105] News of the Liebig's 'opportunity' was greeted with enthusiasm in London, and the Colonial Office swiftly gave its support, even though the difficult question of importing Kenyan meat to the United Kingdom could not be easily resolved. Liebig's were given land for their factory and a ten-year lease on 10,000 acres for their holding ground, with an option on a further 10,000 acres. Government agreed to 'afford all reasonable facilities' for the movement of stock to the Athi River site, thereby committing itself to the creation of stock routes, and gave assurances that everything possible would be done to secure the supply of cattle to the factory. Liebig's estimated that they would process up to 30,000 head of cattle per annum, purchasing the stock at between 2s. 50 and 4s. per 100 lb. live weight, giving a 'fair' price of between 18s. and 30s. to the herder for an animal of 750 lb.[106] The prices were 'fair' only in the sense that Kenya's livestock trade was then in an economic slump, but Liebig's enthusiasm was largely explained by the profits they anticipated at such low prices. Daubney, later to be described by Stockdale as 'a supreme optimist',[107] was confident that Kenya could supply stock in sufficient quantities at these prices to make the factory viable, although it was evident that a marketing infrastructure would have to be hastily assembled. The grant received for the fertilizer factory at Eldalat was therefore returned to the Colonial Development Fund, and a sum of £11,400 received in its place for the development of stock routes.[108] Leaving the Kenya government to worry about supply, Liebig's set about building their factory which was ready to open early in 1938.

[104] De Wade to Ormsby-Gore, 12 September 1936, and subsequent correspondence, PRO CO 852/16/8.
[105] What follows is a brief summary of Liebig's Kenya misadventure. For the full story, see David M. Anderson, 'Uneconomic stock: the development of Kenya's livestock industry, 1918–48' (in preparation).
[106] De Wade to Ormsby-Gore, 12 September 1936, PRO CO 852/16/8.
[107] Minute by Stockdale, 21 December 1939, PRO CO 852/219/12.
[108] De Wade (Ag Gov) to Ormsby-Gore, 20 March 1937, and Ormsby-Gore to Morrison (Board of Trade), 24 July 1937, both in PRO CO 852/105/9.

It was clearly Daubney's hope that the factory would be supplied through culling campaigns mounted in the African reserves. The Rift Valley, including Baringo, the Northern Frontier Province, the Maasai districts and Machakos were all mentioned in discussions with Liebig's as likely areas of supply, and it was on the market prices prevailing in these areas that Liebig's had based their costings in 1936. However, by the time the factory was opened in 1938 the market had recovered, and Liebig's found that it was difficult to buy cattle at even double the earlier estimated prices.[109] Faced with a shortfall of supply, Liebig's threatened to close the plant and the government came under immense pressure from the settlers to assist in securing supplies through compulsory culling.[110] Although there is no evidence that Daubney favoured compulsion from the outset, he had always expected the Provincial Commissioners to support the factory by making every effort to secure cattle from the pastoral areas. Despite the fact that most of these senior officials remained opposed to compulsion, in December 1937 Daubney succeeded in pushing through a decision to mount a compulsory destocking campaign in the Machakos reserve, to the east of Nairobi.[111] Assuming this proved successful, the method could be extended to other reserves. By wooing Liebig's to Kenya, Daubney had, in effect, forced the issue of compulsory culling to a head after more than a decade of official prevarication.

The Kamba areas of Machakos and Kitui stood alongside Baringo as the most notoriously overstocked of Kenya's African reserves.[112] After several years of work on anti-erosion measures in Machakos, a 'Reconditioning Committee' was established in 1935 to oversee the closure and reseeding of pastures along the lines practised by Langridge in Baringo. Perhaps learning from Baringo's failings, the Machakos scheme made greater efforts to involve local farmers and to gain the cooperation of herders. Propaganda in favour of destocking was issued through the Reconditioning Committee, so to some extent it could be argued that the move towards a compulsory cull in Machakos was building upon work already under way. Of more significance, however, were the facts that the Machakos Reserve lay adjacent to the

[109] However, Liebig's did manage to buy some stock in southern Baringo, although the quality of these animals was very poor: Dir. of Vet. to PC/RVP, 3 August 1939, and reply 1 September 1939, KNA PC/RVP.6A/23/13.

[110] Secretariat Circular, no. 23, 20 December 1937, PRO CO 533/496/38184/3, cited in Munro, *Colonial Rule and the Kamba,* 221.

[111] Munro, ibid., cites a note of a discussion held at Government House, 21 December 1937, in KNA VET 2/10/7/1 II, deposit no. 1/23. The catalogue numbers for this series at the Kenya National Archive have subsequently been changed, and I have been unable to locate this file.

[112] The following account of the Kamba destocking is based upon Munro, *Colonial Rule and the Kamba.,* 220–2; Robert L. Tignor, 'Kamba political protest; the destocking controversy of 1938', *International Journal of African Historical Studies,* 4 (1971), 237–51; Bismarck Myrick, 'Colonial intiatives and Kamba reaction in Machakos District: the destocking issue, 1930–38', in L. Spencer (ed.), *Three Aspects of Crisis in Colonial Kenya* (Foreign and Comparative Studies Series, East Africa 21, Syracuse University, Syracuse, 1975).

Liebig's Athi River factory and that the administrative officers in the district were generally more persuaded of the need for compulsion than were their counterparts in other districts. The District Commissioner, A.N. Bailward, was instructed to draw up a scheme for destocking that would allow the animals to be sold in lots at public auction, by which means prices would be held down to a level that Liebig's could afford. To achieve this Bailward set culling quotas for each locality, based on estimated carrying capacity, and left it to the local chiefs and headmen to decide which cattle would be sacrificed to the cull. As the destocking campaign got under way, the settler press was brimming over with self-satisfied delight: Here was the culmination of more than a decade of settler pressure upon government, and once again government had been forced to concede that the settler in fact knew best.[113] The initial phase of the cull appeared to proceed well, but before the end of July the whole programme had been derailed by African protest, with 2,000 Kamba marching to Nairobi to confront the Governor and widespread refusal to cooperate with the chiefs and headmen seeking to organize the cull in the reserve. While settlers called for strong measures to force compliance, the government dallied and eventually backed down. London officials now criticized Nairobi for having been too hasty and urged a slower and less confrontational approach to the problem of overstocking; a policy of 'encouragement', rather than compulsion, should be pursued.[114] Though they did not know it, Kamba resistance had almost certainly saved Baringo's Tugen herders from a similar fate.

The problem of Liebig's supply therefore persisted. Without compulsion, Africans would not offer sufficient cattle to Liebig's buyers at the low prices they were prepared to pay. After stumbling through several more difficult months, by April 1939 supplies had all but dried up, and Liebig's took the decision to close the Athi River factory.[115] Under a barrage of settler criticism, led by the Stock Owners' Association, Daubney sought concessions that would allow the factory to reopen. With drought then affecting the Highlands, settlers offered to supply the factory with a limited number of stock from their own herds. In addition, Daubney worked hard to open up further stock routes from the north and the Rift Valley, and District Officers were instructed to redouble their propaganda efforts in Baringo and the Maasai areas. For their part, Liebig's began to buy cattle in neighbouring Tanganyika and even from Uganda. The Kenyan administration was compelled to agree to unlimited imports to secure the reopening of the factory on 15 July 1939. The government guaranteed the supply of cattle to the factory for six months

---

[113] For a sample from the *East African Standard*, see 'Destocking Sales Continue', 4 June 1938, 28; 'Auctioning Kamba Cattle', 18 June 1938, 7; 'Kenya and Export of Meat: New Chilling Factory May Pave Way', 21 June 1938, 5; 'Impression of a Destocking: Distribution rather than Destruction', 1 July 1938, 3.

[114] Munro, *Colonial Rule and the Kamba*, 226–36, provides an excellent summary of the protest.

[115] Minutes by Melville, 30 May 1939, and Williams, 30 December 1939, both PRO CO 852/219/12.

and agreed to underwrite any losses made through shortfall of supplies in that period.[116] By November, Daubney's plan to bring cattle from Samburu had been thwarted by the diagnosis of bovine pleuropneumonia among the Samburu cattle, and the factory was fast becoming totally dependent upon imported stock. A dejected Daubney attended the meeting of Provincial Commissioners on 13 November 1939, in the hope of persuading them 'that by the exercise of a little pressure' more Kenya cattle could be supplied to the factory.[117] With their fingers so recently burned in Machakos, no Provincial Commissioner was prepared to offer any assistance to Daubney.

By the end of 1939 the irony of the developing situation was becoming clear to the Liebig's management: 'The position has now developed into the ludicrous one that we have a factory in Kenya and that every animal we shall be slaughtering between now and the New Year will be coming from a neighbouring territory.'[118] Before the year was out a steady supply of cattle was entering Kenya from Tanganyika, utilizing Kenya's newly provisioned stock routes to make their way to the Athi River factory. During 1939 the market price of cattle in Tanganyika had fallen steadily, to a level at which Liebig's buyers could compete effectively with Somali and other African traders at the regular markets held in several provinces. Here, without the restrictions imposed by the disease controls that protected settler dairy and beef producers in neighbouring Kenya and without any compulsion, there was a buoyant African livestock trade, which saw more than 100,000 head of cattle sold through the official markets each year.[119] In effect, the Kenya government was now subsidizing the destocking of Tanganyika's pastoral areas. From its reopening in July 1939 until the end of the year, the Athi River factory handled 11,792 head of stock, 3,846 being imported from Tanganyika and the majority of the remainder coming from settler farms in the White Highlands. Over the next three years, the trend was accentuated: in 1940 the factory handled 58,044 cattle, 48,038 from Tanganyika; in 1941 the total increased to 86,414, of which 67,769 head came from Tanganyika; and in 1942 63,465 of the total of 77,537 head of stock processed by Liebig's were imported from Tanganyika.[120] As the absurdity of the situation unfolded, Stockdale could not hide his disappointment at the failure, but minuted for his Colonial Office colleagues that he felt 'the Kenya government did not think out the question of supply carefully enough'.[121]

---

[116] Brooke-Popham to Sec. of State, 29 August 1939, PRO CO 852/219/12. See also *East African Standard*, 'Subsidy for Liebig's Suggested', 28 April 1939; 'Plan to Help Kenyan Stock Industry', 30 June 1939; 'Liebig's Reopening', 7 July 1939.

[117] Daubney to Stockdale, 12 November 1939, PRO CO 852/219/12. Stockdale had supported Daubney throughout the whole Liebig's affair.

[118] Liebig's Manager, Nairobi, to Liebig's Oxted, England, 22 November 1939, copied in PRO CO 852/219/12.

[119] 'Cattle Walk 450 miles to Kenya', *East African Standard*, 19 December 1939.

[120] Calculated from the Athi River slaughter returns.

[121] Minute by Stockdale, 4 June 1940, PRO CO 852/288/14.

In the wake of events in Machakos and the humiliating setbacks with Liebig's, the Kenya government set up an 'Overstocking Committee' to make recommendations for a new set of policies. The committee of seven included four settler members, two of whom, Colvile and Pardoe, were appointed to represent the Stock Owners' Association. At the opening meeting, on 29 May 1939, Colvile made it clear that his Association believed compulsory culling was the only way forward; the cattle should go to Liebig's and the revenue should be used to defray the costs of providing services for the pastoral areas.[122] At the second meeting, on 15 June, he and Pardoe forced the issue again, insisting that the committee could not proceed unless it had a clear statement from government that it was prepared to compel African herders to comply with culling orders. When government refused to give any such assurance, Colvile and Pardoe promptly resigned from the committee.[123] With their departure the debate over compulsion was effectively closed. When the committee produced its interim report, in April 1941, the recommendations essentially concurred with the policies advocated by the Provincial Commissioners: formal and regular stock auctions would be established in greater numbers in the African reserves; stock routes would be opened by the Veterinary Department from these markets to give an outlet for the cattle; education, propaganda and persuasion were to be the weapons to combat overstocking; and, where culling was to be introduced, it would be done only with the cooperation of the local African authorities.[124] This was to be the basis of postwar development policy. Already, before the end of 1939, branding of cattle for census purposes had taken place in parts of southern Baringo and in Samburu, and some stock had been cull-branded and sold to Liebig's as part of this process.[125] By such gradualist methods progress would be slower, but confrontation would be avoided.

The economic changes brought by the Second World War gave those advocating gradualism grounds for optimism. In the evidence given to the Overstocking Committee by the Provincial Commissioners the price offered

[122] 'Note of a discussion of the first meeting of the Overstocking Committee', 29 May 1939, KNA CS 1/5/1.

[123] 'Overstocking Committee Circular', to all Members of Executive Council, 15 June 1939; Colvile to Ag. Chief Secretary, 23 June 1939; Pardoe to Ag. Chief Secretary, 24 June 1939, all in KNA ARC(MAWR)–3 VET–1/8.

[124] *Interim Report of a Committee Appointed to Advise as to the Steps to be Taken to Deal with the Problem of Overstocking in Order to Preserve the Future Welfare of the Native Pastoral Areas* (Nairobi, 1941). For the interim report, and related papers, see KNA ARC(MAWR)–3 VET–1/13ii. The final membership of the committee was G.M. Rennie (Chief Secretary), E.B. Hosking (Chief Native Commissioner), R. Daubney (Director of Veterinary Services), Major H.D. White, H.R. Montgomery and the redoubtable F.O.B. Wilson. The committee was terminated before producing any further report.

[125] See 'Notes of discussion at first meeting of the Overstocking Committee', 29 May 1939, KNA CS 1/5/1.

to the African herder was identified as the crucial element in determining the level of support for destocking. This was brought into sharp relief by the remarkably successful activities of the Meat Control Board, set up in Kenya after the outbreak of war to secure beef supplies for the military. In the six months between September 1941 and March 1942, the Meat Controller purchased 89,000 head of cattle from Kenya's African reserves. Over the same period Liebig's were able to secure only 1,842 head of cattle from the same areas. The crucial difference was price: Liebig's were offering only 5s. per 100 lb. weight for First Grade animals, 3s. 50 for Second Grade and 3s. for Third Grade; Meat Control paid 10s. for First Grade, 7s. for Second Grade and 4s. for Third Grade (though they rarely bought animals below the Second Grade).[126] Liebig's complained that the activities of Meat Control, supported as it was by the weight of the state, amounted to requisitioning. There was more than a grain of truth in this, and before the end of the war African opposition to the Meat Control sales was becoming apparent in some districts. The Stock Owners' Association worried that the sale of higher-quality animals to Meat Control was diminishing the breeding stock of the herds without dealing with the more immediate problem of poorer scrub stock. But the clear message was that African herders, far from being 'uneconomic' or 'irrational' in their attitudes to livestock, were highly sensitive to price shifts in the market: they sold stock when they judged the price to be favourable and held on to it when prices were poor.

The culling controversy sharpened the political debate about the development of the pastoral reserves at both the local and the national levels. Whilst a settler at Solai might with just cause complain that the trespass of rinderpest-infected stock on to his dairy farm endangered his 'life's work and savings', was the African herder to stand idle and watch his cattle die while good pasture was visible across the boundary?[127] Both African herder and European settler felt that the responsibility ultimately came to rest in the lap of government. As the Solai settler Caleb Kerby pleaded with the Provincial Commissioner in 1935: 'I sympathise with the Kamasia [Tugen] – we must all live – but we must look to you for help in this.'[128] The damning condemnation of the state's failures in Baringo during the 1930s was a product of an emerging sense that the state ought to encourage better land husbandry. External pressures articulated with local concerns to bring an increased urgency to government policies: the new politics of ecology now demanded intervention in African land husbandry. But how was this to be accomplished?

[126] The prices were reported to the Executive Committee of the Stock Owner's Association, 30 October 1940, KNA Min. of Agri. 2/32. Liebig's raised their Grade prices in April 1942, to 7s. 60, 6s. and 5s. respectively: see 'Summary of discussions re livestock purchases', 9 April 1942, KNA ARC(MAWR)–3 VET–3/28.

[127] BHT/TG/19 and BHT/TG/22; Poestkoke to PC/RVP, 18 April 1932, KNA PC/RVP.6A/15/15.

[128] Kerby to PC/RVP, 13 March 1935, KNA PC/RVP.6A/15/15.

Seven

The Politics of Property
African Land Development in Baringo
1940–63

Before the outbreak of the Second World War the scene was already set for a dramatic acceleration in the pace of rural change in the Baringo lowlands: the Kenya administration was committed to development in the African reserves, but not at the cost of social conflict and political crisis. Informed and alarmed by the failure in Machakos, Baringo's new District Commissioner, Hyde-Clarke, took it upon himself in 1939 to draft a new scheme for the rehabilitation of the district. Taking Colin Maher's earlier proposals as his starting-point, but scaling them down to financially realistic and logistically manageable levels, Hyde-Clarke advocated a more gradual process of education and example, through the establishment of schools and demonstration plots, rather than the immediate sweeping measures of land clearance and legislated control suggested by Maher.[1] With the Veterinary Department now committed to creating stock routes out of Baringo and other reserves, the prospects for development had greatly improved. Maher had observed in 1937 that without Veterinary Department cooperation on this point 'money would be poured into the Reserve like water into sand but no improvement would be seen'.[2] While

---

[1] Governor's Deputy to Sec. of State, 13 August 1939, enclosing Hyde-Clarke, 'Baringo District rehabilitation scheme', January 1939, KNA PC/RVP.6A/11/23.

[2] Maher, *Soil Erosion and Land Utilisation*, 84, 64–9. A similar opinion was expressed by the government commission of inquiry set up to examine the problem of overstocking: see *Interim Report of a Committee Appointed to Advise as to the Steps to be Taken to Deal with the Problem of Overstocking in Order to Preserve the Future Welfare of the Native Pastoral Areas* (East African Pamphlet No. 293, Nairobi, 1941).

his own Draconian proposals had been impossible to digest (especially in the light of the Kamba destocking experience), the milder palliatives of Hyde-Clarke were acceptable. Stressing tactfully that, while more radical measures might be considered necessary in the long term, the present circumstances were such that 'the situation is deteriorating daily, and at present funds are so limited for reconditioning that the effect is almost negligible', Hyde-Clarke's scheme was well received in Nairobi.[3] At an estimated cost of £16,540, to be spread over a five-year period, the Baringo District Rehabilitation Scheme was given the blessing of the central administration and a grant was sought from the Colonial Development Fund for its implementation.[4]

When the war intervened, Hyde-Clarke's proposals were suspended and from 1940 to 1944 the district administration had only £450 per annum to spend on reconditioning works, all drawn from the funds of the Local Native Council. When, in 1944, the district administration was invited to prepare a new development plan for postwar reconstruction, the rehabilitation scheme was taken up as the basis of the wider African lands development programme in Baringo.[5] Although modifications would be introduced as a consequence of wartime events, the experience of the 1930s had profoundly influenced the formulation of the development policies that would be implemented in Baringo in the postwar period.[6]

This chapter will examine the succession of development programmes introduced in southern Baringo from the 1940s up to the ending of colonial rule in 1963. The continuities with earlier government projects from the 1930s were strong. The areas of the African reserve closest to the European-owned farmlands, along the Solai border to the east, and the southern border area of Esageri, between Mogotio and Ravine, continued to be the places where development efforts were concentrated. The postwar history of development in these two zones up to the early 1950s will be examined in detail, before the final section of the chapter focuses upon the movement for individual tenure and smallholdings. But, first, it is necessary to take a broader view of the political and economic context in which Baringo's postwar development plans were shaped.

---

[3] Ibid.

[4] Ibid. Also, MacDonald (S of S), Despatch no. 810, 11 October 1939; and Sweatman (DC/BAR) to PC/RVP, 22 January 1940, both KNA PC/RVP.6A/11/23.

[5] For a catalogue of the development work undertaken between 1940 and 1944, see 'Preparation for Baringo's 5-year Development Plan', R.T. Lambert, 28 June 1944, KNA DO/ER/2/2/2.

[6] BHT/ES/1 and BHT/ES/3; R.O. Hennings, 'The African Land Development Organisation, 1946–62', in Cone & Lipscomb (eds), *History of Kenya Agriculture*, 91–6; Lambert (DC/BAR), 'Interim Development Plan, Esageri Lands', 17 March 1946, KNA PC/RVP.6A/11/34.

Development plans, developing problems, 1940–50

The commitment of the British government to a more interventionist approach to rural development in its African colonies had been signalled in 1940, with the passing of the Colonial Development and Welfare Act. This new bill grew directly out of the debate surrounding the Moyne report on the disturbances in the West Indies during the 1930s, but it was also connected with wider discussions of the need for more active programmes for economic development in all the dependent territories. The 1940 bill replaced the Colonial Development Act of 1930, which had tied British assistance for the colonies primarily to capital projects that brought direct gain to British industry and had precluded all except a few infrastructural projects in the area of welfare. The initial financial provisions of the bill allowed for expenditure of up to £5,000,000 per annum, and revisions in 1943 and again in 1945 substantially increased these sums. These millions would ultimately be dwarfed by the amounts that were raised through local taxation in late colonial Africa to fund rural development, but their availability gave an essential initial stimulus to planning and implementation. To be awarded these development monies, colonies were invited to submit bids for support, showing how the individual projects fitted within wider development programmes. By 1948, the whole process by which colonies planned for economic development had been radically overhauled, and each territory had been encouraged to prepare a formal development plan of a wide-ranging and integrated nature. This shift toward a more centrally planned and coordinated programme of development became the guiding principle of postwar colonial policy throughout British Africa, providing the *raison d'être* for what Low & Lonsdale have so vividly termed 'the second colonial occupation'.[7]

In response to the new demands of the Colonial Office, the Kenya government separated its postwar plans for the White Highlands (the Scheduled Areas) from those for the African reserves. New administrative and financial structures were created to further the development of African areas. The African Land Development Organisation (ALDEV) was set up in 1945 as an agency of the Development and Reconstruction Authority (DARA), at the time when Kenya's 'Ten Year Development Plan, 1946–55'

---

[7] Low & Lonsdale, 'Towards the new order', 12–16. The momentous shift in British colonial financing has spawned a very full literature. For the essential primary documents, see Morgan, *Official History of Colonial Development*, i, 80–123; and for a more accessible account, A.N. Porter & A.J. Stockwell, *British Imperial Policy and Decolonization 1938–64*, Vol. 1, *1938–51* (Basingstoke, 1987), 12–24, 92–100. The best study of the Colonial Development Fund is Constantine, *Making of Colonial Development Policy*. For the impact of the war upon colonial planning, see Lee, *Colonial Development and Good Government*; Lee & Petter, *The Colonial Office*; J.M. Lee, '"Forward thinking" and War: the Colonial Office during the 1940s', *Journal of Imperial & Commonwealth History*, 6 (1977), 64–79; Pearce, *Turning Point in Africa*.

was being prepared.[8] The original intention was that ALDEV would identify suitable lands for the settlement of 'surplus' African population from overcrowded areas. In the event, ALDEV's early emphasis upon settlement gave way by the end of 1947 to a focus upon land utilization, 'when it became clear', in the words of the ALDEV chairman, 'that the root of the evil which had to be tackled was not over-population, but mismanagement of the land'.[9] Although ALDEV operated in all provinces, from the outset much of the development work concentrated in marginal areas of low or previously underdeveloped agricultural potential; and a high proportion of the schemes supported by ALDEV concerned the problems of the pastoral areas, where the relationship between signs of erosion and degradation continued to be closely connected with overstocking. At its establishment, ALDEV received a guarantee of £3,000,000 in funding to be spread over the ten-year plan, £443,000 of which came through a grant from the Colonial Development and Welfare Act, with the larger balance being found through the DARA funded by the Kenya exchequer (initially from revenues, latterly through borrowings). Of the approximately £2,000,000 spent in the districts and provinces over the ten-year period, pastoral-land projects in the Southern Province (£821,270, £713,648 of which was spent in Machakos), the Rift Valley Province (£381,260) and the Northern Province (£68,153) received the lion's share. Baringo District alone received grants totalling £83,720, making it one of the principal centres of ALDEV activity.[10] For these pastoral districts, the analysis of their problems and the suggestions proposed in the mid-1940s were not so very different from those contained in the papers of the Kenya Land Commission a decade earlier.[11] Although ALDEV gave priority to particular kinds

---

[8] The terms of reference are set out in *African Land Utilization and Settlement,* (Government of Kenya Sessional Paper no. 8, Nairobi, 1945). The board underwent four changes of name, reflecting the shifting emphasis of its work: 1945–6, African Settlement Board; 1946–47, African Settlement and Land Utilisation Board; 1947–53, African Land Utilisation and Settlement Board; 1953–63, African Land Development Board. DARA was, in effect, Kenya's first development planning body. See Robert H. Jackson, 'Planning, politics and administration', in Goran Hyden, Robert Jackson & John Okumu (eds), *Development Administration: the Kenyan Experience* (Nairobi, 1970), 176.

[9] ALDEV, *African Land Development,* 2.

[10] For the full figures, see ALDEV, *African Land Development,* appendix H. Central Province receivecd £381,260, but much of this came during the Mau Mau Emergency with the initiation of the Swynnerton Plan from 1953. Excluding Central Province, and deducting the monies given for the special purchase of the Kipkarren and Kaimosi farms in Nandi, more ALDEV money was expended in Baringo than in any district other than Machakos.

[11] The emphasis on these districts in both the Kenya Land Commission and the postwar Development and Reconstruction Authority indicated how little had been achieved by the 1930s inquiry, but was surely reinforced by the fact that J.F.G. Troughton was heavily involved in both. Troughton had assisted Fazan in preparing the précis papers and writing the final report for the Land Commission, and was also the author of the government's *Interim Report on Development* (Nairobi, 1945), which set out the programmes to be followed by DARA. See KNA PC/NKU/2/1/47 for a copy of this government publication.

of problem, such as reconditioning, destocking or the enclosure of lands, it did not impose policies or projects upon districts. Rather, ALDEV oversaw the coordination of policies between the various government departments and the provincial and district administrations, awarded funds for specific projects on application and provided extra technical assistance where this was needed. Its role was therefore essentially facilitative and supervisory, rather than programmatic, and once a project was initiated ALDEV would not commit itself to further recurrent expenditure, withdrawing to leave the district administration to carry the scheme forward. Only partly in jest did one board member suggest that the ALDEV crest 'should be the ALDEV cow being milked by the district team'.[12]

From 1945 until the end of the 1950s every major rural development project mounted in Baringo began its life sheltered under the umbrella of ALDEV funding. Under the ten-year plan, until 1955, reconditioning programmes and controlled-grazing schemes dominated. Most of the schemes begun in this phase were relatively small in scale, many of them being a direct continuation of the reconditioning work carried out before 1939. The starting-point for all this work, in 1946, was Hyde-Clarke's 'rehabilitation scheme', and even in the mid-1950s the thrust of his thinking could still be seen in the emphasis given to the need for local participation and consent.[13] Efforts were made to draw local African authorities into the running of these projects – chiefs and local committees, empowered through local by-laws and rules and enforced through the chief's courts. As we shall see in our detailed discussion of Solai and Esageri below, this quest for local collaborators achieved some limited success, but it also had a number of unintended consequences. Not least, it generated an increasingly intense struggle over access to environmental resources within the communities concerned. In the next phase, from 1955 onwards, ALDEV's key role having been consolidated in the Agriculture Bill of that year, Baringo was given an enhanced priority for development funds with a broader programme of works designed to protect the entire area of the southern lowlands bounded by the Perkerra catchment, from the Mau in the south to Lake Baringo in the north. Ironically, coming so close to the ending of colonial rule in Kenya, these later programmes were characterized by a more coercive and legalistic approach, including an extensive campaign of compulsory culling and a dramatic acceleration in the process of land enclosure and entitlement. With these more confrontational tactics, disputes within Baringo's African communities became more overt and determined around the question of property rights in land.

The economic and ecological climates in which these postwar initiatives

---

[12] Quoted in ALDEV, *African Land Development*, 3.
[13] The scheme was outlined in response to Secretariat Circular no. 44 of 1944, 'Post-war development plans, Baringo district', R.T. Lambert, October 1944, KNA PC/NKU/ 2/1/47.

occurred were as volatile as they had been in the 1920s and 1930s; drought, outbreaks of disease and fluctuating market conditions often proved the turning-points around which success or failure would be determined. The strongest common thread running through both phases of postwar development in southern Baringo was the issue of destocking. This, more than any other concern, dominated colonial thinking in the district, and a survey of livestock marketing is an essential starting-point in any assessment of Baringo's development programmes.

Wartime initiatives in livestock marketing in Baringo had little immediate impact, but their longer-term consequences were significant. Pressure on Tugen herders to accept destocking measures had been building up toward the end of the 1930s, and the new arrangements set in place for the sale of stock during the war created some of the marketing infrastructure that had previously been lacking. In 1939, Hyde-Clarke had succeeded in persuading a reluctant Local Native Council to agree to the cull-branding of nearly 9,000 head of cattle, all initially destined for Liebig's Athi River factory. In fact, only 1,600 head were purchased by Liebig's, the rest being deemed of too poor quality even for their processing plant.[14] In the face of growing Tugen opposition, a further cull was carried out in the following year, this time some 2,000 head of cattle being purchased by Liebig's.[15] At this point the marketing of cattle was placed under the authority of the Meat Controller, through the Livestock Control Board, which was charged with securing the supply of beef to feed the military. As we have seen, the board set prices at a high enough level to bring sellers to the market-place but it was only prepared to purchase better-quality stock. In Baringo relatively few cattle of a higher grade were offered for sale in 1941, but all of these went to Livestock Control, leaving Liebig's with the unwelcome opportunity of paying inflated prices to obtain the poorest animals. Not surprisingly, in these circumstances Liebig's hastily withdrew from the Baringo market. Even with the better prices offered to the producer by the Livestock Control Board, average prices were by no means high: 2,765 cattle bought in Baringo during 1941 averaged 39s. 49 per head, no higher than prices prevailing before 1939, and even this relatively small offtake had virtually exhausted the local supply of suitable bullocks by the end of the year.[16] Sales to Livestock Control continued at a similar level over 1942,[17] but by January 1943 buying had ground to a halt in the midst of drought. When the sale yards opened again in May, the stock remained in very poor condition. By the end of the year Livestock Control had taken only 1,558 head of cattle,[18] in 1944 they purchased only 1,065 head and in 1945 took 2,068 head in

---

[14] Rift Valley Province AR, 1939.

[15] Ibid., 1940.

[16] Ibid., 1941.

[17] Ibid., 1942.

[18] Ibid., 1943.

what was still a very weak market. For herders recovering from drought, prices averaging below 40s. per head in a period of generally high inflation in the cost of living offered no incentive to sell. Wartime sales figures were very far short of what was deemed necessary to destock the district, and Livestock Control purchases were in any case not reducing the numbers of the poorest-quality animals.[19]

Despite the relatively small numbers of cattle exported during the war years, the district administration emerged from the war convinced that livestock marketing could be pushed ahead. There were some grounds for this optimism. After many years in which quarantines had locked up Baringo's stock, the war had allowed the development of new outlets and the loosening of veterinary constraints. The development plans that were framed for the district towards the end of the war loudly proclaimed the importance of maintaining these stock outlets. The Overstocking Committee had advocated similar measures in its interim report, and before the end of the war government pledged further funds for these purposes. Government development monies, provided through the Colonial Development and Welfare Act and from local resources, funded the construction of sale yards and improvements to the controls at holding grounds. To assuage settler anxieties about the disease risk, government undertook to control the movement and holding of cattle on these routes in the same manner as had been developed during the war. From early in 1946, the Meat Marketing Board (MMB) therefore effectively took over the position of the Livestock Control Board as a government agency to regulate the marketing of African stock.[20] The price ceilings imposed during the war were now lifted and the MMB was freed – at least in theory – to buy competitively against other buyers, including local African traders. Postwar conditions were certainly ripe for this liberalization of the market. With meat consumption increasing throughout Kenya, especially in the urban areas, the market for cattle and goats was stronger than ever.

But, having established the outlets and to some extent freed the market, it was up to the local administration to ensure the supply of cattle. In Baringo, Lambert, like Hyde-Clarke before him, was convinced that local chiefs could be cajoled into cull-branding without resort to outright coercion, especially if better prices were offered and so long as drought conditions did not distort the market. In these favourable conditions, Lambert hoped that herders initially drawn into the market through the enforcement of culling would quickly come to see the advantages of a regular pattern of voluntary livestock sales.[21] In September 1946, a livestock census began throughout the locations of southern Baringo to establish a truer picture of the total livestock holdings in order to set an effective annual

---

[19] Baringo District ARs, 1944 and 1945.

[20] For establishment of the MMB, see Raikes, *Livestock Development*.

[21] See the summary in Lambert's 'Political history'.

culling rate – a target figure for the export of stock. The census was approached with unusual thoroughness, especially in the Lembus area, and it seems likely that it represents the most accurate set of statistics on livestock available for Baringo in the colonial period.[22] The stock count was complete by the end of January 1947. The relatively heavy stocking rate for the region as a whole came as no surprise, but officials were alarmed by the pattern of distribution of stock. More than half the total number of cattle and calves were found to be in one location, Lembus, in the south-west corner of the district, adjacent to the European-owned farms of Ravine and the large tracts of land held by the Forest Department as forest reserve. It was accordingly decided to begin culling in Lembus first, and it was reported that the Lembus elders had been persuaded 'without great difficulty' to accept a cull of 30 per cent of cattle in the location. This amounted to a reduction of 7,000 head of cattle in total, and would be achieved within nine months with planned sales of 200 head per week. Enlarged sale yards were speedily constructed at Esageri, Eldama Ravine and Mogotio.[23]

Table 7.1 South Baringo livestock census, 1946

	Cows	Bulls	Oxen	Total adult cattle	Calves	Donkeys & goats	Sheep
Lembus	20,726	1,903	3,327	25,956	6,972	348	26,980
Kakamor	3,030	310	278	3,618	1,306	17	8,830
Keben	4,361	502	455	5,318	1,957	0	14,258
Pokorr	5,139	486	473	6,098	2,264	13	12,490
W. Endorois	1,746	168	143	2,057	686	6	9,201
E. Endorois	4,783	437	530	5,750	1,745	72	16,452
Totals	39,785	3,806	5,206	48,797	14,930	456	88,221

When the sales commenced on 6 February they were an immediate and surprising success.[24] 'A great deal more cattle were produced than had been bargained for' at the first sale, and officials were astonished at 'the cheerful atmosphere which surrounded the whole event'. By the end of February, 1,224 head of cattle had been sold and, although the pace slowed thereafter, good numbers of Lembus stock continued to be offered for sale through the year. By June, sales were started in other locations, beginning with a 30 per cent cull in Pokorr. New sale yards went up at Ngentalel, Mukuyoni and

---

[22] Baringo District AR, 1946, for the figures.

[23] DC Baringo to PC RVP, 16 January, 1947, KNA DO/ER/2/2/2, commenting that it had been difficult to establish who were the owners of animals and that although elders had been persuaded of the cull, younger men had not.

[24] Rift Valley Province AR, 1946.

Emining, as chiefs in other locations 'requested' sales. By the end of the year some fifty-four sales had been held, at which 6,916 head of cattle had been sold.[25]

From 1946 to 1949 considerable progress appeared to be made as these cattle sales became a regular feature throughout all the locations of southern Baringo. Prices fetched for cattle of reasonable quality quickly spiralled upwards with the combination of improved demand and the liberalization of trade. Average prices per head of cattle sold in Baringo doubled between 1941 and 1948, from less than 40s. per head to more than 80s.[26] The sales were generally very well attended, more cattle frequently being offered for sale than the buyers could take. As prices climbed in 1948, more than 5,000 head of cattle were sold for export from the district. In the following year sales were above 10,000 head, with prices remaining good despite the onset of drought. 'It can be said that these sales have now become like fairs,' wrote a delighted Provincial Commissioner in his report for 1948, 'petty traders set up their stalls displaying a very reasonable range of articles. Tea booths sprang up and there was a general holiday atmosphere. The people appeared to be pleased to be there to gossip with their friends.'[27] This idyllic picture of rural merriment glossed over the fact that a sizeable proportion of the sales came through the culling of stock belonging to herders who could hardly be said to have entered the market freely, being pressed to sell by chiefs and headmen. Though the district administration liked to emphasize the income generated by the stock sales – peaking at more than £50,000 from cattle and goat sales in 1949 – resistance was evident in many locations, especially among older herders with larger numbers of cattle. The District Officer charged with affecting the cull in Lembus in 1947 confessed that 'it was necessary to keep a continued eye open for backsliding and subversive propaganda from the reactionaries' – a veiled reference to the fact that stern administrative pressure was in fact needed to maintain the pattern of sales.[28] The 'progessive element' who supported the sales were invariably younger men, especially those whose households had diversified economically and whose needs for cash were more apparent than those of elders, who, as one official lamented, 'desire only to be left alone'.[29] But even the so-called 'progressives' were seldom in complete harmony with government policies. The sale of female stock to the MMB was a particularly sore point, as herders were dissatisfied that only beef prices were paid for breeding stock. When, in 1949, government moved to brand all stock on controlled grazing areas throughout the district this increased anxieties that herders might be forced to cull breeding stock to the MMB.[30]

[25] South Baringo AR, 1947.
[26] Rift Valley Province AR, 1941; Baringo District AR, 1948.
[27] Rift Valley Province AR, 1948.
[28] South Baringo AR, 1947.
[29] Ibid., 1948.
[30] Baringo District AR, 1949.

These were among the early indications of greater troubles to come.

Even as the successes of the 1946–9 period were trumpeted, difficulties were experienced in keeping the stock routes open and in regulating the market through the MMB. The stock routes established out of Baringo by Livestock Control during the war moved African cattle through the settler farms along partially fenced roads and tracks to Nakuru. When a stock route of this kind had first been established as an experiment at Solai in 1936, to bring Samburu stock across Laikipia to the railhead, settlers' fears about the spread of disease had proved completely justified.[31] Over 2,500 head of cattle were brought to Solai by this route in 1936 and 1937, but significant numbers of animals were reported to have strayed on to the farms and several outbreaks of disease were attributed to the Samburu cattle. Under pressure from settler farmers, the route was closed.[32] After the end of the war, settlers along the Nakuru routes now raised similar objections and, one by one, the tracks were closed, until only that running through Mogotio and along the foot of the Menengai Crater to Milton's Sidings remained open.[33] The rate at which the MMB could move cattle out through Menengai depended upon the availability of rolling-stock to then move them on by rail, and by 1949 the general improvement in the economy caused a restriction in the transport available to the MMB. This bottleneck led to serious overcrowding on the Mogotio holding grounds, and the MMB was quickly under criticism for the deterioration in the quality of stock being held there and for contributing to problems of overgrazing.[34]

In the goat trade, where the greater number of transactions arguably had a wider economic impact throughout the district, the apparent postwar boom was marred by similar marketing difficulties. At the end of 1946 the export of goats from Baringo was placed under the exclusive control of the MMB, who exported through Nakuru. The reasons for this were partly related to disease controls, but a more important factor was the desire of the administration to (once again) gain greater control over the Somalis who dominated the itinerant goat trade. During the war years, Kikuyu buyers had paid good prices for Baringo goats, but the Somalis, who flooded back to the markets as independent buyers after 1945, at once found the MMB-controlled prices to be significantly lower. In the early months of 1947 they reacted to what they saw as government suppression of price by withdrawing from the market. The government responded by withholding their trading licences unless they agreed to act as agents for the MMB. Most Somalis refused to comply with this, claiming to hold stock acquired prior

[31] PC/RVP to Deputy Director of Animal Industries, 28 April 1933, KNA PC/RVP.6A/23/5; Chairman, Ngobit Farmers Association to DC/Rumuruti, April 1932, KNA PC/RVP.6A/23/3; BHT/ES/1.

[32] Baringo District ARs, 1936 and 1937, KNA(m) PC/RVP.2/7/; Subukia Farmers Association to DC/Nakuru, 26 June 1936, and reply 3 July 1936, KNA PC/RVP.6A/27/4.

[33] South Baringo AR, 1947.

[34] Baringo District AR, 1949.

to the implementation of the new regulations and which they were not prepared to sell at the controlled price. These goats, which they claimed numbered more than 15,000, were being held in the southern Baringo locations awaiting sale. The administration finally forced the issue in July by threatening to prosecute the Somali traders under the Outlying Districts Ordinance unless they sold their surplus stock on to the MMB by the end of August. The Somali traders had evidently hoped that government would allow them to sell on the open market or that their delaying tactic would force up the MMB price, but in the end they were compelled to pass on the stock to the MMB at the controlled price. Between August and the end of the year, MMB bought a total of 19,440 goats in Baringo, many of which had probably been brought into the district over the previous year from regions to the north.[35] Problems emerged again in 1948, when the MMB could not dispose of the quantity of goats brought to Mogotio for sale by these same traders, now acting as its agents. Earlier in the year it had been agreed that not only would the MMB take all goats from the district, but they would also accept animals through Baringo from Kapenguria and Turkana. Owing to the large accumulation of goats being held at Mogotio in September awaiting export, all further requests by Somalis to sell goats to the MMB through Nakuru had to be refused.[36] The sheer quantity of the African livestock trade had overwhelmed the capacity of the holding ground, the stock routes, the railway rolling-stock and the abattoirs.

Veterinary restrictions were also having an adverse effect upon the cattle market by 1948. Although other buyers could still purchase at the cattle auctions, disease controls were enforced, giving MMB a monopoly on exports from Baringo. This meant, in effect, that, as with the goat trade, the MMB now sought to use other buyers as their agents. Whilst producer prices remained fairly steady over 1948 and into the early months of 1949, this nevertheless made it more difficult for the MMB to regulate the market and to maintain price levels. As prices began to slip, controversy blew up over Baringo cattle, with the head office of the MMB 'claiming that Africans were being bribed to destock by uneconomic prices', while settlers claimed that 'the increased "overheads" of the Board were being met by a drop in prices to the producers'.[37] Baringo's brief dawn of postwar prosperity came to an abrupt end as cattle prices tumbled in 1949 against a background of widespread drought in the Rift Valley and a glut of meat on the market.[38] By the end of the year it was estimated that 30,000 head of cattle had died in Baringo because of drought and starvation, 10 per cent of the total district herd and many more than had been sold for export in the previous three years put together.[39]

[35] Ibid., 1947.
[36] Ibid., 1948.
[37] Ibid., 1949; Rift Valley Province AR, 1948.
[38] Rift Valley Province AR, 1949.
[39] Baringo District AR, 1949.

In 1950, whilst the market was still savagely depressed by the effects of drought, the MMB gave way to a new body, the Kenya Meat Commission (KMC), who took over from Liebig's the running of the Athi River canning factory.[40] This should have further opened up the market for African cattle, by placing the KMC in a position to buy both high- and low-quality stock. In an effort to ensure this, the government also set up the African Livestock Marketing Organization (ALMO) alongside the KMC. ALMO's brief was to develop supplies of cattle specifically from the African pastoral areas for the KMC.[41] To achieve this, new stock routes and holding grounds were established, along the lines set out in Faulkner's 1947 report on the development of the livestock industry.[42] These changes were accompanied by a highly significant shift from the earlier segregationist, quarantine policies, toward a programme of campaigns of disease prevention and inoculation in the pastoral reserves, coupled with efforts to raise the general quality of the animals herded.[43] In the medium term these developments would bring about the most active period of livestock sales in Kenya's modern history until ALMO's financial collapse in 1963, but the initial transition proved awkward.[44] In the process, Baringo's gains of 1946 to 1949 appeared to be squandered. Short of capital and as yet unable to run the factory efficiently, in February 1950 the KMC ceased all purchases in the African areas, closing the markets in Baringo and other districts 'to the bewilderment' of herders.[45]

When the KMC came back into the Baringo market in 1951, through ALMO, it operated a floor-price mechanism at the sale yards, ostensibly to prevent dealers' rings from depressing the prices. In the event, ALMO's prices were found to be up to 50 per cent lower for all classes of stock than those offered by itinerant Somali and Nyanza buyers,[46] and by the end of the year ALMO buyers were simply unable to afford to buy at the prices offered at auction by the African buyers.[47] It is very doubtful whether ALMO really did increase prices to the Baringo herder as against what was on offer from the itinerant traders, but in Kenya overall ALMO's activities certainly 'did lead to a substantial increase in deliveries of cattle to KMC' from the African reserves, from about 80,000 head per anuum in 1954–6

[40] Raikes, *Livestock Development*, 119.

[41] Ibid.

[42] D.E. Faulkner, 'Prospects for the reorganisation of the livestock industry of Kenya' (November 1947), *passim*, PRO CO 852/996.

[43] Raikes, *Livestock Development*, 119. In Southern Baringo 33,500 rinderpest inoculations were carried out: Baringo District AR, 1951.

[44] ALMO was replaced by the Livestock Marketing Division of the Ministry of Agriculture, and the emphasis of its policies turned towards the development of higher-potential livestock areas: Raikes, *Livestock Development*, 120.

[45] Rift Valley Province AR, 1950; Baringo District AR, 1950.

[46] Baringo District AR, 1951.

[47] DO/Eldama Ravine to DC/Baringo, 13 September 1951, KNA DO/ER/2/24/10.

Table 7.2 *Baringo livestock sales, 1939–60*

	Cattle	Sheep/goats	Comments
1939	1,600		Liebig's. Cull branding
1940	2,000+		Liebig's
1941	2,765		LC, av. 39s. 49 p.h.
1942	2,926	5,274	LC
1943	1,558	195	Drought. No sales Jan.–Apr.
1944	1,065		
1945	2,068		
1946	1,400+		
1947	7,231 (£22,984)	19,440	MMB, av. 63s. 57 p.h. 57 sales
1948	5,434 (£24,412)	14,061 (£7,857)	MMB, av. 89s. 85 p.h.
1949	10,078 (£42,471)	17,532 (£10,011)	MMB. av. 84s. 82 p.h. Drought
1950	2,169	2,000+	MMB unable to buy. Goat prices 'poor' (25–35 cents per lb.)
1951	4,000*	10,289	Prices 'poor'. Somali and Nyanza buyers pay av. 150s. p.h. KMC pay 100s. p.h.
1952	6,000		Private buyers only. Drought
1953	7,908 (£48,000)		Av. 125s., higher at Emening, lower at Marigat
1954	5,726 (£38,980)		Foot-and-mouth in mid-year closed all markets periodically. Av. 146s. 24, but 155s. 90 in south.
1955	4,704 (£34,388)	2,319	Foot-and-mouth. Av. 168s. 53. Abattoir built
1956	2,797	20,287	Foot-and-mouth. ALMO buy 50% goats
1957	6,533	21,098	'Prices high'
1958	5,575 †	12,827	Foot-and-mouth quarantine, Jan.–Mar.
1959	14,330	34,320	Compulsory destocking. 'Fantastic' (£85,000 total) prices. Top steer 695s., goat 103s., sheep 65s. Herd of eleven from Kabimoi, 530s. each. 100+ traders attending sales
1960	10,687	21,025	Compulsory destocking until July, then drought. Foot-and-mouth quarantine, 6 months.
1961	8,077		Compulsory destocking disrupted by drought and quarantine
1962	3,889		
1963	5,524		

* This figure from ALDEV reports. Annual reports give 4,200 and 2,740.

† Figures from 1958 onwards include Marigat abattoir and exports on hoof.

NB Peter Little gives 8,792 cattle for 1939, but this is the figure cull-branded, not the figure exported. His figure for 1958 is 13,295, but I cannot work out where this comes from.

LC, Livestock Control, p.h., per head.

to 180,000 in 1962.[48] In Baringo, however, foot-and-mouth disease severely restricted all cattle exports from 1954 onwards, and sales would not again reach the levels of the late 1940s until the government finally resorted to a campaign of compulsory culling in 1959 (see Table 7.2). Through these years the auction sales continued, with African buyers, many of them from Nyanza, competing very effectively with ALMO and itinerant Somalis, despite the limitations imposed by quarantines.[49]

In the years immediately following the war, then, Baringo had appeared on the verge of an 'economic revolution'.[50] For the first time a surplus of cash was evident among southern Baringo's herders, accruing from a combination of stock sales and military remittances. In the middle of 1947 it was estimated that £2,000 per month was entering the district from cattle sales alone.[51] With cash in hand, fewer Tugen volunteered for work on the farms or on the various government development projects starting up throughout the district. To attract labour to the farms, wages were raised from 10s. to 12s. early in 1947, but even then labour shortages persisted. Without the need to find cash to pay their taxes, people preferred to use their labour on their own *shambas*.[52] Investment in new technology also helped to give individual African producers the opportunity to enter the market. The local marketing of milled maize was transformed by the use of hand-turned maize mills. These simple devices became common in other parts of Kenya by the 1930s, but were rare in Baringo before 1945. After the war local demand for the hand-mills rocketed, but supply was pitifully short; in 1948 only three mills were available for purchase in the district.[53] When the situation improved in 1949 and 1950, hand-mills were reported to be in use all over Baringo, though demand still greatly exceeded supply.[54] Ploughs and tractors required much larger investments, but by 1950 these were also making an impact on the southern locations, especially in Lembus where greater acreages of land were being cultivated under cereals.

For those who had accumulated larger sums, trade also presented an attractive investment opportunity. Ex-askaris were prominent among the many new Tugen 'trading companies' applying for plots in the Baringo trading centres, especially at Eldama Ravine. Keen not to thwart the entreprenuerial zeal of Tugen applicants, the District Commissioner (DC) granted twenty-eight new licences to 'native' traders by early in 1947, most being given plots at four newly declared trading centres at Kabartonjo, Tenges, Pororr and Esageri.[55] Even this dramatic expansion could not meet

[48] Raikes, *Livestock Development*, 194–5.
[49] For details of cattle sales in the period 1951 to 1957, see KNA DO/ER/2/24/10.
[50] South Baringo AR, 1947.
[51] Baringo Distrcit AR, 1947.
[52] South Baringo AR, 1947.
[53] Baringo District AR, 1948.
[54] Ibid., 1950.
[55] Ibid., 1947.

local demand for plots, with fifty further applications coming in by November 1947. The general shortage of consumer goods still being experienced in Baringo, as elsewhere, with the continuation of wartime controls, discouraged the DC from awarding any further licences that year: with an estimated accumulated cash surplus in the district of £21,500 by the end of 1947, there simply was not enough to spend the money on.[56] By 1949, all applications for licences from traders 'alien' to the district were being automatically refused by the Local Native Council in favour of local Tugen traders, who were by then established in all the main trading centres throughout Baringo.[57]

The commercial activities of these new Tugen shopkeepers very quickly emerged to challenge the previously dominant position of Indian and Nubian traders. The distribution of controlled goods in Baringo after the war was still managed by the two leading Indian traders, F.D. Patel (based at Mogotio) and C.B. Patel (at Ravine), and, from their substantial shops at Ravine, Alidan Visram and Juma Hajee underwrote a number of other trading stores throughout the district.[58] These long-established traders were secure in their control of wholesaling, but they did not welcome the new competition in retailing, least of all at a time when goods were in short supply. During 1947 there were signs of friction between Indian and Tugen traders. This came to a head when a group of Tugen from the Lembus area muscled their way into the grain trade, for long controlled by the leading Indian traders. Since the 1930s, Indian merchants had acted as agents for the government in the wholesale distribution of maize to the various trading centres throughout the district at controlled prices. This monopoly on distribution had been tightened by wartime regulations preventing the free movement of cereals between one district and another.[59] The Lembus Trading Company, a new and entirely Tugen-owned concern, effectively undercut this controlled market by buying up around 1,000 bags of maize from the 1946 harvest in southern Baringo at very cheap prices, and then offering to distribute it at the controlled price. With the controlled price estimated to be almost double the price prevailing in the local Baringo market, this was surely a most opportunistic venture. The initiative created a dilemma for the administration, for whilst they were keen to foster local African commerce, they were not keen to permit 'an exorbitant profit' to be made. But there was nothing that could legally be done to prevent the sale of the Lembus maize at whatever price, so long as it did not leave the district. To prevent an oversupply, the government therefore suspended its contract with the Indian merchants and allowed the Lembus traders to take over the supply to the district. All went well until October, by which time

---

[56] South Baringo AR, 1947; Baringo District AR, 1947.
[57] Baringo District AR, 1949.
[58] Ibid., 1947; BHT/SW/1, interview with Juma Hajee.
[59] Mosley, *Settler Economies*, ch. 4, for a description of the system.

the locally grown maize was in short supply and government imports had to be restarted. However, to encourage local enterprise it was decided that the distribution of this imported maize should now be entirely in African hands,

> subject to the condition that the natives should deposit the price of the imported maize in advance, and that if it was found that they were not capable of managing their business satisfactorily, the distribution would be reinvested in the Indian wholesalers concerned.

Although the administration was suspicious that the Lembus Trading Company acquired some of its grain supply through illegal purchases of maize grown by forest squatters outside the district – produce that could legally be traded only through the Forest Department – maize distribution in Baringo 'worked well' throughout 1947.[60]

The Lembus Trading Company was less successful the next year, when there was a poor harvest, especially in the north. By May there were serious shortages of supply in the Pokot and Il Chamus areas. The Tugen traders had grossly underestimated the overall district requirements, and their network of distributors seemed unable to get the maize through to the northern areas where it was most needed. Lacking experience and with no free capital to buy in other markets (thanks to the government's insistence upon the payment of the bond), the Lembus traders were unable to resolve the situation. In May, faced by the possibility of localized famine in the north, the government handed back the distribution contract to F.D. Patel at Mogotio, who immediately brought in 1,000 bags of imported maize.[61]

Tugen traders may have lacked experience and capital, but they did not lack enterprise. Although the Tugen chiefs on the Local Native Council were sternly critical of the traders for their failure, the setback to the emergence of a strong Tugen entrepreneurial class in the south of the district was only temporary. Over the 1950s, Tugen traders gradually displaced Indians as a dominant force in all areas of retailing. Those who could not obtain trading-centre plots or government contracts turned to other commercial activities in the years after 1945. The old mainstay of Baringo's commerce, the trade in hides and skins, enjoyed a revival in the 1940s and early 1950s, despite wildly fluctuating prices. Here, again, there was rivalry between established Indian traders, who commonly used African agents to buy in bulk – F.D. Patel exported 20,000 hides and skins in 1951 alone – and Tugen traders who had insufficient capital to match them.[62] In other areas Indian competition was less in evidence. Transport was a popular alternative to retailing, with several Tugen groups forming to raise the capital necessary for the initial investment in a lorry. The vehicles purchased were usually elderly and in a sorry state of repair, but by 1950

---

[60] South Baringo AR, 1947.
[61] Baringo District AR, 1948.
[62] Ibid., 1951.

a number of regular bus and taxi services were running, including a Ford V8 converted pick-up offering what must have been a hair-raising ride from Kabartonjo to Eldoret.[63] At the other end of the commercial scale, an 'enterprising few' in southern Baringo began charcoal burning in the 1940s to supply the demands of Nakuru's burgeoning African locations.[64]

Whilst on one level Peter Little is surely right in his contention that 'market centres in Baringo grew in response to the demands of the colonial state',[65] it is quite clear that from at least 1945 onwards the demands of the state were widely perceived as a constraint upon African commercial activities. Africans sold their livestock in greater numbers when prices were favourable, characteristically at times when market restrictions were eased; demand for trading licences and shop plots remained stronger than supply throughout the last two decades of colonial rule, despite greatly increased competition between traders; and an emergent class of African entrepreneurs embarked upon an ever-widening range of commercial activities both within and beyond the district boundaries, taking advantage of every opportunity. Although none of this had much impact in the north of the district, southern Baringo did indeed undergo an 'economic revolution' of sorts in the years between 1945 and 1963. But it was not attended by the kind of social transformation the state had intended, for it was achieved without any significant degree of destocking, although the average numbers of livestock held by the majority of households certainly continued to decline over the period. A few had become considerably richer, but many, many more were slowly becoming poorer. African commercial ambition vastly outstripped colonial planning for economic development in these years as the state struggled to maintain its control over the pace and management of 'modernization'. And even before 1950, Africans in the more prosperous southern locations were investing in the wider welfare and development of their own communities: to give only two examples, a cess of 2s. per head of cattle sold in West Lembus was introduced to pay for the building of a school, and 8,932s. was donated by the herders of Pokorr location for the provision of a borehole.[66] But the emergent African entrepreneurs and modernizers of southern Baringo were by no means in the majority, and their demands were often hotly contested by others, who rejected the lure of commercial opportunities and who were less convinced of the need to be 'progressive'. Nor did the so-called 'progressives' always agree as to the direction that progress should take. Nowhere was this more apparent than in the crucially important area of land reform: ironically, it was in this sphere, where the colonial state had so long nurtured its own ambitions for radical change, that the pace of African initiatives would

[63] Ibid., 1950.
[64] Ibid., 1948.
[65] Little, *Elusive Granary*, 40.
[66] South Baringo AR, 1947.

become overwhelming. Closer examination of the history of postwar development projects at Esageri and Solai between 1945 and 1955, the first two schemes to be funded through DARA under ALDEV, will illustrate the roots of this more clearly, and then an analysis of the subsequent ALDEV Perkerra Catchment Scheme will show the way in which the politics of land were transformed.[67]

Esageri & Solai, 1945–54

> In the south, cooperation in local rehabilitation plans has increased in spite of the attitude of a recalcitrant minority which, as in every community, is concerned only with its own problems irrespective of the plans and wishes of the group amongst which it lives.[68]

Comments such as this are to be found in almost every administrative report on southern Baringo from 1945 through to the early 1960s. They tell us a great deal more about the nature of colonial government than about the views of Africans. The attitude of the colonial administration to signs of opposition to its plans for modernization and development was to dismiss those complaining as backward-looking traditionalists, unable to see the benefits that modern, scientific methods of land husbandry would bring. They were usually styled a 'minority', and their protests presented as only a temporary impediment to more rapid and widespread acceptance of colonial projects. The untenability of this interpretation is apparent from its annual repetition, as one official after another confronted the same 'recalcitrant minority', still in stubborn opposition. For some officials, it is possible that they believed that acceptance, cooperation and policy success lay just around the corner; for others, such claims were surely recognized as a necessary insurance if higher authorities were to be satisfied that government programmes were achieving something. Like Langridge in the 1930s, the officials who followed him into Baringo after 1945 understood the value of well-dressed windows.

Delving beyond the platitudes of the annual reports and into the daily record of colonial interactions, a rather different story comes into focus: a story in which resistance to colonial development projects is a constant, even growing element in the politics of ecology in postwar Baringo, with the most 'progressive' and modernizing Tugen consistently agitating for quicker and more dramatic reform than the colonial state was prepared to willingly concede. Nowhere was this more starkly evident than along the Esageri and Solai borders. In the interwar years, it was here that African trespass into European-owned farmlands had prompted the appointment of a Reconditioning Officer to Baringo. After 1945, both areas were again to be the focus of major development initiatives.

---

[67] Papers in KNA DO/ER/2/2/2 provide background to the initial drafting of the schemes.
[68] Baringo District AR, 1949.

Surrounded on all sides by African lands, the Esageri block of European farms was a notorious trespass trouble spot, its absentee landlords infamous for their various practices of 'Kaffir farming'.[69] Aware of the difficult history of the farms and looking for land that could be used as a holding ground to allow the reconditioning programme to be advanced more speedily, the Kenya Land Commission had recommended in 1932 that the Esageri block should be repossessed by government and leased to the Tugen as a holding ground, along with the Kisokon and Kabimoi areas to the east (which had originally been designated as the Uasin Gishu Maasai Reserve).[70] But despite the fact that all but one of these eight farms in the Esageri block were unoccupied in the mid-1930s, the owners refused to sell at the market price then offered by government. In 1945, DC Lambert revised the earlier proposals and again raised the question of Esageri, suggesting that the land be exchanged for the Kiplombe area, farm LO501/R, lying to the south of the Ravine–Nakuru road. Although designated for European settlement, Kiplombe had long remained unoccupied and was treated by local Tugen herders as if it were part of the reserve, many Tugen in effect 'squatting' on the land. Isolated from the rest of the Tugen reserve lands, Kiplombe was difficult to police and was a favourite jumping-off point for herders trespassing on nearby farms. The proposal of an exchange with Kiplombe was more favourable to settler opinion than the simple sale of the Esageri farms, as it did not entail the actual loss of acreage in the White Highlands – a matter of principle upon which settler political leaders stood firm. Lord Francis Scott led an investigation into the proposal on behalf of the settlers of Esageri and Rongai and which came out in favour of the exchange, primarily on the grounds that the road would then mark a well-defined boundary to the settled area, that the trespass problem would be greatly alleviated and (perhaps most significantly) that the Kiplombe area was anyway potentially better farmland than the Esageri block.[71] The local settlers finally agreed to the move and, in the expectation that an exchange could be carried through without significant delay, Lambert pushed ahead with wider plans for the development of the area. In the event, the Esageri–Kiplombe exchange was not completed until 1950. Delay and procrastination were in part caused by settlers, who wrangled over the details of the transaction, but were also fomented by local Tugen herders, who

---

[69] BHT/ES/3 and BHT/TG/9; *KLC:EM*, ii, evidence of Welby (PC/RVP), 1921–2; Maher, *Soil Erosion and Land Utilisation*, 103–5.

[70] These are farms 488, 489, 490, 5249, 5276, 6262, 5461 and 493, shown on Map 2.2, Chapter Two.

[71] Lambert (DC/BAR) to PC/RVP, 2 January 1942; Commissioner of Lands and Settlement to PC/RVP, 19 January 1942; and Lord Francis Scott, 'Report on proposed exchange between the Kamasia Native Reserve and the highland area of Esageri', 9 May 1944, all in KNA PC/RVP.6A/11/34. For further papers on the exchange, see KNA PC/RVP.6a/11/33.

mobilized to protect their own interests and to oppose the loss of Kiplombe.[72]

Tugen resistance to the Kiplombe exchange was partly derived from their own perception that they were being asked to sacrifice better land for worse, but their opposition was deepened by the knowledge that exchange would be linked to the implementation of controlled rotational grazing on the Esageri block, at Kisokon and at Kabimoi. To accomplish this, the carrying capacity of the land needed to be greatly improved and the numbers of stock then grazing the area greatly reduced so as to make way for the incoming cattle. In effect, this meant that the numbers of herders and livestock permitted to remain in these areas would be strictly controlled. Inevitably, fewer herders than had grazed Kiplombe would gain access to Esageri when the exchange went through – this was precisely the intention of government – and the restrictions were likely to force herders to hold only a portion of their animals in the rehabilitated lands. Many would be excluded from all three blocks of land in the short term and all would find access limited in the longer term.

Lambert put the scheme up to the DARA, along with similar proposals affecting the Solai border (see below), and the funding of the development work was approved and went ahead in early 1946 under the auspices of ALDEV.[73] From 1946 to 1950 some £23,000 was allocated to the scheme, paying for the clearing of some 800 acres of bush by a variety of mechanical means, and a further 1,000 acres by ring-barking and burning; the drilling of three boreholes, two of which failed to produce water; the construction of a new dam at Kisokon and the improvement of an existing dam at Esageri; and the ring-fencing of the area with 48 miles of barbed wire.[74] In conjunction with the stock census of southern Baringo in 1946, a system of temporary grazing permits was to be introduced to regulate stock on Kisokon, Kabimoi and Kiplombe and cattle to be permitted into these areas would be branded.[75]

The news that these measures would be linked to a cull of cattle was explained to herders at a *baraza* at Eldama Ravine in November 1946, attended by the Provincial Commissioner (PC). On hearing that a 30 per

[72] The exchange was agreed under the Crown Lands Ordinance in October 1948, but was held up until 1950 by the refusal of the Tugen being moved from Kiplombe to accept a voluntary cull of their stock. See KNA PC/RVP.6A/11/34.

[73] See 'Development of Reserves, Baringo 1945–47', KNA PC/RVP.6A/11/24, for full correspondence on proposals.

[74] For a summary of the work undertaken, see ALDEV, *African Land Development,* 115–16. For details of bush-clearing experiments, see 'ASLUB Report, Schemes in operation or proposed', 27 March 1947, KNA PC/RVP.6A/11/43; BDAR, 1948; 'Record of meeting held in office of PC, RVP, 27 October 1949', KNA PC/RVP.6A/11/43.

[75] For details, see Lambert's 'Development plan for Esageri', March 1946, in KNA PC/RVP.6A/11/34, and Lambert to DO/Ravine, 5 November 1946, and subsequent notes, in KNA PC/RVP.6A/11/24. The legal authority for this was Government Notice 838 of 1942, under which stock limits were set for each area.

cent cull was planned, Chief Cherono of Lembus asked for time to organize a voluntary cull before government took any dramatic steps. Sensing prevarication, the PC sternly informed the *baraza* that 'the time for discussion about the overstocking problem was past: government was contributing handsomely and it was time the Tugen played their part'.[76] At the Local Native Council meeting that followed the *baraza* discussion of the proposals was more heated, with the Council coming out strongly against any steps to remove Tugen from Kiplombe. Chief Cherono was all too aware that both the cull and the grazing controls would be fiercely resisted.

When controls were formally introduced in 1947, the problems began almost immediately: local herders actively sought to avoid branding and the issuing of permits. So few locals were willing to join the scheme that Tugen had to be recruited from other areas. This strategy backfired when it became clear that trespass into all of the controlled areas had increased markedly as a consequence of herders with permits bringing in unbranded stock and assisting other 'unregistered' herders to enter the controlled areas. Friction between local herders and those from further north became acute. Additional grazing guards were posted along the boundary within the first few months, but in response to this herders armed themselves and incidents of intimidation against grazing guards became frequent. Many grazing guards resigned, reportedly having been 'frightened off', and by July 1948 the entire staff of grazing guards at Esageri had twice been dismissed *in toto* to try to prevent bribery. Fencing was hastily constructed in June, but the barbed wire was soon cut and removed in several places. When confronted by the District Officer from Eldama Ravine, trespassing Tugen defiantly declared their intention to continue grazing the land for as long as they wished. Control was never effectively established at any point on the scheme, despite periodic claims by District Officers over the following months that 'things were improving'. In reality, disobedience of government orders was 'flagrant', widespread and, to a certain extent, orchestrated by a vocal and energetic group of herders.[77] In October 1949, an embarrassed provincial commissioner finally admitted before the ALDEV board that the scheme had proved 'completely futile' due to the 'lawlessness and non-cooperation' of the Tugen. The problem was essentially 'one of enforcement'. Moreover, experiments with bush clearing had proved highly expensive and unsustainable in the longer term, being abandoned in 1950. This failure rendered the target stocking level unobtainable, and added to the problems of controlling trespass. The only success had been in the cull of cattle, with voluntary sales achieving close to the targets set. However,

---

[76] Report of meeting in South Baringo AR, 1946, and in KNA PC/RVP.6A/11/24. Lambert's proposals for a cull were first set out in Lambert to Izard (PC/RVP), 24 January 1944, KNA PC/RVP.6A/11/45.

[77] See the quarterly reports and related correspondence in 'Agricultural Development, Esageri, 1947–58', KNA PC/NKU/2/2/30. Also, various papers in KNA PC/RVP.6A/11/24, KNA DO/ER/2/2/2 and KNA DO/ER/2/2/5.

even this had not yet achieved any noticeable impact upon the extent and frequency of cattle trespass and it was doubted whether the cull had even matched the natural increase of the herds. With promises from the PC that stricter controls would be enforced, the ALDEV board only grudgingly agreed to press on with the scheme.[78]

But over the next four years there was no improvement in the situation and local resistance remained deeply entrenched, especially over Kiplombe. The Kiplombe–Esageri exchange was finally completed on 31 January 1951, with the forcible removal of the last Tugen herders from Kiplombe hill.[79] The evictions only intensified political feelings, especially when the land remained unoccupied more than three years later. Trespass into Kiplombe continued on a massive scale every dry season, accompanied by skirmishing with grazing guards and Tribal Police and a seasonal spate of Tugen herders appearing before the courts to be fined. By 1954, the issue was still 'a bone of contention, brought up at every baraza': 'One can sense the antagonistic feelings of the people', wrote the DC.[80] Severe drought conditions from 1952 right through 1953 finally brought matters to a head, with trespass reaching record proportions by October–November 1953. Settlers complained loudly that Kiplombe was being used to gain access to farms further to the south in Nakuru District and asked for stricter controls. Extra Tribal Police were posted to the area in January 1954, but they met such a hostile reaction from Tugen herders on Kiplombe that the administration began to fear that there would be 'serious unrest'. With the Mau Mau emergency then at its height, the wider political climate had a bearing upon the situation, and the decision was taken to avoid confrontation and grant the Tugen permission to use Kiplombe, 'in view of the prevailing drought conditions'. The Nakuru District Council, whose responsibility Kiplombe now was, reluctantly backed down. From 1 March 1954, Tugen were legally allowed to rent Kiplombe on the payment of a temporary grazing fee of 2s. per head per month, up to a limit of 1,000 cattle, and on condition that no trespass occurred on to the farms beyond.[81] In 1955, and again in 1956, permission to graze Kiplombe was granted in the dry season, but only in the face of trenchant resistance from local European settlers.[82]

---

[78] 'Record of a meeting held at office of PC/RVP, 27 October 1949', KNA PC/RVP.6A/11/43; PC to ALDEV, 28 February 1949, KNA PC/RVP.6A/11/45; South Baringo AR, 1947. On the failure of bush clearing, see Commissioner of ALUS to PC/RVP, 4 April 1950, KNA PC/RVP.6A/11/33.

[79] DC/BAR to PC/RVP, 9 February 1951, KNA PC/RVP/6A/11/33. Huts, stores and bomas on the Kiplombe land were all destroyed, to prevent people moving back.

[80] 'Report on south Baringo grazing areas, 1953', 27 February 1954, KNA PC/NKU/2/2/30. See also MacLeod's comments, 'Report on South Baringo grazing areas', 5 January 1955, KNA PC/RVP.6A/11/15.

[81] Simpson (DC/BAR) to PC/RVP, 16 November 1953 and 11 January 1954, and subsequent correspondence, KNA PC/RVP.6A/11/15.

[82] Wainwright to various Baringo officers, 15 November 1955, and Wainwright to Secretary for African Affairs, 5 January 1956, both in KNA PC/RVP.6A/11/33.

The politics of resistance to postwar development schemes along the Solai border was slower to take root, but just as fiercely contested as at Esageri. By 1945, trespass was scarcely less prevalent at Solai than it had been in 1930 and, if anything, the problems had deepened, with increasing numbers of Tugen homesteads settled near to the boundary at Kisanana and Ngentalel. When, in the closing months of 1945, DC Lambert drafted his plans for postwar development, it was hardly surprising that he should single out the Solai border as one of the district's most pressing problems. The scheme he had in mind for Solai involved the fencing of the boundary, partly paid for by local settlers and partly by the African District Council, the closure of areas for reconditioning, paddocking of the land with the introduction of rotational grazing blocks, the branding of stock and a forced reduction of stock numbers through culling, all to be accomplished under the supervision of a European Development Officer. Where the interwar schemes here had aimed at restoring the open range through temporary closure for reconditioning, these postwar schemes saw the introduction of permanent systems of rotational grazing, thus reducing the commons.[83]

The proposed scheme at Solai initially centred upon the neighbouring areas of Ngentalel in East Endorois location and Kisanana in Pokorr location, both in the vicinity of the Ngentalel borehole. This borehole provided the only water in the reserve for 12 miles up to the Solai border, and in the dry season this drew substantial numbers of stock into the area from surrounding locations – in the dry season of 1942 the borehole had been reported to be in use 23 hours a day.[84] Ngentalel covered approximately 13,000 acres and was permanently inhabited by some 400 Tugen, not including those who arrived seasonally. Kisanana was a smaller area to the immediate south. At only 11,000 acres it held a permanent population of 600 people and their animals. Grazing controls had first been introduced at Kisanana in 1939 under the District Crop and Produce Livestock Rules, limiting the cattle in the area to 1,300 head. Wartime supervision of the area had been minimal, however, and by 1945 it was apparent that there had been no effective effort by the local chief to enforce this limit. Lambert now hoped to reduce the stock in Kisanana to 650 head and to impose a limit of 750 head at Ngentalel. The Solai proposals were presented as a model that might eventually be extended to other areas of the southern lowlands and, although Lambert made light of the issue, this clearly amounted to a full-scale assault upon the principle of common land in southern Baringo.[85]

From the very outset of the scheme, Lambert anticipated some 'local opposition' but was determined to force matters, hoping to carry the Local

---

[83] Lambert to PC/RVP, 22 September 1945, KNA PC/RVP.6A/11/24. For a summary of this and related schemes, see de Wilde et al., *Experiences with Agricultural Development*, ii, 177–83.

[84] Director/PWD to PC/RVP, 24 February 1942, KNA PC/RVP.6A/11/27.

[85] Lambert to PC/RVP, 16 May 1946, 'Kamasia–Solai Border Scheme', KNA PC/RVP.6A/11/24.

Native Council and a few of the senior elders with him.[86] 'If they support it, well and good,' he wrote in February 1946. 'If they do not, I feel their attitude should not be allowed to stand in the way of progress.'[87] The battle lines were drawn on the maps in the DC's office as the new restricted areas were planned. In the closing weeks of 1945, the outline of the scheme was approved by the provincial administration and a grant application was put before the DARA board.[88]

On learning, in early January, that the Pokorr boundary at Ngentalel was to be fenced as well as the boundary with the settler farms, local elders immediately protested. By the end of February the persistence of DC Lambert had persuaded the chiefs on the Local Native Council to remove their objections to fencing and to other aspects of the scheme, but there was still little evidence of support from local herders. Survey work continued over the next few months, and by August a detailed map of the border area had been completed and the award of a DARA grant of £7,500 for the scheme was confirmed. Fencing work finally began in September 1946.[89] Within a matter of weeks serious local resistance to the scheme was manifest. The objections were loudest from those who now realized they were to be excluded from access to the borehole at Ngentalel, although those within the scheme were also unwilling to move their settlements to allow the implementation of closed grazing areas. As the work ground to a halt, the DC summoned a *baraza* at Pokorr, where Chief Chesire, who himself lived within the betterment area, did his best to quell the protests. To those outside the scheme his vested interest was all too clear. Herders from Endebess and Mugurin, who would now be excluded from their only source of water for their stock, insisted that the government should first put down a borehole at Mugurin and even offered to pay 324 bullocks toward the cost.[90]

By December 1946, grazing controls had already 'all but broken down'. Locally recruited Tribal Police would not report local elders who trespassed,[91] and in March and April 'malicious damage' was done to the fencing along the scheme boundary. By September the fence was reported to be in so bad a state of repair that it was 'literally falling down'. Later in the year it was discovered that survey beacons along the boundary had been removed.[92]

[86] Lambert, 'Solai Border Development Plan', February 1946, KNA DO/ER/2/2/4.
[87] Lambert to PC/RVP, 22 February 1946, PC/RVP.6A/11/24. See also, Lambert, 'Solai Border Plan', February 1946, KNA DO/ER/2/2/4.
[88] Colonial Secreatry to PC/RVP, 15 November 1945; Provincial AO/RVP to D. of Ag., 17 December 1945, both in KNA PC/RVP.6A/11/24. Lambert put the scheme before the LNC meeting on 12 January: DC to PC, 12 January 1946, KNA PC/RVP.6A/11/24.
[89] 'Report on DARA Reconditioning Schemes', 16 January 1947, KNA PC/RVP.6A/11/24.
[90] Baringo District AR, 1946; Morgan (PC/RVP) to DC/BAR, 8 February 1947, and subsequent correspondence, in KNA PC/RVP.6A/11/27, on provision of cattle to pay for borehole; see also letters in DO/ER/2/2/2.
[91] 'Progress report on Solai', December 1946, KNA PC/RVP.6A/11/24.
[92] Various papers in KNA DO/ER/2/2/4.

Trespass along the Solai boundary reached new heights during the dry season of the early months of 1947, and Lambert contemplated applying for a Police Levy; but even though the Nakuru courts frequently passed the maximum punishments upon convicted herders, the frustrated DC could only record his irritation that the Tugen herders seemed happy to 'simply pay the fines'.[93] Much to the discomfiture of the district administration, Governor Mitchell made an unofficial and unscheduled visit to Kisanana at the height of these troubles in February 1949. He was not impressed. Mitchell described what he saw as a 'deplorable desert'. Advocating forced culling of Tugen stock in the area, he urged that government should be prepared:

> to take the most drastic action. The problem is a relatively simple one, and if it has to come to a rumpus it is a very good wicket, because we have shown the greatest generosity and patience to these people, and given them the greatest help over a very long time.[94]

The areas of Kisanana and Ngentalel in which controlled grazing had been tried since 1946 were by the end of 1949 in worse condition than originally, because of the extent of trespass. The most obvious reason for failure lay in the problems of the water-supply to the Mugurin and Endebess areas. After several unsuccessful attempts to establish boreholes around Mugurin in 1948, it was decided to experiment with tank dams. By August 1949, ten dams had been constructed in the Mugurin area, and all bar one continued to operate successfully over the next few years.[95] This eased pressure upon the Ngentalel borehole to some extent, but it did not halt the local resistance to every aspect of the Solai scheme. Governor Mitchell may have been prepared for a 'rumpus', but his district staff now took a more sober view, retreating from Lambert's postwar optimism and seeking to gradually build a base of local support for grazing control and destocking through the encouragement of 'progressive farmers' and modernizers. The man appointed to replace Chesire, Chief Morogo, was to be the leading figure in this. Over the 1950s Morogo took up government plans for reform with apparent enthusiasm, being especially keen on rotational grazing schemes.[96] But he had few allies among Tugen herders, and there was little sign of progress on the Solai border for much of the early 1950s.

The 'can-do' optimism of the administration in the immediate postwar years had given way by the early 1950s to a lethargic acceptance of the apparent intractability of Baringo's problems. Between 1946 and 1951,

---

[93] South Baringo AR, 1947; Lambert to AI Police/Solai, 11 April 1947, KNA PC/NKU/2/15/50.

[94] Mitchell to CNC, 8 February 1949, KNA DO/ER/2/2/4.

[95] In 1949, DARA funded the Solai scheme to the tune of £1,245, including £638 for the Mugurin dams: Baringo District AR, 1949.

[96] Ibid., 1950. Morogo was placed in sole charge of grazing control from February 1954. See 'Notes on the ALDEV meeting, Kabarnet, 5 February 1954', KNA PC/NKU/2/2/29.

ALDEV had allocated £35,684 to the south Baringo grazing areas, but to little effect.[97] When the ALDEV board toured the district in 1954, it was conceded that the various schemes had 'muddled along' since 1949 without significant progress being made. The results of the money spent at Solai and Esageri over nine years since 1946 had been 'negligible'. The collapse of livestock sales after 1949 was undoubtedly a key factor in the disillusionment of the district administration, as was the lack of local support for government projects. To revive the schemes and to try to foster a greater degree of local support and participation, the ALDEV board recommended that policy now be moved away from reconditioning for rotational relief of the grazing and that instead the controlled areas should be turned into permanent ranches with the graziers paying fees which could then be used as a development fund. A start had been made to introduce this at Esageri from 1950.[98] This type of scheme, it was argued, would give graziers a stronger vested interest in the success of the ranches. In addition, the enclosure of individual farms, which was already happening spontaneously in some areas would be encouraged but only where these were thought to be economically viable. These changes were to have a dramatic impact upon the local politics of ecology.

Enclosing the range, 1950–63

> The foundation of all good husbandry was the enclosure of the land: this was the unanimous opinion of all leaders of farming thought.[99]

No colonial official in Kenya during the 1950s would have seriously disputed the wisdom of Robert Trow-Smith's stress upon the significance of enclosure, but there was considerable discussion about how it should be best achieved. Most analysis of this to date has focused upon the Central Province, where consolidation of lands, enclosure and the registration of titles was rapidly pushed through during the Mau Mau emergency as a key element of the Swynnerton Plan for agricultural development.[100] Taking advantage of the powers available under the emergency regulations and drawing upon handsome provision of funds and manpower, land reform became a potent weapon in the battle against Mau Mau, as those loyal to government were assisted to secure title whilst those in rebellion were systematically excluded from the process of registration. Whilst it has been widely acknowledged that this rapid transformation of land tenure – the

---

[97] Hennings to PC/RVP, 21 December 1951, KNA PC/RVP.6A/11/33.

[98] Baringo District AR, 1950.

[99] Robert Trow-Smith, *English Husbandry* (London, 1951), quoted with approval in the introduction to ALDEV, *African Land Development*.

[100] *A Plan to Intensify the Development of Agriculture in Kenya [Swynnerton Plan]* (Nairobi, 1954); Anne Thurston, *Smallholder Agriculture in Colonial Kenya: the Official Mind and the Swynnerton Plan* (Cambridge, 1987); M.P.K. Sorrenson, *Land Reform in Kikuyu Country* (London, 1967).

entire process was rushed through within six years – laid the foundation for the successes of Kenya's agricultural sector after independence, less attention has been paid to the impact of the spontaneous enclosure that took place in many other parts of Kenya from the 1940s.[101] Spontaneous enclosure was already widespread in the Kipsigis and Kisii districts by 1950, and in the years that followed it quickly developed in many other areas, including Nandi, Elgeyo and Baringo, as well as in some of the Luo locations to the west. Commenting briefly upon this trend, de Wilde suggested that it was driven primarily by growing land hunger, but it is also clear that in many districts colonial officials gave tacit encouragement to spontaneous enclosure even where it contradicted the thrust of prevailing local policies for rural development.[102] The debacle hinged upon a dilemma: Should the 'more progressive elements' in the district be allowed to set the pace of development by spontaneously enclosing land, even where this was unregulated and might amount to little more than a 'land grab' by an enterprising few, and even if it might be ecologically and economically unsound in the longer term? Or should properly formulated plans for consolidation and registration be drawn up first, and then carefully implemented so as to ensure a fairer and more sustainable distribution of lands amongst all those with legitimate claims? Agricultural and veterinary staff generally argued for planned and supervised settlement schemes, but, in practice, local district officials found it expedient to allow spontaneous enclosure where it suited the politics of the moment, and to let someone else worry about the future consequences.

So it was in southern Baringo. Spontaneous enclosure first became apparent in the district during 1950. Officials were keen to encourage this in the arable-farming regions of the Tugen Hills as an example of what could be achieved by 'improved methods of husbandry', even though consolidation had not taken place.[103] As an incentive, small loans were made available to farmers who enclosed and, by 1952, the district office was receiving a steady stream of requests for assistance. The first two loans were granted to hill farmers in 1951 and another six in 1952, each with small-holdings of more than 8 acres, which were laid out and planned under the guidance of African Agricultural Instructors.[104] Over the next two years, the enclosure movement picked up 'astonishing momentum' throughout the district, but most especially in the southern lowlands, where 'enclosure of individual holding gained impetus at so fast a rate that little control [was] exerted'.[105] Here, spontaneous enclosure bred conflict between the younger

[101] Sorrenson, *Land Reform*.

[102] De Wilde, *Experiences with Agricultural Development*, ii, 170–71.

[103] DC/BAR to PC/RVP, 26 October 1950, KNA PC/RVP.6A/11/43.

[104] Baringo District AR, 1952. By 1954 there were thirty-four male and seven female Agricultural Instructors in the district, virtually all based in the hills and more the three-quarters of them in northern Baringo; Baringo District AR, 1954.

[105] Ibid., 1953 and 1954 (for the quote).

generation, who led the movement, and the elders, who defended 'long-established communal grazing rights'. Elders were not alone in their opposition and, in some places, newly erected fences were torn down by *murran* herding stock, who objected to the restriction to common grazing.[106] Officials, who saw enclosure as a beneficial development over the longer run, were initially happy to sit back and watch these conflicts emerge, seeing the struggles as a helpful contribution to finding the solution to Baringo's problems.[107] But the situation ran out of control very much more rapidly than anyone had anticipated. In the hills it soon proved difficult to persuade farmers to dedicate their efforts and investment to the enclosed plot when they still maintained several other patches of land scattered over the hillside.[108] Where loans had been made to hill farmers, government could exert at least some control over how the enclosed land was developed. On the lowlands, requests for loans were rarely entertained, as Tugen here were considered to be wealthy enough in stock to meet any capital costs of development from their own resources. Once spontaneous enclosure had been permitted here, there was little that officials could do about it.

Much of the land that was spontaneously enclosed on the lowlands by the mid-1950s was considered to be ecologically better suited to ranching and officials worried that the smallholdings claimed were often economically unviable. 'The fact cannot be disregarded', wrote the DC in 1956, 'that the majority of the more educated Tugen prefer the idea of smallholdings and look upon the idea of a manyatta with abhorrence.' Ranching was 'the ideal medium of introducing them gradually to the principles of correct land management', he argued, but they increasingly rejected this option. This he attributed to the influence of European farms, noting that spontaneous enclosure was most widespread in areas adjacent to the settler lands: 'Thus, in the areas from Chemogoch to Kabimoi and northwards within the Emening Triangle, there has been a tremendous increase in the acquisition of smallholdings.' People were pushing ahead in this area without survey or proper planning, with 'chaotic' results and considerable conflict among themselves.[109] The European farms may well have been a model for some, but for others the move to enclose was a protective strategy rather than an acquisitive one. The fencing of the reserve boundary at Solai and Esageri after 1945 emphasized the permanence of the denial of access to the highland grazing, and many lowland Tugen, especially those with some resources to invest in the development of a farm, had undoubtedly come to the view that it was a sensible move.[110] As early as 1950, it had been noted that Tugen generally

---

[106] Ibid., 1953 and 1954.

[107] See, for example, DC/BAR to PC/RVP, 26 October 1950, KNA PC/RVP.6A/11/43.

[108] Baringo District AR, 1955. All but one of the hill farmers given loans were in default on repayments by 1955.

[109] Baringo District AR, 1956.

[110] BHT/TG/76 and BHT/TG/88.

did not see enclosure as an alternative to common land use, but as an option to be exercised alongside it:

> Most people who enclose do not play the game. They also graze on the commons, thus getting the most advantage both ways at the expense of others. If a man encloses grazing he should reduce his cattle accordingly. Most people who enclose would rather abandon enclosure than sell off the rest of their stock which continue to be farmed out and graze on the commons.[111]

While they could 'get it both ways – by putting stock on their enclosures and grazing on the common as well', they did not even need to reduce their commitment to herding;[112] and, for many, enclosure allowed them to escape the increased control and supervision that was evident in the ranching schemes then being advanced by government, with the branding of stock, enforced culling and the issuing of grazing permits. By 1957, most lowland Tugen expressed 'active opposition or complete apathy' towards ranching. Enclosure had become the popular demand: 'Judging from the antics of the more vocal members of the community, everyone wants an individual holding and none want the ranching system.'[113]

The enclosure movement was supported by the most 'progressive' and modernizing Tugen, but in their opposition to ranching schemes they found themselves in alliance with more conservative herders, who wished only to avoid government controls or to preserve open access to the commons. This powerful, if somewhat improbable, coalition of interests systematically undermined the implementation of controlled grazing schemes and ranches throughout southern Baringo from the mid-1950s onwards.

A new ranching scheme had been launched at Esageri in November 1954, using a paddocking system of rotational grazing blocks over some 26,000 acres. Cattle numbers were limited to ten per grazier, and only 260 graziers were registered for the scheme. A permit was issued for each branded animal on the ranch, with a grazing fee charged for each head of stock, the fees to be used for the development of services on the ranch.[114] Heavy policing restricted the degree of trespass and goats were completely eliminated from the area, with heavy fines being imposed for transgression of the rules. All trespassing stock was confiscated under local by-laws, with the cases coming before the District Officer at Eldama Ravine and, although the herders had initially been told that the proceeds from the sale of trespassing stock would be returned to them, this proved legally

---

[111] DC/BAR to PC/RVP, 26 October 1950, KNA PC/RVP.6A/11/43.

[112] Baringo District AR, 1955.

[113] Ibid., 1957.

[114] The proposal originated from R.O. Hennings, 'South Baringo: Esageri', 26 June 1954, KNA PC/RVP.6A/11/33. Interestingly, Hennings advocated that some land be made available for individual holdings from the outset, although this suggestion was not initially implemented.

impossible.[115] Through the collection of fees and the accumulation of fines, by 1956 the scheme was self-financing and the graziers even agreed to an increase in the fees to allow further development. The Esageri scheme was now paraded as a model that could be applied in other parts of the district. But, when a survey of the stock on the ranch was conducted in 1956, a possible reason for the graziers' compliance became apparent. Of the animals on the Esageri paddocks, 81 per cent were found to be female and only 19 per cent male: the ranch was evidently a breeding-ground for young stock, which were then being returned to unregulated lands within the reserve to the north. In effect, the improved pastures of Esageri were being used 'as an incubator'; the ranch was assisting in the restocking of herds throughout the district, and turning a handsome profit for the graziers in the process. To control this it was decided to prevent ranch stock from returning to the reserve by insisting that the offtake be sold on to outside buyers, whether adult or immature. As soon as this intention was revealed to the graziers, agitation for the subdivision of the ranch into smallholdings reached clamorous proportions.[116] The Tugen attitude to the ranch was clear enough. The ranch held attraction for herders only when it could be utilized in conjunction with the existing system of communal grazing. Once restrictions prevented this, the herders preferred to request smallholdings, which they hoped to manage without the interference of government.

Despite these difficulties, the creation of many more large ranches of the Esageri type formed the central element of the new district development programme for Baringo put forward under ALDEV during 1956. The Perkerra Catchment Scheme was based upon an integrated, ecological-systems approach to the development of the district, drawing together plans for reafforestation on the Mau, in Lembus and along the spine of the Tugen Hills, with the development of large ranches on the lowlands, and the protection of the whole Perkerra River catchment area so as to secure the water-supply for the development of large-scale irrigation at Lake Baringo (see Chapter Nine). Championed by the ALDEV secretary, R.O. Hennings, the scheme greatly enlarged the number of European officers to be posted to the district and marked the return of a more determined approach to the whole question of overstocking and carrying capacity. Under these proposals, individual smallholdings were to be restricted to the ecologically more favoured areas, mostly in the extreme south of the district and in the hills. For the vast majority of herders, the ecology of the lands on which they lived dictated that their fate would be to join collectively in a large ranch, where the numbers of cattle would be restricted. Surplus animals

---

[115] The District Commissioner only agreed to implement the controls once money to pay for forty additional grazing guards was assured. Swann (ActPC/RVP) to Min for African Affairs, 10 August 1954, and related papers, KNA PC/NKU/2/2/35.

[116] DO/Ravine to PC/RVP, 3 December 1956, KNA PC/NKU/2/2/35. For a brief history of the scheme, Edmondson, 'South Baringo Grazing Scheme', 25 August 1956, KNA PC/NKU/2/2/35.

would be excluded from the ranches, and it was intended that a destocking programme would eventually be introduced to deal with the problem of those excess animals left on the unregulated rangelands. These proposals were deeply unpopular.[117]

Resistance to the ranching idea was particularly intense along the Solai border, where Chief Morogo had long battled against the opponents of government controls. The first signs of organized opposition had been apparent at Solai in 1952, when herders from Endebess and Ngentalel had excluded government servants and mission supporters from meetings to discuss the imposition of dipping fees. Among the leaders of this opposition were Chepto Ruto and Changwany Cheruiyot of Endebess, arap Chebegen of Ngentalel and Cherutich Chelelgo of Kisanana, all of whom were politically active in the district and known to be advocates of enclosure.[118] More prominent still were Cheptiony arap Lelmen and Musa arap Chesire, men who in all other respects might have been considered progressive by colonial officials. Each had been an outspoken member of the African DC, arap Lelmen having served as a member from 1947 and Chesire being elected in 1953; both were active in local commerce; and both were staunch opponents of grazing controls. As early as 1956, before tensions surrounding the ranching schemes overflowed, the district commissioner had requested arap Lelmen's removal from the African District Council (ADC). 'He is an influential man', he wrote to the provincial commissioner, who 'has set himself up in opposition to the local chief' and 'quietly makes propaganda against government land use schemes'. Within a few weeks, Lelmen had been removed from the ADC for alleged 'misbehaviour'.[119] None of these men could be styled as 'traditionalists', least of all Lelmen or Chesire, and yet all opposed government schemes. Under their guidance, Tugen stockowners at Kisanana refused to pay the dipping fees in 1952 and many removed livestock temporarily from the location to avoid the Veterinary Department's inspectors. There was also evidence throughout the 1950s that trespass into controlled grazing in this area was systematically organized so as to cause maximum disruption to government schemes, and again the same 'ringleaders' were suspected. When the 5,000 acres of controlled grazing at Kisanana was designated as an Esageri-style ranch in November 1955, there was immediately massive and coordinated trespass into the ranch from herders opposed to its creation or excluded from its membership.[120]

---

[117] Baringo District AR, 1956, for a summary of the scheme, and papers in KNA PC/NKU/2/2/29, for financing and operation over the first two years. The project had been drawn up in close consultation with the District Team, which had first met in January 1952. Arguments for the extension of the ranching schemes had first been made by the District Agricultural Officer, Iain MacLeod, 'Memo on agricultural policy in South Baringo', 19 August 1952, KNA PC/RVP.6A/11/15.

[118] Jones (DO/Eldama Ravine) to DC/Baringo, 4 July 1952, KNA DO/ER/2/2/4.

[119] DC/BAR to PC/RVP, 19 June 1956, KNA PC/NKU/2/1/104.

[120] Baringo District AR, 1956.

In January 1957, when a stock census along the border was imminent in preparation for the extension of the ranching scheme, there was a mass movement of cattle out of Ngentalel and into Waseges, again inspired and organized by local activists. As a consequence, some 1,000 head of cattle died in Waseges by the end of March from tsetse and East Coast fever. Herders blamed the government – and especially Chief Morogo – for their losses, but by April most had returned to Ngentalel, much the poorer for their adventure.[121]

The deepening divisions between opponents and supporters of government at Solai were compounded by the politics of clientage. Chief Morogo was judged to be 'a man of outstanding ability and energy' and the most successful of all the African agents of government in Baringo. From his appointment, in September 1950, opposition to him at Kisanana and Ngentalel was 'vigorous and well nigh violent', but Morogo dealt with the 'belligerent old men and lazy youths' with a firm hand. When trespass cases came before the chief in the Native Tribunal Court, Morogo was notoriously severe in his treatment of offenders.[122] But Morogo and his headmen were widely believed to use their privileged positions to advantage themselves, infringing grazing-control rules by trespassing with their own cattle and exploiting opportunities to place their own nominees within the ranching schemes. It is evident that colonial officers were generally aware of this, but tended to see it as an inevitable consequence of the confrontational politics that the schemes provoked; this was certainly the view taken by Edmondson, the European officer responsible for the ranching schemes at Solai in the mid-1950s and the official who worked most closely with Chief Morogo.[123] From time to time, even officials were embarrassed by the more public aspects of this clientage. In May 1957, for example, a raid into the Kisanana ranch caught 100 head of trespassing cattle, including animals belonging to Chief Morogo, his office clerk and all his senior headmen.[124] Massive dissatisfaction with the allocation of permits to graziers at the time of the Kiplombe-Esageri exchange was proved to have been well founded several years later, when, in June 1958, a group of 174 Tugen made representations through a Nakuru-based firm of advocates to claim they had been made landless as a consequence of the exchange. The District Officer at Eldama Ravine took over the investigation of this from Chief Joel Chirmirmir, and after carefully scrutinizing some 133 of the claimants – all of those who could be traced – reached the conclusion that at least thirty-three had legitimate claims. These persons appeared on the original

[121] Various monthly intelligence reports, 1956–7, in KNA DO/ER/2/3/6.
[122] For the failings of his predecessor, see March 1950, KNA PC/NKU/2/2/32; and PC/NKU/2/2/30, for trespass cases before Native Courts from 1949; also Baringo District AR, 1949.
[123] Interview with Edmondson, BHT/ES/3.
[124] See various papers, KNA DO/ER/2/3/6.

Kiplombe register of squatters and should have been made provision for in the exchange.[125] Episodes such as this did little to inspire confidence that land-use regulations would be fairly applied.

The most intense episode of resistance to the ranching schemes flared up in Mugurin and Gobat, as the Perkerra Catchment Scheme was introduced there between 1957 and 1959. The flames were fanned by Musa Chesire. A week after government officials had explained the advantages of the ranching proposals to a *baraza* at Mugurin, sixty herders attended a second meeting organized by Chesire in opposition to the scheme.[126] The District Officer dismissed the protesters as 'a few half-educated people who want smallholdings', but was aware that trouble was likely.[127] Opponents of the ranches had been successful in getting themselves nominated on to the local committee set up to oversee the issuing of grazing permits and, through their membership, tried to forestall the control measures. When this proved futile and officials arrived to implement the scheme in July 1957, the people refused to move their homesteads or their stock. Several arrests were made on charges of 'obstructing government business', and one Mugurin herder, Kipsunui arap Beres, was sentenced to six months' hard labour as an example to other protesters.[128] This confrontation only intensified the resistance of what the DC was still pleased to dismiss as 'a handful of malcontents'. The people of Mugurin now organized the collection of money to employ lawyers from Nakuru, with a view to taking out an injunction to prevent the imposition of grazing controls. This proved costly and ineffective, but for several months it caused great irritation to the increasingly beleaguered district administration. Meanwhile, from August 1957, agitation against the scheme spread over a widening area and all voluntary cooperation with the administration in the Mugurin and Solai areas collapsed. Within a few weeks there was disruption on every ranching scheme in southern Baringo.

Local chiefs, led by the redoubtable Morogo, were now pushed into the firing-line to gain the confidence of the majority, whom the administration persisted in assuming were being swayed by a minority of agitators. *Barazas* were speedily held all over the district to set out the official view, but reactions were so hostile that it was feared the protests might become violent. Before the end of September, a platoon of the General Service Unit (GSU) – the paramilitary wing of the Kenya Police – was posted to Mugurin to restore order. A Kenya Police detachment replaced them from 14 to 21 November, and another GSU platoon then came and patrolled the area until the end of November. By the end of the month, these intimidatory

[125] A full account of the investigation appears in KNA DO/ER/2/10/7. The timing of this complaint was almost certainly influenced by political developments in the neighbouring Lembus Forest. See Chapter Eight.

[126] Papers in KNA PC/NKU/2/1/105.

[127] Papers in KNA DO/ER/2/3/6.

[128] Ibid.

tactics appeared to be working and the DC was able to report 'indications of a change of heart' among the people of Mugurin.[129] But Mugurin continued 'to be a very sore spot' throughout all of the next year, with serious trouble brewing up in neighbouring Gobat, where the people mounted a 'mass civil disobedience' campaign to resist all efforts to impose ranching controls.[130] From June to August the GSU were again called in to the Mugurin and Gobat areas. 'Almost all the people do not accept control and do not obey orders unless forced to', reported the District Officer.[131] Towards the end of the year, it was even rumoured that a *laibon* had visited the area and 'stirred up certain Tugen to take illegal action against grazing control measures'.[132]

By 1959, protest against the ranching schemes appeared to be universal. Opposition to all kinds of collective activity was everywhere led by those who were most determined to have individual holdings. Musa Chesire, in particular, continued to busy himself against the schemes, setting up the Baringo Independence Party in April 1959 and regularly raising protests through the ADC. He was briefly suspended from the Council, ostensibly because of a false accusation made against an Indian trader, but throughout the year the administration had plotted to persuade other councillors to censure him. Despite the best efforts of the officials, Chesire was voted back on to the Council with a resounding majority in the elections of February 1960.[133] His popularity was undoubtedly based upon his opposition to government, and he continued to support the protests that rippled across all of the ranching schemes. At Kisanana and Ngentalel, herders refused to pay for grazing permits and revolted against the Special Rate levied to maintain the boreholes, so both were closed down for part of the year.[134] At Gobat, eighty herders unilaterally enclosed land in the best grazing paddock during 1960, and police had to be sent in to rip the fences down.[135] At Ngendalel and Ol Kokwe, there was much agitation to divide the land into smallholdings and at neighbouring Kisanana, people refused to accept the issuing of grazing permits, only cooperating when a proper survey and formal allocation of individual holdings were promised.[136]

Faced by this widespread resistance from 1957 onwards, the administration gradually capitulated, making provision for smallholdings on most of the ranching schemes and allowing title to be confirmed to the lands that had been spontaneously enclosed on the lowlands. The price to be paid for

---

[129] South Baringo AR 1957; Baringo District AR, 1957.
[130] Baringo District AR, 1958. DC/BAR to Hennings, 10 June 1958, KNA PC/NKU/2/2/36.
[131] Papers in KNA PC/NKU/2/2/36.
[132] Baringo District AR, 1958.
[133] See KNA PC/NKU/2/1/104 and PC/NKU/2/1/105.
[134] DC/BAR to DO/Eldama Ravine, 16 June 1959, KNA PC/NKU/2/18/7.
[135] Baringo District AR, 1960.
[136] DC/BAR to DO/Eldama Ravine, 16 June 1959, KNA PC/NKU/2/18/7.

Table 7.3 Livestock census, 1957: South Baringo locations

	Owners	Cattle	Sheep and goats	Total units*	Surplus units
Lembus	1,243	18,946	28,842	24,734	16,734
Kakamor	735	9,857	30,126	15,882	12,992
Pokorr-Keben	1,419	31,355	56,112	32,577	25,122
Endorois	1,306	20,208	76,744	35,557	20,891
Totals	4,703	80,366	191,824	108,750	75,739

* Five sheep or goats = 1 stock unit

Source: '1957 Baringo Stock Census', KNA DO/ER/2/24/7. The census was taken in December 1957 and was estimated to be 95 per cent accurate for the cattle count and 90 per cent accurate for sheep and goats.

this was Tugen agreement to yet another destocking campaign: if individual holdings were to go ahead, then there would have to be cull of cattle. Preparations for a cull had begun late in 1957, with the most painstaking livestock census undertaken since 1946. With a new field abattoir built at Marigat in the same year, officials now had a means of disposing of stock within the district. The 1957 census revealed a remarkably different distribution of stock in the southern locations, the decline in cattle numbers in Lembus being the most notable feature, but showed that all these locations were more heavily stocked than before, with a particularly marked increase in the numbers of sheep and goats (Table 7.3). On the estimates of the Livestock Officer, a massive cull would be needed – above 40 per cent in some locations – to bring the livestock holdings within the carrying capacity of the land. The decision was taken to enforce a five-year culling programme from 1959, but to do so through the agency of the Baringo Rules Committee. This body had initially been set up in 1958, comprising the DC and six African members (drawn from the ADC; members included Chief Morogo and Chief Joel Chirmirmir of Lembus), to administer the controls to be enforced on the grazing schemes. The committee was now given a broader role in adjudicating on individual holdings and in setting cull quotas for livestock sales in each location.[137] This linked the two processes of enclosure and destocking, making it difficult for those supporting enclosure to actively campaign against destocking. The Rules Committee toured the district to win support for the cull, and negotiated quotas with local subcommittees in each location. For the administration,

[137] The new Rules Committee was constituted under Government Notice 2162, 6 June 1958, to comprise six members of the African District Council, along with the District Commissioner. Its powers replaced orders in force under Government Notices 383 of 1939 and 838 of 1942, which had given government powers to control land use only in 'B' areas (that is, land opened to African use by the recommendation of the Land Commission of 1932: Esageri, Kisanana, Churo), the Emening triangle, Gobat and the Lembus Forest. See Butler (DC/BAR) to Wolff (PC/RVP), 20 April 1959, KNA PC/NKU/2/18/7.

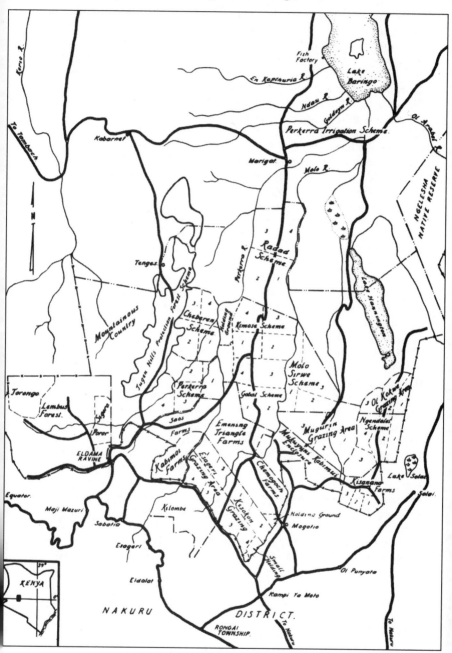

Map 7.1 Grazing schemes, southern Baringo, 1945–63

this at first proved a successful strategy, but this was largely because the 'prices paid for good stock were little short of fantastic'. By the end of the year, more than a hundred traders were attending each sale, mostly from Nyanza and Central Province. Once again, as in the immediate postwar years, Baringo's stock-owners were happy to sell in a buoyant market and the Rules Committee had little trouble persuading herders to participate. The sales in 1959 realized £85,000.[138] The market remained strong into the early months of 1960, but then disaster struck: a foot-and-mouth outbreak brought a quarantine to the district, and in July the compulsory cull was formally halted because of a severe drought. By the end of the year, many herders were suffering serious losses and the Marigat field abattoir was unable to pay its way. By 1961, it was clear that drought had achieved a cull as effectively as the destocking campaign had intended, with losses over the entire district estimated to be above 50 per cent, but, instead of providing an influx of cash to herders that could be used for the further development of the district, it had caused massive losses. For the first time since the 1930s, 1960 saw the distribution of famine relief to some 500 families on the Baringo lowlands.[139]

With the destocking campaign getting off to a good start in 1959, government now greatly speeded up the process of survey and registration of Baringo's smallholdings. In the Emening triangle, immediately to the north-east of Esageri, smallholdings that had been set up by the people themselves at Nguberetti and Saos were adjudicated for registration during 1959 and 1960.[140] At Chemogoch the people had seized the initiative and marked out their own enclosures, farms varying from 35 to 250 acres in size; in 1959 these lands were surveyed and formalized into plots averaging 50 acres, with considerable readjustment to many of the claims.[141] Individual holdings were allowed on part of Kisokon from 1958, and this was extended to the entire Esageri ranching scheme from 1961. At Kisanana, fifty-two farms were marked out and, at Ngentalel, 200 graziers secured claims to smallholdings by the end of 1960. By this time, more than 800 smallholdings had been registered on the lowlands of southern Baringo, the vast majority of these on lands that had originally been designated for the development of ranching schemes.[142] Even at Mugurin, government finally gave way, retaining 30,300 acres as ranch land but excising 6,540 acres of more productive land towards the Molo River for enclosure. The success of this initiative restored some modicum of local support. Linked with the decision to allow smallholdings was the recognition that it would be impossible to

---

[138] Baringo District AR, 1959. See 'Baringo District Rules, 1954–60', KNA PC/NKU/2/18/7.

[139] Baringo District ARs, 1959, 1960 and 1961. Cf. Little, *Elusive Granary*, 52.

[140] Butler (DC/BAR) to DO/Eldama Ravine, 20 November 1958, KNA PC/NKU/2/2/36.

[141] Baringo District ARs, 1956, 1957 and 1958.

[142] Ibid., 1958, 1959 and 1960. See also Butler (DC/BAR), 'Short notes on betterment schemes in South Baringo', n.d. [Feb. 1959?], KNA PC/NKU/2/18/7.

Table 7.4 Grazing schemes, southern Baringo, 1945–63

	Acreage	Graziers	Stock units per scheme	Stock units per grazier (av.)	Comments
1. Solai border/Mugurin					
Ngentalel	11,700	186	800	5	Began under DARA, 1946. ALDEV control from 1958 Block rotation began 1957
Kisanana	5,000	31	240	8	Began under DARA, 1946. Ranching developed from 1955. ALDEV control from 1958, then divided into individual holdings
Mugurin	17,325	249	1,175	5	Began under ALDEV 1957. Better land removed for enclosure, 1959. Abandoned 1962
Molo Sirwe	10,000	103	522	5	Separated from Mugurin in 1960, abandoned in 1962
Ol Kokwe	9,500	144	658	4.5	Begun 1958. ALDEV
Kabimui	8,800	187	676	3.5	Divided into individual holdings from 1955
2. South Baringo (Esageri)					
Kisokon	14,500	87	860	10	Formerly known as Esageri ranch. Divided into individual holdings from 1961
Kiptuin	13,600	197	1,946	10	
Kilombe	13,205	100	1,000	10	Transferred to White Highlands 1950. Rented to Tugen from 1954
3. Perkerra Catchment					
Gobat South	16,800	267	1,680	6	Began 1958, divided 1960. ALDEV
Kimoset	16,200	208	1,157	5.5	
Radad	25,000	211	1,250	6	Began 1960. ALDEV
Perkerra	16,750	333	1,333	4	Began 1958, under ALDEV
Cheberen	19,000	351	1,200	3.4	Began June 1960

destock in Mugurin because this would leave too many families with too few cattle for their livelihood. Some thirty years earlier, Crewe-Read had come to the same conclusion: colonial administration had a short memory.[143]

Even with acceptance of smallholdings, the politics of control and exclusion still rumbled on. The issuing of grazing permits had never been popular with herders, who maintained that the land should be part of the open range, regulated by the elders and the community, not by government. In the tensions of 1957–9, refusal to pay fees or to accept permits became the easiest and most direct means of protest. Among smallholders there was anxiety that government would try to maintain the permits even on enclosed lands. This fear was fuelled by the knowledge that when the first official smallholdings had been allowed at Kisokon, the holders were obliged to continue to buy permits for their stock. The steps taken to prevent herders at the Esageri ranch from returning cattle to the reserve also implied that smallholders may not be free to dispose of their livestock as they wished; those Tugen establishing smallholdings were now determined not to be cut off from the reserve in the same way. But, when the Baringo Rules Committee was set up early in 1958, the power to exert controls over any part of Baringo, with regard to herding or cultivation, was extended within the discretion of the committee. In effect, any area, whether held communally or individually, could now be subject to control. The fears of smallholders appeared to be well founded.

The controversy over this wide extension of authority to impose controls drew the elected African Member of the Legislative Council for the Northern Rift Valley into the Baringo debate for the first time, and gave the politics of the crisis a sharper edge, as Kenya moved into the post-Mau Mau phase of negotiation that would culminate in independence in 1963. It was rather surprising that Daniel Toroitich arap Moi had not become involved sooner. A Tugen from the hills around Tenges, in central Baringo, and the claimant to a smallholding at Kabimoi, he was undoubtedly fully aware of the struggles on the Baringo lowlands throughout the 1950s. He was even a member of the ALDEV board, which oversaw the implementation of development policies, so he had seen all of the proposals within the Perkerra Catchment Scheme in advance of their implementation; he was present at the ALDEV meeting of 20–21 January 1958, when the draft proposals for the new Baringo Rules Committee were discussed in detail. It was not until March 1959, after he had himself refused to accept the issuing of a permit for his own land at Kabimoi, that Moi entered the fray.[144] Raising the matter with the Baringo DC, and through the ALDEV executive officer, Moi argued that, in maintaining the permit system, the

---

[143] Paragraph from Baringo District AR, 1959.
[144] Kiplagat Chesire to Governor, 12 March 1959; Moi to Butler (DC/BAR), 30 March 1959; Wolff (PC/RVP) to Butler (DC/BAR), 7 April 1959, and related correspondence; for Moi's refusal of the permit, see Butler (DC/BAR) to Wolff (PC/RVP), 20 April 1959, all in KNA PC/NKU/2/18/7.

government was 'hampering the African farmer' by seeking 'to control him'. In principle, no smallholder should be subjected to such controls: if smallholdings were to be a success, then the farmer must manage his own lands, argued Moi. Moreover, there already existed regulations to prosecute farmers and herders under the land-usage by-laws, enforceable through the ADC. But permits were equally objectionable to Moi when imposed on ranching schemes, where they tended to rigidify the pattern of stock holding: unless the number of stock held on permit were regularly reviewed, 'the result would be that a rich man would have a guarantee that he remained rich and a poor man would be unable to increase his wealth'.[145] Where the administration argued that the permits were a protection to ensure that every herder was allowed to graze at least some stock on ranch lands and that this needed to be regulated through the Baringo Rules Committee, which could arbitrate local disputes, Moi wanted all of the controls and regulatory devices placed at the local level, entirely in African hands. Over the next two years he was to get his way, as preparations were made for independence and an increasing degree of authority was handed down to local African government.

Around the same time, Kiplagat Chesire had submitted to the government a more populist version of Moi's criticisms of the permits. The brother of Musa Chesire, and a shop-owner at Emening trading centre and smallholder in Chemogoch, Kiplagat Chesire lacked Moi's elected status, but none the less expressed views that were widely shared by other Tugen. In his lengthy letter to the governor, Kiplagat Chesire offered a wide-ranging critique of government land policies and accused the chiefs and elected members of local government committees of high-handedness and favouritism. His strongest complaint was that the ranching schemes – the '*manyatta*' system, as he termed it – were deeply unpopular with the people, who 'have to abandon their homes [to] follow the cattle' between the various blocks of grazing on the orders of government. This had never been the Tugen practice in the past, and they did not want it imposed upon them now. DC Butler, still keen to enforce government programmes, disputed the veracity of this assertion; but Chesire's words echoed the sentiments of many colonial officials, who now, in the wake of such wide-spread opposition, were uncertain of the advantages of the ranching schemes.[146] On safari through Baringo in September 1957, with the troubles at Mugurin reaching crisis point, the provincial veterinary officer gave vent to his doubts about rotational ranching schemes that inevitably restricted the carrying capacity of the wider rangeland to the tolerance level of the worst block of land within the rotation. Although he doubted

---

[145] The quoted phrase is not Moi's own, but a paraphrase of his statement, rendered by the Provincial Commissioner: Wolff (PC/RVP) to Butler (DC/BAR), 7 April 1959, KNA PC/NKU/2/18/7.

[146] Butler to Wolff, 30 April 1959, KNA PC/NKU/2/18/7, dismissed Kiplagat Chesire as someone 'who is always causing trouble and will not listen to reason'.

whether smallholdings on the lowlands would bring much of an economic return to the majority of farmers, it could be no worse than the effects of ranching and would have other, social benefits. Not least, it would have local support. 'The people of Baringo ... cannot fancy being moved around in areas of 10 or 20 or 30,000 acres,' he argued. 'They want, like you or I, to have their house, a piece of land as a permanent thing, and their living (their shamba and their stock) near at hand.'[147] Kiplagat Chesire could not have put it better himself.

The enclosure of land had come about not from a positive policy decision of government, but through pressure from the people themselves. Colonial images of Baringo's Tugen people styled them as a pastoral people, and their presumed inability to farm effectively led many officials to argue that controlled grazing schemes were a necessary first step in 'teaching' them better husbandry in preparation for the eventual move to smallholdings. While it is surely the case that many of the Tugen who first came out of the hills with their few cattle in the early years of the twentieth century nurtured hopes of establishing themselves as prosperous herders of cattle, it is to be doubted that they ever intended to fully adopt a Maasai-style pattern of widespread seasonal movements. Rather, they hoped to occupy higher, wetter grazing lands to the east and south of the lowlands, from where they could replicate a pattern of mixed husbandry similar to that in the Tugen hills, but from a more advantageous ecological base and with a greater dependence upon livestock. By the 1950s, the descendants of those first migrants certainly had no desire to adopt a pattern of seasonal movements within government-controlled grazing schemes. Not all wanted smallholdings, but a significant and active minority saw the enclosure of land as a means of escaping government controls and improving their own material conditions of life.

It is difficult to avoid the conclusion that postwar colonial developers in Baringo were trapped within there own limited perceptions of the district's problems and the capabilities of its peoples. Colonial officials tried to 'manage' development along ecological lines, so as to restore and preserve the productive capacity of the land. In the face of a growing body of evidence to the contrary, the policies to restore grazing lands and maintain sustainable carrying capacities under controlled conditions in ALDEV's Perkerra Catchment Scheme perpetuated the myth that the Baringo lowlands had in the recent past been considerably more productive. Among officials in the technical departments of government, especially those with expertise in rangeland ecology and livestock husbandry, there were growing murmurs of dissent. Iain MacLeod was one veterinary officer who doubted that the Baringo lowlands had ever held productive grazing: 'It is easy, but illogical for want of proof, to say that this zone has depreciated through

---

[147] PVO/RVP to Exec Off/PAO, 16 September 1957, KNA PC/NKU/2/2/35.

over-stocking,' he argued.[148] Such viewpoints were expressed from time to time, but they had little impact upon policy. The wider politics of Baringo's image as 'a land in decay' continued to drive the development effort; and trespass on to European-owned farms and, increasingly embarrassingly, on to the government's own 'controlled' ranching schemes was the issue that sharpened that politics. For Governor Mitchell, for the ALDEV secretary R.O. Hennings, for District Commissioners like Lambert and Butler, for the European settlers, and for many others besides, Baringo's problems continued to be laid at the feet of 'ignorant' farmers and herders and the inability or unwillingness of government to exert adequate controls over their activities. Even as independence loomed and enclosure moved ahead at a pace on the lowlands, district commissioner Butler could still argue that African farmers in Baringo would not improve their enclosed land 'unless made to do so'.[149] Protest and opposition had forced the government to make concessions on the lowlands, but this did not mean that they were prepared to retreat everywhere. In the Lembus Forest, to the west of Esageri, the government faced a similar wave of opposition to its development programmes. Here, as we shall see in the next chapter, colonial officials were more determined to hold their ground.

[148] Macleod, 'Memo on agriculture in Baringo', KNA PC/RVP.6A/11/15.
[149] Butler to Wolff (PC/RVP), 20 April 1959, KNA PC/NKU/2/18/7.

Eight

The Captured Forest
Lembus, 1904–63

The history of the Lembus Forest stands at one remove from the broader pattern of events on the lowlands to the east, yet it is also integral to an understanding of the politics of ecology in Baringo. In the first years of this century, whilst the colonial conquest of the region was still under way, the government of the East Africa Protectorate awarded Lembus to a commercial company for the development of a timber industry. It was to prove one of the largest and most favourable land concessions made to Europeans in colonial Kenya. Through this concession, the Lembus Forest was separated from the subsequent administration of the native reserves of the adjoining districts, and indeed also separated from the direct jurisdiction of the Forest Department, who were responsible for forest reserves in other parts of the colony.

This chapter will examine the history of this concession over the colonial period, culminating in the transfer of control of the forest to the Baringo African District Council in 1958. This marked a political victory for those Tugen in southern Baringo who had long campaigned for their rights in Lembus to be formally recognized. At the end of the nineteenth century, herders from many communities, including Uasin Gishu Maasai, Nandi and Elgeyo, as well as Tugen, had grazed their animals within Lembus. Some of these were permanent residents of Lembus, clearing land on the forest fringes and in the more favourable glades for cultivation, and all were hunters and gatherers of forest products. Some Dorobo (Okiek) families had their homes within the forest at the turn of the century, although their numbers were relatively small.[1] For all those who used the

[1] Roderick H. Blackburn, 'The Okiek and their history', *Azania*, 9 (1974), 39–57.

forest, whether permanent residents or seasonal migrants, it had considerable ecological importance, and all were in some senses dependent upon access to it.[2] Colonialism would bring a severe curtailment of that access, and ultimately one group, the Tugen of Baringo, were able to assert rights over the forest that would exclude all others.

The political struggles of Baringo's Tugen against the commercial company who held legal tenure over the forest, against the forest department who sought to impose reafforestation and conservationist programmes limiting access to Lembus, against the district administration of Baringo who tried to establish a firmer grip on the politics of the area, and ultimately against other Africans who sought to exercise their own 'rights' in Lembus, will be the focus of this chapter. In these struggles, the ecology of the forest, and especially its relationship to the surrounding grazing lands, played a crucial role. The opening section of the chapter will provide the historical background to the alienation of the forest and the operation of the commercial lease to the end of the Second World War, revealing the sharp contradictions between private and public interests under colonialism. The crucial issue of 'native rights' in Lembus over the same period will be examined in the next section. The final part of the chapter will detail the political struggle to 'capture' the Lembus forest after 1945, illustrating the means by which Tugen agitation had brought Lembus back into the mainstream of Baringo's politics of ecology by the eve of independence.

Alienation & commercial forestry

> The forests of the Mau, Nandi Plateau, and the slopes of Mt Elgon contain hundreds of thousands of magnificent conifers – juniper and yew. The timber of the juniper is to all intents and purposes like cedar-wood. The mere thinning of these woods which is necessary for their improvement, and which might be carried out concurrently with the establishment of European settlements, would provide millions of cubic feet of timber, which would find a ready market on the east coast of Africa.[3]

Sir Harry Johnston's glowing description of the potentials of forestry was typical of the optimism that brought European settlers to East Africa in the early years of this century. Seldom substantiated by anything more than the passing glance of the traveller's eye, large tracts of East Africa were heralded as being rich in the resources that, with some initial investment, could support a new white settler colony. Among the greatest supporters of this view of the future was the High Commissioner for East Africa from 1900 to 1904, Sir Charles Eliot. Aware that investment on a large scale would be necessary to establish the new colony on a sound footing, Eliot used his position to encourage 'men of capital', both large and small, by offering

---

[2] Matson, *Nandi Resistance*, 17–19, 224–34, for comments on Lembus prior to 1900.

[3] Johnston, *Uganda Protectorate*, i, 291–2.

land concessions on highly favourable terms.[4] Agreements he entered into, often without consulting his political masters in London, forced the hand of a British government initially reluctant to sanction white settlement in East Africa, but they also proved to be Eliot's nemesis: as the extent of the commitments made became apparent in 1904, Eliot tendered his resignation in the face of mounting criticism of his actions.[5]

One proposal then already in an advanced stage of negotiation was for the establishment of a timber industry on the forested escarpments to the west of Eldama Ravine, whose economic potential had been so vividly announced by Sir Harry Johnston. A South African speculator named Charles Grant had briefly visited the area with his business partner George Fotheringhame in January 1904, and on returning to Nairobi had entered into negotiations with Eliot on the terms of a fifty-year lease to be granted over some 64,000 acres of forest. In common with other European observers in the early years of the present century,[6] Grant was hopelessly optimistic in his assessment of the economic potential of lumbering in Lembus. He told Eliot that he was prepared to meet the costs of constructing a mill immediately, and would also build a narrow-gauge tramway that would link the commercial forest to the railway some 20 miles to the south. Having whetted Eliot's appetite for investment, Grant returned to South Africa to raise additional capital for the project, entering into an agreement with Lingham & Neame's timber company of Johannesburg. Lingham then engaged an agent to represent his interests in the scheme, and it was in this capacity that Ewart Grogan arrived in Nairobi in May 1904.[7]

The murky dealings between Grogan, Lingham and Grant over the next few weeks were to result in legal suits amongst themselves rumbling over the next decade, and even attempts by Grant to sue the Secretary of State for breach of contract.[8] It is not entirely clear what transpired between them, but the outcome was that a counter-bid from Grogan, in partnership with Lingham, was lodged with the government of the British East Africa Protectorate. Where there had been worries about Grant's ability to raise the necessary capital, Grogan's ambitious proposals for the wider development opportunities of the infant colony drew the warm support of the High

---

[4] Sorrenson, *Origins of European Settlement* remains the best account.

[5] Matters can be followed in detail in *Correspondence Relating to the Resignation of Sir Charles Eliot and to the Concession to the East Africa Syndicate*, Cd 2099 (1904). Bennett's, 'Settlers and politics', 267–73, provides a useful summary.

[6] Johnston, *Uganda Protectorate*; Charles Eliot, *The East African Protectorate* (London, 1905).

[7] Papers in KNA AG4/2313 give a very full record of Grant's involvement in the Lembus contract.

[8] Grant succeeded in bringing Grogan to court, in April 1906, to contest legal ownership of the Lembus concession, but lost the case. Papers in KNA AG4/2313 give the background to this case, and the *East African Standard*, 4 May 1906, reports the court proceedings. Edward Paice rather unfairly dismisses Grant as 'a well-known malcontent', *Lost Lion of Empire: The Life of 'Cape-to-Cairo' Grogan* (London, 2001), 192.

Commissioner, Sir Charles Eliot. The two men had first met in Mombasa the day after Grogan's arrival in East Africa, and they then shared a carriage on the train journey to Nairobi. Although Lembus was at this time closed because of imminent military operations against the Nandi, Eliot gave Grogan permission to inspect the forest. While touring the Mau escarpment forests in June, Grogan also cast his entrepreneurial eye upon the undeveloped farmlands of the Uasin Gishu Plateau to the north, convincing himself that speculation in the development of the colony would bring considerable rewards. Before leaving East Africa, Grogan therefore purchased two large blocks of land for development within the township of Nairobi, secured Eliot's commitment to the forest concession and linked all of this to a promise of '100 acres of prime land in Mombasa' – 50 acres for a timber yard and 50 acres of water-frontage where port facilities could be built. This would all support the export of the timber to be milled. The Mombasa grant, according to Grogan's biographer Edward Paice, proved to be 'the crowning achievement of Grogan's two-month tour of British East Africa'. Eliot 'had been charmed out of his wits' by the enterprising Grogan.[9]

The two men departed together by steamer from Mombasa to England in early July 1904. Just a few days later, on 9 July 1904, the Acting High Commissioner, Charles Hobley, signed the licence agreement giving Ewart Grogan and his partner Lingham a timber concession of 64,000 acres 'near Eldama Ravine'.[10] The grant of wharfage land at Mombasa remained unsigned, as horrified Whitehall officials sought the legal means to renege upon Eliot's casual but costly agreement. In the meantime and before the steamer reached England, Eliot had resigned as High Commissioner, stung by official criticism of his overly cosy land dealings.[11]

The forest that Grogan had secured by these means covered a total area of approximately 100 square miles (see Map 8.1), immediately to the west of Eldama Ravine and north of Sclater's Road. It was, and is, an area of immense ecological importance to the surrounding region: Lembus lies across the watershed dividing the river systems of the Rift Valley and western Kenya, with the Perkerra River and its larger tributaries rising in the hilly downlands above the forest line at around 9,000 feet. Several smaller, but equally important, streams flow northwards, feeding into the Kerio River valley running toward Lake Turkana.[12] In 1903, Lembus was

---

[9] Paice, *Lost Lion*, 149–59, quotations from 159.

[10] Crown Advocate, 'Memorandum on the Lingham and Grogan timber concession', 11 October 1910, enclosure A, 'Original Licence', 9 July 1904; and all related correspondence in KNA AG4/2313.

[11] Paice, *Lost Lion*, 159–63, for a discussion that is sympathetic to Eliot. For the official papers, see *Correspondence Relating to the Resignation of Sir Charles Eliot,* Cd. 2099.

[12] Descriptions are to be found in D.E. Hutchins, *Report on the Forest of British East Africa* (London, 1909); J.F. Hughes, 'Forest and water supplies in East Africa', *Empire Forestry Journal,* 28 (1955), 31–42; Colony and Protectorate of Kenya, *An Economic Survey of Forestry in Kenya and Recommendations Regarding a Forest Commission* (Nairobi, 1950); ALDEV, *African Land Development.*

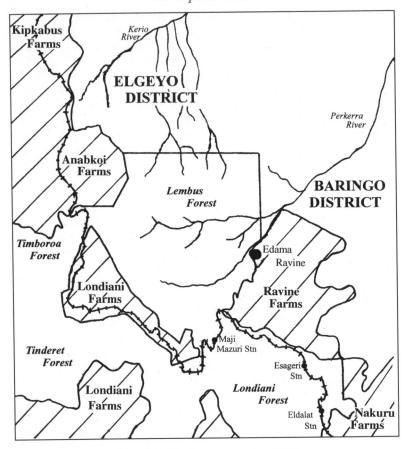

Map 8.1 The Grogan concession, 1916

made up variously of valuable economic forest land, some scrub and bush areas and a large number of glades. The individual glades varied from 30 to 300 acres in size, and offered valuable upland seasonal grazing to herders inhabiting the surrounding lowlands. The best of this grazing was to be found in the high and cold Torongo glades in the north-west portion of Lembus. Another extensive block of glades at Pororr, in the lower and warmer south-east corner of the forest near to Eldama Ravine, offered better conditions for mixed farming. Large areas of the forest proper were dense, consisting mainly of *podo* and cedar woods, with considerable quantities of bamboo to be found in clumps on the higher parts.[13]

---

[13] Cowley, 'Memorandum on agricultural aspects of the main forest-free areas of the Lembus Forest', KNA PC/NKU/2/1/31.

On first hearing, in February 1904, of the proposed development of a timber industry, officials in London had approved the idea in principle and provided Eliot with a forest licence from colonial Burma as a model. They much preferred this form of larger-scale capital enterprise, as against the individual settler farmers whose cause Eliot had so often championed. He was warned, however, that several clauses in the Burma contract would need emendation if the government's interests were to be protected in the particular conditions of East Africa.[14] It was a warning that appears to have been ignored. In his haste to secure forestry investment in the colony, Eliot promised substantial powers and inducements to the concessionaires, largely neglecting the requirements of the Forest Department and giving government very little control over the formal definition of the extent of the concession or its future working. Far from re-establishing the government's interests in these matters, Eliot's successor, Sir Donald Stewart, turned out to be an equally keen supporter of the forest enterprise. Dazzled by Grogan's grand plans for development of the Mau escarpment and the Uasin Gishu Plateau, in March 1905 Stewart agreed to a further lease of 64,000 acres to the Grogan and Lingham syndicate, doubling the size of the initial concession. He also 'agreed in principle to Grogan's demands' regarding the working of the concession.[15]

Difficulties in the administration of the concession first surfaced when, in 1907, having finally succeeded in getting the forest surveyed and mapped, Grogan then attempted to formally define the full extent of his rights. Grogan insisted that key clauses in the licence should be interpreted so as to exclude non-forested areas from the acreage accounted within the terms of the agreement. This implied a vast extension of the area over which the concessionaire might choose to work. Next, Grogan determined and sought to enforce a method of calculating royalty payments that seriously disadvantaged government and gave the concessionaire a significant economic advantage over all other sawyers in the colony. The Forest Department dug their heels in and refused to accept the terms as interpreted by Grogan. Having allowed Grogan and Lingham 'to create what amounted to their own principality' to the west of the Rift Valley, Eliot and Stewart had between them sown the seeds of what would be a long-running and rancorous squabble.[16]

For the next few years, protracted legal wrangling held back the development of the timber industry in Lembus. Grogan's position was bolstered by his claim to the valuable wharf-frontage at Mombasa, which

[14] Lansdowne to Eliot, 25 April 1904, KNA AG 4/2313.

[15] See correspondence between Stewart and Lansdowne from January to March 1905, including Grogan's enlarged scheme (dated 8 January 1905), in PRO CO 533/1. Quotation from Paice, *Lost Lion*, 167.

[16] Correspondence in KNA AG 4/2313 covers these initial disputes. Paice, *Lost Lion*, 167, for the quotation. By the end of 1905, Grogan had secured the backing of the financier, C.S. Goldman, and the political support of Sir George Goldie. See *Lost Lion*, 172–3.

Eliot had rashly offered to facilitate the export of merchantable timber to South Africa. In reality, it was this and not the forest concession that held greater economic value to Grogan in the longer run. As the colony's economy grew and the pressure on Mombasa's poorly developed harbour mounted, Grogan knew his bargaining position would strengthen,[17] whilst the Forest Department pressed for the foreclosure of the lease. His prominence as a leader among the white settler community (he was elected president of the Colonists' Association in January 1907) and his energy in hounding government on several fronts simultaneously made the politics of the situation even more difficult to resolve.[18] When, in 1910, the Crown Advocate finally advised that government would be unlikely to win if it went to law against Grogan to seek termination of the contract, the Conservator of Forests was compelled to renegotiate a new licence without altering the financial provisions of the original agreement.[19]

When the renegotiated lease was finally signed in March 1916, it pleased Grogan rather more than the government. During 1912, Grogan had spent £8,000 on establishing a sawmill at Maji Mazuri, and then no less than £20,000 on the construction of a 20-mile tramway linking it to the mainline station at Mau Summit. But subsequent exploitation of the forest 'proved a nightmare', Grogan's lumbering company, Equator Sawmills (ESM) being severely hampered by labour shortages and adverse weather.[20] Although by February 1914 Grogan was able to claim orders to a value of £30,000, his timber business required constant investment and he lacked the capital;[21] and the outbreak of war later that year saw ESM teeter towards the verge of bankruptcy by 1918.[22] Whilst Grogan felt he should be given the easiest possible terms for the profitable working of the concession in order to combat his difficulties, the Conservator of Forests was still appalled by the extent of the freedoms given to the concessionaire.[23]

---

[17] The lease on the Mombasa land was not in fact agreed until November 1920, and then Grogan received only 50 acres, not the 100 originally promised. Paice, *Lost Lion*, 318–19.

[18] Ibid., 210. In addition to Paice, two other biographies chart Grogan's political career: Norman Wymer, *The Man from the Cape: The First Trek from Cape to Cairo* (London, 1959); and Leda Farrant, *The Legendary Grogan: Kenya's Controversial Pioneer* (London, 1981). Paice's account is by far the most critical and the more informative.

[19] Crown Advocate, 'Memo, on the Lingham and Grogan Timber concession', 11 October 1910, and other papers, KNA AG 4/2313.

[20] Paice, *Lost Lion*, 251–2. By the end of 1911, Grogan was the sole concessionaire of Lembus, having taken over Lingham's interests (after Lingham took his businesses into voluntary liquidation) and bought out Goldman's share. By the early 1920s, Lord Howard de Walden had bought in to the company as a minority shareholder; Paice, *Lost Lion*, 248, 326 n20.

[21] Ibid., 254–5.

[22] Ibid., 278.

[23] Acting Conservator of Forests to Attorney-General, 3 November 1920, 'Copy of Forest Lease, 1 March 1916', and related correspondence, KNA AG 4/2313; Conservator of Forests to Osborne (Senior Commissioner, Kerio), 31 July 1925, KNA ARC(FOR) 7/2/128, for a summary of the department's criticisms of the early operation of the concession.

The reasons for his outrage were partly commercial and partly conservationist. Colonial forestry in Kenya, as throughout British Africa, was initially modelled on the example of colonial India.[24] During the second half of the nineteenth century, Indian forestry had been established on a sound commercial base, raising revenue for government while also being able to finance extensive programmes of reafforestation.[25] Forestry in India paid for itself and, from this position of strength, gained support in government circles for a conservationist strategy that would ensure continued revenue surpluses. In short, commercial viability had facilitated conservation and reafforestation in India, to the benefit of the state exchequer. In the early 1900s, Indian-trained foresters were recruited to the African colonies in the hope of achieving the same results. But it soon became apparent that the lower yield of merchantable timber in the majority of African forests made it impossible to generate sustained revenue surpluses on the scale experienced in India. Unable to realize their revenue-raising potential and therefore in need of subsidy in order to mount programmes of reafforestation and preservation, Forest Departments quickly came to be seen as a drain on the limited financial resources of the colonial state in Africa.[26] In these circumstances, the Lembus concession was particularly galling to the Kenya Forest Department. Not only was the department being denied income because of the ludicrously low rates of royalties fixed under the lease, but the preservation work of the department was being hampered by the manner in which Grogan's agents and contractors were exploiting the forest, endangering its longer-term sustainability.[27] To understand the attitude of the foresters we need to examine more closely the financial arrangements under the Lembus Forest lease and the working of the lease by the concessionaire from 1912 onwards.

An important feature of the early negotiations over the Lembus concession was the agreement that the normal royalties payable to government on all merchantable timber extracted from the forest would be set at a reduced rate. Therefore, despite the protests of the Conservator of Forests, the final agreement of 1916 set royalty payments at only two rupees per 100 cubic feet of milled timber and double that for timber in the round (unmilled), with an additional sum payable on each acre clear-felled.[28] These rates were less than half those payable by sawyers working other

---

[24] E.P. Stebbing, *The Forests of West Africa and the Sahara* (London, 1937); A.H. Unwin, *West African Forests and Forestry* (London, 1920).

[25] E.P. Stebbing, *The Forests of India,* 3 vols (London, 1922); E.P. Stebbing, 'Forestry in Africa', *Empire Forestry Journal,* 20 (1947), 126–44.

[26] N.V. Brasnett, 'Finance and the Colonial Forest Service', *Empire Forestry Journal,* 21 (1942), 7–11; Stebbing, 'Forestry in Africa', 126–44; T.P. Ofcansky, 'Kenya forestry under British colonial administration, 1895–1963', *Journal of Forest History,* 28 (1984), 136–43.

[27] J.H. Nicholson, *The Future of Forestry in Kenya* (Nairobi, 1931). This paragraph is taken from Anderson, 'Managing the forest', 253.

[28] With the currency conversion in 1921, these rates became 2s. and 4s. respectively.

Kenyan forests. After 1919, from when sawmill concessions in the colony were granted only by competitive tender, the disparity between the terms operating in the Lembus concession and elsewhere in the colony became even more marked. In 1928, Grogan's sawyers were paying only 6 cents per cubic foot of timber, while sawyers elsewhere in Kenya paid 50 cents per cubic foot. Furthermore, ESM[29] paid a fixed annual licence fee of only Ks.12,000 (initially 6,000 rupees), against which royalty payments were offset. Timber to the value of Ks.12,000 had therefore to be felled before the department saw any revenue for the timber extracted from the concession.[30] For the four years 1921–4 the total revenue deriving to government from the concession was £2,753, whereas the costs to the Forest Department of managing the area amounted to £3,306. Nowhere else in Kenya were forests being worked at a commercial loss to the state. By the mid-1920s, ESM were cutting more timber than all the other sawyers in Kenya's forests put together and yet were paying considerably less for the privilege.[31]

Forest Department antagonism towards ESM was deepened further by the suspicion that the company was infringing the already generous terms of its licence. The commercial working of the Lembus concession had begun with the opening of the first mill in 1912, but due to shortages of finance and staff, it was not until 1921 that the Forest Department began to carefully monitor the activities of ESM.[32] Even at this stage the only detailed map of the forest was still held by Grogan, having been drafted by a surveyor in his employment in 1906–1907. This gave Grogan and ESM a much clearer knowledge of the potential of the forest than had the Forest Department.[33] The persistent unwillingness of ESM to furnish the department with their working plans for Lembus raised the suspicions of the Conservator of Forests, and by 1923 he had uncovered evidence of irregularities in ESM's calculation of royalties due and of areas clear-felled. It seemed that ESM were stretching the terms of the lease to their absolute limit. On their own admission, the policy of the company was 'to pick the eyes out of the forest', rather than to clear-fell.[34] Consequently, when the department sought to

[29] Paice, *Lost Lion*, 248–9.

[30] 'Report of the Select Committee of the Legislative Council appointed to consider Forest Royalties', 1919, KNA AG 4/919; Crown Advocate to Acting Chief Secretary, 23 April 1912 and Conservator of Forests to Attorney General, 3 November 1920, both KNA AG 4/2313; Nicholson to Colonial Secretary, 2 February 1928, KNA ARC(FOR) 7/2/128. The licence was formally transferred to the Equator Sawmills Ltd in March 1921: see Ag. Chief Secretary to Commissioner of Lands, 10 March 1921, KNA ARC(FOR) 7/2/128.

[31] Battiscombe (Conservator of Forests) to Senior Commissioner/Kerio, 31 July 1925; and Nicholson (CO Forest Adviser) to Chief Secretary, 2 February 1928, both in KNA ARC(FOR) 7/2/128.

[32] See the Kenya Forest Department Annual Reports, 1913–21.

[33] 'ESM Ltd Forest Concession', unsigned, 1923, KNA AG 4/2332. Tannahill to Commissioner of Lands, 20 January 1921; and Acting Chief Secretary to Commissioner of Lands, 10 March 1921, both in KNA ARC(FOR) 7/2/128.

[34] Bradley (ESM) to Battiscombe (Conservator of Forests), 26 February 1924, KNA

reafforest areas that they believed ESM to have clear-felled, they invariably discovered that trees had been left standing. Under a clause that gave the company rights to re-enter any areas not clear-felled for a further twenty years after their original working, ESM avoided making any additional royalty payments while also preventing reafforestation.[35] To the eyes of an experienced forester, the lumbering practices of ESM's contractors in Lembus were deplorable:

> The forest work carried on in the felling area here is almost beyond conception. No one seems to be in charge of the boys who are doing the forest work and they go along cutting and felling in any way they like. Trees are felled across the hill, others are felled down (hill) on top of them and broken. Trees are felled into other standing ones which get broken and bare stumps thirty feet high are seen everywhere. In cross-cutting logs they are cut to suit the logging contractors without any consideration of economy.[36]

At a conservative estimate, it was reckoned that more than 15 per cent of the timber felled by the company up to the mid-1920s had been left to rot in the forest.[37] The terms of the concession allowed ESM to be grossly inefficient, 'slashing down forest uncontrolled' and 'pouring money … into the pockets of their contractors', and yet still flooding the market with cheap timber at prices the smaller mills could not hope to match.[38]

The Forest Department relentlessly pursued ESM over these practices into the 1930s, while pressing for the Attorney-General to declare foreclosure on the concession in view of the company's apparent infringements of the lease.[39] As a result of these pressures, from 1926 ESM were compelled to submit monthly returns on their activities, to settle all outstanding royalties promptly, and to hand over a number of clear-felled areas for replanting. The licence was amended at this time to raise the royalty rates to 4s. per 100 cubic feet of milled timber, and 8s. on timber in the round, in return for which alteration the government conceded the claims for clear-felling payments in the hope of encouraging ESM to adopt better forestry practices.[40] But, while it was widely acknowledged by the late 1920s that

---

[34 (cont.)] ARC(FOR) 7/2/127; Battiscombe to Osborne (Senior Commissioner/Kerio) 31 July 1925, both in KNA ARC(FOR) 7/2/128.

[35] 'Grogan Forest Licence – Royalty Payments 1920–9', KNA ARC(FOR) 7/2/127; 'Grogan Forest Licence, 1921–8', KNA ARC(FOR) 7/2/128; 'Equator Saw Mills, 1923–9', KNA ARC(FOR) 7/1/41 II.

[36] Quoted in Battiscombe (Conservator of Forests) to Osborne (Senior Commissioner/Kerio), 31 July 1925, 'Grogan Forest Licence', KNA ARC (FOR) 7/2/128, from the Londiani forester's AR, 1917–18.

[37] Ibid.

[38] Assistant Forester, Londiani to ESM Agent, Maji Mazuri, 2 October 1928, KNA ARC (FOR) 7/1/41 II.

[39] 'Grogan Forest Licence and Royalty Payments, 1920–29', KNA ARC(FOR) 7/2/127, charts the disputes.

[40] See Tannahill's 'Memorandum' on the meeting with government officials to discuss this,

the forest concession had been 'a most unfortunate error', the government had at no time been prepared to challenge Grogan by attempting to terminate the agreement.[41] Grogan then still held ownership of several very strategic plots of land, including areas of central Nairobi and valuable pastures adjacent to the railway at Athi River. In the boom of the 1920s land values on all these sites climbed sharply, and as Kenya's agriculture began to expand and its exports increase, Grogan's hold over the Mombasa waterfront land at Mbaraki became more important. Having successfully developed the facilities at Mbaraki, in direct competition with the government's own port at nearby Kilindini, Grogan sold the port to the government in 1926 for the sum of £350,000. Grogan then offered to sell a further bundle of assets to the government for another £300,000, this including the Lembus concession and its four sawmills.[42] He soon withdrew this offer, and by 1928 his negotiations had taken a different tack when he expressed his willingness to give up certain plots in Nairobi in return for an extension of the Lembus concession. Only a very firm intervention from the Colonial Office's forestry adviser brought these latter discussions to an end.[43]

When the tables turned with the recession of the early 1930s, and the timber trade collapsed, the government's foresters again saw an opportunity to claw back control of Lembus.[44] Even though the advantages of low royalties allowed the Lembus concessionaires to weather the depression much better than their competitors, Grogan's seven mills had annual running costs of £25,000 but no market for their timber. By 1933, ESM were unable to make the payment of the annual licence fee.[45] This breach of the licence gave government the opportunity to seek legal termination of the contract, but wider political concerns again intervened: in the circumstances of the

[40] (cont.) dated 21 December 1925, and a copy of the revised agreement, signed by Governor Grigg, both in KNA ARC(FOR) 7/2/128. Tannahill, previously an official in the Land Office, was by then acting as Grogan's attorney and managing agent for ESM.

[41] Nicholson to Chief Secretary, 2 February 1928, and Grigg to Amery (Secretary of State), 12 November 1925, both in KNA ARC(FOR) 7/2/128. Governor's Deputy to Secretary of State, May 1926; Battiscombe (Conservator of Forests) to Tannahill (ESM), 25 July 1924; and 'Monthly Returns, 1924', all KNA ARC(FOR) 7/1/41 II. The licence in fact contained no penalty clauses, and it was doubtful whether foreclosure was ever a realistic legal option. Grigg to Amery, 12 October 1925, KNA ARC(FOR) 7/2/128.

[42] Grogan to Felling (Kenya and Uganda Harbours and Railways), 12 August 1926, and subsequent correspondence, KNA ARC(FOR) 7/2/128. Paice, *Lost Lion*, 334 n6, cites what appears to be the same letter, but with a different file number – KNA/LO/43/33/1/6. For contrasting views of the Mbaraki transactions, see Paice, *Lost Lion*, 327–30, and McGregor Ross, *Kenya From Within*, 162–3.

[43] J.W. Nicholson to Chief Secretary, 2 February 1928, KNA ARC(FOR) 7/2/128.

[44] Kenya Forest Department, ARs 1930–34. The licence was transferred to a holding company, East Africa Ventures Ltd, during 1927, but the concession continued to be managed by ESM; see ESM to Battiscombe (Conservator of Forests), 13 January 1927, KNA ARC(FOR) 7/2/127.

[45] 'Grogan Forest Licence – Timber Payments, 1931–6', KNA ARC(FOR) 7/2/129.

Table 8.1 Equator Sawmills Ltd: timber milled and royalty payments, 1912–35

	Timber milled (cu.ft.)	Royalty payment (incl. licence fee)*
1912	56,450	6,000 rupee
1913	52,758	6,000 rupee
1914	143,166	6,000 rupee
1915	282,703	6,000 rupee
1916	151,175	6,000 rupee
1917	99,020	6,000 rupee
1918	90,701	6,000 rupee
1919	188,262	6,000 rupee
1920	176,926	6,000 florin
1921	222,186	13,313 sh
1922	462,249	14,103 sh
1923	47,590†	12,000 sh
1924	121,111	12,000 sh
1925	223,260	14,467 sh
1926	397,148	25,150 sh
1927	582,102	36,163 sh
1928	475,279	30,363 sh
1929	548,723	33,594 sh
1930	498,239	30,500 sh
1931	167,809	12,000 sh
1932	83,324	12,000 sh
1933	111,600	12,000 sh
1934	109,357	12,000 sh
1935	?	12,000 sh

* From 1912 to 1920 the licence fee = 6,000 rupees p.a; 1920 = 6,000 florins; 1921 onwards = 12,000 shillings p.a.
† Mills were shut down for part of 1923 because of a collapse in the timber market.
Source: KNA, various Forest Department and Attorney-General files, 1902–39.

Table 8.2 Kenya Forest Department: wartime revenue, 1938–45

	Revenue (£)	Expenditure (£)	Surplus (£)
1938	41,550	31,323	10,227
1939	43,702	31,051	12,651
1940	57,170	30,800	26,370
1941	75,136	29,473	45,663
1942	119,020	36,608	82,412
1943	140,492	45,646	94,846
1944	142,079	60,920	81,159
1945	156,314	74,363	81,951

Source: Kenya Forest Department Annual Reports, 1938–47.

depression, the Kenya government was more intent on persuading businesses to remain in the colony than expelling them. All of Grogan's businesses in the colony were in serious trouble, and by 1935 ESM ceased trading. Having given up his mills, Grogan still held his forest lease but was no longer directly involved in its exploitation. Sawmill activities in Lembus were now subcontracted to other firms, headed by the East African Timber Co-operative Society, which by 1935 produced 70 per cent of the colony's timber.[46] By the eve of the Second World War, then, the Forest Department had succeeded in asserting only nominal control over the management of Lembus, and one of Kenya's richest and most heavily lumbered forests continued to add only negligibly to their revenues (see Table 8.1).

Ironically, it was the rampant exploitation of Kenya's forests triggered by the Second World War that was to transform the revenue base of the Forest Department. Timber production in the colony as a whole climbed from 19,750 Hoppus tons in 1938 to 116,500 Hoppus tons in 1945, and in Lembus Forest alone a further six mills came into operation over this period. The boom in lumbering, subsidized by the high guaranteed prices offered by government for milled timber, left 'chaotic conditions' in many forests; but the revenues accrued were substantial (see Table 8.2).[47] In an initiative unique to Kenya, early in the war government established a Forestry Sinking Fund. Taking the surplus revenue raised for 1940 as the baseline, and placing all annual revenues raised by the department above the 1940 figure in the Sinking Fund, it was intended that the fund would be used to subsequently replenish and develop the forests exploited during the wartime boom. By the end of the war the Sinking Fund stood at over £300,000.[48] To match their new-found financial clout, the Forest Department was also given a more prominent role in rural development policies from the 1940s onwards, public awareness of the role of forest cover in preventing erosion and protecting catchments having been sharpened by the erosion scare and land-husbandry debates of the 1930s.[49] After 1945, the department was therefore able to regulate the activities of the sawyers in Lembus more effectively and could afford to mount a more systematic programme of reafforestation in preparation for taking over full responsibility for the Lembus Forest on the expiry of the concession at the end of

---

[46] Paice, *Lost Lion*, 360–1, n13.

[47] Kenya Forest Department, ARs 1945–7.

[48] For details of wartime timber production in the colony, see H.M. Gardner, 'Kenya forests and the war', *Empire Forestry Journal*, 21 (1942), 45–7; R.M. Graham, 'Forestry in Kenya', *Empire Forestry Journal*, 24 (1945), 156–75; and Kenya Forest Department, ARs 1945–7.

[49] Anderson, 'Depression, dust bowl', 321–43; K.P.W. Logie, *Forestry in Kenya. A Historical Account of the Development of Forest Management in the Colony* (Nairobi, 1962); Nancy U. Murray, 'The other lost lands: the administration of Kenya's forests, 1900–52', History Department Staff Seminar Paper, Kenyatta University College, Nairobi (1982); Ward, *Deserts in the Making*.

1957. But those Africans whose rights to graze their animals, to cultivate and to cut timber and fuel wood in Lembus had fallen victim to the commercial exploitation by ESM had by then other ideas on the future of the forest.

'Native rights'

I could tell you something about the distribution of the peoples up in the Kamasia [Tugen] and Elgeyo and Nandi in the early days. I think it was in 1903 [1904] when I first went there. The government had advertised forest rights up there, and I was induced to go and have a look at it. At that time, beyond one Dorobo family, in the areas between the Kamasia [Tugen] Hills, Londiani mountain, the Nandi and the [Uasin Gishu] Plateau, there were no natives at all, except a certain number of Kamasia [Tugen] who slipped over the edge of the hills there and were living a little down the river (the stream that runs into Baringo) and up the slopes of the hills near Ravine Station. It was not a tribal movement at all, but the ordinary aggregation of oddments that always collects around a government station. The only other natives were one or two families of Dorobo whom I got to know because I used them when I was opening up that forest.[50]

This was how Ewart Grogan recalled the 'early days' in Lembus when giving evidence before the Kenya Land Commissioners in 1932. His opinion that the area was uninhabited remained consistent with the argument he had advanced in the protracted negotiations over the confirmation of the licence between 1904 and 1916. He had, in fact, visited Eldama Ravine for only a few days in May 1904. He returned, briefly again, late in 1906, when his surveyor was mapping the forest. This second visit came only a few months after the military campaign against the Nandi, during which the British forces had swept through Lembus and into the Nandi Hills, pushing all Africans and their livestock to the north and west. Elgeyo and Tugen in this area were suspected of complicity with Nandi, and many who had been living close to Ravine moved away to protect themselves from the randomness of colonial violence.[51] For these reasons, it is quite possible that Grogan might have encountered surprisingly few people in his exploratory tramps through Lembus. On the other hand, Grogan had reason enough to deny the significance of any potential African claims. Under the terms of the Lands Ordinance of 1902, compensation was to be paid to Africans dispossessed by Europeans; to admit to prior occupation was to invite a claim for compensation. Moreover, Grogan would have been well aware that officials in London were consulted over

---

[50] *KLC:EM*, iii, evidence of Major Ewart S. Grogan, 3041.
[51] For the details of the campaigns against Nandi, see Matson, *Nandi Campaign;* Matson, *Nandi Resistance;* Matson, *Nandi Resistance – the Volcano Erupts;* Gold, 'Nandi in transition'; Mwanzi, 'Koitalel and Kipchomber'.

such large concessions and that they would need to be assured that the lands to be awarded were not densely settled.[52]

Even if the Nandi campaign had caused a temporary flight from the forest in 1905–6, other evidence indicates that the occupation of Lembus was much greater than Grogan was prepared to admit. The question of possible 'native rights' had been raised at an early stage in the negotiations, the government concerned to ensure that Africans living within the concession would continue to enjoy their customary rights. Believing that such claims were limited to a few families of Dorobo, Grogan initially raised no objection to a clause that would protect the interests of these few 'traditional' forest dwellers.[53] But officials were by then already aware that the reality was rather different. As early as March 1906, the Conservator of Forests had acknowledged that there were large acreages of Tugen cultivation on some of the unforested lands within the concession, and he suggested that these areas should be declared 'as a native reserve' and removed from the terms of the licence. Reiterating this point in October 1911, the District Commissioner at Eldama Ravine pointed out that the concession 'took in land where the Kamasia were living' and asked for clarification as to their future status.[54] At the same time, it was realized that Elgeyo grazed cattle in the glades above the neck of the Kerio Valley, in the northern portion of Grogan's claim. In 1910, kraals inhabited by Elgeyo and their stock were to be found within the concession, the 'deep cattle tracks from top to bottom' of the escarpment indicating that their use of the area was long-established.[55]

Once Grogan's agents established the first operating sawmill in Lembus in 1912, they must have quickly appreciated the true extent of African occupation, although there is no account of this in the surviving documentary record. However, during the final stages of the renegotiation of the lease – between June 1913 and March 1916 – Grogan now argued for a severe limitation of 'native rights', reiterating his contention that non-forested land (i.e. glades) should be excluded from the acreage of the licence and alternative forest land offered instead. A compromise was agreed that the Governor should, in the near future, 'be required to endeavour to ascertain and define the nature and extent of free grazing rights and other such customary rights as may have been exercised in the [forest] prior to the dates of the concession'.[56] In 1917, the District Commissioner investi-

[52] Eliot had given such an assurance in 1904 – see Lansdowne to Eliot, 25 April 1904, KNA AG 4/2313. In the event, African claims for compensation were nowhere entertained: see Sorrenson, *Origins of European Settlement*, ch. 1.

[53] Hyde-Clarke, 'Lembus Forest: Appreciation of the Position', 28 July 1938, KNA PC/NKU/2/1/31.

[54] Legal Department, 'ESM Ltd Forest concession', 1923, drawing upon original of Barton memorandum, KNA AG 4/2332.

[55] 'Précis of Barton memorandum', 1923, KNA AG 4/2332.

[56] 'Copy of Forest Lease, 1 March 1916', KNA AG 4/2313.

gated the nature (but not the extent) of 'native rights' in Lembus, and reported these to Grogan as: the free grazing of livestock; the right to build houses and cut wood for fuel; the right to cut down trees for the manufacture of honey boxes; the use of all watercourses and salt-licks; the right to cultivate gardens within and outside the forested areas; and the right to use all paths and roads without hindrance. This amounted to complete freedom of action for all Africans who could establish a claim to have rights in the forest, except in so far as the milling operations might restrict their temporary use of specified areas. Grogan did not reply to the District Commissioner's letter.[57]

In the absence of Grogan's response, for the next six years the definition of rights appears to have been forgotten whilst African access to Lembus was dealt with in an ad hoc manner by Grogan's sawyers and their contractors.[58] While his agents did much as they pleased, Grogan had no reason to remind government of its responsibilities. The matter only came up again when the Baringo district administration intervened to protest at the rough-and-ready treatment of Africans by ESM's contractors and the zeal with which the local Forest Officer sought to enforce the regulations of the Forest Ordinance, without reference to the status of the Lembus occupants. While the timber contractors and the Forest Department shared the view that these were 'unauthorized persons' who should be removed from the forest, district officials insisted that nothing could be done until the Governor had proclaimed a formal definition of native rights in the forest.[59]

It was the district administration, therefore, and not the Forest Department or Grogan, who finally requested that the formal definition of rights be established. A census of the forest was conducted in 1923, and in December Governor Coryndon issued his definition of native rights in Lembus. This document, known as the Coryndon Definition, laid down eleven specific rights, which concurred closely with those first proposed to Grogan in 1917, including the rights to construct dwellings, to graze animals, to cultivate and to gather forest produce (see Table 8.3). The rights were granted to all those Africans who were able to satisfy the administration that they had enjoyed use of the forest, 'according to native law and custom', prior to the initial signing of the lease in 1904 or between then and the beginning of lumbering operations in 1912. Appended to the Coryndon Definition was a full list of all the named 'right-holders', as they now became known. The list was viewed with horror by both Grogan and the Forest Department, for it identified no fewer than 485 Tugen and eleven Dorobo right-holding families, and further stipulated that such rights were

---

[57] The original correspondence does not survive, but it is reported in detail in the précis of the Barton memorandum, attached to the Legal Department's draft commentary headed 'ESM Ltd Forest Concession', of 1923, in KNA AG 4/2332. The absence of Grogan's reply is reported here.

[58] Legal Department, 'ESM Ltd Forest Concession', 1923, KNA AG 4/2332.

[59] Ibid.

Table 8.3 Coryndon Definition: rights granted in Lembus

---

1. Rights to reside and erect all necessary buildings, shelters and fences for the accommodation of themselves, their families and their animals.
2. Rights to graze and other vegetable products required by them or their stock of every description or their other domesticated beasts or birds for their support or for customary purposes.
3. Rights to salt required by their stock of every description.
4. Rights to water for themselves and their animals for all domestic and agricultural purposes and to fish in any water subject to the fishing laws of the Colony.
5. Rights to as much cultivable land as they can cultivate.
6. Rights to as much fuel as is required for their own consumption.
7. Rights to as much forest produce as may be required for the construction of their huts, or furniture, or cattle 'bomas', or for bridges, or for any other customary purpose whatsoever.
8. Rights to stone, soil, sand or gravel, or other such products for use by themselves and for customary purposes.
9. Rights to hunt or snare game, animals or birds, subject to the game laws of the Colony.
10. Rights to collect honey and to put up honey barrels.
11. Such other rights as may hereafter be proved to the satisfaction of the Governor to have been exercised by them within the said area prior to the date of the said indenture.

Such rights shall be exercisable at all times and in all places within the area marked on the plan attached hereto, subject to the limitation of the aforesaid Indenture, by all these families, their heirs or representatives, according to native law and custom of the Lembus clan of the Kamasia tribe and of the Dorobo tribe who are now living in the area as specified in the Schedules attached hereto.

Source: 'Coryndon Definition', 12 December 1923, KNA PC/NKU/2/1/30

to be passed down to the descendants of each right-holder named. The children of listed right-holders already numbered 650 and around 40 per cent of the adult males listed were either as yet unmarried or married but without children (see Table 8.4). It was clear that the future management of the forest was going to be highly problematic.[60]

The Coryndon Definition was to remain a bone of contention throughout the colonial period. To the sawyers and to the foresters it represented a serious hindrance to the economic and ecological management of the forest. Both constantly sought to exploit other clauses in the lease to place firmer controls upon the right-holders, the Forest Department trying to override the terms of the Definition through applying the rules of the Forest Ordinance. Having fought for the Definition, the Baringo district administration

---

[60] Governor Coryndon, 'Definition of Native Rights', 12 December 1923, KNA PC/NKU/2/1/31.

Table 8.4 Lembus right-holders, 1923, 1951 and 1959

| | | 1923 | | |
| | | Men | | |
	Unmarried	With wives	Women	Children
Tugen	109	376	483	637
Dorobo	1	10	10	13
	110	386	493	650
		(496)		

	1951	
	Families inside forest	Families elsewhere
Tugen	518	300
Dorobo	30	
Elgeyo	72	
	620	300
		(920)

1959
Right-holding families
(households with claims to a smallholding)

Tugen	841

Sources:

1923: Coryndon Definition, 12 December 1923: Schedule 2, KNA PC/NKU/2/1/30.

1951: Cumber (DC/BAR) to Cowley (PAO/RVP), 14 August 1951, KNA PC/NKU/2/1/30.

1959: Wolff (PC/RVP) to Perm. Sec, Afr. Affs, 21 April 1959, KNA PC/NKU/2/13/3.

had, in effect, become the guardian of the right-holders' interests against the sawyers and foresters. They had a vested interest in playing this role, for if Tugen were to be evicted from Lembus then they would be pushed eastwards on to the already overstocked southern Baringo lowlands. But, as we shall see, even those District Officers who defended the principle of African access to the forest sometimes thought it better not to inform those in Lembus of the full extent of their rights. For the Africans of Lembus, the Definition was a charter of undeniable rights to be exercised in perpetuity, an absolute guarantee of their security in the forest. However, they were not at first made aware of the strength of their position. At first, indeed, the imposition of the Definition amounted to tighter controls and not increased freedoms for the right-holders. By securing the rights of those families listed, the Coryndon Definition had effectively closed the forest to all others. Many who made periodic use of the forest,

but were not listed as right-holders, now found themselves legally excluded from the forest.

The exclusion of Elgeyo was to prove a highly significant decision in the political future of Lembus. E.B Hosking, who served as a District Officer in both Baringo and Elgeyo before 1920, expressed his surprise before the Land Commission that Elgeyo claims to Lembus should have been overlooked. To his knowledge, they 'had grazed animals in the northern portions of Lembus for years' and were only 'forced out' by the Tugen right-holders.[61] The reasons for their total exclusion in 1923 remain obscure, although in 1926 one senior official was to assert that their case had been misrepresented by a member of the Land Office, who then went on to work in Grogan's employ, and that subsequently ESM's contractors had systematically 'evacuated' them from the northern glades to clear the area for the grazing of the loggers' working oxen.[62] The effect of the denial of Elgeyo claims was to turn Lembus into a Tugen forest and, to a large degree, this suited the convenience of the administrators at Eldama Ravine. By the terms of the definition, the rights were to apply exclusively to 'the Lembus clan of the Kamasia [Tugen] tribe and the Dorobo tribe who are now living in the area'. Tugen and Dorobo elders were consulted in compiling the lists of right-holders, although it must be doubted that they were fully aware of the implications of this process. By the early 1930s, however, Tugen right-holders actively complained of the illegal presence of Elgeyo cattle within Torongo and had them evicted.[63] At this stage, then, it might seem that the colonial state had captured the forest for Tugen, but they were already playing some part in capturing it for themselves. In the process, ethnic identity had taken on a new, sharper significance.

Because the concession lay in lands originally designated as forest reserve, the Forest Department and not the Baringo District administration held jurisdiction over Lembus. It was the responsibility of the Forest Officer based at Londiani or (latterly) Maji Mazuri to oversee the running of the lumbering operations. This included clearing glades required by the contractors, for grazing or for logging or milling purposes, and implementing schemes of reafforestation and conservation. Inevitably, the presence of the right-holders often impeded these operations. In other forests, the department engaged squatters as labourers, directing the settlement and cultivations of such persons under the Forest Ordinance. The position of the right-holders in Lembus precluded the engagement of squatters, and it was intended that the terms of the Coryndon Definition should take precedence over the Ordinance. This was fine in theory, but

---

[61] *KLC:EM*, ii, evidence of E.B. Hosking, 1909–10.

[62] Osborne (SC/Kerio) to Ag Chief Secretary, 3 August 1925, KNA ARC(FOR) 7/2/128. A.C. Tannahill must surely be the officer implicated by Osborne's accusation, but no record of the original reports has been traced. Paice, *Lost Lion*, 298, n5.

[63] Brown (DC/Baringo) to Welby (PC/RVP), 13 March 1933, KNA PC/NKU/2/13/3.

in practice it removed the only legal authority that the forester had to regulate the movement and activities of the right-holders, and it greatly increased the costs of reafforestation. By 1925, both ESM and the Forest Department were complaining that it was impossible to manage the concession effectively within the legal terms set.

Rights could be legally curtailed in Lembus only in relation to the direct requirements of the working of the concession, but the forester was soon ignoring these fine distinctions. Already by 1925, a number of glades had been set aside by the forester for the exclusive use of Dorobo families, whose numbers had climbed sharply since the census of 1923. Many of the non-right-holders were former forest squatters, allowed into Lembus because they were known to the forester and likely to be compliant in following the requirements of the Forest Ordinance.[64] Two years later this ad hoc arrangement was vastly extended to limit and regulate the access of right-holders to all the major glades within Lembus. The proposal for a more workable management plan for Lembus was broached by Rammell, the forester at Londiani, who was concerned that the freedoms given to the right-holders were contributing to erosion in some parts of Lembus, while in other areas there had been damaging forest fires. His intention was to confine the right-holders 'into definite areas', creating buffer zones between areas open to the right-holders and those to be closed in the interests of forest conservation. He advocated restricting the rights to cut poles and bamboo in the higher parts, using the Forest Ordinance to prosecute transgressors. In the Poror area, in return for Tugen being permitted 'to do what they like' in the south-eastern portion, they were to be prevented from entering other glades. Up in Torongo and in the larger glades near the centre of Lembus, 'no cultivation will be allowed' and only grazing permitted. Several glades would be closed to right-holders simply on the grounds that they were 'inaccessible and difficult to control', and others because they might be used as springboards for trespass into neighbouring forests or farms. These proposals were accepted by Bailward, the District Officer at Ravine, in November 1927, when an inventory of glades was drawn up, detailing restrictions and conditions. 'We agree', reported Rammell to his Conservator of Forests, 'that in these authorized interior glades the detection of any offence shall be followed by the punishment of the offender if caught, and (or) the closing of the glade to grazing.'[65] All of this contravened the rights set down in the Coryndon Definition and had no legal authority, and yet from 1927 until 1938 Lembus was administered on the basis of the agreement drawn up between Bailward and Rammell.

There were occasional rumblings about these restrictions, but for the

---

[64] Rammell (Forester/Londiani) to Ag Conservator of Forests, 22 November 1927; Bond (DC/Baringo) to Ag PC/RVP, 8 December 1937; Graham (Forester/Londiani) to Bond (DC/Baringo), 14 December 1937, all KNA PC/NKU/2/1/30.

[65] Rammell to Battiscombe (Conservator of Forests), 22 November 1927, KNA PC/NKU/2/1/30. This became known as the 'Bailward Agreement'.

most part Tugen in Lembus seem to have been unaware of the true extent of their rights and were happy simply to exploit the advantages that being legally resident in the forest brought. And these advantages came to be increasingly valued over the 1920s and 1930s. First, during the mid-1920s the administration completed the final demarcation of the Native Reserves: African populations were either to remain in their designated Native Reserve or to take temporary labour contracts on European farms. Movement now required a passbook – the hated *kipande* – and the closer monitoring of Africans served to accentuate the role of the forest as a place of refuge. Africans wishing to move livestock around from one area to another, and particularly those with labour contracts seeking to smuggle extra cattle on to European farmlands, did so under cover of the forests. Strategically placed at the heart of the White Highlands between several European farming areas and coupled with the advantages of concealment and good grazing, the Lembus Forest became a particularly important entrepôt for Africans and their livestock.[66] Occasional raids by the police confirmed suspicions that the forest was heavily used by non-right-holders in this way: one raid on Torongo Glade, in 1929, uncovered more than 400 head of cattle herded illegally in the forest.[67] Secondly, and accentuating this trend, in the drought years between 1926 and 1935, more and more livestock were herded into the forest in search of better grazing and fodder. By the 1930s it was common practice for southern Baringo's herders to 'loan' animals to friends and relatives among the right-holders. Thirdly, others moved animals into Lembus to avoid the limitations set on the government's reconditioning schemes and the threat of destocking on the lowlands, often providing the right-holder with 'a consideration' for his trouble.[68] Over these years, Lembus therefore became an increasing asset to Baringo's herders, the right-holders ever more closely bound up with the political economy of the Tugen reserve to the east.

By the mid-1930s the presence of growing numbers of non-right-holders, and especially their cattle and goats, was widely acknowledged. Colin Maher highlighted the overstocking of the Lembus glades in his 1937 report, prompting the foresters to take a closer look at the situation in those glades they had opened up to Tugen under the Rammell–Bailward agreement.[69] This coincided with renewed attempts by government to move the many scattered communities of forest-dwelling Dorobo, including those in Lembus, into two specially designated reserves. The removal of Dorobo had first been mooted by a committee set up to consider their future in 1929,

---

[66] Murray, 'The other lost lands'; David M. Anderson, 'Stock theft and moral economy in colonial Kenya', *Africa*, 56 (1986), 399–416.

[67] Hyde-Clarke, 'Lembus Forest', 28 July 1938, KNA PC/NKU/2/1/31.

[68] Graham (Forester/Londiani) to Bond (DC/Baringo), 23 December 1937, KNA PC/NKU/2/1/30.

[69] Maher, *Soil Erosion and Land Utilisation*; Graham (Forester/Londiani) to Bond (DC/Baringo), 23 December 1937, KNA PC/NKU/2/1/30.

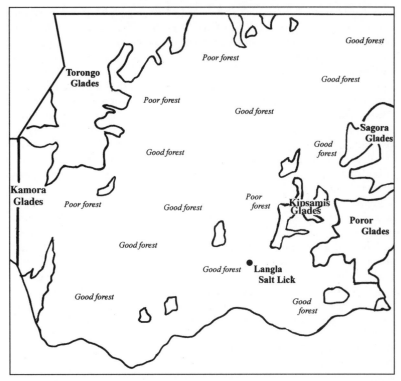

*Map 8.2 Lembus forest glades, c.*1928

and was endorsed by the Land Commission of 1932.[70] So it was that, when, in 1937, the forester, Graham, gave closer attention to 'the Lembus question', he had two aims in mind: first, to get the Lembus Dorobo to agree to move to the Chepalungu Forest, far to the south, in fulfilment of the recommendations of the Land Commission; and, secondly, to establish firmer controls over Africans remaining in the forest and to expel those who had no right to be there. Although he would fail in both endeavours, his probings were to awaken the Tugen right-holders as to the true strength of their position.

At a *baraza* of Lembus Dorobo held in the Arama glade in September 1937, the proposal to move them all to Chepalungu was announced. Of the seventy-two Dorobo interrogated that day, only ten turned out to be right-holders. The majority of the rest were Dorobo who admitted to having only recently come into Lembus under the 'protection' of the headman,

---

[70] Rita M. Breen, 'The Kenya Land Commission (1932–33) and Dorobo land issues', seminar paper, History Department, University of Nairobi (1972).

arap Teriko; others were persons believed to be Tugen, Elgeyo and Nandi, also claiming the 'protection' of arap Teriko. The non-right-holding Dorobo were told they would be removed to Chepalungu, and arrangements were made to take the non-Dorobo, with their stock, under escort back to their own reserves. Though pressed by the forester to join the other Dorobo in Chepalungu, the remaining ten right-holders and their families refused to leave Lembus. Determined to clear the Dorobo out of the Arama glades, which he judged to be overstocked and also used to trespass into other adjacent forest areas, Graham then tried to compel arap Teriko and his remaining followers to vacate the Arama glades.[71] Old Teriko had been an interpreter at Eldama Ravine in the days following the British conquest of Baringo, and was well known to all in the forest and to many European officials besides. He had used his favoured position as a right-holder to establish a large following of clients, a fact several officials prior to Graham had chosen to ignore. He sheltered people and their stock in the Arama glades, and was handsomely rewarded for doing so; in return he was reliable and loyal in government service.[72] But the new forester's intervention had undermined arap Teriko's power base and threatened to fracture his authority irreparably. Knowing something of how to play the politics of local government, he now appealed to the Baringo District Commissioner, Bond, to defend the Dorobo rights under the Coryndon Definition. At first apparently unaware of the Rammell–Bailward agreement, Bond blundered into the fray on behalf of the government's old retainer, criticizing the Forest Department for their 'high-handed' actions and pointing out that they had no power to remove Tugen or Dorobo right-holders from the Arama glades north of Sclater's Road. Once again, the district administration had been cast as the unlikely defenders of 'native rights': 'It may be inconvenient for the forest department to have stock in the Arama,' wrote Bond in December 1937, 'but the right-holders seem, to me, to be entitled to graze there.' He went on to comment that the rights defined in 1923 'seem very wide … and it is doubtful if the natives themselves know the full extent of them nor at the moment may it seem advisable that they should'. But he had by then already informed arap Teriko of his firm opinion that the Dorobo right-holders did not have to obey the forester's instructions to move from Arama or anywhere else.[73] The genie was out of the bottle.

---

[71] Graham was at first under the misapprehension that Dorobo rights under the definition were tied to specific glades, and thought that by removing them he would forever clear the issue of 'rights' from those areas. Graham (Forester/Londiani) to Conservator of Forests, 24 September, 12 October and 30 November 1937, KNA PC/NKU/2/1/30.

[72] Hodge (PC/RVP) to Fazan (PC/Nyanza), 21 September 1938, PC/NKU/2/1/30. The same arap Teriko was one of a small group of Dorobo who gave evidence before the Land Commission in 1932: *KLC:EM*, ii, 1868–72.

[73] Bond (DC/Baringo) to Ag PC/RVP, 8 December 1937, KNA PC/NKU/2/1/30. Bond was aware of arap Teriko's manipulation, commenting that 'he has undoubtedly been endeavouring to play off the forest department against the administration'. In a personal

Politics in the forest, 1938–63

The word spread with astonishing speed. Within a few weeks of arap Teriko's interview with District Commissioner Bond, right-holders throughout Lembus were refusing to obey the orders of the forester. Glades that had been 'closed' since 1927 were now quickly occupied by Tugen cattle; in Kamora, Dorobo herders threatened forest guards sent to evict them from temporary grazing; and in the Arama glades instructions to withdraw cattle to allow the sawyers to graze their oxen, a legitimate request under the terms of the licence, were ignored.[74] Seizing the moment, herders brought ever more animals into the glades, disregarding the limitations previously set by the foresters. A census undertaken in January 1939, revealed 8,054 cattle and 22,034 sheep and goats within Lembus, the Torongo glades being especially heavily grazed. By then the forest was more heavily overstocked than any of the Native Reserve lands within Baringo.[75]

This rapid loss of government control in Lembus alarmed district officials as much as it did the Forest Department. It remained the view of the administration that the legal position of the right-holders should be respected, and that the Forest Ordinance could not be used to override the terms of the Coryndon Definition. But unless land use was regulated in Lembus there was a danger that the entire rehabilitation and reconditioning programme for the neighbouring Baringo lowlands would be placed in jeopardy: the erosion and deforestation of Lembus might threaten the Perkerra catchment and, whilst the forest provided an easy bolt-hole for Tugen cattle, there was little prospect of enforcing a cull of stock anywhere on the lowlands.[76] Somehow, the genie needed to be put back into the bottle.

With these concerns to the fore, it was decided early in 1939 to reimpose controls within Lembus, through the same Baringo Crop and Production Rules that had been used to remove livestock from overgrazed lands on the lowlands. With the agreement of the Forest Department, this was enacted through government notice in May 1939. District Commissioner Hyde-Clarke now busied himself at *barazas* at Eldama Ravine and in the forest, explaining the position to all in an effort to re-establish government

---

[73 (cont.)] letter to the provincial commissioner, Rammell attempted to go above Bond's head to have the 1927 agreement restored: Rammell (Forester, Londiani) to Hodge (PC/RVP), 27 June 1938, KNA PC/NKU/2/1/30.

[74] Rae (Forester) to Asst Conservator of Forests, 29 July 1938; Hyde-Clarke (DC/Baringo) to Hodge (PC/RVP), 28 July 1938, both KNA PC/NKU/2/1/31.

[75] Murray, 'Census of Lembus Forest (Grogan Concession) Stock, January 1939', KNA PC/RVP.6A/11/15; Hyde-Clarke (DC/Baringo) to Hodge (PC/RVP), 25 June 1939, KNA PC/RVP.6A/23/13.

[76] Hyde-Clarke, 'Lembus forest: appreciation of position', 28 July 1938, KNA PC/NKU/2/1/31.

authority. Right-holders were told that the government now had powers to limit livestock numbers and regulate cultivation throughout the concession. In effect, the informal Rammell–Bailward 'agreement' had given way to a more formal control, with authority passing from the Forest Department to the Baringo District administration. This last point was noted with satisfaction by the right-holders themselves, who viewed their closer association with the administration of Baringo District as a positive step in their efforts to bolster Tugen claims to Lembus.[77]

Over the next ten years the precise legal position of the right-holders continued to be debated among often confused officials, few of whom were as aware of the history of the situation as they should have been and each of whom seemed to take a differing view of the legal interpretation to be placed upon the various orders governing the forest. Increasingly it was the right-holders themselves who forced the issue, asserting their own interests, manoeuvring to strengthen their position and exploiting the uncertainty of officials. Every government order was contested and the outcome usually subject to negotiation before the right-holders would give up any ground. When, for example, in 1943, the sawyers requested substantial areas of grazing for working oxen in the Pororr glades there was massive Tugen resistance to the suggestion that they should vacate lands some had cultivated there for more than 20 years.[78] Within the terms of the lease, the sawyers were entitled to access for these purposes and the right-holders had no legal defence. However, so sensitive had the politics of the forest become that the district administration convinced the Forest Department that those to be removed should be compensated with land elsewhere and that, as a sign of goodwill, their huts and stores should be left standing for them to return to at a future date. The Kamora glades, lying outside the concession, were accordingly opened to those evicted from Poror, although with livestock numbers limited under the Baringo District rules.[79] Five years later, the right-holders cultivating in the Muringwa glades won an even greater victory against an attempt by the Forest Department to evict them all from land they had farmed for more than ten years. Here the point at issue was that, under the Rammell–Bailward 'agreement', Tugen had been allowed to graze in the Muringwa glades but not to cultivate. The forester now argued that the arable farms were 'illegal' and that the farmers should be

---

[77] Conservator of Forests to Hodge (PC/RVP), 18 January 1939, KNA PC/RVP.6A/23/13; 'Baringo Crop and Production Rules (1939)', *Government Gazette*, 17 May 1939, extended to include Lembus. See also, Conservator of Forests to Hopkins (PC/RVP), 11 April 1938, and Hyde-Clarke (DC/Baringo) to Hopkins (PC/RVP), 19 May 1938, KNA PC/NKU/2/1/30.

[78] Conservator of Forests to Izard (PC/RVP), 19 August 1943; and Forester/Londiani to Lambert (DC/Baringo), 19 August 1943, KNA PC/NKU/2/1/30.

[79] Izard (PC/RVP) to Conservator of Forests, 8 September 1943, and reply, 21 September 1943, KNA PC/NKU/2/1/30; DO/Baringo to Forester/Londiani, 7 October 1943, KNA DO/ER/2/2/17.

prosecuted. Notices to quit were issued to the right-holders in Muringwa before the District Commissioner intervened to point out firmly that it was the 'rules' of the Forest Department that lacked legality. 'To prosecute without being assured of a conviction and with an acquittal resulting would', he warned:

> open the eyes of the Kamasia [Tugen] to the fact that they have been fooled for years and that until rules are framed and made law, they can exercise their rights indiscriminately to the detriment of the forest and to loss of power behind administrative order.

The Muringwa eviction orders were withdrawn.[80]

By the end of the 1940s, the right-holders were no longer being fooled. Their political awakening had been furthered after 1945 by broader currents of change sweeping through lowland Baringo. Lembus played a prominent part in Baringo's brief period of economic prosperity after the Second World War. Many right-holders were amongst those seeking to establish retail outlets, trading concerns and transport businesses at this time; and the dramatic increase in cultivation in the forest was driven in large part by the opportunity to sell grain on to the African-owned Lembus Trading Company at advantageous prices (see Chapter Seven). It had long been recognized that, although the right-holders were 'amongst the most progressive' people in the region, the anomalous position of the Grogan concession disallowed the development of schools, dispensaries, shops or other services within the forest.[81] Despite this, the people of Lembus were charged a supplementary tax, which was supposed to assist the Forest Department in providing just these facilities. By 1952, the right-holders still lacked any of the services that these taxes were supposed to pay for and that were by then common in other African locations. This came to be increasingly bitterly resented, and it fuelled the politics of protest, for the right-holders came to see the lack of services as a sure sign that the Forest Department intended to expel them on the termination of the concession-aire's lease at the end of 1957.[82] Aware by 1948 that the people of Lembus were determined to make the future of the forest a political issue, District Commissioner Simpson warned that government needed to move forward cautiously. The old ad hoc arrangements would no longer do: 'it is essential that we proceed now strictly according to the law'.[83]

In Simpson's view, the excision of the larger glades from the terms of

---

[80] Simpson (DC/Baringo) to Forester/Londiani, 19 May 1948, KNA PC/NKU/2/1/30.

[81] Bond (DC/Baringo) to Hopkins (PC/RVP), 19 May 1938, KNA PC/NKU/2/1/30.

[82] During 1952, the right-holders formally requested the provision of shops, butcheries and schools in Torongo and Poror, and offered to fund the building of a welfare hall in Muringwa from their own resources: Denton (DO/Eldama Ravine) to Forester/Londiani, 8 September 1952, KNA PC/NKU/2/13/3.

[83] Simpson (DC/Baringo) to Divisional Forester, Londiani, 28 August 1948, KNA PC/NKU/2/1/30.

the concession was the only way forward. Tugen had persistently requested this at *barazas* and council meetings from the late 1930s onwards. Not surprisingly, then, the idea was 'warmly welcomed' by right-holders when Simpson raised it at a *baraza* in September 1948. But they insisted that any excision should only be seen 'as a temporary measure'. The right-holders made it clear that 'they were reluctant to agree to anything which might prejudice their claim for the Lembus forest area north of Sclater's road to be in due course incorporated within Baringo district'.[84] Simpson entirely supported the Tugen position. To allow excisions would create the administrative difficulty that the Torongo glades would be separated from Baringo. The political repercussions might also be serious, for it was widely believed that the government had promised in 1922 that the forest would revert to their control on the termination of the lease. Tugen 'agitators' were already fuelling the rumour that lands were only being improved to be taken away and given to Europeans; for the government to be perceived as having 'changed its words' would only do damaged to the wider development efforts throughout southern Baringo. It was the economic argument in favour of incorporation that held the real sting, however. If the forest were incorporated within Baringo District, the revenues from saw-milling would accrue to the Baringo African District Council (ADC). They, and not the Forest Department, would then be the beneficiaries of substantial income, which could be used for the accelerated development of the entire district. Armed with these arguments, Simpson sallied forth to do battle with the Forest Department.

As the right-holders were well aware and as Simpson was soon to find out, the Forest Department was not prepared to contemplate the loss of the entire forest. Its gaze, too, was fixed upon the likely income to be generated from Lembus once it was returned to the status of a Crown Forest: that income was likely to be greater if the troublesome right-holders could be removed from the forest altogether. The Conservator of Forests therefore offered to support immediate excision of the glades in return for Tugen giving up their rights over all other parts of the forest and agreeing to its return to Forest Department control on expiry of the lease.[85] Simpson was disappointed and frustrated by this stance, but it was exactly what the right-holders had anticipated all along.

While officials batted around memoranda on the pros and cons of excisions, the right-holders focused their campaign on the goal of perma-

---

[84] Simpson (DC/Baringo) to Chairman of Forest Boundary Commission, 28 September 1948, KNA PC/NKU/2/1/30, proposing excisions. This was supported by the concessionaire's agents, Visoi Sawmills. See correspondence, September 1948 to June 1949, in KNA PC/NKU/2/13/3. For details of the *baraza*, and the sections quoted, see Simpson to Morgan (PC/RVP), 19 July 1949, KNA PC/NKU/2/1/30.

[85] Simpson (DC/Baringo) to Morgan (PC/RVP), 19 July 1949, KNA PC/NKU/3/1/30; Rammell (Conservator of Forests) to Simpson (DC/Baringo), 20 November 1948, KNA PC/NKU/2/1/30.

nently incorporating all of Lembus within Baringo. A small but very active group of right-holders, headed by Reuben Bomett and Willie Chumba, took a lead in this.[86] Regular meetings were held in the forest to discuss the latest developments, and support for the campaign appears to have been remarkably solid. Among their many allies in southern Baringo were the young Chief Joel Chirmirmir, who was responsible for overseeing Lembus, and the ADC member and prominent Lembus trader Joseph Sadalla. This group now widened the political scope of the campaign beyond Baringo, making contact with the Kenya African Union (KAU) and with Joseph Chemallen, then an African member of the Legislative Council, and canvassing the Forest Boundary Commission. The Boundary Commission predictably supported the line taken by the Forest Department, confirming in its recommendations of 1950 that the Lembus residents would legally 'have no rights after 31 December 1957', but giving approval to the excision of non-forest land.[87] The continuing recalcitrance of the Forest Department was all too clear in March 1951, when the Conservator of Forests replied to Chemallen's enquiry on Lembus; Chemallen was outraged by the deliberately misleading response that the right-holders had only 'ill-defined rights' that 'could be extinguished at the will of government'.[88] The attempt at deception was embarrassing to government and greatly inflamed sentiments in the forest.[89] Only when representatives of the KAU visited the forest to speak at public meetings a few months later was the Forest Department finally prevailed upon, by an increasingly nervous district administration, to push ahead with the surveys required for the excisions.[90] These tactics brought little direct gain to the right-holders, but each served to heighten political consciousness of the Lembus issue.

The agricultural survey of Lembus conducted during July 1951 identified the Torongo and Pororr glade systems as the areas most suitable for excision and the permanent settlement of the right-holders. Tugen cultivation in Pororr was long-standing and some farmers had already begun enclosing their land. The prospects for intensive arable farming here seemed very good. The higher and drier Torongo glades would accommodate fewer families on larger, more extensive holdings, and here mixed farming was advocated. It was proposed that these lands should be divided into

---

[86] Others included Eric Bomett, Tarakwa Cheborer and Chepsala Chepkuria. The bulk of the surviving papers concerning the resettlement committee are in KNA PC/NKU/2/2/77.

[87] Ag. Conservator of Forests to Johnston (PC/RVP), 20 July 1950, KNA PC/NKU/2/1/30.

[88] Conservator of Forests to Chemallen, 29 March 1951, and reply, 24 April 1951, KNA PC/NKU/2/1/30.

[89] On reactions to the comment, see Johnston (PC/RVP) to Chief Native Commissioner, 4 October 1952, KNA PC/NKU/2/1/30.

[90] Low (DC/Baringo) to Ryland (PC/RVP), 13 May 1951, and Low to Cowley (Provincial Agricultural Officer/RVP), 14 August 1951, both KNA PC/NKU/2/1/31. 'Meeting re Lembus excision', 14 July 1951, KNA PC/NKU/2/1/30.

smallholdings to be allocated to named right-holders, and both areas declared part of Baringo District. Cultivation rules would be applied, however, and the numbers of animals held by the smallholders would be limited by permit. These proposed regulations would be staunchly opposed in Lembus, as elsewhere in southern Baringo, but there was another, more fundamental difficulty to be overcome. The latest census of the forest had identified some 920 right-holders and their families, 620 of whom were resident within Lembus and another 300 who lived outside the concession. Although it was suspected that some of the claimants might not be legitimate, there was no escaping the reality that only around half the right-holding families could be accommodated on smallholdings of an economically viable size in Torongo and Pororr.[91] The nature of the dilemma was clear enough. 'If we announce our intention to remove families and to deny rights to those presently in the reserve, we will stir up the KAU,' wrote the District Commissioner in August 1951, but, without expulsions, the right-holders could not all be given land within Lembus.[92] 'Whatever the legal position may now be,' wrote another official six months later, 'even if we could evict these people, we have nowhere to put them.'[93]

As the wider context of emerging nationalist politics impinged upon the Lembus question, the administration found their hands tied ever more tightly. In May 1952, the right-holders addressed a petition to the Secretary of State for the Colonies, requesting his intervention to secure all of the forest for Tugen on expiry of the concession.[94] This brought no change to government policy, but, when a 'working committee' with four African members (including Joel Chirmirmir and Reuben Bomett) was set up in August 1952 to assist the District Officer in adjudicating the claims of right-holders to smallholdings in Poror and Torongo, it was evident that local cooperation was now being actively sought for the first time.[95] Before the committee had a chance to meet, J.M. ole Tameno, then the African Member of the Kenya Legislative Council representing the Rift Valley, visited Lembus at the invitation of the right-holders. Tameno found what he described as 'genuine unrest' in Lembus. On returning to Nairobi, he accused the government of giving 'twisting answers' to the Tugen to avoid

[91] Cowley, 'Memo on agricultural aspects of main forest-free areas of the Lembus forest', 24 July 1951, KNA PC/NKU/2/1/30.

[92] Cumber (DC/Baringo) to Cowley (Provincial Agricultural Officer/RVP), 14 August 1951, KNA PC/NKU/2/1/30.

[93] Jones (DO/Eldama Ravine) to Simpson (DC/Baringo), 26 February 1952, and 'Memo on the Lembus Forest by the Solicitor General', 15 November 1952, both KNA PC/NKU/2/1/31.

[94] Low (DC/Baringo) to Ryland (PC/RVP), 13 May 1951, and reply, 18 May 1951, in KNA PC/NKU/2/1/30.

[95] Ag. Divisional Forester, Londiani to Denton (DO/Eldama Ravine), 22 July 1952; and reply, 30 July 1952, KNA PC/NKU/2/1/30.

telling the truth about their rights and about plans for the future of the forest. On 5 November 1952, only a fortnight following the Declaration of Emergency in Kenya, Tameno tabled a question in the Legislative Council on the situation in Lembus.[96] The political point was timely. A fortnight later the legal opinion of the Solicitor-General confirmed that the right-holders were correct in asserting that their privileges would not be expunged with the termination of the Grogan concession. Government could only remove the right-holders from Lembus by revoking the agreements that had secured those privileges.[97]

Despite the tense political circumstances of the Mau Mau emergency, senior Forest Department officials persisted over the next three years in their efforts to compel government to do just this. The district administration now openly sided with the right-holders, notifying them of the legal position and even encouraging those with capital enough to afford it to fence their lands in the forest glades.[98] During 1954, stout cedar fences sprang up all over Poror and Muringwa with such rapidity that officials began to worry that the movement for spontaneous enclosure here would quickly become as chaotic as in other parts of southern Baringo.[99] In an effort to stem the rising tide, the forester ordered the fences to be destroyed and tried to prosecute the Tugen concerned before the District Officer from Eldama Ravine intervened on their behalf.[100] While playing one part of government off against the other, Tugen busily 'packed the area' with livestock to maximize their claims. By the end of 1955, the situation in Lembus was 'thoroughly out of control'. Feeling against the Forest Department had so intensified that violent resistance was feared.[101]

Finally, in February 1956, a meeting of all the government offices involved was convened in Nakuru to resolve matters once and for all. No representatives of the Lembus people were invited to attend the meeting, but their presence as the determining factor reverberated throughout the discussion. The argument in favour of transferring the entire forest to the Baringo ADC was plainly stated. On the political side, the historic claims of the Tugen were accepted as strong; Tugen leaders would accept nothing other than placing the forest under ADC authority, and any other policy would meet 'with the bitterest opposition from the entire tribe and it might require a levy force to impose the government's orders upon the people';

---

[96] J.M. ole Tameno to Chief Native Commissioner, 12 September 1952, and related correspondence, KNA PC/NKU/2/1/31.

[97] 'Memo on the Lembus Forest by the Solicitor-General', 15 November 1952, KNA PC/NKU/2/1/30.

[98] Swann (PC/RVP) to Sec. for African Affairs, 15 January 1955, KNA PC/NKU/2/1/30.

[99] Risley (DC/Baringo) to Swann (PC/RVP), 23 December 1954, KNA PC/NKU/2/1/30.

[100] Risley (DC/Baringo) to Swann (PC/RVP), 25 November 1954, and 3 January 1955, KNA PC/NKU/2/1/30.

[101] Conservator of Forests to Swann (PC/RVP), 21 May 1955, and Risley (DC/Baringo) to Swann, 20 October 1955, KNA PC/NKU/2/1/30.

destocking throughout southern Baringo would then be 'well nigh impossible' without local cooperation; and any denial of rights in Lembus would leave the problem of where to resettle those expelled. On the economic side, the future development of the entire district could be handsomely improved if the forest royalties were available; and the Forest Department could still retain its role in reafforestation even if the forest were under ADC control, so there would be no threat to conservation. In response, the Forest Department could only lamely argue that annual revenues in the region of £15,000 to £20,000 should not be siphoned away 'for the use of one tribe', but instead be used 'for the general revenue of the colony'. The meeting took little time to resolve that the transfer of Lembus to the Baringo ADC should go ahead.[102]

After a struggle spanning more than fifty years, it seemed that the Tugen of southern Baringo had at last won a decisive victory over the Forest Department. They had successfully 'captured' Lembus for themselves, in the process negating the claims of other African rivals – the Dorobo and the Elgeyo to the north. In their victory the people of Lembus had secured land for their own permanent settlement and potentially sustainable revenues that might underwrite the development of the whole District of Baringo for many years to come. But there was to be a final twist in the colonial history of Lembus that would leave a bitter taste for those who had campaigned so long and hard.

Although many of the right-holders appear at first to have thought that they had seen the last of the Forest Department in Lembus with the 1956 decision, this was not in fact the case. The terms of the transfer to Baringo brought royalties from commercial forestry to the ADC, but did not alter the supervisory role of the Forest Department: the forest still had to be protected, conservation measures imposed and reafforestation undertaken. The forester would have no powers to interfere on the smallholdings in Torongo and Pororr, which would be regulated under the authority of the Baringo administration in common with the rest of the district, but the forested areas of Lembus would now be subject to the rules of the Forest Ordinance governing African-controlled forests. In effect, this amounted to a limitation upon the freedoms of the right-holders, removing many of the privileges they had enjoyed – albeit intermittently and partially – under the old Coryndon Agreement.

It was, of course, some consolation to those Africans on the District Council that the revenues from the management of the forest would now be used for the benefit of the district, not the Forest Department or the shareholders of the saw-milling companies. But even here the new, post-

---

[102] Sec. for African Affairs to Swann (PC/RVP), 1 March 1956, 'Minutes of meeting to consider future of Lembus Forest, 24 February 1956', KNA PC/NKU/2/1/30. The secretary to the ALDEV board, R.O. Hennings, strongly supported the decision, as he saw this as a means of obtaining greater sums of money for district development: Hennings to Colchester (Minister for Forestry), 10 March 1956, KNA PC/NKU/2/1/30.

Grogan concession arrangements imposed unwelcome restrictions. The Perkerra Catchment Scheme, launched in 1956 as part of the African Land Development Organization's (ALDEV) programme of conservation measures in the Rift Valley Province, identified the Lembus Forest as having a critical role in the protection of water flow to the irrigation project planned on the shores of Lake Baringo far to the north. Before the transfer of the forest was legally approved, the ADC was therefore asked to help secure this programme by agreeing that they would use the bulk of the royalty accruing from Lembus for the development works within the catchment scheme for the first fifteen years of its operation. The ADC found this unobjectionable in principle, as it ensured that revenues raised from Lembus would be distributed amongst other locations. This condition was strongly advocated by the board of ALDEV and supported by Daniel arap Moi, who sat on the board representing African interests.[103] None the less, these restrictions were an uncomfortable reminder that Baringo's peoples had as yet little direct voice in the development that their district received: others would still decide how their monies would be spent. This tarnished the glow of victory in Lembus. But there was much worse to come.

In the negotiations to precisely define the areas of the smallholdings that got under way following the 1956 decision, the Forest Department raised a string of objections and restrictions that severely delayed the process. The arguments they advanced were invariably linked to the conservation of the catchment and the need to protect particular islands of forests on hillsides and within valleys adjacent to or within the zones intended for settlement. There was also a dispute as to the total amount of land that should be set aside for settlement and the size of holdings to be granted to each farmer.[104]

It was decided from the outset that the existing pattern of holdings in Pororr, where the majority had fenced land by 1957, and also in Torongo, where fewer had fenced but the plots spontaneously enclosed were very extensive, should not be allowed to remain. On the advice of Cowley, the Provincial Agricultural Officer, and with the support of ALDEV, which agreed to meet part of the costs of establishing the smallholdings, plans were laid to survey the areas concerned and to lay out farms on 'scientific lines'. At first it was calculated that farms of 25 acres would be needed for economic viability in Pororr, and considerably larger holdings in Torongo. This was based upon Cowley's careful agronomic assessment of each zone, but when the census of the right-holders was complete and the local committee had checked the credentials of claimants, it was found that 841

[103] Wainwright (PC/RVP) to Permanent Sec. African Affairs, 30 September 1958; and 'Notes of a meeting to discuss the allocation of lands in the Lembus Forest', 25 September 1959, both KNA PC/NKU/2/2/77.

[104] 'Notes of a meeting to discuss the allocation of lands in the Lembus Forest', 25 September 1959; and Butler (DC/Baringo) to Wainwright (PC/RVP), 19 January 1960, KNA PC/NKU/2/2/77.

families had a legitimate claim to be settled in Lembus. There was not enough land to go round.[105]

To gain the additional acreage needed, it was suggested that the Forest Department sacrifice other forested areas within Lembus. This they firmly refused to do, on the grounds that it would jeopardize the conservation of the catchment. Unable to gain support against the conservationist arguments, Cowley reluctantly recalculated the size of the smallholdings to get an average holding of 18 acres. He doubted whether these plots were viable, especially those located at higher altitude, but acknowledged that there now seemed no political alternative but to accept the situation.[106]

As these negotiations dragged on, the right-holders became frustrated by the seemingly interminable delays; and they had concerns of their own over the process of land allocation. In order to adjudicate the allocation of the 18-acre plots, the district administration established a local resettlement committee. This body inevitably comprised those who had been most active in the political campaign in Lembus – Reuben and Eric Bomett, Willie Chumba, Tarakwa Cheborer and Chepsala Chepkuria, along with Joel Chirmirmir.[107] These men had been in the vanguard of protest over several years, and each of them had enclosed their own lands in Pororr. Their holdings were each considerably in excess of the 18-acre plots now planned within the resettlement area. For Cowley's plan to be effectively implemented, the leading members of the resettlement committee, and many others besides, would have to give up acreages they had fenced and farmed for several years past.

The district administration baulked at the political implications of this. At a private meeting in November 1958, District Commissioner Butler had agreed to give the resettlement committee considerable powers over the process of land allocation. The committee was to have authority to determine the grades of holdings to be allocated to individuals and to decide who should be resettled where. Butler further agreed that holdings already marked out in Torongo should be left unaltered. This concession had foolishly been agreed before Cowley's survey and assessment of agricultural potential.[108] Many holdings in Torongo were considerably larger than the 18-acre-sized plots eventually decided upon. The problem now confronting the district administration was how to square Butler's agreement with the resettlement committee with Cowley's planned scheme for resettlement.

[105] Cowley, 'Memo on agricultural aspects of the main forest-free areas of the Lembus Forest', 24 July 1951, KNA PC/NKU/2/1/30; Wolff (PC/RVP) to Permanent Sec. African Affairs, 21 April 1959, KNA PC/NKU/2/13/3, and 28 July 1959, KNA PC/NKU/2/2/77.

[106] Wolff (PC/RVP) to Permanent Sec. African Affairs, 21 April 1959 and 28 July 1959; and notes of discussion in Nairobi, 25 September 1959, all in KNA PC/NKU/2/2/77.

[107] Wolff (PC/RVP) to Permanent Sec. African Affairs, 28 July 1959, KNA PC/NKU/2/2/77.

[108] Butler (DC/Baringo) to Wolff (PC/RVP), 6 November 1958, PC/NKU/2/2/77.

The solution was found in a politically motivated compromise. A small group of farmers in Pororr were formally defined as 'progressive farmers', and on this basis were permitted to keep larger holdings as a model of development for others to follow. As Butler explained, this would retain 'the goodwill of these sensible and influential people'.[109] But, to allow for the additional land this would take up, less experienced (and presumably less influential) farmers found that they were given holdings considerably smaller than 18 acres. Similarly, in Torongo, wealthier livestock owners were allowed to retain their large plots, on the grounds that successful stock farming could not be effectively managed on holdings of 18 acres or less. In return for these concessions, which greatly favoured a small but vocal and politically active group, the committee agreed to resolve all the other disputes arising in the process of resettlement.[110] All this kept the committee sweet and ensured that the allocation process went ahead without further disruption, but it was the cause of considerable rancour among those right-holders who found that their individual interests had been sacrificed.

Delays in implementation did nothing to ease the tricky process of allocation. The transfer of the forest had been agreed in March 1956, but it was not until September 1958 that the planning of the resettlement actually got under way.[111] At the end of 1959 the Forest Department was still haggling over the precise acreage to be given up, and only in January 1960 did the Lembus resettlement committee finally agree to the allocations of plot sizes then proposed.[112] Only at this stage could the transfer be officially approved, and this was done by government notice on 23 February 1960 – nearly four years after the initial decision.[113] It was more than a further year before a surveyor was assigned to Lembus to lay out the plots, and no resettlement in fact took place in Pororr or Torongo until the middle of 1963, just a few months prior to Kenya's independence.[114]

The right-holders finally got their land, but the bitterest blow of all was yet to hit them: they would be denied the promised riches from the commercial exploitation of the forest. It had been assumed all along by the right-holders and the Baringo District staff that the revenues from the forest would come to the ADC as soon as the Grogan licence came to an end on 31 December 1957. The costs of the Lembus resettlement scheme were to be met in part from these monies and, as we have seen, the ADC was already early in 1958 provisionally allocating sums to other development projects within the district, including the Perkerra Irrigation Scheme, on

[109] Ibid.

[110] Ibid.

[111] Wolff (PC/RVP) to Cowley (Provincial Agricultural Officer, RVP), 25 September 1958, KNA PC/NKU/2/2/77.

[112] Notes of the meeting held in Nairobi, 25 September 1959; and Butler (DC/Baringo) to Wolff (PC/RVP), 19 January 1960, both KNA PC/NKU/2/2/77.

[113] Legal Notice no. 98 of 1960, *Kenya Gazette Supplement* no. 13, 23 February 1960.

[114] For correspondence on the land survey, see KNA PC/NKU/2/2/77.

the basis of projected income. But in September 1958 the district administration was informed that no monies could be accumulated in the ADC coffers until the formal notice of transfer was approved. Until that could be accomplished, the Forest Department would continue to get the benefit of the revenues raised in Lembus. There is little doubt that this fact influenced the Forest Department in their procrastination over the following two years.

When arguing for the retention of the forest within the Crown Lands in 1956, the Conservator of Forests had claimed that revenues of up to £25,000 per annum could be derived from Lembus; by the end of 1958 he was far more pessimistic, claiming that a maximum of only £5,000 per annum could be anticipated for the ADC. By 1959, the actual revenues shown on the Forest Department's returns for Lembus had actually dropped to only £2,000.[115] How had this depressing reduction come about? Although some district officials and many members of the ADC harboured the belief that the department 'milked the forest' of its commercial value over these last years, there is scant evidence to support this claim. The more plausible explanation lies in the fact that the initial estimated economic value of the forest in the early 1950s had been vastly inflated by the Forest Department merely to empower the arguments for retention of Lembus as an asset to the exchequer of the colony. This tactic ultimately failed to win the argument, but in the process it served to create an undue degree of optimism among the members of the Baringo ADC, and indeed within the district administration and on the ALDEV board, that the forest could generate a substantial annual income.

When it was realized that annual revenues would be less than one-tenth of those estimated, the financial bases of the future development of the Lembus resettlement schemes and many other projects throughout the district were dealt a fatal blow. With or without the capture of the Lembus Forest, the poverty of Baringo District was to be as acute after independence as it had been under colonialism. It was hardly surprising that many in southern Baringo thought this to have been the intention of the colonial government all along.

[115] The legal difficulties in securing income from the forest for the ADC are discussed in KNA NKU/2/2/77. See especially Wolff (PC/RVP) to Permanent Sec. African Affairs, 30 September 1958.

Nine

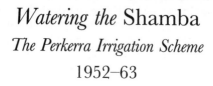

Watering the Shamba
The Perkerra Irrigation Scheme
1952–63

During the 1950s, Baringo became a favoured location for the rural development programmes of the African Land Development Board (ALDEV). There were no fewer than twenty-five ALDEV projects still active in the district on the eve of independence in 1963; and in direct grants only Machakos, Kitui and Kwale Districts received more than the £188,709 spent by ALDEV in Baringo between 1946 and 1962.[1] Given the extent of this expenditure, the results were meagre. Confronted by repeated and mounting failure in grazing-control and conservation schemes, colonial officials tended to see the problem as one of implementation. Instead of questioning their approach, the 'limited success' of development initiatives in Baringo only drove ALDEV's members on to more coercive methods and more ambitious plans.

This reached its peak in the mid-1950s with the grand design of the Perkerra Catchment Scheme. For ALDEV the Catchment Scheme was an opportunity to promote an 'ecological systems' approach to the management of rural development, whilst the more integrated strategy this emphasized fitted well with the enhanced role then being given to the 'District Team' in coordinating programmes across the various government departments.

The Catchment Scheme was a new idea, then, but it drew together three elements of the district's development programmes that were already under way.[2] The first was the protection of the forested parts of Lembus and the

---

[1] ALDEV, *African Land Development*, 117–36, 304–5.

[2] Ibid., 132–5. The idea for a 'catchment' scheme arose from a report by the Chief Conservator of Forests, sent to the Minister for Forest Development, 27 March 1956, KNA PC/NKU/2/2/33. See also papers in KNA DO/ER/2/15/2.

southern portion of the Tugen Hills, where the Perkerra River and its several smaller tributaries rose. Apart from the Lembus Forest (discussed in Chapter Eight), a further six areas of forest below Tenges, totalling 19,174 acres, were to be demarcated for protection, the population being moved from the steep-sided hills to allow for reforestation. Progress on these forest areas was slow, but by 1961 the demarcated zones had been surveyed and some trial plantings had been made. The second element was the extension of grazing controls on the lowlands to cover the full course of the Perkerra River from Lembus to Lake Baringo. This entailed the imposition of block-rotation grazing schemes on five areas, each of between 16,000 and 25,000 acres. As we have described in Chapter Seven, although all five schemes had been put in place by 1959, local resistance was so entrenched that the grazing controls were largely rendered ineffective by lack of cooperation and persistent trespass.

The third element of the Catchment Scheme was the development of a large-scale irrigation project, to be situated at the point where the Perkerra River entered the alluvial flats on the southern shore of Lake Baringo. The Perkerra Irrigation Scheme began in the early 1950s amid optimistic claims that its grain would feed the district, and that the export of its cash crops would generate high incomes to fuel wider economic growth and development.[3] A decade later the scheme was struggling to survive, subsidized by central government at a staggering rate of £24,000 per annum – more than double the annual sums spent on grazing schemes in the district between 1946 and 1962. A conservative estimate suggested that, by 1964, over £325,000 of government money had been spent on the scheme. In the words of Robert Chambers, the Perkerra Irrigation Scheme 'had become a mature dwarf, confirmed in its dependence ... and sustained in its search for economic viability by the hope that a near miracle would overcome its structural impediments'.[4] Far from bringing the intended benefits to Baringo, Peter Little argues that in the longer term the scheme 'impoverished the area and increased its dependence on food imports'.[5]

This chapter will examine the history of the Perkerra Irrigation Scheme, from its initial conception in the 1930s, through its construction and operation during the 1950s, up to 1963, when the decision was taken to maintain it despite the huge losses still being made. The first part of the chapter will explain the process by which such a disastrous scheme as this was proposed and implemented, offering a critique of the failings of colonial planning and management. As with pasture reconditioning, grazing control and resettle-

---

[3] Cowley (PAO/RVP) to DC, 6 March 1952, and subsequent correspondence in KNA PC/RVP.6A/11/21, and Cowley's correspondence April–May 1952, KNA PC/RVP.6A/11/15.

[4] Robert Chambers, *Settlement Schemes in Tropical Africa: a Study in Organizations and Development* (London, 1969), 351. See also, de Wilde et al., *Experiences with Agricultural Development*, 221.

[5] Little, *Elusive Granary*, 163.

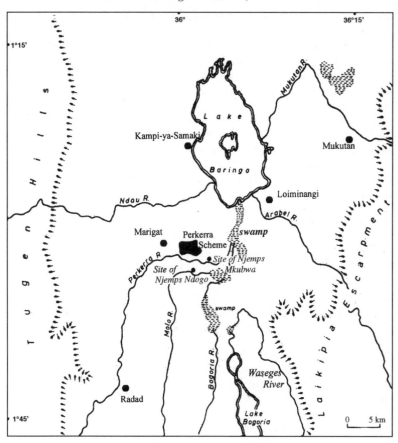

Map 9.1 Lake Baringo and its environs, c.1960

ment in the Baringo lowlands and in Lembus, government intentions on the Perkerra Irrigation Scheme shifted over time and were undermined by a combination of opposition from the local population and dissent among colonial officers themselves. In the second part of the chapter we shall reconsider the response of local people to the irrigation scheme, looking at the deeper history of indigenous irrigated cultivation at Baringo.

The perils of planning

It first occurred to colonial officials that they might encourage irrigation in Baringo during the drought of *Kiplel kowo*, when they noticed that some Chamus families were successfully irrigating small gardens from the spate

269

waters of the rivers flowing into the lake. District staff saw in this an opportunity to foster permanent cereal cultivation and so lessen Baringo's growing dependence upon famine relief. When a Senior Agricultural Chemist, V.A. Beckley, visited the Rift Valley during 1933, he was persuaded to make a tour of a number of the smaller indigenous irrigation sites near Lake Baringo to assess their scope for expansion and replication. Beckley was unimpressed by the potential for extension of these indigenous cultivations, as he thought them too primitive in construction and haphazard in method; but he did put forward the proposition that a barrage across the Perkerra gorge, above the trading centre of Marigat, might create 'a very good prospect of a really big project being successfully run'.[6] Provincial Commissioner Welby seized upon these comments, hoping that irrigated cultivation might secure the subsistence production of the entire district. He therefore pressed for a full investigation of the potential of modern irrigation on the Perkerra.[7]

A survey of the hydrology of the Perkerra River and the geology of the alluvial flats below the gorge was undertaken in 1936 by a specialist irrigation engineer (Carrick) and a hydrological surveyor (Tetley) from the Public Works Department.[8] They made a remarkably detailed study of the river and its environment, measuring the flow and calculating seasonal adjustments from the available rainfall records to model the potential for a permanent system of irrigation. Carrick and Tetley confirmed that the river flow fluctuated hugely, falling below 3 cusecs at some point during most years, though maintaining a flow above 70 cusecs with good rains in wetter seasons. They were encouraged to find no evidence that the river had ever dried up below the gorge; but in full spate it presented a terrifying spectacle. On the evening of 7 March 1936, while Carrick and Tetley's team were based at Marigat, they observed a high flood on the Perkerra after heavy rains in Lembus. Standing that night at the site chosen for the weir, they estimated the surface velocity of the flood to be 24 feet per second and the discharge in the river channel at an astonishing 49,900 cusecs. This flood raised the river gauge at Marigat from 1.1 ft. to 15.32 ft. in less than one hour, and it had arrived at the proposed intake site with a 'bore' 2 ft. high. By the next morning, twelve hours after the arrival of the flood, the Marigat gauge had fallen to 1.98 ft. and the discharge to 327 cusecs.[9]

These tremendously fierce but short spates were a common occurrence during the rainy season. Carrick and Tetley were in no doubt that a substan-

---

[6] Chambers, *Settlement Schemes*, 347: 'Soil Survey of Perkerra Irrigation Scheme', 29 April 1933, KNA PC/RVP.6A/11/15.

[7] Welby (PC/RVP) to Chief Native Commissioner, 13 June 1933, KNA PC/RVP.6A/11/43.

[8] 'Report on the Perkerra River Irrigation Project', Carrick and Tetley, 25 June 1936, KNA PC/RVP.6A/11/15. A preliminary survey had been completed by two Public Works Department (PWD) engineers, Harris and Sampson, in 1934.

[9] Ibid., 6–7.

tial weir could be constructed that would withstand these floods, but engineering works of this kind would certainly be uneconomic on a subsistence scheme of the kind wanted by the district staff. The profitable export of high-income cash crops would be needed to meet such substantial overheads, but with no road to the lake, and so no easy access to a market, this did not seem feasible. With these considerations in mind, they recommended the construction of a temporary weir, with only the head regulator and the culverts to be in masonry. They identified a suitable site, on the left bank of the river, and mapped out a line for the main canal from this intake point that would permit the irrigation of up to 3,000 acres. With a temporary weir, they estimated the establishment costs of the scheme to be £16,000. The recurrent costs of repairing the weir each year were estimated at £1,600, but the annual savings to the district in famine relief expenditure would offset this.[10]

This proposal rested upon two very important assumptions, both of which were founded in the particular problems of the district in the 1930s. First, Carrick and Tetley framed the scheme around the subsistence cultivation of mixed cereals (maize, sorghum and millets), because this would find a ready local market among pastoralists and because such cultivation was already familiar to the local population. This could work well enough, but its success would inevitably depend upon good yields being obtainable under irrigation – and without proper field tests no accurate assessment could be made of yield potential. Secondly, Carrick and Tetley opted for high-density settlement to make maximum use of the 3,000 acres available for irrigation. They calculated that holdings of only 1 acre of irrigable land per family would be adequate, but only if the irrigation was worked twenty-four hours each day. Families would have to be housed in villages outside the irrigable area, and not permitted to live on their farms. By these means, some 2,900 families could be brought on to the scheme – implying a total of perhaps 11,600 persons. This amounted to maybe one-quarter of Baringo's entire population in 1936.

These proposals left many questions unanswered. Would the local population be willing to settle in such large numbers? Would they accept the demands of a round-the-clock system of cultivation? What would the tenants do with their livestock? Despite the many uncertainties, district officials embraced the proposal with enthusiasm. Promotion of the irrigation scheme became a *leitmotif* for the Baringo administration over the next few years. An application based on Carrick and Tetley's recommendations was first put up to the Colonial Development Fund (1929) in 1937, but other projects received a higher priority in London and the Perkerra proposal was shelved.[11]

[10] Ibid., 1–3, 10.

[11] Grants under the Colonial Development Fund were expected to carry a high level of expenditure in Britain. See Constantine, *Making of British Colonial Development Policy*. This would not have been achievable with the Perkerra proposal, and this discouraged the Kenya government.

Two years later Hyde-Clarke's 1939 integrated scheme for district development included irrigation on the Perkerra. This received wide support within
the colonial government, but no provision could then be made for funding
due to the outbreak of war. In 1940, an application under the new Colonial
Development and Welfare Act (CDWA) was briefly considered, but again
no action was taken.[12] Between 1941 and 1946 the scheme was put forward
on no fewer than five separate occasions, including a suggestion that Italian
prisoners of war could be utilized as a source of cheap labour on the project,
and yet another hydrological investigation of the river was undertaken in
1943. None of these proposals received financial backing. As the failures
mounted, interest in the project waned among district staff.[13]

It was not until 1952 that the potential of irrigation in Baringo was again
raised, and this was done in total ignorance of the earlier proposals. On his
first tour through the district, the new Provincial Agricultural Officer,
Cowley, came across some Chamus women cultivating fields irrigated with
the overflow from a small river running through the alluvial flats to the
south of the lake. He was excited by what he saw:

> They employ a simple system of box terracing and cultivation consists of
> roughening the top 3 inches of silt with wooden planting sticks. Considering
> the people are so extraordinarily primitive, pre-stone age, in manner and
> appearance, the accuracy of their bank construction was extraordinary; also
> their apparent ability to site their box terraced lands so that an even flow
> of overflow water was received on the plots. It appears they can get a crop
> of maize (flat white) in between 3 and 4 months under these conditions,
> providing that a supply of overflow water comes down about 4 times and
> with not more than three week intervals between any flood. The procedure
> is chancy, as it depends upon natural flooding which may or may not occur,
> but it is evident that the land will grow satisfactory crops still, providing that
> water is made available.[14]

---

[12] DC/BAR to Hodge (PC/RVP), 19 March 1940; Hodge (PC/RVP) to Chief Secretary, 2
May 1940, stating that money could more usefully be spent on general rehabilitation
programmes than on an irrigation scheme; both KNA PC/RVP.6A/11/27.

[13] By 1941, Tetley was Director of the Public Works Department, and used his position to
promote the scheme once again: Chief Secretary to Director of Agriculture, 23 December
1941, and related correspondence, KNA PC/RVP.6A/11/27. In 1943 the idea was revived
as a possible means of increasing agricultural production as part of the war effort: Chief
Secretary to PC/RVP, 20 April 1943, and reply 14 May 1943, both KNA PC/RVP.6a/
11/27. Towards the end of 1943, with food shortages in Baringo, a decision was taken to
investigate the scheme again: R. Chance (Irrigation Advisor), 'Note on irrigation in Kenya',
11 January 1944, KNA PC/RVP.6A/11/27. And between 1944 and 1946 District
Commissioner Lambert did his best to promote the scheme: see, for example, Lambert to
PC/RVP, 15 January 1944, and Lambert to PC, 23 September 1946, both KNA
PC/RVP.6A/11/27. In 1946, PC/RVP pushed for the Development and Reconstruction
Authority (DARA) to 're-examine' question of irrigation schemes in Baringo: PC to Ch
DARA, 24 January 1946, KNA PC/RVP.6A/11/21. Chambers, *Settlement Schemes*, 347.

[14] Cowley to PC/RVP, 5 April 1952, KNA PC/RVP.6A/11/21.

Like Beckley, some nineteen years before, Cowley saw in this indigenous practice the potential for a modern development project. But, where the early 1930s had been marked by the spectre of famine and the need for improved subsistence, Cowley was full of the development opportunities heralded by the 'new colonialism' of the postwar years. His enthusiastic report to the District Commissioner made the case for a large-scale irrigation scheme with 'marketable crops' – maize, beans, sorghum, cassava and bananas might all be grown for local consumption, and lucerne, citrus, cotton, tobacco and groundnuts were possible export crops. Within a couple of weeks of his visit, a formal proposal for a pilot project was put before ALDEV.[15]

It is ironic, but by no means surprising, that Cowley seems to have been unaware at this stage of Beckley's 1933 report or Carrick and Tetley's 1936 report on the Perkerra. There is no mention of these investigations in his original correspondence on the matter[16] or in the application made to ALDEV. By 1952 the district was staffed by an entirely new group of officers, none of whom had any memory of the previous proposals, and no one bothered to look through the district files. The ALDEV board therefore treated the application *de novo*. A grant of £2,500 for capital expenditure on the pilot project was made by ALDEV in April 1952 and, by July, some 15 acres on the left bank of the Perkerra had been set out for crop trials.[17] Initial plantings of maize, groundnuts, sorghum and sugar cane were successful,[18] but before a second season of trials could begin in 1953 Cowley's carefully laid plans were overtaken by events.

In October 1952, Kenya's Governor declared a State of Emergency. Over the next year, as the campaign against Mau Mau grew in intensity, large numbers of suspects were placed in detention. Among these detainees were Kikuyu squatters from the settler farming districts to the south of Baringo. In August 1953 it was decided to hold these prisoners in camps within the Rift Valley Province, and the administration was asked to immediately find suitable locations. Confronted with this urgent request, the Provincial Commissioner grabbed the opportunity: Marigat was offered as a possible site for a Mau Mau detention camp, with the understanding that prisoners' labour would be used on the construction of the Perkerra Irrigation Scheme.[19] Neither Cowley nor others in the district administration were consulted on this decision, but it is doubtful that anyone would

---

[15] Cowley to DC, 6 March 1952, KNA PC/RVP.6A/11/21; Cowley to PC, 5 April 1952, KNA PC/RVP.6A/11/21. Also Cowley's correspondence, April–May 1952, KNA PC/RVP.6A/11/15. Cowley hoped that a successful trial would enable an approach to be made to the Overseas Food Corporation for funding.

[16] Low to ALUS, 4 April 1952; Cowley to Dir. of Agriculture, 9 April 1952, both KNA PC/RVP.6A/11/21.

[17] Hennings (ALUS) to Cowley, 3 July 1952, KNA PC/RVP.6A/11/21. £70 was spent in 1952, and a further £743 from the ALDEV grant in 1953.

[18] ALDEV, *African Land Development*, 121–2.

[19] Telegram, PC to DC, 19 September 1953, KNA PC/RVP.6A/11/21.

have opposed the idea of acquiring a free labour force for the construction of the scheme. This appeared to be the boost that the project had always needed to secure its success.

Before the end of the month an engineer had arrived at Marigat to survey the area and lay out the camp and the irrigation works. In the rush, Carrick and Tetley's careful survey of 1936 – with its detailed survey maps – remained hidden away in the deep litter of the district office. Working in haste, the engineer overlooked the intake site on the left bank of the Perkerra, chosen by Carrick and Tetley because it would allow for a gravity flow system, and instead selected a site on the right bank, which required a pump to raise the water. It was only a few months later, after considerable work had already been undertaken, that the 1936 report was 'rediscovered' and the preferred site identified from Carrick and Tetley's map. In February 1954, work began again to relocate both the camp and the irrigation works on the left bank, closer to Cowley's experimental plot.[20] This costly false start set the tone for the stumbling progress of the Perkerra Scheme over the next decade.

Tenants & technicians

The decision to house Kikuyu detainee labourers at Marigat dramatically altered the political context in which the Perkerra Irrigation Scheme would be developed. District staff now found several other fingers in their pie. The Department of Agriculture was responsible for crop trials, cultivation and marketing on the Perkerra Scheme, while the Public Works Department constructed, managed and maintained the irrigation works. The labour for all these activities was controlled and supervised by the Prison Department, who ran the Marigat Camp where Mau Mau detainees were housed. From 1954, the Community Development Department ran part of the Perkerra Scheme as a rehabilitation project, taking some prisoners into a separate 'open' village. From 1956, oversight of the whole scheme was placed under the newly created Central Irrigation Board, with its headquarters in Nairobi. Each of these five departments of government had their own priorities, and none of them were formally required to report to Baringo's District Commissioner or to consult with the District Team. This quickly bred conflicts. While district staff saw Perkerra, according to one Provincial Commissioner, as 'a settlement and land rehabilitation scheme' for the benefit of the people of Baringo, the other departments involved saw it as 'a government estate for the making of money, growing produce and employing labour'.[21] And between them all, responsibilities frequently overlapped

---

[20] Richardson, Engineer to Exec. Off., ALUS, 3 October 1953, and Exec. Off. ALUS to DC, 15 September 1952, both KNA PC/RVP.6A/11/21; Minutes of ALDEV meeting, Lake Baringo, 4 February 1954, KNA PC/NKU/2/2/33. Chambers, *Settlement Schemes*, 348.

[21] Provincial Commissioner Wainwright, quoted in Chambers, *Settlement Schemes*, 360.

and aims came into conflict. Agricultural staff lamented the poor work of Prisons labour; Community Development and Prisons staff fell to squabbling over the designation and management of prisoners; the Public Works Department were criticized by everyone for delays and poor standards of work; the Central Irrigation Board was thought 'irrelevant but meddlesome'; and the District Team, for their part, treated everyone else with the greatest suspicion.[22] At Perkerra, as in Lembus, colonial government was a house divided against itself.

For the district staff and for the local African population, the struggle at Perkerra came to centre upon the granting of tenancies. The 1936 proposal had intended the settlement of Chamus and Tugen farmers, who would cultivate cereals for their own subsistence. Cowley's pilot project of 1952 shifted the focus to commercial cash cropping, and this raised doubts as to the capabilities of local farmers. While he was prepared to try out local farmers as tenants, Cowley stressed the importance of having an experienced and competent labour force on the scheme, regardless of their origins. Roddan, the Director of Agriculture, firmly endorsed this view, insisting upon the right of his department to select tenants solely on the basis of their farming skills.[23] Other senior officials in the Department of Agriculture and on the board of ALDEV also expressed their doubts as to the capacity of Chamus or Tugen farmers to cope with the demands of a large-scale, modern irrigation scheme.[24] To the horror of the District Team, many of these commentators favoured the option of settling Kikuyu or Kamba farmers as permanent tenants at Perkerra.[25]

District officials in Baringo were quick to jump to the defence of 'local interests' when the question of future tenancies was first raised during 1952. 'Response may be slow at first,' cautioned District Commissioner Low:

> but we should not have to go outside the district to find men. Each year the shortage of good arable land in the Kamasia hills is becoming more acute and for this reason there would be the strongest opposition to any rights of occupancy being offered to members of other tribes.[26]

With the support of the Provincial Commissioner, Low initially won agreement that Chamus and Tugen farmers would be given an opportunity to prove their worth as tenants once the scheme was fully operational.[27] But

---

[22] See, for example, Simpson to Hennings, 11 December 1953; PC to Hennings, 16 December 1953, both in KNA PC/RVP.6A/11/21.

[23] Roddan to Hennings, 10 April 1956, KNA PC/NKU/2/2/34.

[24] PC to DC Low, 7 July 1952, and minute by Cowley, 1 August 1952, KNA PC/RVP.6A/11/21.

[25] Hennings to Simpson (DC/BAR), Dec 1953, and Simpson's reply, 11 December 1953, KNA PC/RVP.6A/11/21; correspondence between Hennings and PC (RVP), January 1956, in KNA PC/NKU/2/2/34.

[26] Low to Johnson, 18 July 1952. Low was supported by the Provincial Team – PC to Exec. Office, ALUS, 13 August 1952, all in KNA PC/RVP.6A/11/21.

[27] PC to Exec. Officer, ALUS, 13 August 1952, KNA PC/RVP.6A/11/21.

this was overtaken by the construction of the prison camp and the arrival of 1,800 Kikuyu prisoners before the end of 1953. Over the next three years the district administration fought a running battle to prevent Kikuyu tenants being settled permanently on the scheme. From October 1953, prison labour was used in the construction and maintenance of the irrigation works and in the agricultural work on the crop trials. With no programme devised to award tenancies to local farmers, and none likely whilst the administration of the scheme was so closely linked to the needs of the Emergency, the prospects for 'local interests' appeared bleak. Things looked worse with the arrival of the Community Development Department in 1954, whose staff assumed from the outset that Kikuyu prisoners in the process of rehabilitation could be settled as permanent tenants.[28] To that end, and without consulting district officials, an experimental 'open village' of Kikuyu detainees was established adjacent to the scheme before the end of 1955.[29] This 'village' might easily have turned into a successful seed-bed for Kikuyu tenants, were it not for the fact that virtually all the Kikuyu placed there sought ways of obtaining work in other areas of the Rift Valley as soon as the opportunity arose.[30] For released detainees, a farm at Marigat, adjacent to their former prison, must have seemed an inhospitable and uncongenial home. When it became clear that rehabilitated detainees would not stay, a scheme was devised to recruit some 200 Kikuyu families from the Central Province as contract labourers. Fervent opposition from the District Commissioner could not prevent the first of these labourers arriving in 1956, but they came without their families and all had returned to Central Province within a year.[31] The 'Kikuyu menace' – as one District Officer somewhat emotively termed it[32] – was raised yet again in 1957, when Special Commissioner C.M. Johnson tried to send seventy-five 'hard-core' Mau Mau to be settled on the Perkerra Scheme: only the desperate pleas of District Commissioner Palmer thwarted this plan at the eleventh hour.[33]

---

[28] DC to PC, 26 July 1954, KNA PC/NKU/2/2/33.

[29] Baringo District AR, 1956.

[30] Hennings to Chief Secretary, 6 November 1956; monthly reports for 1955, General Manager, Perkerra Irrigation Scheme (PIS), and related correspondence. And for continuing opposition to this idea, Wainwright (PC) to Manager PIS, 1 October 1956, and DC to Wainwright, 28 September 1956, all in KNA PC/NKU/2/2/34.

[31] Hennings to Chief Secretary, 6 November 1956; PC to Sec. for Community Development, 12 April 1957, both in KNA PC/NKU/2/2/34. These migrants were almost certainly not rehabilitated Mau Mau, as the district staff believed, but loyalist families. This would explain the many conflicts that arose after their arrival, especially in regard to Mau Mau detainee labourers from the Marigat Camp: monthly reports for 1956 and 1957, General Manager, Perkerra Irrigation Scheme, KNA PC/NKU/2/2/34. I am grateful to Caroline Elkins for much useful information on this.

[32] DO to DC, 29 June 1957, KNA PC/NKU/2/2/34.

[33] The crucial letter is Palmer to PC, 1 May 1957, but see also related papers in KNA PC/NKU/2/2/34.

Some of these attempts to settle Kikuyu on the Perkerra Scheme represented nothing more than naked opportunism: released detainees and refugee Kikuyu 'loyalists' had to be put somewhere and, to beleaguered officials, Marigat must have seemed a better destination than many others. But the political expediency of the Mau Mau Emergency obscured both Cowley's emphasis on the need to find suitably skilled and energetic tenants and the district administration's insistence upon the need to secure local interests.

The shifting sands of government policy at this time hardly provided a secure foundation for district development. Advancement of the scheme came to depend primarily upon the operations of the prison camp. By the early months of 1956 fewer detainees were being sent to Marigat and the labour available to the scheme was in decline. Plans laid to increase the area under irrigation to 1,500 acres by 1957 required a labour force in excess of 2,500 men, but it now seemed that fewer than 1,800 would be available.[34] At the same time, the scheme manager was increasingly dissatisfied with the work carried out by the detainee labourers; the numbers of men available fluctuated unpredictably, mainly due to sickness, and progress was sporadic; labourers were unenthusiastic and worked slowly; they took little care over tasks, and supervision by prison staff was often inadequate. There were problems of control and discipline. For all these reasons, the Department of Agriculture wanted permanent tenants brought on to the scheme. But by 1956, their earlier preference for Kikuyu labour had been tarnished by the experience of the Emergency, and the manager at Perkerra was of the opinion that 'no good Kikuyu tenants' could anyway be persuaded to come to Perkerra.[35] In these circumstances, local tenants appeared the only option.

With acute shortage of labour threatening the scheme in the early months of 1956, and with the tacit support of the scheme manager, the Provincial Commissioner pressed the case for allowing 'Tugen and Njemps [Chamus] in at the earliest possible time under the easiest possible terms'.[36] A compromise was agreed, allowing Chamus and Tugen 'temporary settlers' on to the scheme as an experiment – 'a few guinea pigs … to help us assess what a family is capable of working' was how Roddan now saw it.[37] The 'temporary settlers' were to be made to sign a statement saying they had no rights in the land and could be removed at will. This was deemed necessary because the land for the scheme had not yet been legally excised from the Native Reserve, but it also served to underline the insecurity of the tenants' position. Each 'temporary settler' was given 2 acres

[34] Reports of General Manager, PIS, in PC/NKU/2/2/34.
[35] Koch (Hydaulic Engineer, PWD), 'Report of Inspection', 8 August 1956, KNA PC/NKU/2/2/34.
[36] PC to Sec for Ag [Hennings], 19 January 1956, KNA PC/NKU/2/2/34.
[37] Roddan to Hennings, 10 April 1956, KNA PC/NKU/2/2/34.

of land, but permitted only to grow crops specified by the scheme management. They paid no rent, but were allowed to keep their own crops.[38] The first thirty families joined on these terms on 11 May 1956, all of them Tugen. By the end of the year their number had grown to forty-seven families, including some Chamus.[39]

Having won this concession to local interests, the District Team now lobbied hard to secure permanent contracts for the tenants. The good progress of the 'temporary settlers' in the first few months helped to make the case, but it was the heightening of political tensions in other parts of the district toward the end of 1956 that decisively swung the argument. With trouble brewing in Lembus, the Kiplombe exchange being resisted by many herders in the Esageri area, and a breakdown of control threatened at Solai over the issuing of grazing permits, it was easy to see that a decision to evict the 'temporary settlers' from Perkerra and bring in 'outsiders' would be likely to further fuel the fires of local dissent. The plans for the Perkerra Catchment Scheme were approved by the ALDEV board in November, and were seen, in large part, as a means of regaining control of the several development programmes then under its guidance in Baringo. With the Perkerra Irrigation Scheme now to be reintegrated within the district development plan, the confirmation of tenancies for local farmers seemed a more logical step.[40] By the end of the year the ALDEV board had grasped the nettle, and the decision to allow permanent local tenancies was confirmed. The question now was whether the Tugen and Chamus could make an economic success of it.

Between 1952 and 1956 government officials remained bullish about the scheme's prospects. Their optimism was buttressed by the calculations of F.A. Brown, the Colonial Office Adviser on Irrigation and former manager of the Sudan Gezira Scheme, who visited Perkerra at the end of 1954. Brown thought it possible to generate gross annual revenues of £96,000 from the scheme: with plots of 4 acres, this would give 740 tenants an average annual income of £94 (1,880s.). Brown's estimates were widely cited in ALDEV's literature[41] and became part of the folklore of the project, justifying more expansive plans to construct more substantial masonry headworks and to enlarge the acreage between 1954 and 1956. However, underlying these grand designs was the unresolved question of whether a profitable cash crop could be found.

There were several failed experiments. The most embarrassing – and costly – was a scheme to grow tomatoes for sale directly to a canning company. Early crop trials indicated that yields of up to 8 tons per acre

[38] Gen Manager, PIS, 30 April 1956; PC/RVP to DC/BAR, 2 May 1956, KNA PC/NKU/2/2/33.

[39] PC/RVP to Sec for Ag., 19 June 1956; DC/BAR to Ag. Dir. Agri., 7 July 1956, both KNA PC/NKU/2/2/33. Chambers, *Settlement Schemes*, 348.

[40] Hennings to CS, 6 November 1956, KNA PC/NKU/2/2/34.

[41] ALDEV, *African Land Development*, i, 122.

might be expected, and on this basis Kabazi Canners contracted to purchase the harvest from up to 500 acres of tomatoes grown by the labour from the detention camp. With two crops in each year, Kabazi calculated that a yield of above 5 tons per acre would allow them to break even. This margin turned out to be too tight. In the first season of 1956 labour shortages meant that only 8 acres could be planted, realizing a yield of only 4 tons per acre. The second crop was expanded to 60 acres, but blight, mildew and eelworm reduced the yield to just over 1 ton per acre. Over 100 acres were planted to tomatoes in 1957, but the crop fared no better. At the end of the year, Kabazi Canners withdrew from the enterprise amid rancorous exchanges over the failure of government to fulfil its side of the bargain.[42]

No reliable cash crop had yet been found when the first local 'temporary settlers' were engaged in 1956. At this point, experiments in effect shifted from the demonstration plot to the tenant's own fields – the tenants would indeed become the 'guinea-pigs' Roddan had described. In the first year it was decided that the tenants should grow groundnuts. On the basis of earlier trials, yields of 20 cwt an acre were anticipated, but by April 1957 it was evident that even on the best plots the 'temporary settlers' had managed only 5 cwt.[43] These farmers had done well with their first crop of maize, and the poor performance with groundnuts came as a surprise to the scheme management. The problems were thought to lie with the unfamiliarity of the crop, and managers believed that tighter control of water management and weeding would bring about improved results.

When the first seventy-five permanent tenants joined the scheme in May 1957[44] – including in their number around thirty of the original 'temporary settlers'[45] – they were given 4 acres of land each, 3 acres of which was to be planted to crops twice a year, the remaining acre to be left fallow. The first crop each year was to be a maize crop, for subsistence, and the second crop a cash crop – groundnuts. The scheme management took responsibility for the mechanical preparation of the fields for the maize crop; tenants sowed, weeded and harvested this crop themselves.[46] Groundnuts were then to be planted as a second crop. In an effort to overcome the problems

---

[42] For negotiation of the contract, see KNA PC/NKU/2/2/33. Manager, PIS, Report for 15–30 August 1957, KNA PC/NKU/2/2/34; Richardson to Irrig. Man., Min. of Ag., 6 September 1957, KNA PC/NKU/2/2/34; Richardson, 'PIS: Dispute with Kabazi canners', 3 October 1957, KNA PC/NKU/2/2/34; *East African Standard*, 6 September 1957; de Wilde et al., *Experiences with Agricultural Development*, 223.

[43] DC to PC, 13 April 1957, KNA PC/2/2/34.

[44] Hennings to Sec. for African Affairs, 23 January 1957; DO to DC, 12 January 1957; Hennings to Sec. for Ag., 23 January 1957; PC to Ch PIS Committee, 22 February 1957, all in KNA PC/NKU/2/2/34; ALDEV, *African Land Development*, ii, 134.

[45] Chambers, *Settlement Schemes*, 356, reports that the others were evicted because of 'poor husbandry'.

[46] Hennings to Sec. for African Affairs, 23 January 1957, KNA PC/NKU/2/2/34.

experienced with the groundnut crop in the previous year, the scheme management contracted to prepare and sow this crop in the first year, as well as completing the first weeding; tenants would then complete a second weeding and harvest the crop, under the supervision of management.[47]

As in 1956, things got off to a very good start. In June 1957 the scheme manager reported that the new tenants were 'doing well': 'results to date are very encouraging indeed. They have sown, watered, re-sown and weeded in a manner few people imagined they would be capable of.'[48] An ad hoc tenants' committee was formed, led by a Tugen headman and a Chamus chief, through whom the management could convey agricultural instructions; and, to encourage the tenants to settle with their families, each was permitted to bring two milch cows or a calf into the scheme.[49] The maize crop ultimately produced a lower yield that season than had been hoped, achieving around twelve bags an acre rather than thirty, but this was still sufficient to give the tenants a good surplus for sale to neighbouring herders. The scheme management were untroubled by this, as they considered it likely that some of the shortfall in apparent yield could be attributed to deliberate under-reporting on the part of tenants (who had sold the produce directly into the local market) and high levels of theft from the fields.[50] With news of the success of the maize crop, more people came forward requesting tenancies and, by the beginning of 1958, the scheme could boast 196 Tugen and forty-five Chamus settlers.[51]

But, even as these new tenants were joining the scheme, trouble was brewing. The scheme management had undertaken the planting and first weeding of the groundnut crop and it was now time for the tenants to engage in the second weeding: the vast majority simply refused to do so. They argued that the combination of low yields and high fixed costs made groundnuts uneconomic.

The logic of their position was plain enough. At 5 cwt an acre, tenants in the previous year had raised only around 330s. per acre from groundnuts.[52] From this income they were expected to pay a 'water rate' to cover the services provided by the scheme. The water rate had been set at 300s. an acre for 1957, which was clearly far too high in relation to the value of the cash crop. The scheme management thought it reasonable that tenants might use any profit from the sale of maize to meet these charges, but the tenants saw the charges as relating only to the cash crop. Their protests against the high charges were supported by the district administration, and the rate was in fact reduced later in the year to 70s. per acre. This brought the charges within the range of profit from the crop, but it did not take

[47] Ibid.
[48] Manager PIS, Report 1–15 June 1957, KNA PC/NKU/2/2/34.
[49] PIS, Report 1–15 June 1957, KNA PC/NKU/2/2/34.
[50] Chambers, *Settlement Schemes*, 356. PIS Report, 15–30 April 1957, KNA PC/NKU2/2/34
[51] ALDEV, *African Land Development*, 135.
[52] DC to PC, 13 April 1957, KNA PC/NKU/2/2/34.

account of the costs of hired labour. Very few tenants had yet brought their families to the scheme, and so virtually all continued to depend upon hired labour for weeding and harvesting at a cost of a further 100s. or more per annum.[53] With these fixed costs and even with a reduction in rates, the majority of tenants could only grow groundnuts at a loss.

The numbers of tenants had reached a peak of 241 during the early part of 1958. As attempts were made to enforce compliance with the cultivation rules for groundnuts and to collect payment of charges, tenants started to leave the scheme. By the end of 1959 there were only 114 left:[54] many had been evicted for 'poor husbandry' (that is, refusing to tend the groundnut crop) and failure to pay rates; parts of the scheme were reverting to bush; no casual labour could be recruited locally to work the land; and the scheme was losing money at an alarming rate.[55] The future of the whole enterprise now appeared bleak.

Coming hard on the heels of the revelation that little income would in fact accrue to the district from the termination of the Lembus Forest concession (see Chapter Eight), the failure of groundnuts at Perkerra in 1958 came as a bitter blow. District staff had won the battle to secure local farmers on permanent tenancies, and they had even been successful in getting African representation on the 'Irrigation Committee', which oversaw the daily running of the scheme.[56] More important still, they had secured income from Perkerra for the Baringo African District Council (ADC). In 1957 the development costs of the project – by then around £126,000 – had been set aside as a grant, and agreement was reached that the Central Irrigation Board (CIB) should lease the land from the ADC at a fixed rent. This meant that no interest burden would fall upon the district coffers and that the ADC could look forward to an accumulating income. Any profit to the scheme remaining after the payment of rent and the charges levied by the CIB for services would then accrue to the province.[57] Success at Perkerra would bring benefits to all, but without a viable cash crop there could be no profit.

[53] Hennings to Sec. for African Affairs, 23 January 1957, KNA PC/NKU/2/2/34. It is indicative of the haphazard progress of the scheme that no legal authority existed under which to charge this rate in 1957, although provision was subsequently made later in the year. The rate of 300s. contrasted sharply with the rate of 7s. per acre suggested in 1936 in Carrick and Tetley's subsistence-based scheme. In the early 1960s, it was estimated that each tenant paid approximately 300s. per annum in labour costs. See de Wilde et al., *Experiences with Agricultural Development*, 234.

[54] ALDEV, *African Land Development*, 135.

[55] Chambers, *Settlement Schemes*, 356. Baringo District ARs, 1958 and 1959.

[56] Wesley arap Tomno, a member of the ADC, was the first African representative on the 'Irrigation Committee', although Provincial Commissioner Wainwright had wanted to appoint Daniel arap Moi. DC to PC, 9 December 1957, and PC to Chairman, Perkerra Irrigation Committee, 14 August 1957, both KNA PC/NKU/2/2/34.

[57] PC to Sec for African Affairs, 20 June 1956; Memo on 'Organisation of irrigation', 16 April 1956, both in KNA PC/NKU/2/2/66; PC to DC, 5 February 1957, and Hennings to PC, 28 February 1957, both KNA PC/NKU/2/2/34.

Numerous technical problems with the hydrology and agriculture of the scheme added to the misery. The weir constructed in 1953 had been quickly and cheaply built, and needed continual repairs over the next eight years. This turned out to be vastly more expensive than Carrick and Tetley had estimated in 1936: flood damage in 1954 alone cost over £6,000 to repair, with larger and more substantial masonry headworks being put in place. Major repairs were again needed in 1957, and a further flood in 1961 required repairs costing £5,000.[58] Leakage from the main canal, caused by its poor construction, reduced the actual area that could be irrigated from 3,000 to around 2,400 acres in the long rains and, at most, 1,200 acres in the short rains.[59] Experiments with both basin and ridge-and-furrow patterns of cultivation had been rendered meaningless by the poor levelling of the basins, which led to waterlogging, and misalignment of the furrows, which caused poor distribution of water.[60] Waterlogging of the basins was a very serious problem in some parts of the scheme, and had caused severe infestations of nut-grass each rainy season.[61]

From 1959 to 1961, the scheme limped along on a 'care and mainte-nance' basis, with the tenants growing only maize.[62] The flood damage of 1961 was a further costly blow and, when the Provincial Agricultural Com-mittee met in Nakuru during April 1962 to discuss the future of the scheme the mood was gloomy. The Hydraulic Engineer described the damage to the weir and 'stressed the unsuitability of the river for a large expansion of acreage'. The economics of the scheme, as reported to the meeting, were clearly unsatisfactory: the total cost to date had been £364,700, and in 1961 only 430 acres were under crop of the 1,750 available for irrigation. An accumulated deficit of at least £50,000 for the period 1960–63 was con-sidered 'inevitable'.[63] Although the Department of Agriculture made a spirited defence of the potential of the scheme, the balance of opinion weighed against the project: too much money had been squandered for too little return. In conclusion, Provincial Commissioner Wolff announced that the scheme would close in April 1963, unless a suitable cash crop could be found in the meantime.[64]

One month later his decision had been rescinded. The reason for the change of heart was that it appeared that a viable cash crop had at last been found – onions. The first small crop of onions had been harvested in

[58] Chambers, *Settlement Schemes*, 352–3; ALDEV, *African Land Development*, i, 123; Perkerra Irrigation Scheme Report, July 1957, KNA PC/NKU/2/2/34).

[59] De Wilde et al., *Experiences with Agricultural Development*, 222; ALDEV, *African Land Development*, 135.

[60] Koch (PWD), 'Report of Inspection', 8 August 1956, KNA PC/NKU/ 2/2/34.

[61] For summaries, see de Wilde et al., *Experiences with Agricultural Development*, 223, and Chambers, *Settlement Schemes*, 358.

[62] Chambers, *Settlement Schemes*, 349; Baringo District AR, 1959.

[63] Joint Irrigation Committee reports, KNA PC/NKU/2/2/66.

[64] Provincial Agricultural Committee, minutes 14 April 1962 and 5 May 1962.

Table 9.1 Perkerra Irrigation Scheme: finance and settlement, 1954–64

	(1) Capital (£)	(2) Recurrent (£)	(3) Depreciation (£)	(4) Revenue (£)	(5) Losses(£) (2)+(3)–(4)	(6) Tenants (No.)
1954 } 1955 }	86,366	21,588	1,727	Nil	23,315	–
1956	33,546	16,490	2,398	Nil	18,888	47
1957	55,061	22,213	3,498	500	25,211	72
1958	32,777	16,145	4,153	800	19,498	241
1959	9,675	31,060	4,347	2,100	33,307	114
1960	2,771	16,313	4,402	2,640	18,075	99
1961	3,045	14,460	4,463	2,405	16,518	128
1962	7,221	20,218	4,608	2,021	22,805	326
1963	14,241	31,906	4,892	13,232	23,566	334
1964	6,198	35,580	5,017	7,114	33,483	362

Source: Chambers, Settlement Schemes, 350.

Table 9.2 Onions on the Perkerra Irrigation Scheme, 1961–4

	1961–2	1962–3	1963–4
No. of acres of onions	62	300	416
Gross sales of onions	£1,682	£11,530	£31,370
No. of tenants	129	326	349

November 1960.[65] Early problems with disease were overcome by spraying, and production increased from 62 acres in 1961 to 416 acres in 1963, with average yields of 3 tons per acre, although the better tenants were able to obtain 4 to 5 tons.[66] Gross sales of onions in the 1962–3 season realized £11,530, and this income at last began to attract tenants back to the scheme. In the next year gross income from onions for the 349 tenants nearly tripled to £31,370.

On the eve of Kenya's independence in 1963, the combination of onions and maize was bringing prosperity to some tenants. In the 1962–3 year, 40 per cent of farmers with a 4-acre plot earned over 3,000s. after deducting charges due, with a similar proportion of 1-acre tenants earning above 1,000s. The income of the very best tenant was above 7,000s. These were very high profits by the standards of Baringo, but there was tremendous variation in performance and around 30 per cent of tenants were acknowledged to be 'doing poorly'.[67] Even amongst the most 'progressive' tenants

[65] Joint Irrigation Committee reports, KNA PC/NKU/2/2/66; de Wilde et al., Experiences with Agricultural Development, 223; Baringo District AR, 1960.
[66] De Wilde et al., Experiences with Agricultural Development, 233; Chambers, Settlement Schemes, 354.
[67] De Wilde et al., Experiences with Agricultural Development, 233.

there was still a tendency to view the scheme as an adjunct to other activities. Fewer than 60 per cent of tenants had built houses on the scheme by 1964 and absenteeism remained a significant problem, while many tenants kept large herds of livestock on the scheme in contravention of the regulations.[68] Even amongst the most successful tenants were many who also ran trading and transport businesses. To some extent, the Perkerra Scheme had become a place for those with capital to speculate.[69]

And those who did so found that their risk was effectively underwritten by the state. Rates were collected specifically for the investment made in lands planted to onions from 1961 onwards, when better incomes began to filter through to the tenants. However, charges for ploughing were never made and, by 1964, payments made by tenants still fell considerably short of the actual costs of the services provided. The most progressive farmers could certainly afford to pay these charges by 1963, but the relatively low level of the charges and their non-payment kept inefficient cultivators in production.[70] At Kenya's independence in 1963, the Perkerra Scheme was therefore still struggling to survive. Its 349 tenants were growing onions as a cash crop and irrigated maize for subsistence and for sale in local markets and kept cattle on irrigated star-grass pastures. Overall, the scheme continued to operate in deficit. A conservative estimate suggested that annual expenditure on the running of the project exceeded income by £16,500.[71] Other estimates put this figure as high as £24,000 per annum – the equivalent of giving each tenant a hand-out of £68 a year in a district where average incomes were less than a quarter of this figure.[72]

Indigenous irrigation

The past experience of irrigation in Baringo held more potential lessons for colonial developers than they were capable of realizing. In Chapter One, we gave a brief description of the part played by Chamus irrigation agriculture in supplying the trading caravans that visited Baringo in growing numbers from the 1840s through to the 1890s. It was noted that the irrigation cultivations probably reached their peak of productivity toward the end of the 1870s, going into a slow decline thereafter. Here we shall elaborate the nineteenth-century workings of this system in greater detail, describing the level of technology employed in the construction and maintenance of the system and the constraints operating upon its expansion and

---

[68] Ibid., 234, reports that by 1964 all attempts to restrict the number of animals kept on the scheme by tenants had failed. Most tenants had between ten and twenty cattle, plus a large number of small stock.

[69] Ibid., 227, 238; Chambers, *Settlement Schemes*, 357.

[70] De Wilde et al., *Experiences with Agricultural Development*, 231.

[71] Ibid., 221.

[72] Chambers, *Settlement Schemes*, 351.

sustainability. We shall also offer a reconstruction of the Chamus nineteenth-century agricultural cycle, with some discussion of cereal production and crop mix under irrigation.[73] The point to be made, in contrast to the characteristics of the Perkerra Scheme, is that Chamus indigenous irrigation agriculture was a sophisticated, well-adapted and flexible system of production. However, it could only function successfully within defined parameters, and once the Chamus themselves began to test those limits the system became unsustainable.

Nineteenth-century irrigation at Lake Baringo was organized around a system of communal labour based upon the two Chamus villages of Njemps Mkubwa (*Leabori*), on the banks of the Perkerra River, and Njemps Ndogo (*Lekeper*), alongside the Molo River. The irrigation complex of each village was constructed, controlled and managed under the authority of an elders' council, the *olamal*, in which each clan was represented.[74] The alignment of the canal running from the river to the fields, which might be over 1000 metres in length, and the selection of the location for the headworks of the dam across the river, demanded a high degree of skill and experience in surveying by eye. The labour to construct and maintain this main canal was organized communally, as was all the necessary work on the dam. Constructed of brushwood, boulders and mud, Chamus dams did not totally block the river, but extended only partially across the flow, diverting water into the canal. The dams required frequent repair, and were often washed out completely when the rivers were in spate. Communal labour was also called out to clear land if the field area was to be extended. Rights to cultivation within the irrigated fields and, more specifically access to water depended upon having contributed to the labour of the main irrigation works.[75] Discipline, regulation and control here were as tight as on any colonial irrigation scheme.

Cultivation of household plots was not subject to community direction. The main canal fed a series of smaller channels, with boulder sluices being used to regulate the supply of water to each area. Within the fields themselves each channel fed an intricate series of furrows that bisected the fields into blocks only 5 to 6 metres square – of the kind Beckley and Cowley had described in 1933 and 1952, respectively.[76] Sluices permitted close control of irrigation from one block to the next. These blocks represented the holdings of individual households. The style of planting was also adapted to suit irrigation, with shallow basins and ridges being constructed

---

[73] The following paragraphs draw heavily upon Anderson, 'Agriculture and irrigation technology'; Anderson, 'Cultivating pastoralists'; Adams & Anderson, 'Irrigation before development'; and Spencer, *Pastoral Continuum*, 129–204.

[74] On the authority of the elders, see Spencer, *Pastoral Continuum*, 141–3.

[75] BHT/CH/1, BHT/CH/6, BHT/CH/10 and BHT/CH/12. See also Dundas, 'Notes on the tribes', 49–72.

[76] We have no precise evidence of the scale of the field system or the exact size of individual plots. This is based upon oral evidence. BHT/CH/4, and others.

to create wetter and drier areas within each block. Chamus informants recalled various forms of intercropping within the fields, some commenting that sorghums were planted around the edge of a basin, whilst millets were planted in the centre.[77] Chamus farmers in the nineteenth century had a good knowledge of the crops they cultivated and a sophisticated under-standing of the management of their irrigation.

The availability of land, labour and water set constraints upon this system of cultivation. The flashy nature of both the Perkerra and the Molo Rivers made it necessary to site the field systems away from the immediate vicinity of the river, to lessen the likelihood of a flood inundating the field area with heavy deposits of debris and silt. In a dry year, therefore, parts of the fields might receive inadequate water. For this reason, households usually culti-vated more than one block of land within the field system. In this, as so much else, Chamus cultivators were balancing a number of factors to mini-mize risk: despite their irrigated cultivation, the people of Lake Baringo were not immune from low yields, crop failures, scarcity of food or even famine.

Chamus villagers had close social linkages, as well as a regular pattern of exchange, with neighbouring Maa-speaking pastoralists, as was described in Chapter One.[78] Many destitute pastoralists were absorbed within Chamus society during the nineteenth century, and evidence from clan and family histories and from European sources implies both an increase in cattle holdings among the Chamus and an expansion of irrigation between the 1850s and 1870s.[79] This was driven not only by the demographics of immigrant pastoralists; it was also determined by the active desire of Chamus cultivators to take advantage of the new market for food crops created by the growth in the Swahili caravan trade. Chamus farmers deliberately sought to increase their surplus production for purposes of exchange rather than consumption. The incentives to do so were consider-able. Apart from the material goods obtainable from the caravan traders in exchange for grain, the Chamus gathered ivory to be exchanged for live-stock.[80] As well as providing substantial wealth in relation to a whole series of social transactions, the accumulation of livestock (especially cattle) through trade with the Swahili gave Chamus households the opportunity to move away from cultivation and into pastoralism. Under the growing influence of the numbers of recent cattle-herding 'immigrants' who had settled at Lake Baringo as a result of destitution, this became a highly desirable goal from the last quarter of the nineteenth century.[81]

[77] BHT/CH/16.

[78] See also Anderson, 'Cultivating pastoralists', 248–9.

[79] Spencer's reconstruction of nineteenth-century history, *Pastoral Continuum*, 150–54, marks this as the beginnings of a Chamus 'pastoral tradition'. BHT/CH/8; BHT/CH/15; Dundas, 'Notes on the tribes', 50–53; and (though less detailed) Gregory, *Great Rift Valley*, 354–56; Thomson, *Through Masailand*, 263; von Hohnel, *Discovery*, ii, 3.

[80] BHT/CH/2; BHT/CH/7. Also von Hohnel, *Discovery*, ii, 5.

[81] Spencer, *Pastoral Continuum*, 158 n7, suggests that the independence of refugee pastoralists,

Increased production at Lake Baringo could be achieved through extending the irrigated area and by intensifying cultivation on existing plots. The former required collective decision-making and the organization of communal labour, while the latter could be achieved by individual households. The Chamus agricultural cycle and the crop mix selected by the farmer could be manipulated conservatively, to shield against famine, or speculatively to maximize yield. There were limits to these strategies however, and risks had to be carefully evaluated.[82]

Let us first consider the degree of flexibility within the agricultural cycle.[83] Like other Maa-speakers, the Il Chamus have divided the year into twelve named periods, or 'months'. In relation to cultivation, flexibility in the actual duration of named periods in the calendar was essential to accommodate the fluctuating nature of seasonality – the unpredictability of rainfall, variation in yields, the incidence of losses through crop disease or predation, and so on. The extent of flexibility was bounded by ritual on the one hand, and by the organization of household labour, on the other. 'Months' in this sense were of irregular length, and it was quite common for an additional named period (month) to be added to the cycle during a prolonged dry season or during an extended period of heavy rains. Some of the breaks between named periods were also linked to the visibility and position of the stars, notably the Pleiades. For example, ceremonies connected with the preparation of fields for cultivation and the first opening of the irrigation channels would invariably be completed before the Pleiades disappeared (towards the end of April), while the main harvest (in theory) would not begin until the Pleiades had appeared again (early in June.)[84]

The named periods of the Chamus year are set out in Table 9.3, in relation to the sequence of the agricultural cycle under irrigated cultivation. The year divides broadly into two parts – the dry season (Il Kulua to L'Neaigok), when the preparatory labour for cultivation was undertaken, and the season of rains and harvest (Purkula to Loirujruj), which effectively ended when the last crops were gathered in. Although the irrigation channels were opened for the first time in the cycle at L'Neaigok, after the blessing of the fields, plantings took place either side of this event. The early planting at Iarat immediately preceded the opening of the channels. At this stage not all fields would be planted. Farmers would have hoped for good early rains immediately following the opening of the channels, but it was their intention to bring on this early crop with irrigation water as an insurance against the failure or late arrival of the rains. Sorghum planted

[81 (cont.)] rather than their full absorption within Chamus society, may have stimulated their rapid acquisition of livestock from the 1880s. At least some of the refugees, in Spencer's words, were 'impatient cultivators and not simply supplementary labourers' (174–5).

[82] For example, the comments of BHT/CH/9 and BHT/CH/10.

[83] The following section draws heavily upon Anderson, 'Agriculture and irrigation technology', 90–95.

[84] Also noted by Dundas, 'Notes on the tribes', 54–55.

Table 9.3 The Chamus agricultural cycle

Il Kulua (November/December)	Beginning of dry season
Rialpala (December /January)	Clearing land and digging fields; repairing of irrigation channels
Iarat (February)	Early sowing of sorghum and millet
L'Neaigok (February/March)	Construction and repair of dams; blessing of fields; opening channels and watering of early-planted fields
Purkula (April)	Beginning of rainy season ('month of heavy rain'); weeding; second planting (before disappearance of Pleiades)
Lapa Longokua (May)	Awaiting harvest; weeding; bird scaring; protection of fields; building and repairing grain stores
Lorikine Ledukuya Lorikine Leware	Beginning of main harvest (following reappearance of Pleiades)
Lorikine Leokine (June/July/August)	
Loirujruj Ledukuya	
Loirujruj Leware	
Loirujtuj Leokine (August/September/ October)	Final harvesting of late plantings

NB. This table, based upon the testimonies of Chamus elders, amplifies that reproduced in Dundas, 'Notes on the tribes', 55. Compare with F. Mol, Maa: *A Dictionary of the Maasai Language and Folklore* (Nairobi, 1978), 186; and Spencer, *Pastoral Continuum*, 147. Although the days of each month were counted in relation to the stage of the moon, this cannot strictly be described as a lunar calendar. There is no sense in which the Chamus kept a careful reckoning of the passage of time by this means. Direct calibration between Chamus names and a twelve-month calendar is apt to give a misleading sense of precision. It is the sequence of the calendar that matters, and not the precise measurement of its constituent parts.

at this time would be intended to mature quickly, in order to replenish the dwindling stores from the previous year, and might then be ratooned with the onset of the rains.[85]

Joseph Thomson was present at Lake Baringo in the early months of 1884, when he witnessed the ceremonies connected with L'Neaigok:

> I was awakened by a great singing and dancing, as if the best of fun was going on in the village across the river. I was settling down to sleep again when I was made aware that the revellers were moving along the river banks. Then they stopped and howled for about an hour to Ngai. This done, they were addressed by some of the elders, and finally they crossed the stream and proceeded up its course. The singing had been a prayer to

---

[85] Described in interviews with BHT/CH/4 and BHT/CH/10, and still practised on indigenous irrigation plots around the lake during the 1980s.

Ngai to assist in the damming up of the stream for the purpose of spreading its waters into their fields. This operation occupied them several days. Their efforts were finally crowned with success, and the canals overflowed with their life-giving fluid.[86]

We can date this event between 1 and 17 February, some two months before the rains would be expected. At this time, the Chamus were nearing the end of their grain supplies from the previous harvest. Thomson was unable to purchase food here, and supplies were also exceedingly difficult to procure from the Tugen country nearby.[87] In 1884, then, as in other years, the Chamus employed irrigation not to provide cultivation all the year round, but to extend the duration of the harvest through early planting, thereby shortening the hungry season. The management of irrigation between L'Neaigok and Purkula would therefore be of considerable importance, especially following a year of poor harvest. Flexibility in the timing of L'Neaigok would allow an earlier or later start to the irrigation cycle. This would also be of greater importance if cultivators had disposed of a high proportion of their grain stores through trade. The early sowing of cereals and the ratooning of sorghum were effective means of intensifying production without placing a greater area of land under cultivation. Thus, increases in the area planted before L'Neaigok was one means of coping with the demands of traders for the supply of grain.

L'Neaigok was 'movable', but the extent to which it could be manipulated was constrained by other factors. During the period when the Pleiades were no longer visible in the sky, roughly 28 April to 10 June, the Chamus were bound by a number of restrictions in ritual and social practice. Over this period it was considered unpropitious to be engaged in either planting or harvesting: the rituals surrounding the completion of the one and commencement of the other could not be carried out until the Pleiades had reappeared. In effect, this meant that the second (or main) planting had to be completed before the end of April, and that the main harvest would not begin until early June.[88] Although it is doubtful that these restrictions were in practice absolute, they did set normal limits within which the cycle was expected to operate. The management and operation of the irrigation system was not, therefore, perfectly elastic: it could be modified to meet the demands of the market, but only within limits.

Market opportunities could also be exploited by seeking to increase yields through altering the crop mix. This carried significant risks. Sorghum (*Sorghum vulgare*), finger millet (*Eleusine coracana*) and bulrush millet (*Pennisetum typhoides*) were the principal cereal crops cultivated by Chamus farmers during the second half of the nineteenth century.[89] We do not know the

[86] Thomson, *Through Masailand*, 312.

[87] Ibid.

[88] BHT/CH/10 and BHT/CH/12.

[89] Spencer, *Pastoral Continuum*, 140, gives information on finger millet (*ndapa* or *mbeke*) and red-grained sorghum (*mosiong*), but does not mention bulrush millet.

relative balance between these crops within the cultivation system; nor do we have a clear picture of preferred cropping combinations. However, insights from oral histories, in combination with analysis of the characteristics of each of these cereals, suggest a number of ways in which nineteenth-century Chamus farmers might either reduce their vulnerability to drought and famine or increase their surplus production above the requirements of subsistence.

Sorghum and bulrush millet are both well adapted to the environmental conditions by Lake Baringo. Sorghum can be ratooned and is relatively drought-resistant, and yet is also more resistant to waterlogging than other cereal crops – an important consideration in an irrigation system where drainage may have been uncertain. Against this, it is liable to heavy predation by *Quelea* birds, and harvesting, threshing and cleaning are more labour-intensive than for maize. Sorghum matures in two to three months at this altitude (towards 1000 m) and equatorial latitude, making the Lake Baringo borders one of the most ideally suited parts of the region for sorghum cultivation.[90] Of the cereals grown in East Africa, sorghum and bulrush millet are the only ones to produce satisfactory yields on soils that have been exhausted by previous cropping. Bulrush millet is equally drought-resistant and is quick-maturing. It is usually harvested between three and four months after sowing. Unlike sorghum, its initial growth is rapid. This short maturation period means that bulrush millet may be termed drought-evading, as well as drought-resistant. That is to say, it can be successfully cultivated in areas with a rainfall of only 500 to 600 mm per annum, provided it is planted at the right time.[91] In many parts of East Africa, bulrush millet was commonly grown as the last crop in the arable break before the land was rested under a bush fallow.

Chamus informants describe fallow periods as having been reduced under the demands of the nineteenth-century caravan trade, and suggest that this factor ultimately contributed to the decline of the irrigation system.[92] Reduced fallows would fit with a movement from bulrush millet to finger millet (*Eleusine*) – the former being employed on fields after sorghum and prior to fallow. Finger millets are less well suited to the Baringo environment. While they can tolerate a dry period in the first month of growth, they subsequently require a steady supply of soil moisture, and generally do well only in areas with an average annual rainfall of at least 850 mm. In a reasonably good year, finger millets would have thrived under irrigation at

---

[90] J.D. Acland, *East African Crops* (London, 1971), 186–91. Bird damage to the crops at Baringo was reported by von Hohnel, *Discovery*, ii, 5. Also, BHT/CH/16. For sorghum, see H. Doggett, *Sorghum* (London, 1970), and on the classification and historical distribution of sorghums, J.R. Harlan & Ann Stemler, 'The races of sorghum in Africa', and J.M. de Wet, R. Harlan & E.G. Price, 'Variability in sorghum bicolor', both in J.R. Harlan (ed.), *The Origins of African Plant Domestication* (The Hague, 1976).

[91] Acland, *East African Crops*, 27–8.

[92] BHT/CH/6.

Lake Baringo, whilst in a year when river levels were low and irrigation therefore less adequate or when rainfall was low and poorly distributed, they would have survived less well than sorghums or bulrush millets.[93]

These cereal crops have markedly differing susceptibilities to a number of common weeds. Weeding is especially labour-intensive with finger millet, which needs very careful attention in the early stages of growth. A combination of bulrush millet and sorghum is particularly effective in securing a minimum level of yield in circumstances where the parasitic weed *Striga hermonthica* presents itself. This weed commonly affects sorghum, but bulrush millet is most resistant among the other cereals to the effects of this parasite.[94] Chamus elders recall that a weed of this description was a serious menace to cultivation at Lake Baringo in the later part of the nineteenth century, and that weeding in general came to present a very acute labour problem.[95] It is quite plausible to suggest that an expansion of cultivation (and/or a decline in labour availability) might have had disastrous results for the whole crop by placing the extent of cultivation beyond the labour capacity. These difficulties would have been compounded if this were combined with the increased cultivation of a crop more vulnerable to weeds and more labour-intensive in the weeding process. An increasing concentration upon finger millets at Lake Baringo would fit this hypothesis.

There is no effective way of calculating the yields obtainable at Lake Baringo in the later part of the nineteenth century, but estimates of yields on non-improved varieties of millets and sorghums in East Africa in the 1960s may provide some clues as to the choices confronting farmers. It was estimated that bulrush millet might achieve 400 lb per acre (450 kg/ha), while finger millet could achieve 400–800 lb per acre (*c.* 450–900 kg/ha), but yields of 1500 lb per acre were considered to be 'easily obtained with good husbandry'. Yields of 500–1500 lb per acre (*c.* 550–1700 kg/ha) were recorded for sorghum.[96] These figures cannot be directly translated to the conditions of Lake Baringo, but as an indication of relative potential they are suggestive of the rationale that may have motivated changes in Chamus cropping patterns in response to the demands of the Swahili caravan trade. These figures reveal that bulrush millet, although well adapted to the local conditions by Lake Baringo and better adapted to a drier environment than finger millet, may have offered a less attractive yield potential than finger millet, especially under careful cultivation practices. The recall of informants on this point showed considerable uncertainty as to the relative importance of these two types of millet in the nineteenth century.[97] No definite answer can be assumed, but it seems likely that the stimulus of the caravan trade may have promoted the cultivation of the higher-yielding

[93] Acland, *East African Crops*, 114–15.
[94] Ibid., 28 and 189.
[95] BHT/CH/10 and BHT/CH/12.
[96] Acland, *East African Crops*, 28, 116 and 189.
[97] BHT/CH/10; BHT/CH/16.

finger millet, with reduced cultivation of bulrush millet. With increased quantities of grain being grown for sale, finger millet would again seem more attractive, owing to its enhanced storage capacity – it lasts much longer in store than bulrush millet or sorghum. Length of storage was an important consideration at Baringo owing to the unpredictability of the caravan trade. Furthermore, finger millet copes much better with low moisture provision in the first month following planting than does either sorghum or bulrush millet.[98] If Chamus wished to increase the extent and yield of their early planting (before L'Neaigok), then finger millet would be the most reliable and high-yielding of those available. However, finger millet is adversely affected by waterlogging, giving best yields on free-draining soils, and might therefore perform less well under irrigation (especially where drainage was inadequate or flooding for even short durations likely – both of these being characteristic features of the Chamus cultivation system). Also, finger millet would require greater labour for weeding.

In summary then, bulrush millet would appear to be a 'safer' crop by Lake Baringo, mixed with sorghum to allow for ratooning of an early-planted crop. But greatly increased storage periods, improved yield and earlier harvesting within the limits of the agricultural cycle were all factors likely to enhance finger millet in the eyes of producers who wished to produce a larger surplus for the market. This implied risk: in conditions of either prolonged drought or waterlogging, finger millet was likely to cope less well than either bulrush millet or sorghum. Irrigation cultivation may therefore have become more vulnerable through the choice of the cultivators to place the supply of the market ahead of the security of a basic level of subsistence production.

Learning from the past?

There is every indication that the Chamus agricultural system of the nineteenth century was manageable and adaptive, that farmers were aware of the flexibility possible within the system and that they were prepared to experiment.[99] But the system came under strain from the 1880s, and by the 1920s the cultivations around both Chamus villages had been abandoned. At the most general level, this can be explained because of two principal factors: a change in the course of the Perkerra River in the flash-flood of 1917, and the rapid accumulation of livestock by Chamus households after 1900 (which precipitated a steady outflow of labour). But increased tendencies to plant a larger early crop for exchange, to trade too great a portion of the harvest, to rely more on the ratooning of sorghum and to

---

[98] Acland, *East African Crops*, 114.

[99] In this respect, note von Hohnel's report that Chamus had already by 1888 experimented with maize cultivation, with seeds supplied by Swahili traders, but that the farmers quickly gave this up. He does not tell us the reason: von Hohnel, *Discovery*, ii, 4.

shorten fallows can all be cited as having contributed to the increased vulnerability of Chamus cultivations to the effects of drought in the last decades of the nineteenth century. These were all indications of the dynamic character of Chamus irrigation.

One of the most startling aspects of the story of the Perkerra Scheme during the 1950s is the disregard shown by colonial officials for the farming capabilities of the local African population, in particular the Chamus. Whilst it is evident in 1952 that Cowley had no knowledge of the extent and history of indigenous irrigation practised at Lake Baringo, it can be demonstrated that other members of the colonial staff did, including some on the board of ALDEV. The Executive Officer of ALDEV, R.O. Hennings, was one. ALDEV's own publications even made reference to Baringo having once been the 'granary' of the region, using this image of a more prosperous past to endorse the interpretation of Baringo's ecological collapse and consolidate support for the interventions mounted by ALDEV to 'restore' good husbandry to the district. For example, the caption to an aerial photograph of the scheme, taken in 1955, reads: 'A general view of the major scheme, reviving what was once a granary for the caravans of Joseph Thomson, Count Teleki and other early travellers.'[100]

If Baringo's African farmers were indeed known to have expertise in irrigation agriculture, why, then, was there such strong opposition to giving local Chamus tenancies within the Perkerra Scheme? The answer was usually couched in terms of technologies: the very real differences between indigenous systems of irrigation and the requirements of a modern scheme were emphasized, especially the discipline of labour and water management, as was unfamiliarity with new cash crops and with their methods of cultivation. Indigenous irrigation was stigmatised as primitive, conservative, haphazard and static. Hennings, Cowley, and many others, simply did not consider the Chamus to be capable of participating in a scheme with modern, 'scientific' methods of agriculture. Behind this view lay a more deeply rooted sense that the Chamus, and also the Tugen, were in fact degenerate pastoralists, their resort to farming only an occasional and temporary response to the desperate conditions brought on by drought and the loss of their livestock. These were not the right kind of peoples to be given the 'gift' of modern development, in the guise of an expensive and technically advanced irrigation scheme, which would best be taken up by communities with a keener entrepreneurial eye and a more obviously developed work ethic.[101] It was symptomatic of the flaws in colonial rural development after 1945 that in setting the agenda for modernization, the past was not ignored but misrepresented.

---

[100] ALDEV, *African Land Development,* 119–121, photograph and caption at 120.
[101] This paraphrases the substance of the debates among the members of ALDEV's board during 1952, summarized in the papers in KNA PC/RVP.6A/11/21, and continued through to 1956, in KNA PC/NKU/2/2/33.

Conclusion

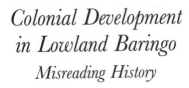

Colonial Development in Lowland Baringo
Misreading History

After Kenya's independence, in 1963, the Perkerra Irrigation Scheme would grow to absorb a full 3,000 hectares of Chamus land by the mid-1970s. Yet nearly 40 years after its inauguration, the scheme was still judged to have brought precious few economic benefits to the local community. At the same time, the scheme's expansion had contributed to the severe shortage of flood-plain grazing, which many herders in this area had relied upon in the dry season, thus diminishing the viability of livestock rearing.[1] In common with the controlled grazing schemes to the south, in most dry seasons since the late 1950s and at times of drought, herders have trespassed with their cattle into the irrigated fields of the scheme on a massive scale.[2] By the 1980s, Peter Little concluded that the Perkerra scheme had 'impoverished the area and increased its dependence on food imports' – exactly the reverse of the intended outcomes when the scheme had first been mooted in 1933. Like the colonial government before it, the Kenyan state has continued to heavily subsidize the irrigation scheme, on a scale that would be unthinkable for the livestock sector in Baringo or anywhere else in eastern Africa. Even by the 1980s, the scheme's revenues still met less than 20 per cent of its production and maintenance costs. And most tenants continued the pattern of the early years of the scheme, treating their participation as an adjunct to other forms of income generation.[3]

Ironically enough, colonial developers in postwar Kenya lacked the hard-nosed economic rationality that had driven Chamus herders to desert

[1] Little, *Elusive Granary*, 136.
[2] Ibid., 137.
[3] Ibid., 163–6.

their villages after 1917. The flood of 1917 was an ecological disaster that came after a prolonged series of economic set-backs. Its parallel can be seen in the 1961 flood that badly damaged the weir at Perkerra, necessitating expensive and difficult repairs. The difference in response to the two events, forty-five years apart, is instructive. Faced by an acute shortage of labour and no prospect of reconstructing the irrigation channels in time for the coming season, Chamus farmers in 1917 had the flexibility and the courage to turn to herding or to take refuge with others. It may be argued that they had little choice, but the close interlinkage between cultivation and herding in Baringo, consolidated socially and economically since at least the middle decades of the nineteenth century, gave them alternatives. In the face of similar disaster in 1961, colonial bureaucrats did not have the flexibility or the courage to close the scheme. Where Chamus herders had limited options, it might be argued that colonial developers had an array of development strategies from which to choose. Instead of adaptation or change, they decided to maintain a modern irrigation scheme on the Perkerra, despite its obvious structural failings and economic shortcomings, in the hope (not the expectation) that it might eventually prove its viability.

As Robert Chambers has observed, 'There was sympathetic backing in the Kenya central government for the vision and enthusiasm of the civil servants at provincial and district level who energetically launched the Perkerra Irrigation Scheme.'[4] These officials repeatedly heralded the imminent success of the venture, the Director of Agriculture, for example, writing boldly in his annual report for 1953 about the potential for '5,000 acres of irrigated cultivation' on the Perkerra.[5] The disjuncture between the hyperbole of government pronouncements regarding the Perkerra scheme and the reality of what was actually happening became more marked over time. The more that expectations were talked up, the more money that was sunk into the floundering project year upon year, the harder it became for officials to accept that the scheme could not succeed. As Chambers concludes, the astonishing thing is that 'a scheme as unpromising as Perkerra should never have been begun'.[6] Once begun, it took on a political life of its own: the Perkerra scheme is still there today, though no more successful than ever.

The behaviour of the colonial administration in respect of the Perkerra scheme was characteristic of a wider pattern. In what still remains the most perceptive account of the period, Michael McWilliam noted in 1975 that 'the key element' in the economic management of Kenya's postwar development 'was a self-confident perfectionism'. 'If Kenya was not quite a social laboratory in the eyes of its administrators,' he lamented, 'it was a country where technically ideal solutions were devised and tried out on a

[4] Chambers, *Settlement Schemes*, 364.
[5] Department of Agriculture AR, 1953, 55.
[6] Chambers, *Settlement Schemes*, 364.

wide range of problems.'[7] This was Iliffe's 'new colonialism' on a grand scale, fostered by the 'divisive threats and promises' of Lonsdale's 'second colonial occupation' in the form of an army of enthusiastic and meddlesome technical staff, and financed in Kenya largely through a combination of increased African taxation and special funding made available as a consequence of the Mau Mau emergency.[8] The costs of this great adventure in development were seldom counted by those on the ground who were busily implementing its ideals.

This book has described a long sequence of colonial interventions in the rural development of Baringo, culminating in the districtwide integrated Catchment Scheme of which the Perkerra Irrigation Scheme was a part. From the 1920s to the 1950s, the rehabilitation and development initiatives mounted in lowland Baringo by the colonial government all, in some way or other, challenged indigenous land tenure. Baringo was by no means unique in this respect. By the 1950s, land-tenure reform was the dominant theme of the 'new colonialism' throughout much of British eastern and central Africa. The colonial ideology of land-tenure reform centred around the principle of entitlement. The creation of individual property in land, protected by a legal title-deed, came to be seen as the essential measure that would allow new investment in African farming to be secured.[9] The state in Kenya became so wedded to this ideology in the 1950s that it allowed farmers and herders to gain title, even in districts such as Baringo, where processes of demarcation and registration of lands had not been properly carried through. Title confirmed land ownership and only through replacing communal landholding with individual tenure, it was believed, could production be increased to a sufficient extent to generate economic wealth. 'Spontaneous' enclosure carried out by some Tugen in Lembus and on the lowlands of southern Baringo in the mid-1950s was therefore welcomed as 'a step in the right direction', even though it was illegal. Entitlement, ownership and increased productivity were the magic ingredients needed for growth in rural economies, according to the litany of colonial rural development, and it was all the better if some Africans sought to initiate these processes for themselves. In rural areas such as Baringo, the 'new colonialism' amounted to nothing less than an assault upon forms of communal tenure.

---

[7] McWilliam, 'The managed economy', 252.

[8] McWilliam, 'The managed economy', 253–7; Iliffe, *Modern History of Tanganyika*, 453–73; Low & Lonsdale, 'Towards the new order'; and John Lonsdale, 'KAU's cultures: imaginations of community and constructions of leadership in Kenya after the Second World War', *Journal of African Cultural Studies*, 13 (2000), 112 for the quotation.

[9] Elizabeth Colson, 'The impact of the colonial period on the definition of land rights', in Victor Turner (ed.), *Colonialism in Africa 1870–1960*, Vol. 3, *Profiles of Change: African Society and Colonial Rule* (Cambridge, 1971), 193–212; Martin Chanock, 'Paradigms, policies and property: a review of the customary law of land tenure', in Kristin Mann & Richard Roberts (eds), *Law in Colonial Africa* (Portsmouth, NH & London, 1991), 61–84.

Although some were willing to seize the opportunity to fence their lands – and their numbers grew as colonial rule drew to a close – prevailing African perceptions of land tenure in Baringo were not generally in sympathy with this push for reform. Title had no place in Tugen or Chamus notions of land use, although the use of land did carry a variety of social responsibilities and obligations. Land in Baringo was communal and was held in trust for a wider community; access to it depended upon membership of that wider community (village and clan among Chamus; *pororosiek* among Tugen), and not to a set of individual rights. In contrast to European notions of 'ownership', in colonial Baringo African herders stressed their rights of 'access'. Land might be controlled by a specific *pororosiek* – whose elders were entrusted with its guardianship – but access to such land was always negotiable, especially in time of greatest need. Therefore, where colonial developers emphasized the need to maximize sustainable production on the land and to gain an economic return, Africans in Baringo stressed the need to guarantee the reproduction of the household. This might entail overexploitation of resources in the shorter term to achieve longer-term security, and it of course implied a radically different perception of the value of livestock as units of reproduction (even when they might be, in European terms, economically unproductive). Where the colonial concept of land-use reforms stressed entitlement, ownership and production, the concepts dominating African views of land use in colonial Baringo can be presented as entrustment, access and reproduction.[10] The contradictions between these two models are very apparent. And in those contradictions lay the roots of African resistance to the rehabilitation schemes of the 1930s and the controlled grazing schemes of the 1940s and 1950s.

Table C.1 Conflicting ideologies of land use

Indigenous	vs	Imposed
Entrustment		Entitlement
Access		Ownership
Reproduction		Production

The determination to push through land-tenure reform was reinforced by colonial misreadings of Tugen and Chamus history. From the early 1900s, colonial officials assumed that both these societies were, by inclination and design, pastoralists who had been held back from an expansive form of livestock husbandry in the nineteenth century only by

---

[10] The writings of Parker Shipton have influenced my thinking on this: see Parker Shipton, 'Debts and trespasses: land, mortgages and the ancestors in western Kenya', *Africa*, 62 (1992), 357–88; and Parker Shipton, 'The Kenyan land tenure reform: misunderstandings in the public creation of private property', in R. Downs & S. Reyna (eds), *Land and Society in Contemporary Africa* (Hanover, 1988), 91–135.

the fear of the dominant Maasai. Colonialism attributed to itself the distinction of having lifted this threat through the *pax Britannica*, opening the door to Chamus and Tugen expansion by the removal of the Maasai on to Laikipia and then finally to the Southern Reserve. While it is true that the *pax Britannica* created this opportunity, the movement of Tugen and Chamus across Baringo towards the upland grazing of Laikipia, Solai and Esageri was not a 'return' to pastoralism, but a new adventure. It was a sign of social adaptability and dynamism, not of blind adherence to tradition or cultural conservatism.

Colonial administrators and European settlers also misread the history of Baringo's landscape – although, for some, at least, this misreading served its own purpose. Erosion and degradation were real enough problems on the lowlands by the 1930s, as no African herder in Baringo would have denied. But the cause of this problem was the compression of Baringo's herders within the semi-arid scrublands between the lake and Menengai, brought about by the denial of access to the upland grazing to the east and south of the lowlands. Baringo's herders had never actually sought to re-create a Maasai model of pastoralism, with its extensive seasonal movements: they had wanted to establish a transhumant system, linking upland dry-season pastures with lowland wet-season areas. European alienation of lands precluded this possibility, leaving the young families who had taken the risk of breaking away and moving out of the Tugen Hills marooned in an ecological niche they could not hope to exploit in the manner they had intended.

Paul Spencer has convincingly argued that among Chamus this rush toward the plains and away from cultivation was, at least in part, an indication of generational struggles.[11] Cattle herding allowed the young to escape the control of elders by finding new, independent means of accumulating wealth and establishing their own households. For Tugen, where the discipline imposed by elders was less rigorous than among Chamus, the evidence for a generational conflict of this kind is hinted at in the oral histories. The 'indiscipline' of Tugen herders along the eastern and southern borders of Baringo in the interwar years is one strong indication that these were young communities, being blamed upon a lack of elders to control and moderate behaviour. These were frontier communities and, in an important sense, they were engaged in reshaping Tugen identity.[12]

These processes of change and the conflicts they have generated did not come to a close with the ending of colonial rule. Among Amnesty International's 'prisoners of conscience' in 1997 was one Juma Kiplenge, from the Endorois location of southern Baringo. Kiplenge had been arrested, along with a dozen others, and badly beaten by the police for his part in

---

[11] Spencer, *Pastoral Continuum*, pt. 2.
[12] For an interesting comparison, see Bill Bravman, *Making Ethnic Ways: Communities and Their Transformations in Taita, Kenya, 1800–1950* (Portsmouth, NH, Nairobi & Oxford, 1998), 252. Spencer makes the same point for Chamus, *Pastoral Continuum*, ch. 6.

organizing an 'unauthorized' cultural festival. As chairman of the Endorois Welfare Management Committee, Kiplenge played an active role in promoting the land claims of Tugen families from the Endorois location. Their dispute with government went back to the mid-1960s, when the Mochongoi Forest within Endorois was gazetted as a forest reserve and access to it denied to local herders. In 1973, the Endorois Tugen suffered further when land around Lake Bogoria was designated as a game reserve and some 400 families were evicted. These families were promised that Mochongoi Forest would then be degazetted for their resettlement and that they would receive a share of the income generated by tourists coming to the Bogoria game reserve. Despite the promises of government, the majority of these families were not allocated any land within Mochongoi Forest and they have never been paid any revenues from the income of the game reserve. In 1974, and again in 1984, some families who attempted to claim and occupy land in Mochongoi were forcibly evicted. In the 1990s, their dispute became entangled in the complex wider politics of President Moi's Baringo constituency, and accusations have been made of 'land-grabbing' in Mochongoi by a wealthy and politically astute few.[13]

In this quarrel, history has been deployed as a weapon to establish the legitimacy of Endorois claims. In a document written in defence of Endorois claims, Juma Kiplenge recites a myth that holds the Mochongoi Forest to be the 'ancestral home' of his people. The Endorois, he claims, have always been 'a nomadic pastoral community depending solely on livestock', moving seasonally between the highlands of Laikipia and the lowlands of Baringo. Contrasting a benign colonial past with the oppression of the national Kenyan government since the 1960s, Kiplenge asserts that 'the colonial government did not interfere' with the pastoralism of the Endorois. All the hardships inflicted upon the Endorois are, by Kiplenge's reckoning, to be located in the years following Kenya's independence:

> Life became harsh for the Endorois. They were restricted to infertile areas and could hardly produce subsistence food. They could not escape droughts and famine, hence watched helplessly their livestock dying during the dry seasons. They became poorer each year since their livelihood is dependent on livestock. They were reduced to relying on relief food from the central government.[14]

Like others before it, this further misreading of Baringo's history serves its own purposes. In blaming the poverty and marginalization of the Endorois community solely upon the neglect of the Kenyan state, Kiplenge places responsibility upon the current government to right the wrongs of the past. In this debate, access to land and the politics of ecology continue to mobilize Baringo's peoples, just as they did under colonial rule.

---

[13] Juma Kiplenge, 'The Endorois community: general profile', unpublished typescript (in possession of author).

[14] Kiplenge, 'Endorois community', 8.

Appendix

The Baringo Historical Texts

The oral histories of Chamus and Tugen form a significant element of the data upon which this study is based. These oral histories have been integrated with evidence from the archival and secondary sources to provide an interpretation of Baringo's past that, wherever possible, allows for corroboration. Establishing a chronological sequence and confirming specific dating within the oral histories largely depended upon an understanding of the age-set systems practised by Chamus and Tugen. This presented a number of methodological problems and requires a brief explanation.

Age-sets

The Chamus age-set system is described by Paul Spencer, being broadly similar to Samburu in structure and operation, but with some elements of Maasai practice.[1] In reconstructing their community history and in ordering their own personal experiences, Chamus senior elders will recall events as having occurred during the period during which a particular named age-set were *murran* – that is to say, between their initiation and their eligibility for marriage as junior elders. This lineal sequence of named sets provides a relatively unproblematic chronology, and for the twentieth century up to the early 1960s it can be corroborated from the colonial archive. However, two features of the system should be noted. First, there were two parallel lines of age-set names among Chamus, which were directly contempo-

---

[1] Spencer, *Pastoral Continuum*, 134–7, 152–8.

raneous. This was explained to me in relation to the residence patterns of the late nineteenth century, it being claimed that each of the two Chamus villages retained separate names for their own subsets of initiates.[2] This refinement needs to be borne in mind, but has no impact upon the chronology. Secondly, although the sequence of named sets denotes cohorts of age-mates, it is possible for individuals to 'climb' a set. Spencer's sophisticated reconstruction of this demonstrates that at certain periods in the past this practice has been more common, although in general terms it is discouraged.[3] What this implies is that the system operates in a flexible way and is not strictly dependent upon biological age. Again, although one must therefore be cautious when reconstructing the life history of an individual, this does not have an impact upon the broader chronological sequence determined by the age-sets. Table A.1 lists the Chamus age-sets in chronological sequence, giving both the principal age-set name (attributed to the Leabori village) and the secondary name (attributed to the Lekeper village). For the nineteenth century, two series of approximate dates are given, one based upon a fourteen-year cycle working back from the corroborated date for the initiation of Kiliako, the other based upon the twelve-year cycle preferred by Spencer.[4]

Table A.1 Chamus age-set chronology

Leabori	Lekeper	12-year		14-year
Twati		*c.* 1841		*c.* 1831
Nyangusi		*c.* 1853		*c.* 1845
Peles	Kilami	*c.* 1865		*c.* 1859
Kidemi	Memiri	*c.* 1877		*c.* 1873
Kinyamal	Tareto	*c.* 1889		*c.* 1887
Kiliako	Parakuo		1901	
Irimpot	Kireo		1913	
Napunye	Takicho		1927	
Parimo	Seuri		1939	
Merisho	?		1948	
Meduti	?		1959	

---

[2] But see Spencer, *Pastoral Continuum*, 134 n4.

[3] Ibid. 181–9.

[4] Ibid., 134–7, 162–5. The only substantive difference in interpretation that emerges if one employs the twelve-year cycle rather than the fourteen-year cycle, is over the involvement of the Chamus in the British punitive attack at Ribo, in the Kerio Valley (see Chapter One, and Spencer, *Pastoral Continuum*, 162). However, Chamus informants are anyway unclear as to whether Kileku or Kinyamal age-sets were involved. Given the numbers of *murran* said to have participated, it is quite likely that members of both age-sets were present. See also Anderson, 'Some thoughts', 113–15.

Tugen age-set organization is cyclical (not lineal), consisting of seven named sets, which rotate and recur.[5] This is constructed upon the principle that when the last old men of one named set have died, the children then being born can be initiated under that same age-set name during adolescence – the new set is literally seen as a reincarnation of the old. All seven age-set names are therefore always in existence, dividing Tugen male society into seven recognized segments. (A parallel cycle operates for women.) In common with Chamus, senior Tugen order their histories through the sequence of the named sets then in the category of *murran*.[6]

The recurrence of the same cycle of age-set names places immediate limitations upon the application of this system in establishing chronology. Time depth is necessarily shallow, and informants displayed a tendency to 'telescope' the memories related to a particular age-set name into the account of events at the time of the most recent manifestation of that named set. For example, a serious famine that might in reality have occurred during the early nineteenth century at the time of the Kaplelach age-set, will be recounted amidst events that took place during the period of the more recently deceased Kaplelach age-set initiated *c.* 1896–1910.[7] The remembered past of Tugen therefore has an effective time depth of only one age-set cycle beyond the generations that are currently alive.

While the duration between Tugen age-sets is notionally a period of fourteen years, this is not fixed and there was in practice considerable overlap between preceding and succeeding sets.[8] For example, when members of the Nyongi age-set began to be initiated in southern Baringo, during 1916, many Kipnikue remained unmarried and continued to be recognized in the status of *murran* until around 1920. Similarly, the Chumo age-set began to be initiated during 1926, before many members of the Nyongi age-set had made the transition to elderhood.[9] This occurs for two reasons. First, the timing of initiations was not uniform throughout all of the Tugen locations. Boys of a locality were normally initiated in a single group, but there might be a considerable time-lag between the opening of initiations in one location and another. This can happen because of fluctuations in the number of boys awaiting initiation in different localities, or because of circumstances such as drought, when the *murran* will resist attempts to begin the initiation of a new age-set until conditions have improved. This was the situation in East Endorois in 1929, immediately after the drought of *Kiplel kowo*, resulting in many members of the

[5] Huntingford, *Nandi of Kenya*, 53–5, is largely applicable to Tugen. See Kettel, 'Passing like flowers', and David W.W. Kettel, 'What's in a name? Age-organisation and reincarnation beliefs of the Tugen-Kalenjin' (unpublished seminar paper, Institute of African Studies, University of Nairobi, April, 1972), for studies of the Tugen example.

[6] Peristiany, *Social Institutions*, 160–75; Huntingford, *Nandi of Kenya*, 76–89.

[7] The same problem is evident in Kipkulei, 'Origin, migration, and settlement'.

[8] This was noted among Nandi by Huntingford, *Nandi of Kenya*, 65.

[9] BHT/TG/22; BHT/TG/32; BHT/TG/34; BHT/TG/39.

prospective Chumo age-set travelling to Lembus and even to the Nandi areas to be initiated.[10] Mobility of this kind is common throughout the Kalenjin-speaking areas of the Western Highlands.[11] Secondly, families may deliberately place brothers or half-brothers in different named sets, effectively 'climbing' a set, in order to avoid competition between them for household resources at a later stage (for example, at marriage). Local demographics can therefore play an important part in 'modifying' the operation of the system.

This obviously raises questions regarding the reliability of age-set affiliation as an indicator of biological age. Interviews were structured so as to carefully compile a history of the initiation set of the informant, but also to gather details of the place of initiation and the circumstances. The dates presented in the right-hand column of Table A.2 give the maximum duration of each age-set, based upon the range evident across all the Tugen interviews in that age-set. Finally, it must be stressed that the operation of the Tugen age-set system in the first half of the twentieth century was the product of an evolutionary process of change that has continued since. And it cannot be assumed that the system as described here functioned in this way throughout the nineteenth century.

Table A.2 Tugen age-set chronology

Age-set name	Estimated dating, on a 14-year cycle	Approximate dating, on actual initiation
Korongoro	1876–1890	
Kipkoimet	1886–1900	
Kaplelach	1896–1910	
Kipnikue	1906–1920	
Nyongi	1916–1930	?1913–1929
Chumo	1926–1940	1926–1940
Sowe	1936–1950	1934–1947
Korongoro	1946–1960	1947–1963

The Interviews

A total of 178 formal interviews were conducted, mostly between January 1980 and April 1981. The interviews were of two different types. The first – the most important category – were conducted by me and recorded on tape in the presence of my research assistant. A total of ninety-three interviews of this type were conducted with men of the senior surviving age-sets, spread throughout more than twenty different localities. Men of

[10] BHT/TG/24; BHT/TG/32; BHT/TG/33.
[11] This is described by Peristiany, *Social Institutions*, 43.

Nyongi and Chumo age-sets were most commonly interviewed among Tugen, although elder members of Sowe and a very few surviving Kipnikue were also consulted. Those of Napunye and Irimpot were predominant among Chamus informants. The second category of interviews number eighty-four in total and these were conducted during the latter part of the initial fieldwork period, between January and May 1981, taking the form of questionnaires conducted by two of my research assistants, Kipronoh Toroitich and Samuel Sekue. The following list provides a key to all 178 interviews, giving the name of the informant, his age-set and his place of residence at the time of the interview. Transcripts of the interviews are in the keeping of the author.

(a) *Baringo Historical Texts/Chamus*

Number		Name	Age-Set	Residence
BHT/CH/	1.	Lekipapui Lekesio	Il Kireo	Eldume
	2.	Ledida	Il Napunye	Eldume
	3.	Lelerupe	Il Napunye	Eldume
	4.	Indi Letakaan	Il Paremo	Eldume
	5.	Lesauroki Loodo	Il Takicho	Eldume
	6.	Parmato Lekesio	Seuri	Eldume
	7.	Lesukoni Lenakure	Il Napunye	Eldume
	8.	Matayo Lentele and Parselelo Lendaperna	both Il Paremo	Ngambo
	9.	Nomoe Lekachuma	Il Paremo	Ngambo
	10.	Matayo Lentele	Il Paremo	Ngambo
	11.	Lekatai	Irimpot	Ngambo
	12.	Ilpisia	Irimpot	Loiminangi
	13.	Meri Leletiren	Il Napunye	Ngambo
	14.	Lemurumpei Lolopich	Il Napunye	Ngambo
	15.	Lekosek Laparsalaach and Lengusurange Lepukaine	both Il Paremo	Salabani
	16.	Ilkeshei Lesaningo	Irimpot	Sintaan
	17.	Kirvam Lesengor	Il Napunye	Ol Kokwe Island
	18.	Ngirokwang Loltagute	Il Napunye	Ol Kokwe Island
	19.	Ntirei Leu~ngi	Il Napunye	Ol Kokwe Island
	20.	Lekaran'oa Loltagule	Il Napunye	Ol Kokwe Island
	21.	Nasolio leparkolua	Irimpot	Loropili
	22.	Letitikany	Irimpot	Loropili
	23.	Karoko Chebii	Chumo	Mukutani
	24.	Loracha Muro Letagila	Il Napunye	Mukutani
	25.	Nenika Leiropo	Il Paremo	Mukutani
	26.	Lekarua Lekoitamet	Il Napunye	Lendarock, nr Mukutani
	27.	Lelopot Lekinoroite	Irimpot	Kirine, nr Mukutani
	28.	Lekipapui Lekesio	IlKireo	Eldume
	29.	Merikoni Lelserkei	Il Paremo	Eldume
	30.	Legilicho Lesikamoi	Il Napunye	Salabani
	31.	Semerian Ntiboko Lesauroki	Il Takicho	Logumgum

32.	Kidogo Lempakony	Il Napunye	Logumgum
33.	Ledida	Il Napunye	Eldume
34.	Tikole Lekinampisia	Seuri	Eldume
35.	Nasolia Leparkolua	Irimpot	Loropili
36.	Letitikany	Irimpot	Loropili
37.	Lelerupe	Il Napunye	Eldume
38.	Lekatoi	Il Napunye	R7 Marigat
39.	Laparkiom	Il Napunye	R7 Marigat

(b) Baringo Historical Texts/ Tugen

Number		Name	Age-Set	Residence
BHT/TG/	1.	Kandagor Lobatan	Chumo	R.5 Marigat
	2.	Chelimo Lotole Chebii	Chumo	Kibingor
	3.	Chelal Koima	Nyongi	Kibingor
	4.	Kipkanen Kiptui	Kipnikue	Lobos
	5.	Chesitoit Kachige	Chumo	Lobos
	6.	Cheboswony A. Kipsotok	Nyongi	Rabai
	7.	Reuben A. Keter (Nandi initiate)	Maina	Kipsogon
	8.	Rongai A. Koborus	Sowe	Kipsogon
	9.	Cherutich Chemutoi	Nyongi	Kipsogon
	10.	Kipkorir A. Kibon	Nyongi	Kipsogon
	11.	Cheptes Kiboito	Chumo	Chemogoch
	12.	Kipngong A. Chepkiyeny	Chumo	Chemogoch
	13.	Kibet Kipmasaidere	Chumo	Chemogoch
	14.	Busi A. Kapbangei	Chumo	Chemogoch
	15.	Chemitei A. Tumo	Nyongi	Chemogoch
	16.	Kiben A. Chebet	Chumo	Chemogoch
	17.	Chepkirui A. Kenei	Nyongi	Chemogoch
	18.	Komen Kokoyo	Nyongi	Chemogoch
	19.	Obike cle Kibon	Chumo	Chemogoch
	20.	Kiplagat A. Kiboito	Chumo	Chemogoch
	21.	Reuben Chebet	Chumo	Kisanana
	22.	Cherutich A. Too	Chumo	Kisanana
	23.	Cheruyot Kiyai	Nyongi	Kisanana
	24.	Chepkerio Chirchir	Chumo	Kisanana
	25.	Cherutich A. Tarta	Nyongi	Ol Kokwe
	26.	Cheruiyot A. Chelal	Chumo	Ol Kokwe
	27.	Rotich A. Cherburet	Nyongi	Ol Kokwe
	28.	Kiptui A. Kutal	Chumo	Ol Kokwe
	29.	Chirchir A. Kigen	Nyongi	Ol Kokwe
	30.	Chepsergon Cherono	Nyongi	Sinende
	31.	Rotich A. Chelanget	Nyongi	Ol Kokwe
	32.	Cherogong A. Chebeyator	Nyongi	Ol Kokwe
	33.	Kigen A. Kipsiabo	Nyongi	Waseges
	34.	Kiperenge A. Xipsiamian	Chumo	Nyalibuch
	35.	Chemitei Chepkoi	Chumo	Emining
	36.	Chesire Sokomo	Kipnikue	Emining
	37.	Philemon Kandie	Chumo	Emining
	38.	Salim Chebungei	Nyongi	Emining
	39.	Chepikiyeng A. Ngetich	Nyongi	Emining
	40.	Chebakwany Cherokony	Chumo	Emining
	41.	Joshua Chesire	Chumo	Emining

42.	Obike ole Kibon	Chumo	Chemogoch
43.	Nderobi Kututwa Sungu	Chumo	Esageri
44.	Lesane A. Cherutich	Chumo	Esageri
45.	Kipketer Chebtubei	Chumo	Esageri
46.	Asera Lungira	Chumo	Kabimoi
47.	Kigen Tuigong	Sowe	Esageri
48.	Cheroneh A. Biwott	Nyongi	Kiptoim
49.	Cheptoo A. Chilewan	Nyongi	Kiplombe
50.	Busi A. Birrir	Sowe	Esageri
51.	Chepkwany A. Kiprop	Chumo	Esageri
52.	Legogo A. k'ipkoret	Nyongi	Muserechi
53.	Kabutie Cherogony	Chumo	R1 Marigat
54.	Kipngetich Kipyoris	Chumo	R10 Marigat
55.	Kimuge Cherogony Kipkewei	Chumo	L1 Marigat
56.	Karani Kamuren	Nyongi	Marigat
57.	Musa Cherogony	Chumo	R14 Marigat
58.	Chepsergon Tonje	Chumo	R1 Marigat
59.	Komen Kokoyo	Nyongi	Chemogoch
60.	Kiptanui Chepkole	Sowe	Mogotio
61.	Teriki Kipkeiyo	(Female)	Koisomo
62.	Chebet Yegon	Chumo	Koisomo
63.	Chebet A. Moei	Chumo	Mogotio
64.	Kigngetich A. Sokwo	Nyongi	Chemogoch
65.	Chepkenger Kimamet	Nyongi	Muserechi
66.	Legogo A. Kipkoret	Nyongi	Muserechi
67.	Kiplagat A. Talai	Nyongi	Poror
68.	Kipngetuny A. Kerich	Nyongi	Poror
69.	Kipkoech Changwany	Chumo	Poror
70.	Kipyegon A. Koima	Nyongi	Muringwa
71.	Cheruiyot Kiriukmet	Nyongi	Muringwa
72.	Chemunung Koima	Chumo	Arama
73.	Cheptalam A. Cheruiyot	Nyongi	Arama
74.	Kipkong Korir	Chumo	Poror
75.	Kipngony A. Sal gong	Chumo	Sinonin
76.	George Kipbunei	Chumo	Poror
77.	Bundotich A. Kimosop	Chumo	Sinonin
78.	Kipkoech A. Kimori	Chumo	Sinonin
79.	Rotich A. Soget	Sowe	Poror
80.	Paul A. Yegon	Sowe	Torongo
81.	Kipsang A. Borimoi	Chumo	Torongo
82.	Kipsonyo A. Chepngeno	Chumo	Torongo
83.	Chepngetich A. Kiprop	Nyongi	Torongo
84.	Rotich Bartenge	Nyongi	Torongo
85.	Kibet A. Mutara	Nyongi	Torongo
86.	Kibet Kiramba	Chumo	Torongo
87.	Limo A. Makong	Nyongi	Murachoni
88.	Kiplagat Tumo	Chumo	Murachoni
89.	Kipletboi A. Koech	Sowe	Murachoni
90.	Chepkeitany A. Bulgat	Nyongi	Murachoni
91.	Jonah A. Sowe	Sowe	Torongo
92.	Paul A. Yegon	Sowe	Torongo
93.	Kimeto Chepngeno	Chumo	Sigoro
94.	Kipngetich Chepyegen	Chumo	Sigoro
95.	Chebliech A. Koror	Kipnikue	Sigoro

96. Jacob Kabor	Chumo	Siriwa
97. Chepberion Barsilip	Kipnikue	Siriwa
98. Chepserigon Chepngetich	Nyongi	Siriwa
99. Kiplipwap Chepkeitany	Nyongi	Siriwa
100. Rotich Cherutich	Chumo	Tenges
101. Elijah Chepkilot	Nyongi	Sacho
102. Chepsui A. Chepngotie	Kipnikue	Tenges
103. Chebserigon A. Cheptarus	Chumo	Mugurin
104. Cheriuyot Kigen	Chumo	Mugurin
105. Kandie A. Talam	Nyongi	Mugurin
106. Tobona A. Cheruiyot	Chumo	Mugurin
107. Kipronoh A. Chepsumbai	Nyongi	Kipkitur
108. Wendet A. Chebet	Chumo	Mugurin
109. Chebet Cheruiyet	Chumo	Mugurin
110. Kimengetch Kigen	Chumo	Mugurin
111. Kipkemei Kipkechem	Nyongi	Kipkitur
112. Toromo Kandie	Chumo	Kipkitur
113. Chebii Suter	Chumo	Mugurin
114. Cherutich Kiptebeny	Chumo	Mugurin
115. Kipngeny Morocco	Chumo	Mugurin
116. Chebii Cheserem	Chumo	Kipketer
117. Chebii A. Kimoguk	Sowe	Lomolo
118. Chesire A. Kandie	Chumo	Lomolo
119. Koech Toroitich	Chumo	Lomolo
120. Ayabei A. Chepkeitany	Nyongi	Loboi
121. Cherutich Kimniywa	Chumo	Loboi
122. Chebii Cherutich	Chumo	Sandai
123. Cheronoh Kentakor	Chumo	Bogoria
124. Chepkoech Cheronoh	Nyongi	Maji Moto
125. Kibowen Cheburet	Nyongi	Kisanana
126. Cheruitich A. Tos	Chumo	Kisanana
127. Kangogo Kigen	Chumo	Kisanana
128. Karinyangei Chepkuto	Chumo	Ngentalel
129. Kutol Cheplagat	Chumo	Ngentalel
130. Kipkoech Kiboiwo	Sowe	Ngentalel
131. Kiperenge A. Kipsiamian	Chumo	Nyalibuch
132. Chepkilot A. Chekiyeng	Nyongi	Nyalibuch

(c) *Baringo Historical Texts/Nubian*

BHT/NB/ 1. Haji Adam Halijab and Ibrahim Fatamuddah, at Eldama Ravine
        2. Suleiman Medi, at Nairobi

(d) *Baringo Historical Texts/Swahili*

BHT/SW/1. Ali bin Salim, at Eldama Ravine

(e) *Baringo Historical Texts/European Settlers*

BHT/ES/ 1. Sir Michael Blundell, at Nairobi
        2. Courtney Curtis and Harold Chapman, at Dundori
        3. Dickie Edmundson, at Ol Punyata

Bibliography

A. Archival Sources

1. Kenya National Archives, Nairobi

The following categories of files were consulted in Nairobi:

PC/RVP	Provincial Commissioner, Rift Valley Province
PC/NKU	Provincial Commissioner, Nakuru
PC/ERD	Provincial Commissioner, Eldama Ravine
DC/BAR	District Commissioner, Baringo District
DC/ERD	District Commissioner, Eldama Ravine
DC/NKU	District Commissioner, Nakuru
GH	Government House, deposit 4
CS	Chief Secretary, deposit 1
CNC	Chief Native Commissioner, deposit 10
MAA	Ministry of African Affairs, deposits 7 and 9
AG	Attorney General, deposits 3, 4 and 5
MAg	Department of Agriculture, deposits 1, 2 and 4
ARC(MAWR)3 Vet	Ministry of Agriculture & Water Resources, Veterinary Division, deposits 1, 2 and 3
ARC(FOR)	Forest Department, deposit 7
ML	Ministry of Labour, deposit 9

The following categories of records, relating to the Kerio Province, Rift Valley Province and Baringo, Eldama Ravine and Nakuku Districts, were consulted on microfilm at the Seeley Historical Library, Cambridge:

ARs	Annual Reports
PRBs	District Political Record Books
HORs	District Handing Over Reports
IRs	Intelligence Reports

2. Public Record Office, London

Series FO 2	(Africa) General
Series CO 519	Original correspondence on the hand-over of the Protectorates from the Foreign Office to the Colonial Office, 1904–05
Series C0 533	East Africa Protectorate/Kenya, correspondence from 1903
Series CO 534	Kings African Rifles
Series CO 544	Sessional Papers, East Africa Protectorate/Kenya, Departmental Annual Reports from 1905.

Series CO 822   East Africa, General files, 1927 onwards
Series CO 852   Economic Department, 1935 to 1963

3. Rhodes House Library, Oxford

MSS. Afr.s.1618	Rongai Valley Farmers' Association papers
MSS. Brit.Emp.t.1 MSS. Afr.s.2024 }	Robert Ogle Barnes papers
MSS. Brit.Emp.s.290	Ernest Gedge papers
MSS. Afr.s.1624	Frederick Jackson papers
MSS. Afr.s.397	Roger Tuke Lambert papers (with additional papers donated by Mrs Lambert)
MSS. Afr.s.510	Vincent Liversage papers
MSS. Afr.s.	Colin Maher papers
MSS. Afr.s.1272	Albert Thomas Matson papers (Parts of this collection are in possession of the author, including Matson's notes on papers seen at the Entebbe Secretariat Archives (ESA), Series A2 to A21, and the Austin Diaries.)
MSS. Afr.s.141	Carl Peters papers
Micr. Afr.568	William Edwin Rumbold papers
MSS. Afr.s.930	Hugh John Simpson papers
MSS. Afr.s.	Oscar F. Watkins papers

B. Official Publications

1. UK Government: Parliamentary Papers & Colonial Reports

1904   Cd. 2099   *Correspondence Relating to the Resignation of Sir Charles Eliot and to the Concession to the East Africa Syndicate.*
1911   Cd. 5584   *Correspondence relating to the Masai, July 1911.*
1925   Cmd. 2387   *Report of the East Africa (Ormsby-Gore) Commission.*
1926   Cmd. 2573   *Reports of Tours in the Native Reserves and on Native Developments in Kenya.*
1929–48   *Colonial Office Lists (London, HMSO).*
1930   Cmd. 3573   *Memorandum on Native Policy in East Africa.*
1932   Cmd. 4093   *Report of the Financial Commissioner (Lord Moyne) on Certain Questions in Kenya.*
1934   Col. 91   *Kenya Land Commission. Evidence and Memoranda. [KLC:EM]*
1934   Cmd. 4580   *Kenya Land Commission: Summary of Conclusions Reached by His Majesty's Government.*
1935   Col. 116   *Report of the Commission appointed to Enquire into and Report on the Financial Position and System of Taxation of Kenya (Sir A. Pim).*
1955   Cmd. 9475   *Report of the (Dow) East Africa Royal Commission, 1953–55.*

2. Kenya Government Publications

Official Gazette of the Colony and Protectorate of Kenya, 1920 onwards (previously *Official Gazette of the East Africa Protectorate,* 1909–1920, and *The Official Gazette of the East Africa and Uganda Protectorates,* 1899–1908).
1905   *Report of the Land Committee.*
1910   *Memoranda for Provincial and District Commissioners.*
1919   *Final Report of the Economic Commission.*
1923   *Final Reports of the Economic and Financial (Bowring) Committee, 1922–23.*
1927   *Report of the Labour Commission.*
1929   *Report of the Agricultural (Hall) Commission.*

1932   *Technical Conferences of the East African Dependencies: Proceedings of a Conference of East African Soil Chemists Held at the Agricultural Research Station, Amani.*

1933   *Report of the Expenditure Advisory Committee, 1933.*

1934   *Report of the Select Committee on Agricultural Indebtedness.*

1935   *Report of the Economic Development Committee, 1934.*

1936   *Report of the Meat and Livestock Enquiry Committee.*

1941   *Interim Report of a Committee Appointed to Advise as to the Steps to be Taken to Deal with the Problem of Overstocking in Order to Preserve the Future Welfare of the Native Pastoral Areas* (East Africa Pamphlet No. 293).

1943   *Report of the Food Shortage Commission.*

1945   *African Land Utilization and Settlement* (Government of Kenya Sessional Paper No. 8).

1947   *Agrarian Problem in Kenya* (Note by Sir Philip Mitchell).

1948   *The Laws of Kenya 1948*, 8 vols.

1954   *A Plan to Intensify the Development of African Agriculture in Kenya* (R.J.M. Swynnerton) [Swynnerton Plan].

1970   *Kenya Population Census, 1969.* 4 vols (Central Bureau of Statistics, Nairobi).

1984   Republic of Kenya, *Baringo Semi-Arid Area Pilot Projects*, Parts 1 and 2 (Ministry of Agriculture, Marigat).

3. Government of South Africa

1932   *Report of the Native Economic Commission, 1930–32* (Pretoria).

C. Secondary Sources

1. Books

Acland, J.D. *East African Crops* (London, 1971).

Adams, William M. *Green Development: Environment and Sustainability in the Third World* (London & New York, 1990).

ALDEV. *African Land Development in Kenya 1946–62* (Nairobi, 1962).

Allan, William. *Studies in African Land Usage in Northern Rhodesia* (Rhodes Livingstone Papers, No. 15; Lusaka, 1949).

Allan, William. *The African Husbandman* (Edinburgh, 1965).

Ambler, Charles. *Kenyan Communities in the Age of Imperialism* (New Haven, 1988).

Anderson, David M. & Vigdis Broch-Due (eds). *The Poor Are Not Us: Poverty and Pastoralism in Eastern Africa* (Oxford, Athens OH & Nairobi, 1999).

Anderson, David M. & Richard Grove (eds). *Conservation in Africa: People, Policies and Practice* (Cambridge, 1987).

Anderson, David M. & Douglas H. Johnson (eds). *Revealing Prophets: Prophecy in Eastern African History* (Oxford, 1995).

Anderson, David M. & David Killingray (eds). *Policing the Empire: Government, Authority and Control, 1830–1940* (Manchester, 1991).

Anon. *The Brands Directory of British East Africa* (Agricultural Department, Nairobi, 1908).

Archer, Sir G. *Personal and Historical Memoirs of an East African Administrator* (Edinburgh, 1963).

Austen, Ralph. *African Economic History* (London & Portsmouth, NH, 1987)

Barber, James P. *Imperial Frontier* (Nairobi, 1968).

Baxter, P.T.W. and U. Almagor (eds). *Age, Generation and Time: Some Features of East African Age Organization* (London, 1978).

Baxter, P. and R. Hogg (eds). *Property, Poverty and People: Changing Rights in Property and Problems of Pastoral Development* (Manchester, 1990).

Beckley, V.A. *Soil Deterioration in Kenya* (Nairobi, 1930).

Bibliography

Beckley, V.A. *Soil Erosion* (Nairobi, 1936).

Beech, Mervyn W.H. *The Suk: Their Language and Folklore* (Oxford, 1911).

Behnke, R.H., I. Scoones and C. Kerven (eds). *Range Ecology at Disequilibrium. New Models of Natural Variability and Pastoral Adaption in African Savannas* (London, 1993).

Beinart, W. (ed.). 'The politics of conservation in Southern Africa', *Journal of Southern African Studies* (special issue), xv (1989).

Bell, W.D.M. *Bell of Africa* (London, 1960).

Bennett, H.H. *Soil Conservation* (New York, 1939).

Bennett, H.H. *Our American Land: The Story of its Abuse and Conservation* (Washington, 1946).

Bennett, H.H. & W.R. Chapline. *Soil Erosion: A National Menace* (Washington, 1928).

Bennett, H.H. & R.C. Pryor. *This Land We Defend* (New York, 1942).

Berman, Bruce. *Control and Crisis in Colonial Kenya: The Dialectic of Domination* (London, Nairobi & Athens, OH, 1990).

Berman, Bruce & John Lonsdale. *Unhappy Valley. Conflict in Kenya and Africa*, 2 vols (London, 1992).

Blaikie, Piers. *The Political Economy of Soil Erosion in Developing Countries* (London and New York, 1985).

Blundell, Michael. *So Rough a Wind: the Kenyan Memoirs of Sir Michael Blundell* (London, 1964).

Blundell, Michael. *A Love Affair with the Sun: a Memoir of Seventy Years in Kenya* (Nairobi, 1994).

Bonnifield, P. *The Dust Bowl: Men, Dirt, and Depression* (Albuquerque, NM, 1979).

Boserup, E. *The Conditions of Agricultural Growth: The Economics of Agrarian Change Under Population Pressure* (London, 1965; reprinted 1993).

Bravman, Bill. *Making Ethnic Ways: Communities and Their Transformations in Taita, Kenya, 1800–1950* (Portsmouth, NH, Oxford & Nairobi, 1998).

Brett, E.A. *Colonialism and Underdevelopment in East Africa: The Politics of Economic Change 1919–39* (London, 1973).

Brink, W. *Big Hugh* (New York, 1951).

Brogdan, A.V. *A Revised List of Kenya Grasses, with Keys for Identification* (Nairobi, 1958).

Brokensha, David, D.M. Warren & O. Werner (eds). *Indigenous Knowledge Systems and Development* (Washington, 1980).

Carson, J.B. *Sun, Sand and Safari* (London, 1957).

Carson, J.B. *Pages from the Past – Kenya* (Braunton, 1990).

Carter, V.G. and T. Dale. *Topsoil and Civilisation* (Oklahoma, 1955, reprinted 1974).

Chambers, Robert. *Settlement Schemes in Tropical Africa: a Study in Organizations and Development* (London, 1969).

Chambers, Robert. *Rural Development. Putting the Last First* (London, 1983).

Chipungu, Samuel N. (ed.). *Guardians in Their Time: Experiences of Zambians under Colonial Rule 1890–1964* (London & Basingstoke, 1992).

Christie, James. *Cholera Epidemics in East Africa* (London, 1876).

Clayton, A. & D.C. Savage. *Government and Labour in Kenya 1895–1963* (London, 1974).

Cone, L.W. & J.F. Lipscomb (eds). *The History of Kenya Agriculture* (Nairobi, 1972).

Constantine, Stephen. *The Making of British Colonial Development Policy, 1914–1940* (London, 1984).

Cooper, Frederick & Randall Packard (eds). *International Development and the Social Sciences – Essays on the History and Politics of Knowledge* (Berkeley, 1997).

Dahl, G. & A. Hjort. *Having Herds: Pastoral Herd Growth and Household Economy* (Stockholm, 1976).

Devendra, C.M. & M. Burns. *Goat Production in the Tropics* (London, 1970).

de Wilde, J.C. et al. *Experiences with Agricultural Development in Tropical Africa*, Vol. 2, *The Case Studies* (Baltimore, 1967).

Dilley, M.R. *British Policy in Kenya Colony* (New York, 1937).

Doggett, H. *Sorghum* (London, 1970).

Ehret, Christopher. *Southern Nilotic History. Linguistic Approaches to the Study of the Past* (Evanston, 1971).

Eliot, Sir Charles. *The East Africa Protectorate* (London, 1905).

Bibliography

Ensminger, Jean. *Making a Market: The Institutional Transformation of an African Society* (Cambridge, 1992).

Fairhead, James & Melissa Leach. *Misreading the African Landscape: Society and Ecology in a Forest-Savanna Mosaic* (Cambridge, 1996).

FAO. *Soil Conservation: an International Study* (Washington, 1948).

Farrant, Leda. *The Legendary Grogan: Kenya's Controversial Pioneer* (London, 1981).

Faulkner, D.E. *Notes on Animal Health and Husbandry for Africans* (Nairobi, 1956).

Feierman, Steven. *Peasant Intellectuals: Anthropology and History in Tanzania* (Madison, 1990).

Ferguson, James. *The Anti-Politics Machine: 'Development', Depoliticization and Bureaucratic State Power in Lesotho* (Cambridge, 1990).

Fieldhouse, David K. *Black Africa 1945–1980: Economic Decolonization and Arrested Development* (London, 1986).

Foran, W.R. *A Cuckoo in Kenya: The Reminiscences of a Pioneer Police Officer in British East Africa* (London, 1936).

Ford, John. *The Role of Trypanosomiasis in African Ecology* (Oxford, 1971).

Giblin, James L. *The Politics of Environmental Control in Northeastern Tanzania, 1840–1940* (Philadelphia, 1993).

Gillett, Mary. *Tribute to Pioneers* (privately published, Oxford, 1986).

Goldschmidt, Walter. *The Culture and Behaviour of the Sebei* (Berkeley, 1976).

Gregory, J.W. *The Great Rift Valley* (London, 1896).

Gregory, J.W. *The Foundation of British East Africa* (London, 1901).

Gregory, Robert G., Robert M. Maxon & Leon P. Spencer (eds). *A Guide to the Kenya National Archives* (Syracuse, 1969).

Grove, Richard H. *Green Imperialism: Colonial Expansion, Tropical Island Edens and the Origins of Environmentalism, 1600–1860* (Cambridge, 1995).

Guha, Rajit. *The Unquiet Woods: Ecological Change and Peasant Resistance* (Delhi, 1989).

Hailey, Lord. *Native Administration in the British African Territories*, Part 1 (HMSO, London, 1950).

Harlow, V.T. and Chilver, E.M. (eds). *Oxford History of East Africa*, ii (Oxford, 1965).

Havinden, Michael & David Meredith. *Colonial Development: Britain and its Tropical Colonies, 1850–1960* (London & New York, 1993).

Havnevik, Kjell. *Tanzania: The Limits to Development from Above* (Uppsala, 1993).

Heady, H.F. *Range Management in East Africa* (Nairobi, 1960).

Helms, D. & Flader, S.L. (eds). *The History of Soil and Water Conservation* (Washington DC, 1985).

Hennings, R.O. *African Morning* (London, 1951).

Hill, Mervyn. *Permanent Way: The Story of the Kenya and Uganda Railway*, 2 vols (Nairobi, 1961).

Hobley, C.W. *Eastern Uganda: An Ethnological Survey* (London, 1902).

Hobley, C.W. *Ethnology of the A-Kamba and Other East African Tribes* (Cambridge, 1910).

Hobley, C.W. *Kenya: From Chartered Company to Crown Colony* (London, 1929).

Hollis, A.C. *The Masai* (Oxford, 1905).

Hollis, A.C. *The Nandi: Their Language and Folklore* (Oxford, 1909).

Holmes, J.M. *Soil Erosion in Australia and New Zealand* (Sydney, 1946).

Homewood, Katherine M. & William A. Rodgers. *Maasailand Ecology: Pastoralist Development and Wildlife Conservation in Ngorongoro, Tanzania* (Cambridge, 1991).

Hunt, Diana. *The Impending Crisis in Kenya: the Case for Land Reform* (Aldershot, 1984).

Huntingford, G.W.B. *Nandi Work and Culture* (London, 1950).

Huntingford, G.W.B. *The Nandi of Kenya: Tribal Control in a Pastoral Society* (London, 1953).

Huntingford, G.W.B. *The Southern Nilo-Hamites* (London, 1953).

Hutchins, D.E. *Report on the Forests of Kenya* (London, 1907).

Hutchins, D.E. *Report on the Forests of British East Africa* (London, 1909).

Huxley, E. *White Man's Country: Lord Delamere and the Making of Kenya*, 2 vols (London, 1935).

Huxley, E. *The New Earth: An Experiment in Colonialism* (London, 1960).

Hyden, Goran. *No Shortcuts to Progress: African Development Management in Perspective* (London, 1983).

Bibliography

Iliffe, John. *A Modern History of Tanganyika* (Cambridge, 1979).

Iliffe, John. *The African Poor: A History* (Cambridge, 1987).

Jacks, G.V. and R.O Whyte. *The Rape of the Earth: A World Survey of Soil Erosion* (London, 1939).

Jackson, Frederick J. *Early Days in East Africa* (London, 1930).

Jahnke, H.E. *Tsetse Flies and Livestock Development in East Africa: a Study in Environmental Economics* (Munich, 1976).

Johnson, Douglas H. & David M. Anderson (eds). *The Ecology of Survival: Case Studies from Northeast African History* (London & Boulder, 1988).

Johnston, H.H. *The Uganda Protectorate*, 2 vols (London, 1902).

Kay, G. *Changing Patterns of Settlement and Land Use in the Eastern Province of Northern Rhodesia* (Hull, 1965).

Kenya Colony and Protectorate. *An Economic Survey of Forestry in Kenya and Recommendations Regarding a Forest Commission* (Nairobi, 1950).

Kershaw, Greet. *Mau Mau From Below* (Oxford, Athens, OH & Nairobi, 1997).

Kerven, Carol. *Customary Commerce: A Historical Reassessment of Pastoral Livestock Marketing in Africa* (London, 1992).

Kimambo, Isaria N. *Mbiru: Popular Protest in Colonial Tanzania* (Nairobi, 1971).

Kimambo, Isaria N. *Penetration and Protest in Tanzania: The Impact of the World Economy on the Pare, 1860–1960* (London, Nairobi, Dar es Salaam & Athens, OH., 1991).

Kipkorir, Benjamin E. *People of the Rift Valley – Kalenjin* (Nairobi, 1978).

Kipkorir, Benjamin E. (ed.). *Imperialism and Collaboration in Colonial Kenya* (Nairobi, 1980).

Kipkorir, Benjamin E. & F.B. Welbourn. *The Marakwet of Kenya* (Nairobi, 1973).

Kitching, Gavin. *Class and Economic Change in Kenya* (New Haven & London, 1980).

Kjekshus, Helge. *Ecology Control and Economic Development in East African History. The Case of Tanganyika 1850–1950* (London, 1977; 2nd edn, Oxford, 1997).

Koponen, Juhani. *People and Production in Late Precolonial Tanzania: History and Structures* (Helsinki, 1988).

Kopytoff, Igor (ed.). *The African Frontier: the Reproduction of Traditional African Societies* (Bloomington & Indianapolis, 1987).

Krapf, Rev. J.L. *Vocabulary of the Engutuk Eloikob* (Tubingen, 1854).

Krapf, Rev. J.L. *Travels, Researches and Missionary Labours* (London, 1860).

Kuczynski, R.R. *Demographic Survey of the British Colonial Empire* (London, 1949).

Lane, Charles R. (ed.). *Custodians of the Commons: Pastoral Land Tenure in East and West Africa* (London, 1998).

Langley, Muriel. *The Nandi of Kenya* (London, 1979).

Leach, Melissa & Robin Mearns (eds). *The Lie of the Land: Challenging Received Wisdom on the African Environment* (Oxford & Portsmouth, NH, 1996).

Lee, J.M. *Colonial Development and Good Government: A Study of the Ideas Expressed by the British Official Classes in Planning Decolonization 1939–64* (Oxford, 1967).

Lee, J.M. & Martin Petter. *The Colonial Office, War and Development Policy: Organisation and the Planning of a Metropolitan Initiative* (London, 1982).

Leys, Colin. *Underdevelopment in Kenya: The Political Economy of Neocolonialism* (London, 1975).

Leys, Norman. *Kenya* (London, 1924).

Little, Peter D. *The Elusive Granary: Herder, Farmer and State in Northern Kenya* (Cambridge, 1992).

Liversage, V. *Land Tenure in Colonies* (Cambridge, 1945).

Logie, K.P.W. *Forestry in Kenya. A Historical Account of the Development of Forest Management in the Colony* (Nairobi, 1962).

Low, D. Anthony & Alison Smith (eds). *Oxford History of East Africa*, Vol. 3 (Oxford, 1976).

Lugard, Frederick D. *The Rise of Our East African Empire*, 2 vols (Edinburgh, 1893).

McCann, James C. *People of the Plow: An Agricultural History of Ethiopia, 1800–1990* (Madison, 1995).

McCann, James C. *Green Land, Brown Land, Black Land: An Environmental History of Africa* (Oxford & Portsmouth, NH, 1999).

Bibliography

McIntosh, Brian G. (ed.). *Ngano: Studies in Traditional and Modern East African History* (Nairobi, 1969).

MacKenzie, Fiona. *Land, Ecology and Resistance in Kenya, 1880–1962* (Portsmouth, NH, 1998).

Maddox, Gregory, James L. Giblin & Isaria N. Kimambo (eds). *Custodians of the Land: Ecology and Culture in the History of Tanzania* (London, 1996).

Maguire, G. Andrew. *Toward Uhuru in Tanzania: The Politics of Participation* (Cambridge, 1969).

Maher, Colin. *Soil Erosion and Land Utilisation in the Kamasia, Njemps, and East Suk Reserves* (Nairobi, 1937).

Maher, Colin. *Soil Erosion and Land Utilisation in the Ukamba (Kitui) Reserve*, Pts I, II and III (Nairobi, 1937).

Masefield, G.B. *A History of the Colonial Agricultural Service* (Oxford, 1972).

Massam, J.A. *The Cliff Dwellers of Kenya* [Keyo] (London, 1927).

Matheson, J.K. & E.W. Bovill (eds). *East African Agriculture* (Oxford, 1950).

Matson, A.T. *Nandi Resistance to British Rule, 1890–1906*, Vol. 1 (Nairobi, 1972).

Matson, A.T. *The Nandi Campaign Against the British, 1895–1906* (Nairobi, 1974).

Matson, A.T. *Nandi Resistance to British Rule, 1890–1906*, Vol. 2, *The Volcano Erupts* (African Studies Centre, Cambridge, 1993).

Meek, C.K. *Land Law and Custom in the Colonies* (Oxford, 1949).

Meyn, K. *Beef Production in East Africa* (Munich, 1970).

Milne, G. *A Provisional Soil Map of East Africa* (Amani, 1936).

Miracle, Marvin. *Maize in Tropical Africa* (Madison, 1966).

Mol, Frans. *Maa: A Dictionary of the Maasai Language and Folklore* (Nairobi, nd)

Monod, Theodore (ed.). *Pastoralism in Tropical Africa* (Oxford, 1975).

Moore, Henrietta L. *Space, Text and Gender: an Anthropological Study of the Marakwet of Kenya* (Cambridge, 1986).

Morgan, D.J. *The Official History of Colonial Development*, 5 vols (London, 1980).

Morgan, W.T.W. & M.N. Shaffer. *Population of Kenya* (Nairobi, 1966).

Morris, H.F. & James S. Read. *Indirect Rule and the Search for Justice: Essays in East African Legal History* (Oxford, 1972).

Mortimore, Michael. *Adapting to Drought: Farmers, Famines and Desertification in West Africa* (Cambridge, 1989).

Morton, Andrew. *Moi: the Making of an African Statesman* (London, 1998).

Mosley, Paul. *The Settler Economies: Studies in the Economic History of Kenya and Southern Rhodesia, 1900–1963* (Cambridge, 1983).

Moyse-Bartlett, H. *The King's African Rifles* (Aldershot, 1966).

Mungeam, Gordon H. *British Rule in Kenya 1895–1912* (Oxford, 1967).

Mungeam, Gordon H. *Kenya: Select Historical Documents, 1884–1923* (Nairobi, 1978).

Munro, J. Forbes. *Colonial Rule and the Kamba: Social Change in the Kenya Highlands, 1889–1939* (Oxford, 1975).

Mwanzi, Henry A. *A History of the Kipsigis* (Nairobi, 1977).

New, Charles. *Life, Wanderings and Labours in Eastern Africa* (London, 1873).

Nicholson, J.H. *The Future of Forestry in Kenya* (Nairobi, 1931).

Ochieng, William R. *An Outline History of the Rift Valley of Kenya up to AD 1900* (Nairobi, 1975).

Ogot, Bethwell A. (ed.). *Hadith 1* (Nairobi, 1968).

Ogot, Bethwell A. (ed.). *Hadith 2* (Nairobi, 1970).

Ogot, Bethwell A. (ed.). *Hadith 4* (Nairobi, 1972).

Ogot, Bethwell A. (ed.). *Kenya Before 1900* (Nairobi, 1976).

Ogot, Bethwell A. (ed.). *Kenya in the Nineteenth Century* (Nairobi, 1985).

Oliver, Roland & Gervais Mathew (eds). *Oxford History of East Africa*, Vol. 1 (Oxford, 1963).

Orchardson, Ian Q. *The Kipsigis* (Nairobi, 1961).

Paice, Edward. *Lost Lion of Empire: The Life of 'Cape-to-Cairo' Grogan* (London, 2001).

Palmer, Robin. *Land and Racial Domination in Rhodesia* (London, 1977).

Pearce, R.D. *The Turning Point in Africa: British Colonial Policy, 1938–1948* (London, 1982).

Bibliography

Peristiany, J.G. *The Social Institutions of the Kipsigis* (London, 1939).

Peters, Carl. *New Light on Darkest Africa* (London, 1891).

Peters, Pauline. *Dividing the Commons: Politics, Policy and Culture in Botswana* (Charlottesville & London, 1994).

Pole-Evans, I. *Report on a Visit to Kenya* (Nairobi, 1939).

Porter, Andrew N. & Anthony J. Stockwell. *British Imperial Policy and Decolonization:* Vol. 1, *1938–51;* Vol. 2, *1951–64* (Basingstoke & London, 1987).

Pratt, D.J. & M.D. Gwynne (eds). *Rangeland Management and Ecology in East Africa* (London, 1977).

Raikes, Philip L. *Livestock Development and Policy in East Africa* (Uppsala, 1981).

Ranger, Terence O. *Voices from the Rocks: Nature, Culture and History in the Matopos Hills of Zimbabwe* (Harare, Oxford, Bloomington & Indianapolis, 1999).

Richards, Paul. *Indigenous Agricultural Revolution: Ecology and Food Production in West Africa* (London, 1985).

Ross, J.C. *Land Utilization and Soil Conservation in the Union of South Africa* (Pretoria, 1947).

Ross, W. McGregor. *Kenya From Within* (London, 1927).

Rotberg, Robert I. (ed.). *Imperialism, Colonialism and Hunger: East and Central Africa* (Lexington, Massachusetts & Toronto, 1983).

Sandford, Stephen. *Management of Pastoral Development in the Third World* (Chichester, 1983).

Schlee, Gunther. *Identities on the Move: Clanship and Pastoralism in Northern Kenya* (Manchester, 1989).

Schoenbrun, David L. *A Green Place, a Good Place: Agrarian Change & Social Identity in the Great Lakes Region to the 15th Century* (Portsmouth, NH, Oxford & Nairobi, 1999).

Sears, P.B. *Deserts on the March* (Norman, 1935).

Sorrenson, M.P.K. *Land Reform in Kikuyu Country* (London, 1967).

Sorrenson, M.P.K. *The Origins of European Settlement in Kenya* (Oxford, 1967).

Spear, Thomas. *Mountain Farmers: Moral Economies of Land and Agricultural Development in Arusha and Meru* (Oxford, Berkeley, Los Angeles & Dar es Salaam, 1997).

Spear, Thomas & Richard D. Waller (eds). *Being Maasai: Ethnicity & Identity in East Africa* (London, 1993).

Spencer, Paul. *The Samburu: a Study of Gerontocracy in a Nomadic Tribe* (London, 1965).

Spencer, Paul. *Nomads in Alliance: Symbiosis and Growth among the Rendille and Samburu of Kenya* (London, 1973).

Spencer, Paul. *The Maasai of Matapato* (Bloomington, 1987).

Spencer, Paul. *The Pastoral Continuum: The Marginalization of Tradition in East Africa* (Oxford, 1998).

Stebbing, E.P. *The Forests of India*, 3 vols (London, 1922).

Stebbing, E.P. *The Forests of West Africa and the Sahara: A Study of Modern Conditions* (London, 1937).

Stockdale, Frank. *Report on His Visit to South and East Africa, Seychelles, The Sudan, Egypt and Cyprus, 1930–31* (London, 1931).

Storey, H.H. *Basic Research in Agriculture: A Brief History of Research at Amani, 1928–47* (Nairobi, n.d. [1950?]).

Sutton, J.E.G. *The Archaeology of the Western Highlands of Kenya* (Nairobi, 1973).

Talbott, Ian D. *Agricultural Innovation in Colonial Africa: Kenya and the Great Depression* (Lewiston, NY, 1990)

Thompson, E.P. *Whigs and Hunters* (Harmondsworth, 1976).

Thomson, Joseph. *Through Masailand* (London 1887).

Throup, David W. *Economic and Social Origins of Mau Mau, 1945–53* (London, Athens, OH & Nairobi, 1987).

Throup, David W. & Charles Hornsby, *Multi-Party Politics in Kenya* (Oxford, Nairobi & Athens, OH, 1998).

Thurston, Anne. *Smallholder Agriculture in Colonial Kenya: the Official Mind and the Swynnerton Plan* (Cambridge, 1987).

Bibliography

Tiffen, Mary, Michael Mortimore & Francis Gichuki. *More People, Less Erosion: Environmental Recovery in Kenya* (Chichester & Nairobi, 1994).

Tignor, Robert L. *The Colonial Transformation of Kenya* (Princeton, 1976).

Tosh, John. *Clan Leaders and Colonial Chiefs in Lango* (Oxford, 1976).

Toweett, Taaitta. *Oral Traditional History of the Kipsigis* (Nairobi, 1979).

Trapnell, C.G. & J.M. Clothier. *The Soils, Vegetation, and Agricultural Systems of North-West Rhodesia* (Lusaka, 1937).

Trow-Smith, Robert. *English Husbandry* (London, 1951).

Unwin, A.H. *West African Forests and Forestry* (London, 1920).

Vail, Leroy (ed.). *The Creation of Tribalism in Southern Africa* (London, Berkeley & Los Angeles, 1989).

Van Zwanenberg, Roger M.A. *Colonial Capitalism and Labour in Kenya, 1919–1939* (Nairobi, 1975).

Van Zwanenberg, Roger M.A. & Anne King. *An Economic History of Kenya and Uganda 1800–1970* (London, 1975).

von Hohnel, L. *Discovery by Count Teleki of Lakes Rudolf and Stephanie*, 2 vols (London, 1894).

Ward, R. *Deserts in the Making: A Study in the Causes and Effects of Soil Erosion* (Nairobi, 1937).

Watts, Michael. *Silent Violence: Food, Famine and Peasantry in Northern Nigeria* (Berkeley, 1983).

Williamson, G. and Payne, W.J.A. *An Introduction to Animal Husbandry in the Tropics* (London, 1965).

Willis, Justin. *Mombasa, the Swahili and the Making of the Mijikenda* (Oxford, 1993).

Wood, Alan. *The Groundnut Affair* (London, 1950).

Worster, Donald. *Dust Bowl: The Southern Plains in the 1930s* (New York, 1979).

Worster, Donald (ed.). *The Ends of the Earth: Perspectives on Modern Environmental History* (Cambridge, 1988).

Wymer, Norman. *The Man from the Cape: The First Trek from Cape to Cairo* (London, 1959).

2. Articles & pamphlets

Adams, William M. & David M. Anderson. 'Irrigation before development: indigenous and induced change in agricultural water management in East Africa', *African Affairs*, 87 (1988), 519–36.

Adams, William M., Tomas Potkanski & John E.G. Sutton. 'Indigenous farmer-managed irrigation in Sonjo, Tanzania', *Geographical Journal*, 160 (1994), 17–32.

Anderson, David M. 'Some thoughts on the nineteenth-century history of Il Chamus of Baringo', *Mila: Bulletin of the Institute for African Studies, Nairobi*, 7 (1984), 107–25.

Anderson, David M. 'Depression, dust bowl, demography and drought: the colonial state and soil conservation in East Africa during the 1930s', *African Affairs*, 83 (1984), 321–43.

Anderson, David M. 'Stock theft and moral economy in colonial Kenya', *Africa*, 56 (1986), 399–416.

Anderson, David M. 'Managing the forest: the conservation history of Lembus, Kenya, 1904–63', in Anderson & Grove (eds), *Conservation in Africa* (Cambridge, 1987), 249–68.

Anderson, David M. 'Cultivating pastoralists: ecology and economy among Il Chamus of Baringo, 1840–1980', in Johnson & Anderson (eds), *Ecology of Survival* (London & Boulder, 1988), 241–60.

Anderson, David M. 'Agriculture and irrigation technology at Lake Baringo in the nineteenth century', *Azania*, 24 (1989), 84–98.

Anderson, David M. 'Policing, prosecution and the law in colonial Kenya', in Anderson & Killingray (eds), *Policing the Empire* (Manchester, 1991), 183–201.

Anderson, David M. 'Cow power: livestock and the pastoralist in Africa', *African Affairs*, 92 (1993), 121–33.

Anderson, David M. 'The "crisis of capitalism" and Kenya's social history: a comment', *African Affairs*, 92 (1993), 285–90.

Anderson, David M. 'Policing the settler state: colonial hegemony in Kenya', in Dagmar

Bibliography

Engels & Shula Marks (eds), *Contesting Colonial Hegemony: State and Society in Africa and India* (London, 1994), 248–66.

Anderson, David M. 'Visions of the vanquished: prophets and colonialism in Kenya's western highlands', in Anderson & Johnson (eds), *Revealing Prophets: History and Prophecy in Eastern Africa*. (London, 1995), 164–95.

Anderson, David M. 'Rehabilitation, resettlement and restocking: ideology and practice in pastoral development', in Anderson & Broch-Due (eds), *The Poor Are Not Us* (Oxford, Athens, OH & Nairobi, 1999), 240–56.

Anderson, David M. 'Master and servant in colonial Kenya', *Journal of African History*, 41 (2000), 459–85.

Anderson, David M. 'Uneconomic stock: the development of Kenya's livestock industry, 1918–48' (forthcoming).

Anderson, David M. & Andrew C. Millington. 'The political ecology of soil conservation in Anglophone Africa', in A.C. Millington, A. Binns and S. Mutiso (eds), *African Resources: Appraisal, Monitoring and Management* (Geography Department, Reading University, Reading, 1987), 48–59.

Anderson, David M. & David Throup. 'Africans and agricultural production in colonial Kenya: the myth of the war as a watershed', *Journal of African History*, 26 (1985), 327–45.

Anderson, David M. & David Throup. 'The agrarian economy of Central Province, Kenya, 1918–39', in Ian Brown (ed.), *The Economies of Africa and Asia and the Interwar Depression* (London, 1986), 8–27.

Anon. 'Overstocking in Kenya', *East African Agricultural Journal*, 1 (July 1935), 16–19, & 1 (Jan. 1936), 309–310.

arap Magut, P.K. 'The rise and fall of the Nandi orkoiyot 1850–1957', in McIntosh (ed.), *Ngano* (Nairobi, 1969), 95–110.

arap Ng'eny, Samuel. 'Nandi resistance to the establishment of British administration, 1893–1906', in Ogot (ed.), *Hadith 2* (Nairobi, 1970), 104–26.

Austin, H.H. 'From Njemps to Marish, Sowe, and Mumias (British East Africa)', *Geographical Journal* (1899), 14, 307–310.

Baker, P.R. '"Development" and the pastoral people of Karamoja, North-Eastern Uganda. An example of the treatment of symptoms', in Monod (ed.), *Pastoralism in Tropical Africa*, (Oxford, 1975), 187–205.

Barber, James P. 'The moving frontier of British imperialism in northern Uganda, 1898–1919', *Uganda Journal*, 29 (1965), 28–30.

Bassett, Thomas J. 'Introduction: the land question and agricultural transformation in Sub-Saharan Africa', in Thomas J. Bassett and Donald E. Crummey (eds), *Land in African Agrarian Systems* (Madison, 1993), 3–34.

Bates, Margaret. 'Social engineering, multi-racialism, and the rise of TANU', in Low & Smith (eds), *Oxford History of East Africa*, Vol. 3 (Oxford, 1976), 157–95.

Beachey, R.W. 'The East African ivory trade in the late 19th Century', *Journal of African History*, 8 (1967), 269–90.

Behnke, R.H. & I. Scoones. 'Rethinking range ecology: implications for rangeland management in East Africa', in Behnke, Scoones & Kervan (eds), *Range Ecology at Disequilibrium* (London, 1993), 1–30.

Beinart, William. 'Soil erosion, conservationism and ideas about development: a southern African exploration, 1900–1960', *Journal of Southern African Studies*, 11 (1984), 52–83.

Beinart, William. 'Introduction: the politics of colonial conservation', *Journal of Southern African Studies*, 15 (1989), 143–62.

Beinart, William. 'Soil erosion, animals and pasture over the longer-term: environmental destruction in southern Africa', in Leach & Mearns, *Lie of the Land* (London and Portsmouth, NH, 1996), 54–72.

Bennett, George. 'The boundary of Uganda in 1902', *Uganda Journal*, 23 (1959), 59–72.

Bennett, George. 'Settlers and politics in Kenya up to 1945', in Harlow & Chilver (eds), *Oxford*

317

History of East Africa, Vol. 2 (Oxford, 1965), 265–332.

Bennett, H.H. 'Land and the Union of South Africa', *Soil Conservation Magazine*, 11 (1945).

Berntsen, John L. 'The Maasai and their neighbours; variables of interaction', *African Economic History*, 2 (1976), 1–11.

Berntsen, John L. 'Maasai age-sets and prophetic leadership, 1850–1912', *Africa*, 49 (1979), 134–45.

Berry, Sara. 'Concentration without privatization? Some consequences of changing patterns of land control in Africa', in S.P. Reyna & R.E. Downs (eds), *Land Society in Contemporary Africa* (Hanover, 1988), 53–75.

Berry, Sara. 'Social institutions and access to resources', *Africa*, 59 (1989), 41–55.

Bisschop, H.R. *The Improvement of Livestock in Kenya* (East African Pamphlet No. 424, Nairobi, 1949).

Blackburn, Roderick H. 'The Okiek and their history', *Azania*, 9 (1974), 39–57.

Blunt, D.L. *Report on the Locust Invasion of Kenya* (Agricultural Department, Nairobi, Bulletin No. 21, 1931).

Bogdan, A.V. 'Bush clearing and grazing trial at Kisokon, Kenya', *East African Agricultural Journal*, 19 (1954), 253–9.

Brandt, F.R. & R.E. Montgomery. 'East Coast fever in the East African Protectorate', *British East African Agricultural Journal*, 4 (1912), 99–102.

Brasnett, N.V. 'Finance and the Colonial Forest Service', *Empire Forestry Journal*, 21 (1942), 7–11.

Brown, Leslie H. 'The biology of pastoral man as a factor in conservation', *Biological Conservation*, 3 (1971).

Campbell, K.O. 'The development of soil conservation programmes in Australia', *Land Economics*, 24 (1948).

Champion, A.M. 'Soil erosion in Africa', *Geographical Journal*, 82 (1933), 130–39.

Champion, A.M. 'The reconditioning of Native Reserves in Africa', *Journal of the Royal Anthropological Society* (1939).

Chanock, Martin. 'Paradigms, policies and property: a review of the customary law of land tenure', in Kristin Mann & Richard Roberts (eds), *Law in Colonial Africa* (Portsmouth, NH & London, 1991), 61–84.

Chirchir-Chuma, Kipketer. 'Aspects of Nandi society and culture in the 19th century', *Kenya Historical Review*, 3 (1975).

Cliffe, Lionel. 'Nationalism and the reaction to enforced agricultural change in Tanganyika during the colonial period', in Lionel Cliffe & John Saul (eds), *Socialism in Tanzania: An Interdisciplinary Reader* (Dar es Salaam, 1972), 17–24.

Collins, Robert O. 'The Turkana Patrol 1918', *Uganda Journal*, 25 (1961), 16–33.

Colson, Elizabeth. 'The impact of the colonial period on the definition of land rights', in Victor Turner (ed.), *Colonialism in Africa 1870–1960*, Vol. 3, *Profiles of Change: African Society and Colonial Rule* (Cambridge, 1971), 193–212.

Conte, Christopher. 'Nature reorganised: ecological history in the plateau forests of the West Usambara Mountains, 1850–1935', in Maddox, Giblin & Kimambo (eds), *Custodians of the Land* (London, 1996), 96–122.

Dawson, Marc. 'Smallpox in Kenya, 1880–1920', *Social Science and Medicine*, 13b (1979).

Dawson, Marc. 'Disease and population decline of the Kikuyu, 1890–1925', in Chrisopher Fyfe & David McMaster (eds), *African Historical Demography*, Vol. 2 (Edinburgh, 1981), 121–38.

des Avanchers, L. 'Esquisse géographique des Pays Oromo ou Galla, des Pays Soomali, et de la Côte Orientale d'Afrique', *Bulletin de la Société de Géographie*, 17 (1859), 153–70.

de Wet, J.M., R. Harlan & E.G. Price. 'Variability in sorghum bicolor', in J.R. Harlan (ed.), *The Origins of African Plant Domestication* (The Hague, 1976).

Dougall, H.W. & A.V. Bogdan. 'Browse plants of Kenya with special reference to those occurring in South Baringo', *East African Agricultural Journal*, 23 (1958), 236–45.

Bibliography

Dundas, K.R. 'Notes on the tribes inhabiting the Baringo District, East African Protectorate', *Journal of the Royal Anthropological Institute*, 40 (1910), 49–72.

Dundas, K.R. 'Notes on the Fauna of Baringo District', *Journal of the East African Natural History Society*, 2 (1911), 63–7.

Edwards, D.C. 'Some notes on the food of goats in semi-arid areas', *East African Agricultural Journal*, 13 (1948), 221–3.

Ensminger, J. & A. Rutten. 'The political economy of changing property rights: dismantling a pastoral commons', *American Ethnologist*, 18 (1991), 683–95.

Fairhead, James & Melissa Leach. 'False forest history, complicit social analysis: rethinking some West Africa deforestation narratives', *World Development*, 23 (June 1995).

Farler, Rev. J.P. 'Native routes in East Africa from Pangani to the Masai country and to the Victoria Nyanza', *Proceedings of the Royal Geographical Society*, 4 (1882), 730–42.

Fearn, Hugh. 'The gold-mining era in Kenya Colony', *Journal of Tropical Geography*, 11 (1958), 43–58.

Fleuret, P. 'The social organization of water control in the Taita Hills, Kenya', *American Ethnologist*, 12 (1985), 103–18.

Gardner, H.M. 'Kenya forests and the war', *Empire Forestry Journal*, 21 (1942), 45–7.

Gartrell, Beverley. 'Prelude to disaster: the case of Karamoja', in Johnson & Anderson, *Ecology of Survival* (London & Boulder, 1988), 193–218.

Giblin, James. 'Trypanosomiasis control in African history: an evaded issue?' *Journal of African History*, 31 (1990), 59–80.

Glover, H.M. 'Soil conservation in parts of Africa and the Middle East: Part 1: Kenya Colony', *Empire Forestry Review*, 33 (1954), 39–44.

Gold, Alice. 'The Nandi in transition: background to the Nandi resistance to the British, 1895–1906', *Kenya Historical Review*, 6 (1978), 84–104.

Graham, R.M. 'Forestry in Kenya', *Empire Forestry*, 24 (1945), 156–75.

Gutto, S.B. 'Law, rangelands, peasantry', *Review of African Political Economy*, 20 (1981), 57–73.

Harlan, J.R. & Ann Stemler. 'The races of sorghum in Africa', in J.R. Harlan (ed.), *The Origins of African Plant Domestication* (The Hague, 1976).

Hardin, G. 'The tragedy of the commons', *Science*, 162 (1968), 1243–8.

Harrison, E. *History and Activities of Locusts in Kenya and Relative Costs of Destruction* (Agricultural Department, Bulletin.No. 9, Nairobi, 1929).

Harrison, E. *The Native Cattle Problem* (Agricultural Department pamphlet, Nairobi, 1929).

Haugerud, Angelique. 'The consequences of land tenure reform among smallholders in the Kenya Highlands', *Rural Africana*, 15/16 (1983), 25–53.

Haugerud, Angelique. 'Land tenure and agrarian change in Kenya', *Africa*, 59 (1989), 62–90.

Hennings, R.O. 'The furrow-makers of Kenya', *Geographical Magazine*, 12 (1941), 268–79.

Hennings, R.O. 'Grazing management in the pastoral areas of Kenya', *Journal of African Administration*, 13 (1961), 191–203.

Hennings, R.O. 'The African Land Development Organization, 1946–62', in Cone & Lipscomb (eds), *History of Kenya Agriculture* (Nairobi, 1972), 91–6.

Herskovits, M.J. 'The cattle complex in East Africa', *American Anthropologist*, 28 (1926), 230–72, 361–88, 498–528, 633–64.

Hetherington, Penelope. 'Explaining the crisis of capitalism in Kenya', *African Affairs*, 92 (1993), 89–105.

Hoben, Alan. 'The cultural construction of environmental policy: paradigms and politics in Ethiopia', in Leach & Mearns, *Lie of the Land* (Oxford & Portsmouth, NH, 1996), 186–208.

Hobley, C.W. 'Notes on the geography and people of Baringo District of the East Africa Protectorate', *Geographical Journal*, 28 (1906).

Hodges, G.W.T. 'African manpower statistics for the British Forces in East Africa, 1914–18', *Journal of African History*, 19 (1978), 101–16.

Hodgson, Dorothy L. 'Images and interventions: the "problem" of pastoralist "development"', in Anderson & Broch-Due (eds), *The Poor Are Not Us* (Oxford, Athens, OH & Nairobi, 1999),

319

221–39.

Hodgson, Dorothy L. 'Taking stock: state control, ethnic identity and pastoralist development in Tanganyika, 1948–58', *Journal of African History*, 41 (2000), 35–54.

Hogendorn, Jan S. & K.M. Scott, 'Very large-scale agricultural projects: the lessons of the East African Groundnut Scheme', in Rotberg (ed.), *Imperialism, Colonialism and Hunger* (Lexington, MA & Toronto, 1983), 167–98.

Hogg, Richard. 'The New Pastoralism: poverty, and dependency in Northern Kenya', *Africa*, 56 (1986), 319–33.

Hogg, Richard. 'Development in Northern Kenya: drought, desertification and food scarcity', *African Affairs*, 86 (1987), 47–58.

Hogg, Richard. 'Settlement, pastoralism and the commons: the ideology and practice of irrigation development in Northern Kenya', in Anderson & Grove (eds), *Conservation in Africa* (Cambridge, 1987), 293–306.

Homewood, Katherine & A. Hurst. 'Comparative ecology of pastoralist livestock in Baringo, Kenya', *Pastoral Development Network Paper*, 21b (1986).

Homewood, Katherine & J.G. Lewis. 'Impact of drought on pastoral livestock in Baringo, Kenya, 1983–85', *Journal of Applied Ecology*, 24 (1987), 615–31.

Homewood, Katherine & William A. Rodgers. 'Pastoralism, conservation and the overgrazing controversy', in Anderson & Grove (eds), *Conservation in Africa* (Cambridge, 1987), 111–26.

Hornby, H.E. 'Overstocking in Tanganyika Territory', *East African Agricultural Journal*, 1 (1935–6), 353–60.

Hughes, J.F. 'Forest and water supplies in East Africa', *Empire Forestry*, 28 (1955), 31–42.

Ingham, K. 'Uganda's old Eastern Province: the transfer to the East African Protectorate in 1902', *Uganda Journal*, 21 (1957), 41–7.

Isaac, F.W. 'The early days', *Kenya Weekly News*, 14 May & 25 June 1954.

Jackson, Frederick J. 'Journey to Uganda via Masailand', *Proceedings of the Royal Geographical Society*, 13 (1891), 193–208.

Jackson, Robert H. 'Planning, politics and administration', in G. Hyden, Robert H. Jackson & John Okuma (eds), *Development Administration: the Kenyan Experience* (Nairobi, 1970), 171–200.

Jacobs, Alan H. 'A chronology of the pastoral Maasai', in Ogot (ed.), *Hadith* 1 (Nairobi, 1968), 10–32.

Jones, B. 'Desiccation and the West African colonies', *Geographical Journal*, 91 (1938), 401–23.

Knowles, Joan and David Collett. 'Nature as myth, symbol and action: notes towards an historical understanding of development and conservation in Kenya Maasailand', *Africa*, 59 (1989), 433–60.

Lang'at, S.C. 'Some aspects of Kipsigis history before 1914', in McIntosh (ed.), *Ngano* (Nairobi, 1969), 73–94.

Lee, J.M. '"Forward thinking" and the war: the Colonial Office during the 1940s', *Journal of Imperial and Commonwealth History*, 6 (1977), 64–79.

Little, Peter D. 'Absentee herdowners and part-time pastoralists: the political economy of resource use in Northern Kenya', *Human Ecology*, 13 (1985), 131–51.

Little, Peter D. 'Social differentiation and pastoralist sedentarization in Northern Kenya', *Africa*, 55 (1985), 242–61.

Little, Peter D. 'Domestic production and regional markets in Northern Kenya', *American Enthnologist*, 14 (1987), 295–308.

Little, Peter D. 'Land use conflicts in agricultural/pastoral borderlands: the case of Kenya', in Peter D. Little & Michael H. Horowitz (eds), *Lands at Risk in the Third World: Local-level Perspectives* (Boulder, 1987), 195–212.

Little, Peter D. 'Women as Ol Payian (Elder): the status of widows among the Il Chamus (Njemps) of Kenya', *Ethnos*, 52 (1987), 81–102.

Little, Peter D. & David W. Brokensha. 'Local institutions, tenure and resource management in East Africa', in Anderson & Grove (eds), *Conservation in Africa* (Cambridge, 1987), 193–210.

Bibliography

Liversage, V.L. 'Some observations on farming economics in Nakuru District', *East African Agricultural Journal*, 4 (1938), 195–204.

Lonsdale, John M. 'The politics of conquest in Western Kenya, 1894–1908', *Historical Journal*, 20 (1977), 841–70.

Lonsdale, John M. 'KAU's cultures: imaginations of community and constructions of leadership in Kenya after the Second World War', *Journal of African Cultural Studies*, 13 (2000).

Lonsdale, John M. & Bruce Berman. 'Coping with the contradictions: the development of the colonial state in Kenya, 1895–1914', *Journal of African History*, 20 (1979), 487–505.

Low, D. Anthony. 'The northern interior, 1840–84', in Oliver & Mathew (eds), *Oxford History of East Africa*, Vol. 1 (Oxford, 1965), 297–351.

Low, D. Anthony. 'British East Africa: the establishment of British rule, 1895–1912', in Harlow & Chilver (eds), *Oxford History of East Africa*, Vol. 2 (Oxford, 1965), 1–56.

Low, D. Anthony & John M. Lonsdale. 'Introduction: towards the new order 1945–63', in Low & Smith (eds), *Oxford History of East Africa*, Vol. 3 (Oxford, 1976), 1–64.

Luckham, M.E. 'The early history of the Kenya Department of Agriculture', *East African Agricultural Journal*, 25 (1959), 97–105.

Maack, Pamela. '"We don't want terraces!" Protest and identity under the Uluguru Land Usage Scheme', in Maddox, Giblin & Kimambo, *Custodians of the Land* (London, 1996), 152–68.

McCabe, J.T. 'Turkana pastoralism: a case against the tragedy of the commons', *Human Ecology*, 18 (1990), 81–103.

McCracken, K. John. 'Experts and expertise in colonial Malawi', *African Affairs*, 81 (1982), 101–16.

McCracken, K. John. 'Colonialism, capitalism and ecological crisis in Malawi: a reassessment', in Anderson & Grove (eds), *Conservation in Africa* (Cambridge, 1987), 63–78.

Mackenzie, Fiona. 'Political economy of the environment, gender and resistance under colonialism: Murang'a District Kenya, 1910–1950', *Canadian Journal of African Studies*, 25 (1991), 226–56.

McWilliam, Michael. 'The managed economy: agricultural change, development and finance in Kenya', in Low & Smith (eds), *Oxford History of East Africa*, Vol. 3 (Oxford, 1976), 251–89.

Maher, Colin. 'Land utilisation as a national problem, with special reference to Kenya Colony', *East African Agricultural Journal*, 2 (1936), 134–44.

Maher, Colin. *A Visit to the United States to Study Soil Conservation* (Agricultural Department pamphlet, Nairobi, 1940).

Maher, Colin. 'African labour on the farm in Kenya Colony', *East African Agricultural Journal*, 7 (1942), 228–35.

Maher, Colin. 'The people and the land: some problems', *East African Agricultural Journal*, 7 (1942–3), 63–9, 146–51.

Maher, Colin. *Peasantry or Prosperity?* (East African Problems Series, No. 3, *East African Standard*, 1945).

Maher, Colin. 'The goat: friend or foe?', *East African Agricultural Journal*, 11 (1945), 115–21.

Maher, Colin. 'A note on the economic and social problems in Kenya and their relationship to soil erosion', *Soils and Fertilizers*, 13 (1950), 1–6.

Maher, Colin. 'Soil conservation in Kenya Colony: Part 1, factors affecting erosion: Part II, soil conservation in practice, organization and legislation; present position and outlook', *Empire Journal of Experimental Agriculture*, 18 (1950), 137–49 & 233–48.

Matson, A.T. 'Uganda's old Eastern Province and East Africa's federal capital', *Uganda Journal*, 22 (1958), 43–53.

Matson, A.T. 'Harry Johnston and Clement Hill', *Uganda Journal*, 23 (1959), 190–91.

Matson, A.T. 'The eastern boundary of Uganda in 1902', *Uganda Journal*, 24 (1960), 128–9.

Matson, A.T. 'Famine in the nineties', *Kenya Weekly News*, 18 August 1961.

Matson, A.T. 'The early history of the Uasin Gishu', *Kenya Weekly News*, 23 February 1963.

Bibliography

Mettam, R.W.M. 'A short history of rinderpest, with special reference to Africa', *Uganda Journal*, 1 (1937), 22–6.

Migot-Adholla, S.E. & Peter D. Little. 'Evolution of policy toward the development of pastoral areas in Kenya', in J. Galaty et al. (eds), *Future of Pastoral Peoples* (Ottowa, 1981), 144–56.

Mukerji, R.K. 'The relations between human and bovine population pressure in India', *Indian Journal of Economics*, 17 (1937).

Muriuki, Godfrey. 'Kikuyu reaction to traders and British administration, 1850–1904', in Ogot (ed.), *Hadith 1* (Nairobi, 1968), 101–18.

Mwanzi, Henry A. 'Koitalel arap Samoie and Kipchomber arap Koilege: southern Kalenjin rulers and their encounters with British imperialism', in Kipkorir (ed.), *Imperialism and Collaboration* (Nairobi, 1980), 15–36.

Myrick, Bismarck. 'Colonial initiatives and Kamba reaction in Machakos District: the destocking issue, 1930–38', in Leon Spencer (ed.), *Three Aspects of Crisis in Colonial Kenya* (Syracuse, 1975).

Newland, R.N. 'Review of the cattle trade in BEA, 1904–08', *British East African Agricultural Journal*, 1 (1908), 264–8.

Ofcansky, Thomas P. 'Kenya forestry under British colonial administration, 1895–1963', *Journal of Forest History*, 28 (1984), 136–43.

Ogot, Bethwell A. 'The role of the pastoralist and the agriculturalist in African history', in Terence O. Ranger (ed.), *Emerging Themes in African History* (Nairobi 1968), 125–33.

Ogot, Bethwell A. 'African ecology in historical perspective', in Bethwell A. Ogot (ed.), *Hadith 7* (Nairobi, 1979), 1–8.

Okoth-Ogendo, H.W.O. 'Agrarian reform in Sub-Saharan Africa: an assessment of state responses to the African agrarian crisis and their implications for agricultural development' in Thomas J. Basset & Donald E. Crummey, *Land in African Agrarian Systems* (Madison, 1993), 247–73.

Otieno, Asenath & Kate Rowntree. 'A comparative study of land degradation in Machakos and Baringo districts, Kenya', in A.C. Millington, A. Binns and S. Mutiso (eds), *African Resources: Appraisal, Monitoring and Management* (Geography Department, Reading University, Reading, 1987), 30–47.

Overton, John D., 'War and economic development: settlers in Kenya, 1914–18', *Journal of African History*, 27 (1986), 91–7.

Peters, Pauline. 'Embedded systems and rooted models', in B. McKay and J. Acheson (eds), *The Question of the Commons: the Culture and Ecology of Communal Resources* (Tuscon, 1987), 171–94.

Peters, Pauline. 'Struggles over water, struggles over meaning: cattle, water and the state in Botswana', *Africa*, 54 (1987), 24–59.

Phimister, Ian. 'Meat and monopolies: beef cattle in southern Rhodesia, 1890–1928', *Journal of African History*, 19 (1978), 391–414.

Phimister, Ian. 'Discourse and the discipline of historical context: conservation and ideas about development in Southern Rhodesia, 1930–1950', *Journal of Southern African Studies*, 12 (1986), 263–75.

Pole-Evans, I., 'The veld: its resources and dangers', *South African Journal of Science*, 17 (1920), 1–34.

Pole-Evans, I., 'Pastures and their management', *Rhodesia Agriculture Journal*, 29 (1932), 912–20.

Pratt, D.J. 'Reseeding denuded pasture land in Baringo District, Kenya, I. Preliminary trials', *East African Agricultural Journal*, 29 (1963), 78–91.

Pratt, D.J. 'Bush control studies in the drier areas of Kenya', *Empire Journal of Experimental Agriculture*, 32 (1964), 18–25.

Pratt, D.J. 'Reseeding denuded land in Baringo District, Kenya: techniques for dry alluvial sites', *East African Agriculture and Forestry Journal*, 30 (1964), 117–25.

Pratt, D.J. & J. Knight. 'Reseeding denuded land in Baringo District, Kenya: techniques for capped red loam soils', *East African Agriculture and Forestry Journal*, 30 (1964), 117–25.

Bibliography

Quam, Michael D. 'Cattle-marketing and pastoral conservatism; Karamoja District, Uganda, 1948–1970', *African Studies Review*, 21 (1978), 49–71.

Ranger, Terence O. 'European attitudes and African realities: the rise and fall of the Matola chiefs of south-east Tanganyika', *Journal of African History*, 20 (1979), 63–82.

Ranger, Terence O. 'The invention of tradition in colonial Africa', in Eric Hobsbawm and T.O. Ranger (eds), *The Invention of Tradition* (Cambridge, 1983).

Ranger, Terence O. 'The communal areas of Zimbabwe', in Thomas J. Basset & Donald E. Crummey (eds), *Land in African Agrarian Systems* (Madison, 1993), 354–87.

Ravenstein, E.G. 'Messrs. Jackson and Gedge's journey to Uganda via Masailand', *Proceedings of the Royal Geographical Society*, 13 (1891), 193–208.

Richards, Paul. 'Ecological change and the politics of African land use', *African Studies Review*, 26 (1983), 1–72.

Rigby, Peter. 'Pastoralism and prejudice: ideology and rural development in East Africa', in Peter Rigby (ed.), *Society and Social Change in Eastern Africa* (Kampala, 1970), 42–52.

Roberts, Andrew D. 'The gold boom of the 1930s in eastern Africa', *African Affairs*, 85 (1986), 545–62.

Roe, Emery. '"Development narratives" or making the best of blueprint development', *World Development*, 19 (1991), 287–300.

Roe, Emery. 'New framework for an old tragedy of the commons and an aging common property resource management', *Agriculture and Human Values*, 11 (1994), 29–36.

Roe, Emery. 'Except Africa' [introduction to special section on development narratives], *World Development*, 23 (1995), 1065–70.

Rogers, Peter. 'The British and the Kikuyu, 1890–1905: a reassessment', *Journal of African History*, 20 (1979), 255–69.

Sambrook, F. & W. Gisherford. 'Cattle and the meat industry in southern Rhodesia', *Rhodesian Agricultural Journal*, 33 (1935–36), 853–5.

Sampson, H.C. 'Soil erosion in tropical Africa', *Rhodesian Agricultural Journal*, 33 (1935–36), 197–205.

Savage, D.C. & J. Forbes Munro. 'Carrier corps recruitment in the British East Africa Protectorate, 1914–18', *Journal of African History*, 7 (1966), 313–42.

Schlee, Gunther. 'Interethnic clan identities among Cushitic-speaking pastoralists', *Africa*, 55 (1985), 17–38.

Scoones, Ian. 'Range management, science and policy: politics, polemics and pasture in southern Africa', in Leach & Mearns, *Lie of the Land* (Oxford & Portsmouth, NH, 1996), 34–53.

Shipton, Parker. 'The Kenyan land tenure reform: misunderstandings in the public creation of private property', in R. Downs & S. Reyna (eds), *Land and Society in Contemporary Africa* (Hanover, 1988), 91–135.

Shipton, Parker. 'Debts and trespasses: land, mortgages and the ancestors in western Kenya', *Africa*, 62 (1992), 357–88.

Showers, Kate. 'Soil erosion in the kingdom of Lesotho: origins and colonial response, 1830s–1950s', *Journal of Southern African Studies*, 15 (1989), 263–86.

Smith, G.E. 'The Survey of British East Africa', *British East African Agricultural Journal*, 1 (1908), 69–73.

Smith, G.E. & A.C. MacDonald. 'Rapid allotments of farms in the Uasin Gishu', *British East African Agricultural Journal*, 1 (1909), 103–14.

Sobania, Neal W. 'Pastoral migration and colonial policy: a case study from northern Kenya', in Johnson & Anderson (eds), *Ecology of Survival* (London & Boulder, 1988), 219–40.

Sobania, Neal W. 'Fisherman herders: subsistence, survival and cultural change in northern Kenya', *Journal of African History*, 29 (1988), 41–56.

Sobania, Neal W. 'Social relationships as an aspect of property rights: Northern Kenya in pre-colonial and colonial periods', in P.T.W. Baxter and Richard Hogg (eds), *Property, Poverty and People* (Manchester, 1990), 1–19.

Sobania, Neal W. 'Defeat and dispersal: the Laikipiak and their neighbours at the end of the

nineteenth century', in Spear & Waller (eds), *Being Maasai* (London, 1994), 105–19.

Sommer, Gabriele & Rainer Vossen. 'Dialects, sectiolects, or simply lects? The Maa language in time perspective', in Spear & Waller, *Being Maasai* (London, 1994), 25–36.

Soper, Robert. 'A survey of the irrigation systems of the Marakwet', in Benjamin E. Kipkorir, Robert Soper & J.W. Ssennyonga (eds), *Kerio Valley: Past, Present and Future* (Nairobi, 1983), 75–9.

Spencer, Ian R.G. 'Settler dominance, agricultural production and the Second World War in Kenya', *Journal of African History*, 21 (1980), 497–514.

Spencer, Ian R.G. 'The first assault on Indian ascendancy: Indian traders in the Kenyan Reserves, 1895–1929', *African Affairs*, 80 (1981), 327–43.

Spencer, Ian R.G. 'Pastoralism and colonial policy in Kenya, 1895–1929', in Rotberg (ed.), *Imperialism, Colonialism and Hunger* (Lexington, MA & Toronto, 1983), 113–40.

Spencer, Paul. 'Drought and the commitment to growth', *African Affairs*, 73 (1974), 419–27.

Stamp, L.D. 'The southern margin of the Sahara: comments on some recent studies on the question of desiccation in West Africa', *Geographical Review*, 30 (1940), 297–300.

Staples, R.R. 'Bush control and deferred grazing as a measure to improve grazing', *East African Agricultural Journal*, 11 (1945), 43–6.

Staples, R.R., H.E. Hornby & R.M. Hornby, 'A study of the comparative effects of goats and cattle on a mixed grass–bush pasture', *East African Agricultural Journal*, 8 (1942), 62–70.

Stebbing, E.P. 'The encroaching Sahara: the threat to the West African colonies', *Geographical Journal*, 85 (1935), 506–24.

Stebbing, E.P. 'The threat of the Sahara', *Journal of the Royal African Society* (Extra Supplement, May, 1937), 3–35.

Stebbing, E.P. 'The man-made desert in Africa: erosion and drought', *Journal of the Royal African Society* (Supplement, Jan. 1938), 3–40.

Stebbing, E.P.'Forestry in Africa', *Empire Forestry Journal*, 20 (1947), 126–44.

Stockdale, Frank. 'Soil erosion in the colonial empire', *Empire Journal of Experimental Agriculture*, 5 (1937), 1–19.

Stocking, Michael. 'Soil conservation policy in colonial Africa', *Agricultural History*, 59 (1985), 148–61.

Sutton, J.E.G. 'Some reflections on the early history of Western Kenya', in Ogot (ed.), *Hadith 2* (Nairobi, 1970), 17–29.

Sutton, J.E.G. 'The Kalenjin', in Ogot (ed.), *Kenya Before 1900* (Nairobi, 1976), 21–52.

Sutton, J.E.G. 'Irrigation and soil conservation in African agricultural history: with a reconsideration of the Inyanga terracing (Zimbabwe) and Engaruka irrigation works (Tanzania)', *Journal of African History*, 25 (1984), 25–41.

Sutton, J.E.G. 'Towards a history of cultivating the field', *Azania*, 24 (1989), 98–112.

Swai, Benaventure. 'Colonial development policy and agrarian protest in Tanganyika territory: the Usambara case, 1920–1960', *Transafrican Journal of History*, 12 (1983), 153–74.

Tempany, H.A., H.A. Roddan, & L. Lord. 'Soil erosion and soil conservation in the colonial empire', *Empire Forestry*, 23 (1944), 142–59.

Theiler, A. & J.M. Christy. 'The prevention and eradication of East Coast fever', *British East African Agricultural Journal*, 4 (1911), 30–41.

Throup, D.W. 'The origins of Mau Mau', *African Affairs*, 84 (1985), 399–433.

Tignor, Robert L. 'Kamba political protest: the destocking controversy of 1938', *International Journal of African Historical Studies*, 4 (1971), 237–51.

Trapnell, C.G. 'Ecological methods in the study of native agriculture', *East African Agricultural Journal*, 2 (1937), 491–4.

Vossen, Rainer. 'Linguistic evidence regarding the territorial history of the Maa-speaking peoples: some preliminary remarks', *Kenya Historical Review*, 6 (1978), 34–52.

Wakefield, T. 'Routes of native caravans from the coast to the interior of Eastern Africa', *Journal of the Royal Geographical Society*, 40 (1870), 303–38.

Waller, Richard D. 'The Maasai and the British, 1895–1905: the origins of an alliance', *Journal*

of African History, 17 (1976), 529–53.

Waller, Richard D. 'East African age organization', *African Affairs*, 79 (1980), 257–60.

Waller, Richard D. 'Interaction and identity on the periphery: the Trans-Mara Maasai', *International Journal of African Historical Studies*, 17 (1984), 243–84.

Waller, Richard D. 'Ecology, migration, and expansion in East Africa', *African Affairs*, 84 (1985), 347–70.

Waller, Richard D. 'Economic and social relations in the Central Rift Valley: the Maa-speakers and their neighbours in the nineteenth century', in Ogot (ed.), *Kenya in the Nineteenth Century* (Nairobi, 1985), 83–151.

Waller, Richard D. 'Emutai: crisis and response in Maasailand 1883–1902', in Johnson & Anderson (eds), *Ecology of Survival* (London & Boulder, 1988), 73–112.

Waller, Richard D. 'Tsetse fly in Western Narok', *Journal of African History*, 31 (1990), 81–102.

Waller, Richard D. 'Acceptees and aliens: Kikuyu settlement in Maasailand', in Spear & Waller, *Being Maasai* (London, 1994), 226–57.

Waller, Richard D. 'Kidongoi's kin: prophecy and power in Maasailand', in Anderson & Johnson (eds), *Revealing Prophets* (London, 1995), 28–64.

Watson, G.C. 'Erosion and the Empire', *East African Agricultural Journal*, 1 (1936), 305–8.

Watt, M. 'The dangers and prevention of soil erosion', *Rhodesian Agricultural Journal*, 10 (1913).

Weatherby, J.M. 'Inter-tribal warfare on Mt. Elgon in the 19th and 20th centuries', *Uganda Journal*, 26 (1962), 200–212.

Weatherby, J.M. 'Nineteenth century wars in Western Kenya', *Azania*, 2 (1967), 133–44.

Were, Gideon S. 'The Maasai and Kalenjin factor in the settlement of Western Kenya: a study in ethnic interaction and evolution', *Journal of East African Research and Development*, 2 (1974).

Westcott, Nicholas J. 'The East African sisal industry, 1929–49: the marketing of a colonial commodity during depression and war', *Journal of African History*, 25 (1984), 445–61.

Williams, Gavin. 'Taking the part of the peasant: rural development in Nigeria and Tanzania', in P. Gutkind & I. Wallerstein (eds), *The Political Economy of Contemporary Africa* (Beverley Hills, 1976), 131–54.

Williams, J.H. *Historical Outline and Analysis of the Work of the Survey Department, Kenya Colony, 1 April 1903 to 30 Sept. 1929* (Government pamphlet, Nairobi, 1931). [Copy seen at Foreign and Commonwealth Office Library, London.]

Wolfe, H. *Memorandum on Native Agricultural Development in the Native Reserves* (Agricultural Department pamphlet, Nairobi, 1936).

Wrigley, C.C. 'Kenya: the patterns of economic life, 1902–1945', in Harlow & Chilver (eds), *Oxford History of East Africa*, Vol. 2 (Oxford, 1965), 209–65.

3. Unpublished papers, dissertations & theses

Agriculture Department. 'A history of the fluctuation of the cattle population in Kajiado, Maasailand, during the last 20 years leading to the disastrous losses of 1961–62' (Nairobi, 1963).

Aldington, T.J. & F.A. Wilson. 'The marketing of beef in Kenya', seminar paper, Institute of Development Studies, University of Nairobi (1968).

Anderson, David M. 'Expansion or expediency: the British in Baringo to 1902', unpublished typescript, Trinity College (1979).

Anderson, David M. 'Herder, settler, and colonial rule: a history of the peoples of the Baringo Plains, Kenya, *c.* 1890–1940' (PhD thesis, University of Cambridge, 1982).

Berntsen, John L. 'Pastoralism, raiding and prophets: Maasailand in the nineteenth century' (PhD thesis, University of Wisconsin–Madison, 1979).

Bille, J.C. & H.H. Heemstra, 'An illustrated introduction to the rainfall patterns of Kenya', ILCA Kenya, Working Document No. 12 (Nairobi, 1979).

Breen, Rita M. 'The Kenya Land Commission (1932–33) and Dorobo land issues', unpublished seminar paper, History Department, University of Nairobi (1972).

Bibliography

Breen, Rita M. 'The politics of land: the Kenya Land Commission 1932–3 and its effects on land policy in Kenya' (PhD thesis, Michigan State University, 1976).

Brown, Leslie H. 'The development of the semi-arid areas of Kenya' (Agricultural Department, Nairobi, 1963).

Carswell, Grace. 'Farmers, agricultural change and sustainability in colonial Kigezi, south-western Uganda' (PhD thesis, SOAS, University of London, 1997).

Cashmore, T.R.H. 'Studies in district administration in the East African Protectorate, 1895–1918' (PhD thesis, University of Cambridge, 1962).

Dalleo, Peter. 'The economic factor in the history of the Somali of Kenya', unpublished seminar paper, History Department, University of Nairobi (1972).

Distefano, John A. 'Lagokap Miot (the children of Miot): an enquiry into Kalenjin pre-colonial history', unpublished seminar paper, History Department, University of Nairobi (1976).

Doyle, Shane. 'Disease and demography in Bunyoro' (PhD thesis, University of Cambridge, 1998).

Edmundson, R. 'Forts of Baringo', manuscript, privately held by Mrs Betty Roberts, Kampi-ya-Samaki, Kenya.

Kettel, Bonnie L. 'Time is money: the social consequences of economic change in Seretunin, Kenya' (PhD thesis, University of Illinois at Urbana-Champaign, 1980).

Kettel, David W.W. 'What's in a name? Age-organisation and reincarnation beliefs of the Tugen-Kalenjin', unpublished paper, Discussion Paper No. 32, Institute of African Studies, University of Nairobi (1972).

Kettel, D.W.W. 'Passing like flowers: the marriage regulations of the Tugen of Kenya and their implications for a theory of Crow Omaha' (PhD thesis, University of Illinois at Urbana–Champaign, 1975).

Kettel, B.L. & D.W.W. Kettel. 'The Tugen of Kenya: a brief ethnographic report', unpublished report, Institute of African Studies, University of Nairobi (1971).

Kinyanjui, K. & N. Ng'ethe. 'Training with underdevelopment: the case of the Baringo Development Training Centre (B.D.T.C.) – an evaluation', Institute of Development Studies, University of Nairobi, Occasional Paper No. 24 (1976).

Kipkorir, Benjamin E. 'The Alliance High School and the making of an African elite, 1926–62' (PhD thesis, University of Cambridge, 1969).

Kipkorir, Benjamin E. 'The Kalenjin phenomenon and the Misri legends', unpublished seminar paper, History Department, University of Nairobi (1971).

Kipkulei, B.K. 'The origin, migration, and settlement of the Tugen people, with special reference to the Aror, from the earliest times to the turn of the twentieth century' (BA dissertation, History Department, Nairobi, 1972).

Kiplenge, Juma. 'The Endorois community: general profile', unpublished typescript (in possession of author).

Little, Peter D. 'Pastoralism and strategies: socio-economic change in the pastoral sector of Baringo District, Kenya', Institute of Development Studies, University of Nairobi, Working Paper No. 368 (April 1980).

Little, Peter D. 'The effects of increased crop production on livestock investments in a semi-arid area: some examples from Baringo District, Kenya', Institute of Development Studies, University of Nairobi, Working Paper No. 386 (August 1981).

Livingstone, Ian. 'Economic irrationality among pastoral peoples in East Africa; myth or reality?', Institute of Development Studies, University of Nairobi, Discussion Paper No. 245 (1977).

Milton, Shaun. 'South African beef industry and Western Transvaal' (PhD thesis, Institute for Commonwealth Studies, University of London, 1996).

Moore, R.O. 'Unraveling the Kalenjin riddle', unpublished seminar paper, History Department, University of Nairobi (1977).

Murray, Nancy U. 'The other lost lands: the administration of Kenya's forests, 1900–52', unpublished seminar paper, History Department, Kenyatta University College, Nairobi (1982).

Ott, Richard. 'Decisions and development: the lowland Tugen of Baringo District, Kenya' (PhD thesis, City University of New York at Stoney Brook, 1979).

Overton, John D. 'Spatial differentiation in the colonial economy of Kenya: Africans, settlers and the state, 1900–1920' (PhD thesis, University of Cambridge, 1983).

Polak, Ben. 'Rinderpest and Kenya in the 1890s' (MA dissertation, Northwestern University, 1985).

Redley, Michael G. 'The politics of a predicament: the white community in Kenya, 1918–1932' (PhD thesis, University of Cambridge, 1976).

Sobania, Neal P. 'The historical traditions of the peoples in the Eastern Lake Turkana Basin, *c*. 1840–1925' (PhD thesis, SOAS, University of London, 1980).

Spencer, Ian R.G. 'The development of production and trade in the reserve areas of Kenya, 1895–1929' (PhD thesis, Simon Fraser University, 1975).

Spencer, Paul. 'Pastoralists and the ghost of capitalism', ILCA conference paper, Nairobi (1977).

Stannar, W.E.H. 'The Kitui Kamba: a critical study of British administration', unpublished report (Nairobi, 1939). [Copy held by J.M. Lonsdale.]

Talbot-Smith, L. 'Leroghi Plateau and notes on the tribes of Baringo District', unpublished manuscript (*c*. 1908). [Copy with Matson papers, Rhodes House.]

Tarus, Isaac. 'An outline history of the Keiyo people from 1700 to 1919' (BA dissertation, University of Nairobi, 1988).

Turton, E.R. 'The pastoral tribes of Northern Kenya, 1800–1916' (PhD thesis, University of London, 1970).

Waller, Richard D. 'The lords of East Africa: the Maasai in the mid-nineteenth century (*c*. 1840–*c*. 1885)' (PhD thesis, University of Cambridge, 1978).

Weatherby, J.M. 'Discussion on the Nandi-speaking peoples', unpublished paper, East Africa Institute of Social Research Conference (Kampala, 1963).

Index

328

Index

Index